SPECIMENS

OF

ENGLISH DRAMATIC POETS,

WHO LIVED

ABOUT THE TIME OF SHAKSPEARE.

WITH NOTES.

BY CHARLES LAMB

NEW EDITION, COMPLETE IN ONE VOLUME.

WILLIS P. HAZARD, 190 CHESTNUT ST.,
PHILADELPHIA.
1857.

PREFACE.

More than a third part of the following specimens are from plays which are to be found only in the British Museum and in some scarce private libraries. The rest are from Dodsley's and Hawkins's collections, and the works of Jonson, Beaumont and Fletcher, and Massinger.

I have chosen wherever I could to give entire scenes, and in some instances successive scenes, rather than to string together single passages and detached beauties, which I have always found wearisome in the reading in selections of this nature.

To every extract is prefixed an explanatory head, sufficient to make it intelligible with the help of some trifling omissions. Where a line or more was obscure, as having reference to something that had gone before, which would have asked more time to explain than its consequence in the scene seemed to deserve, I have had no hesitation in leaving the line or passage out. Sometimes where I have met with a superfluous character, which seemed to burthen without throwing any light upon the scene, I have ventured to dismiss it altogether. I have expunged, without ceremony, all that which the writers had better never have written, that forms the objection so often repeated to the promiscuous reading of Fletcher, Massinger, and some others.

The kind of extracts which I have sought after have been, not so much passages of wit and humor, though the old plays are rich in such, as scenes of passion, sometimes of the deepest quality, interesting situations, serious descriptions, that which is more nearly allied to poetry than to wit, and to tragic rather than comic poetry. The plays which I have made choice of have been, with few exceptions, those which treat of human life and manners, rather than masques, and Arcadian pastorals, with their train of abstractions, unimpassioned deities, passionate mortals, Claius, and Medorus, and Amintas, and Amarillis. My leading design has been, to illustrate what may be called the moral sense of our ancestors. To show in what manner they felt, when they placed themselves by the power of imagination in trying situations, in the conflicts of duty and passion, or the strife of contending duties ; what sort of loves and enmities theirs were ; how their griefs were tempered, and their full-swoln joys abated : how much of Shakspeare shines in the great men his contemporaries, and how far in his divine mind and manners he surpassed them and all mankind.

Another object which I had in making these selections was, to bring together the most admired scenes in Fletcher and Massinger, in the estimation of the world the only dramatic poets of that age who are entitled to be considered after Shakspeare, and to exhibit them in the same volume with the more impressive scenes of old Marlowe, Heywood, Tourneur, Webster, Ford, and others. To show what we have slighted, while beyond all proportion we have cried up one or two favorite names.

The specimens are not accompanied with anything in the shape of biographical notices.* I had nothing of consequence to add to the slight sketches in Dodsley and the Biographica Dramatica, and I was unwilling to swell the volume with mere transcription. The reader will not fail to observe from the frequent instances of two or more per

* The few notes which are interspersed will be found to be chiefly critical.

sons joining in the composition of the same play (the noble practice of those times), that of most of the writers contained in these selections it may be strictly said, that they were contemporaries. The whole period, from the middle of Elizabeth's reign to the close of the reign of Charles I., comprises a space of little more than half a century, within which time nearly all that we have of excellence in serious dramatic composition was produced, if we except the Samson Agonistes of Milton.

TABLE OF REFERENCE TO THE EXTRACTS.

WILLIAM ROWLEY, THOMAS DECKER, JOHN FORD, ETC.

CYRIL TOURNEUR.

JOHN WEBSTER.

SPECIMENS

OF

ENGLISH DRAMATIC POETS

GORBODUC, A TRAGEDY. BY THOMAS SACKVILLE, LORD BUCKHURST, AFTERWARDS EARL OF DORSET; AND THOMAS NORTON.

Whilst king Gorboduc in the presence of his councillors laments the death of his eldest son, Ferrex, whom Porrex, the younger son, has slain; Marcella, a court lady, enters and relates the miserable end of Porrex, stabbed by his mother in his bed.

GORBODUC, AROSTUS, EUBULUS, *and others.*

Gorb. What cruel destiny,
What froward fate hath sorted us this chance?
That even in those where we should comfort find,
Where our delight now in our aged days
Should rest and be, even there our only grief
And deepest sorrows to abridge our life,
Most pining cares and deadly thoughts do grave.
Arost. Your grace should now, in these grave years of yours,
Have found ere this the price of mortal joys,
How full of change, how brittle our estate,
How short they be, how fading here in earth,
Of nothing sure, save only of the death,
To whom both man and all the world doth owe
Their end at last; neither should nature's power
In other sort against your heart prevail,

Than as the naked hand, whose stroke assays
The armed breast where force doth light in vain.
Gorb. Many can yield right grave and sage advice
Of patient sprite to others wrapt in wo,
And can in speech both rule and conquer kind,*
Who, if by proof they might feel nature's force,
Would show themselves men as they are indeed,
Which now will needs be gods: but what doth mean
The sorry cheer of her that here doth come?

MARCELLA *enters.*

Marc. Oh where is ruth? or where is pity now?
Whither is gentle heart and mercy fled?
Are they exil'd out of our stony breasts,
Never to make return? is all the world
Drowned in blood, and sunk in cruelty?
If not in women mercy may be found,
If not (alas) within the mother's breast
To her own child, to her own flesh and blood;
If ruth be banisht thence, if pity there
May have no place, if there no gentle heart
Do live and dwell, where should we seek it then?
Gorb. Madam (alas) what means your woful tale?
Marc. O silly woman I, why to this hour
Have kind and fortune thus deferr'd my breath,
That I should live to see this doleful day?
Will ever wight believe that such hard heart
Could rest within the cruel mother's breast,
With her own hand to slay her only son?
But out (alas) these eyes beheld the same,
They saw the dreary sight, and are become
Most ruthful records of the bloody fact.
Porrex, alas, is by his mother slain,
And with her hand, a woful thing to tell,
While slumb'ring on his careful bed he rests,
His heart stabb'd in with knife is reft of life.

* Nature; natural affection.

Gorb. O Eubulus, oh draw this sword of ours,
And pierce this heart with speed. O hateful light,
O loathsome life, O sweet and welcome death.
Dear Eubulus, work this we thee beseech.
Eub. Patient your grace, perhaps he liveth yet,
With wound receiv'd but not of certain death.
Gorb. O let us then repair unto the place,
And see if that Porrex live, or thus be slain. [*Exit.*
Marc. Alas he liveth not, it is too true,
That with these eyes, of him a peerless prince,
Son to a king, and in the flower of youth,
Even with a twink* a senseless stock I saw.
Arost. O damned deed!
Marc. But hear his ruthful end.
The noble prince, pierced with the sudden wounds,
Out of his wretched slumber hastily start,†
Whose strength now failing, streight he overthrew,
When in the fall his eyes ev'n now unclosed,
Beheld the queen, and cried to her for help;
We then, alas, the ladies which that time
Did there attend, seeing that heinous deed
And hearing him oft call the wretched name
Of mother, and to cry to her for aid,
Whose direful hand gave him the mortal wound,
Pitying alas (for nought else could we do)
His rueful end, ran to the woful bed,
Despoiled streight his breast, and all we might
Wiped in vain with napkins next at hand
The sudden streams of blood, that flushed fast
Out of the gaping wound: O what a look,
O what a ruthful stedfast eye methought
He fixt upon my face, which to my death
Will never part from me,—wherewith abraid‡
A deep-fetch'd sigh he gave, and therewithall
Clasping his hands, to heaven he cast his sight;
And streight, pale death pressing within his face,

* Twinkling of the eye. † Started.
‡ Awaked; raised up.

The flying ghost his mortal corps forsook.
Arost. Never did age bring forth so vile a fact.
Marc. O hard and cruel hap that thus assign'd
Unto so worthy wight so wretched end:
But most hard cruel heart that could consent,
To lend the hateful destinies that hand,
By which, alas, so heinous crime was wrought;—
O queen of adamant, O marble breast,
If not the favor of his comely face
If not his princely chear and countenance,
His valiant active arms, his manly breast,
If not his fair and seemly personage;
His noble limbs, in such proportion cast
As would have rapt a silly woman's thought;
If this might not have mov'd the bloody heart,
And that most cruel hand the wretched weapon
Even to let fall, and kist him in the face,
With tears, for ruth to reave such one by death;
Should nature yet consent to slay her son?
O mother, thou to murder thus thy child!
Even Jove with justice must with light'ning flames
From heaven send down some strange revenge on thee.
Ah noble prince, how oft have I beheld
Thee mounted on thy fierce and trampling steed,
Shining in armor bright before the tilt,
And with thy mistress' sleeve tied on thy helm,
There charge thy staff, to please thy lady's eye,
That bow'd the head piece of thy friendly foe!
How oft in arms on horse to bend the mace,
How oft in arms on foot to break the sword,
Which never now these eyes may see again.
Arost. Madam, alas, in vain these plaints are shed.
Rather with me depart, and help to assuage
The thoughtful griefs, that in the aged king
Must needs by nature grow, by death of this
His only son, whom he did hold so dear.
Marc. What wight is that which saw that I did see,
And could refrain to wail with plaint and tears?

Not I, alas, that heart is not in me;
But let us go, for I am griev'd anew,
To call to mind the wretched father's wo. [*Exeunt.*

Chorus of aged men. When greedy lust in royal seat to reign
Hath reft all care of gods and eke of men;
And cruel heart, wrath, treason, and disdain,
Within th' ambitious breast are lodged, then
Behold how mischief wide herself displays,
And with the brother's hand the brother slays.

When blood thus shed doth stain this heaven's face,
Crying to Jove for vengeance of the deed,
The mighty God even moveth from his place
With wrath to wreak; then sends he forth with speed
The dreadful Furies, daughters of the night,
With serpents girt, carrying the whip of ire,
With hair of stinging snakes, and shining bright
With flames and blood, and with a brand of fire:
These, for revenge of wretched murder done,
Doth cause the mother kill her only son.

Blood asketh blood, and death must death requit;
Jove by his just and everlasting doom
Justly hath ever so requited it.
This times before record and times to come
Shall find it true, and so doth present proof
Present before our eyes for our behoof.

O happy wight that suffers not the snare
Of murderous mind to tangle him in blood:
And happy he that can in time beware
By others' harms, and turn it to his good:
But wo to him that fearing not to offend,
Doth serve his lust, and will not see the end.

[The style of this old play is stiff and cumbersome, like the dresses of its times. There may be flesh and blood underneath, but we cannot get at it. Sir Philip Sydney has praised it for its morality. One of its authors might easily furnish that. Norton was an associate to Hopkins, Sternhold, and Robert Wisdom, in the Singing Psalms. I am willing to believe that Lord Buckhurst supplied the more vital parts. The chief beauty in the extract is of a secret nature. Marcella obscurely intimates that the murdered prince Porrex and she had been lovers.]

THE SPANISH TRAGEDY; OR HIERONIMO IS MAD AGAIN. A TRAGEDY BY THOMAS KYD.

Horatio, the son of Hieronimo, is murdered while he is sitting with his mistress Belimperia by night in an arbor in his father's garden. The murderers (Balthazar, his rival, and Lorenzo, the brother of Belimperia) hang his body on a tree. Hieronimo is awakened by the cries of Belimperia, and coming out into his garden, discovers by the light of a torch, that the murdered man is his son. Upon this he goes distracted.

HIERONIMO *mad.*

Hier. My son! and what's a son?
A thing begot within a pair of minutes, there about:
A lump bred up in darkness, and doth serve
To balance those light creatures we call women;
And at the nine months' end creeps forth to light.
What is there yet in a son,
To make a father doat, rave, or run mad?
Being born, it pouts, cries, and breeds teeth.
What is there yet in a son?
He must be fed, be taught to go, and speak.
Ay, or yet? why might not a man love a calf as well?
Or melt in passion o'er a frisking kid, as for a son?
Methinks a young bacon,
Or a fine little smooth horse colt,
Should move a man as much as doth a son;
For one of these, in very little time,
Will grow to some good use; whereas a son
The more he grows in stature and in years,
The more unsquar'd, unlevell'd he appears;
Reckons his parents among the rank of fools,
Strikes cares upon their heads with his mad riots,
Makes them look old before they meet with age;
This is a son; and what a loss is this, considered truly!
Oh, but my Horatio grew out of reach of those
Insatiate humors: he lov'd his loving parents:
He was my comfort, and his mother's joy,
The very arm that did hold up our house—
Our hopes were stored up in him,

None but a damned murderer could hate him.
He had not seen the back of nineteen years,
When his strong arm unhors'd the proud prince Balthazar;
And his great mind, too full of honor, took
To mercy that valiant but ignoble Portuguese.
Well heaven is heaven still!
And there is Nemesis, and furies,
And things call'd whips,
And they sometimes do meet with murderers:
They do not always 'scape, that's some comfort,
Ay, ay, ay, and then time steals on, and steals, and steals,
Till violence leaps forth, like thunder
Wrapt in a ball of fire,
And so doth bring confusion to them all. [*Exit.*

JAQUES *and* PEDRO, *Servants.*

Jaq. I wonder, Pedro, why our master thus
At midnight sends us with our torches light,
When man and bird and beast are all at rest,
Save those that watch for rape and bloody murder.
Ped. O Jaques, know thou that our master's mind
Is much distract since his Horatio died:
And, now his aged years should sleep in rest,
His heart in quiet, like a desperate man
Grows lunatic and childish for his son:
Sometimes as he doth at his table sit,
He speaks as if Horatio stood by him.
Then starting in a rage, falls on the earth,
Cries out Horatio, where is my Horatio?
So that with extreme grief, and cutting sorrow,
There is not left in him one inch of man:
See here he comes.

HIERONIMO *enters.*

Hier. I pry thro' every crevice of each wall,
Look at each tree, and search thro' every brake,
Beat on the bushes, stamp our grandame earth,
Dive in the water, and stare up to heaven;
Yet cannot I behold my son Horatio.

How now, who's there, sprights, sprights ?
Ped. We are your servants that attend you, sir
Hier. What make you with your torches in the dark ?
Ped. You bid us light them, and attend you here.
Hier. No, no, you are deceiv'd, not I, you are deceiv'd:
Was I so mad to bid you light your torches now ?
Light me your torches at the mid of noon,
When as the sun god rides in all his glory ;
Light me your torches then.
Ped. Then we burn day light.
Hier. Let it be burnt ; night is a murd'rous slut,
That would not have her treasons to be seen:
And yonder pale fac'd Hecate there, the moon,
Doth give consent to that is done in darkness.
And all those stars that gaze upon her face,
Are aglets* on her sleeve, pins on her train :
And those that should be powerful and divine,
Do sleep in darkness when they most should shine.
Ped. Provoke them not, fair sir, with tempting words,
The heavens are gracious ; and your miseries
And sorrow make you speak you know not what.
Hier. Villain, thou lyest, and thou doest nought
But tell me I am mad : thou lyest, I am not mad :
I know thee to be Pedro, and he Jaques.
I'll prove it to thee ; and were I mad, how could I ?
Where was she the same night, when my Horatio was murder'd ?
She should have shone : search thou the book :
Had the moon shone in my boy's face, there was a kind of grace,
That I know, nay, I do know had the murd'rer seen him,
His weapon would have fallen, and cut the earth,
Had he been fram'd of nought but blood and death ;
Alack, when mischief doth it knows not what,
What shall we say to mischief?

ISABELLA, *his wife, enters.*

Isa. Dear Hieronimo, come in a doors,
O seek not means to increase thy sorrow.

* Tags of points.

Hier. Indeed, Isabella, we do nothing here;
I do not cry, ask Pedro and Jaques:
Not I indeed, we are very merry, very merry.
Isa. How? be merry here, be merry here?
Is not this the place, and this the very tree,
Where my Horatio died, where he was murder'd?
Hier. Was, do not say what: let her weep it out.
This was the tree, I set it of a kernel;
And when our hot Spain could not let it grow,
But that the infant and the human sap
Began to wither, duly twice a morning
Would I be sprinkling it with fountain water:
At last it grew and grew, and bore and bore:
Till at length it grew a gallows, and did bear our son.
It bore thy fruit and mine. O wicked, wicked plant.
See who knocks there. [*One knocks within at the door.*
Ped. It is a painter, sir.
Hier. Bid him come in, and paint some comfort,
For surely there's none lives but painted comfort.
Let him come in, one knows not what may chance.
God's will that I should set this tree! but even so
Masters ungrateful servants rear from nought,
And then they hate them that did bring them up.

The Painter enters.

Pain. God bless you, sir.
Hier. Wherefore? why, thou scornful villain?
How, where, or by what means should I be blest?
Isa. What wouldst thou have, good fellow?
Pain. Justice, madam.
Hier. O ambitious beggar, wouldst thou have that
That lives not in the world?
Why, all the undelved mines cannot buy
An ounce of justice, 'tis a jewel so inestimable.
I tell thee, God hath engross'd all justice in his hands,
And there is none but what comes from him.
Pain. O then I see that God must right me for my murder'd son.

Hier. How, was thy son murder'd?
Pain. Ay, sir, no man did hold a son so dear.
Hier. What, not as thine? that's a lie,
As massy as the earth: I had a son,
Whose least unvalued hair did weigh
A thousand of thy sons, and he was murder'd.
Pain. Alas, sir, I had no more but he.
Hier. Nor I, nor I; but this same one of mine
Was worth a legion. But all is one.
Pedro, Jaques, go in a doors, Isabella, go,
And this good fellow here, and I,
Will range this hideous orchard up and down,
Like two she lions, 'reaved of their young.
Go in a doors I say. [*Exeunt.*
(*The Painter and he sit down.*)
Come let's talk wisely now.
Was thy son murdered?
Pain. Ay, sir.
Hier. So was mine.
How dost thou take it? art thou not sometime mad?
Is there no tricks that come before thine eyes?
Pain. O lord, yes, sir.
Hier. Art a painter? canst paint me a tear, a wound?
A groan or a sigh? canst paint me such a tree as this?
Pain. Sir, I am sure you have heard of my painting;
My name 's Bazardo.
Hier. Bazardo! 'fore God an excellent fellow. Look you, sir.
Do you see? I'd have you paint me in my gallery, in your oil colors matted, and draw me five years younger than I am: do you see, sir? let five years go, let them go,—my wife Isabella standing by me, with a speaking look to my son Horatio, which should intend to this, or some such like purpose; *God bless thee, my sweet son;* and my hand leaning upon his head thus, sir, do you see? may it be done?
Pain. Very well, sir.
Hier. Nay, I pray mark me, sir.

Then, sir, would I have you paint me this tree, this very tree:
Canst paint a doleful cry?

Pain. Seemingly, sir.

Hier. Nay, it should cry; but all is one.
Well, sir, paint me a youth run thro' and thro' with villains' swords hanging upon this tree.
Canst thou draw a murd'rer?

Pain. I'll warrant you, sir; I have the pattern of the most notorious villains that ever lived in all Spain.

Hier. O, let them be worse, worse: stretch thine art,
And let their beards be of Judas's own color,
And let their eye-brows jut over: in any case observe that;
Then, sir, after some violent noise,
Bring me forth in my shirt and my gown under my arm, with my torch in my hand, and my sword rear'd up thus,—
And with these words; *What noise is this? who calls Hieronimo?*
May it be done?

Pain. Yea, sir.

Hier. Well, sir, then bring me forth, bring me thro' alley and alley, still with a distracted countenance going along, and let my hair heave up my night-cap.

Let the clouds scowl, make the moon dark, the stars extinct, the winds blowing, the bells tolling, the owls shrieking, the toads croaking, the minutes jarring, and the clock striking twelve.

And then at last, sir, starting, behold a man hanging, and tott'ring, and tott'ring, as you know the wind will wave a man, and I with a trice to cut him down.

And looking upon him by the advantage of my torch, find it to be my son Horatio.

There you may show a passion, there you may show a passion.

Draw me like old Priam of Troy, crying, the house is a fire, the house is a fire; and the torch over my head; make me curse, make me rave, make me cry, make me mad, make me well again, make me curse hell, invocate, and in the end leave me in a trance, and so forth.

Pain. And is this the end?

Hier. O no, there is no end: the end is death and madness;
And I am never better than when I am mad;

Then methinks I am a brave fellow;
Then I do wonders; but reason abuseth me;
And there's the torment, there's the hell.
And last, sir, bring me to one of the murderers;
Were he as strong as Hector,
Thus would I tear and drag him up and down.
(*He beats the Painter in.*)

[These scenes, which are the very salt of the old play (which without them is but a caput mortuum, such another piece of flatness as Locrine), Hawkins, in his republication of this tragedy, has thrust out of the text into the notes: as omitted in the Second Edition, "printed for Ed. Allde, amended of such gross blunders as passed in the first:" and thinks them to have been *foisted in by the players.*—A late discovery at Dulwich College has ascertained that two sundry payments were made to Ben Jonson by the Theatre for furnishing additions to Hieronimo. See last edition of Shakspeare by Reed. There is nothing in the undoubted plays of Jonson which would authorize us to suppose that he could have supplied the scenes in question. I should suspect the agency of some "more potent spirit." Webster might have furnished them. They are full of that wild solemn preternatural cast of grief which bewilders us in the Duchess of Malfy.]

THE LOVE OF KING DAVID AND FAIR BETHSABE, WITH THE TRAGEDY OF ABSALOM. BY GEORGE PEELE.

Bethsabe, with her maid, bathing. She sings: and David sits above, viewing her.

The Song.

Hot sun, cool fire, temper'd with sweet air,
Black shade, fair nurse, shadow my white hair:
Shine sun, burn fire, breathe air and ease me,
Black shade, fair nurse, shroud me and please me;
Shadow (my sweet nurse) keep me from burning,
Make not my glad cause, cause of mourning.
Let not my beauty's fire
Enflame unstaid desire,
Nor pierce any bright eye
That wandereth lightly.

Bethsabe. Come gentle Zephyr trick'd with those perfumes
That erst in Eden sweetened Adam's love,
And stroke my bosom with the silken fan:
This shade (sun-proof) is yet no proof for thee,
Thy body smoother than this waveless spring,
And purer than the substance of the same,
Can creep through that his* lances cannot pierce.
Thou and thy sister soft and sacred Air,
Goddess of life, and governess of health,
Keeps every fountain fresh and arbor sweet;
No brazen gate her passage can repulse,
Nor bushy thicket bar thy subtle breath.
Then deck thee with thy loose delightsome robes,
And on thy wings bring delicate perfumes,
To play the wantons with us through the leaves.
David. What tunes, what words, what looks, what wonders pierce
My soul, incensed with a sudden fire!
What tree, what shade, what spring, what paradise,
Enjoys the beauty of so fair a dame!
Fair Eva, plac'd in perfect happiness,
Lending her praise-notes to the liberal heavens,
Struck with the accents of Arch-angels' tunes,
Wrought not more pleasure to her husband's thoughts,
Than this fair woman's words and notes to mine.
May that sweet plain that bears her pleasant weight,
Be still enamell'd with discolor'd flowers;
That precious fount bear sand of purest gold;
And for the pebble, let the silver streams
That pierce earth's bowels to maintain the source,
Play upon rubies, sapphires, chrysolites;
The brim let be imbrac'd with golden curls
Of moss that sleeps with sound the waters make
For joy to feed the fount with their recourse;
Let all the grass that beautifies her bower
Bear manna every morn instead of dew;
Or let the dew be sweeter far than that

* The sun's rays.

That hangs like chains of pearl on Hermon hill,
Or balm which trickled from old Aaron's beard.

Enter CUSAY.

See Cusay, see the flower of Israel,
The fairest daughter that obeys the king
In all the land the Lord subdued to me,
Fairer than Isaac's lover at the well,
Brighter than inside bark of new-hewn cedar,
Sweeter than flames of fine perfumed myrrh;
And comelier than the silver clouds that dance
On Zephyr's wings before the king of Heaven.
Cusay. Is it not Bethsabe the Hethite's wife
Urias, now at Rabeth siege with Joab?
David. Go now and bring her quickly to the King;
Tell her, her graces hath found grace with him.
Cusay. I will, my Lord. [*Exit.*
David. Bright Bethsabe shall wash in David's bower
In water mix'd with purest almond flower,
And bathe her beauty in the milk of kids;
Bright Bethsabe gives earth to my desires,
Verdure to earth, and to that verdure flowers,
To flowers sweet odors, and to odors wings,
That carries pleasures to the hearts of Kings.

* * * * * * * * *

Now comes my Lover tripping like the Roe,
And brings my longings tangled in her hair.
To joy her love I'll build a kingly bower,
Seated in hearing of a hundred streams,
That, for their homage to her sovereign joys,
Shall, as the serpents fold into their nests,
In oblique turnings wind the nimble waves
About the circles of her curious walks,
And with their murmur summon easeful sleep
To lay his golden sceptre on her brows.

[There is more of the same stuff, but I suppose the reader has a surfeit; especially as this Canticle of David has never been suspected to contain any pious sense couched underneath it, whatever his son's may. The Kingly bower "seated in hearing of a hundred streams," is the best of it.]

LUST'S DOMINION; OR, THE LASCIVIOUS QUEEN. A TRAGEDY, BY CHRISTOPHER MARLOWE

*The Queen Mother of Spain loves an insolent Moor.**

QUEEN.—ELEAZAR, *the Moor*.

Queen. Chime out your softest strains of harmony,
And on delicious Music's silken wings
Send ravishing delight to my love's ears;
That he may be enamor'd of your tunes.
Eleaz. Away, away.
Queen. No, no, says aye; and twice away, says stay.
Come, come, I'll have a kiss; but if you'll strive,
For one denial you shall forfeit five.
Eleaz. Be gone, be gone.
Queen. What means my love?
Burst all those wires; burn all those instruments;
For they displease my Moor. Art thou now pleas'd?
Or wert thou now disturb'd? I'll wage all Spain
To one sweet kiss, this is some new device
To make me fond and long. Oh, you men
Have tricks to make poor women die for you.
Eleaz. What, die for me? Away.
Queen. Away, what way? I prithee, speak more kindly.
Why dost thou frown? at whom?
Eleaz. At thee.
Queen. At me?
O why at me? for each contracted frown,
A crooked wrinkle interlines my brow:
Spend but one hour in frowns, and I shall look
Like to a Beldam of one hundred years.
I prithee, speak to me, and chide me not,
I prithee, chide, if I have done amiss;
But let my punishment be this, and this,
I prithee, smile on me, if but a while;
Then frown on me, I'll die. I prithee, smile.

* Such another as Aaron in Titus Andronicus.

Smile on me; and these two wanton boys,
These pretty lads that do attend on me,
Shall call thee Jove, shall wait upon thy cup
And fill thee nectar: their enticing eyes
Shall serve as crystal, wherein thou may'st see
To dress thyself; if thou wilt smile on me.
Smile on me; and with coronets of pearl
And bells of gold, circling their pretty arms,
In a round ivory fount these two shall swim,
And dive to make thee sport:
Bestow one smile, one little little smile,
And in a net of twisted silk and gold
In my all-naked arms thyself shalt lie.

[Kit Marlowe, as old Izaak Walton assures us, made that ***smooth song*** which begins "Come live with me and be my love." The same romantic invitations "in folly ripe in reason rotten," are given by the queen in the play, and the lover in the ditty. He talks of "beds of roses, buckles of gold:"

> Thy silver dishes for thy meat,
> *As precious as the Gods do eat,*
> Shall on an ivory table be
> Prepared each day for thee and me.

The lines in the extract have a luscious smoothness in them, and they were the most temperate which I could pick out of this Play. The rest is in King Cambyses' vein; rape, and murder, and superlatives; "huffing braggart puft" lines,* such as the play writers anterior to Shakspeare are full of, and Pistol "but coldly imitates." *Blood* is made as light of in some [illegible]

* Take a specimen from the speech of the Moor's:—

> Now Tragedy, thou minion of the night,
> Rhamnusia's pue-fellow, to thee I'll sing
> Upon an harp made of dead Spanish bones,
> The proudest instrument the world affords;
> When thou in crimson jollity, shall bathe
> Thy limbs as black as mine, in springs of blood
> Still gushing from the conduit head of Spain.
> To thee that never blush'st, though thy cheeks
> Are full of blood, O Saint Revenge, to thee
> I consecrate my murders, all my stabs,
> My bloody labors, tortures, stratagems,
> The volume of all wounds that wound [illegible]
> Mine is the Stage, thine is the Tragedy

these old dramas as *money* in a modern sentimental comedy; and as *this* is given away till it reminds us that it is nothing but counters, so *that* is spilt till it affects us no more than its representative, the paint of the property-man in the theatre.]

TAMBURLAINE THE GREAT; OR, THE SCYTHIAN SHEPHERD. IN TWO PARTS. BY CHRISTOPHER MARLOWE.—PART FIRST.

Tamburlaine's person described.

Of stature tall, and straightly fashioned;
Like his desire, lift* upwards and divine.
So large of limbs, his joints so strongly knit,
Such breadth of shoulders, as might mainly bear
Old Atlas' burthen. 'Twixt his manly pitch
A pearl more worth than all the world is placed:
Wherein by curious soverainty of art
Are fixed his piercing instruments of sight:
Whose fiery circles bear encompassed
A heaven of heavenly bodies in their spheres:
That guides his steps and actions to the throne
Where Honor sits invested royally.
Pale of complexion, wrought in him with passion
Thirsting with soverainty and love of arms.
His lofty brows in folds do figure death;
And in their smoothness amity and life.
About them hangs a knot of amber hair,
Wrapped in curls, as fierce Achilles' was;
On which the breath of heaven delights to play,
Making it dance with wanton majesty.
His arms and fingers long and sinewy,
Betokening valor and excess of strength;
In every part proportioned like the man
Should make the world subdue to Tamburlaine.

His custom in war.

The first day when he pitcheth down his tents,

* Lifted.

White is their hue ; and on his silver crest
A snowy feather spangled white he bears ;
To signify the mildness of his mind,
That, satiate with spoil, refuseth blood :
But when Aurora mounts the second time,
As red as scarlet is his furniture ;
Then must his kindled wrath be quenched with blood,
Not sparing any that can manage arms :
But if these threats move not submission,
Black are his colors, black pavilion,
His spear, his shield, his horse, his armor, plumes,
And jetty feathers, menace death and hell ;
Without respect of sex, degree or age,
He raseth all his foes with fire and sword.

[I had the same difficulty (or rather much more) in culling a few sane lines from this as from the preceding Play. The lunes of Tamburlaine are perfect "midsummer madness." Nebuchadnazar's are mere modest pretensions compared with the thundering vaunts of this Scythian Shepherd. He comes in (in the Second Part) drawn by conquered kings, and reproaches these *pampered jades of Asia* that they can *draw but twenty miles a day.* Till I saw this passage with my own eyes, I never believed that it was anything more than a pleasant burlesque of Mine Ancient's. But I assure my readers that it is soberly set down in a Play which their Ancestors took to be serious. I have subjoined the genuine speech for their amusement. *Enter Tamburlaine, drawn in his chariot by Trebizon and Soria, with bits in their mouths, reins in his left hand, in his right hand a whip, with which he scourgeth them.*

Tamb. Holla, ye pamper'd jades of Asia:
What can ye draw but twenty miles a day,
And have so proud a chariot at your heels,
And such a coachman as great Tamburlaine ?
But from Asphaltis, where I conquered you,
To Byron here, where thus I honor you ?
The horse that guide the golden eye of heaven,
And blow the morning from their nostrils,
Making their fiery gate above the glades,
Are not so honor'd in their governor
As you ye slaves in mighty Tamburlaine.
The headstrong jades of Thrace Alcides tamed,
That King Egeus fed with human flesh,
And made so wanton that they knew their strengths,
Were not subdued with valor more divine,

Than you by this unconquer'd arm of mine.
To make you fierce and fit my appetite,
You shall be fed with flesh as raw as blood,
And drink in pails the strongest muscadel:
If you can live with it, then live and draw
My chariot swifter than the racking clouds:
If not, then die like beasts, and fit for nought
But perches for the black and fatal ravens.
Thus am I right the scourge of highest Jove, &c.]

EDWARD THE SECOND. A TRAGEDY, BY CHRISTOPHER MARLOWE.

Gaveston shows what pleasures those are which the King chiefly acl-ights in.

Gav. I must have wanton poets, pleasant wits,
Musicians, that with touching of a string
May draw the pliant King which way I please.
Music and poetry are his delight;
Therefore I'll have Italian masks by night,
Sweet speeches, comedies, and pleasing shows;
And in the day, when he shall walk abroad,
Like Sylvan nymphs my pages shall be clad;
My men, like satyrs grazing on the lawns,
Shall with their goat-feet dance the antick hay.
Sometimes a lovely boy in Dian's shape,
With hair that gilds the water as it glides,
Crownets of pearl about his naked arms,
And in his sportful hands an olive tree
To hide those parts which men delight to see,
Shall bathe him in a spring, and there hard by,
One like Acteon, peeping thro' the grove,
Shall by the angry goddess be transform'd,
And running in the likeness of an hart,
By yelping hounds pull'd down, shall seem to die;
Such things as these best please his majesty.

The younger Mortimer repines at the insolence of Gaveston.

Mort. sen. Nephew I must to Scotland, thou stay'st here.

Leave now to oppose thyself against the King.
Thou seest by nature he is mild and calm,
And seeing his mind so doats on Gaveston,
Let him without controlment have his will.
The mightiest kings have had their minions:
Great Alexander lov'd Hephestion;
The conquering Hercules for his Hilas wept,
And for Patroclus stern Achilles droop'd.
And not kings only, but the wisest men;
The Roman Tully lov'd Octavius;
Grave Socrates wild Alcibiades.
Then let his grace, whose youth is flexible,
And promiseth as much as we can wish,
Freely enjoy that vain light-headed earl,
For riper years will wean him from such toys.

Mort. jun. Uncle, his wanton humor grieves not me;
But this I scorn, that one so basely born,
Should by his sovereign's favor grow so pert,
And riot with the treasure of the realm.
While soldiers mutiny for want of pay,
He wears a lord's revenue on his back,
And Midas-like, he jets it in the court,
With base outlandish cullions at his heels,
Whose proud fantastic liveries make such show,
As if that Proteus, god of shapes, appear'd.
I have not seen a dapper jack so brisk;
He wears a short Italian hooded cloak,
Larded with pearl, and in his Tuscan cap
A jewel of more value than the crown.
While others walk below, the king and he,
From out a window, laugh at such as we
And flout our train, and jest at our attire.
Uncle, 'tis this that makes me impatient.

The Barons reproach the King with the calamities which the realm endures from the ascendency of his wicked favorite Gaveston.

KING EDWARD, LANCASTER, WARWICK. *The* MORTIMERS *and other* LORDS.

Mort. jun. Nay, stay, my lord, I come to bring you news.
Mine uncle is taken prisoner by the Scots.
Edw. Then ransom him.
Lan. 'Twas in your wars, you should ransom him.
Mort. jun. And you shall ransom him, or else——
Kent. What, Mortimer, you will not threaten him?
Edw. Quiet yourself, you shall have the broad seal,
To gather for him throughout the realm.
Lan. Your minion Gaveston hath taught you this.
Mort. jun. My Lord, the family of the Mortimers
Are not so poor, but would they sell their land,
Could levy men enough to anger you.
We never beg, but use such prayers as these.
Edw. Shall I still be haunted thus?
Mort. jun. Nay, now you are here alone, I'll speak my mind.
Lan. And so will I, and then, my lord, farewell.
Mort. The idle triumphs, masks, lascivious shows,
And prodigal gifts bestow'd on Gaveston,
Have drawn thy treasure dry, and made thee weak;
The murmuring commons, overstretched, break.
Lan. Look for rebellion, look to be depos'd;
Thy garrisons are beaten out of France,
And lame and poor lie groaning at the gates.
The wild Oneyle, with swarms of Irish kerns,
Live uncontrol'd within the English pale.
Unto the walls of York the Scots make road,
And unresisted draw away rich spoils.
Mort. jun. The haughty Dane commands the narrow seas,
While in the harbor ride thy ships unrigg'd.
Lan. What foreign prince sends thee embassadors?
Mort. Who loves thee, but a sort of flatterers?
Lan. Thy gentle queen, sole sister to Valoys,
Complains that thou hast left her all forlorn.

Mort. Thy court is naked, being bereft of those,
That make a king seem glorious to the world :
I mean the peers, whom thou shouldst dearly love.
Libels are cast against thee in the street :
Ballads and rhimes made of thy overthrow.
Lan. The Northern brothers seeing their houses burnt,
Their wives and children slain, run up and down
Cursing the name of thee and Gaveston.
Mort. When wert thou in the field with banner spread ?
But once : and then thy soldiers march'd like players,
With garish robes, not armor ; and thyself,
Bedaub'd with gold, rode laughing at the rest,
Nodding and shaking of thy spangled crest,
Where women's favors hung like labels down.
Lan. And thereof came it, that the fleering Scots,
To England's high disgrace, have made this jig :
Maids of England, sore may you moorn,
For your lemmons you have lost at Bennock's born,
With a heave and a ho.
What weened the king of England,
So soon to have woon Scotland,
With a rombellow ?
Mort. Wigmore* shall fly to set my uncle free.
Lan. And when 'tis gone, our swords shall purchase more.
If ye be mov'd, revenge it as you can ;
Look next to see us with our ensigns spread.
[*Exeunt Nobles.*

The King being deposed, surrenders his crown into the hands of the Bishop of Winchester and the Earl of Leicester at Killingworth Castle.

Lei. Be patient, good my lord, cease to lament,
Imagine Killingworth castle were your court,
And that you lay for pleasure here a space,
Not of compulsion or necessity.
Edw. Leister, if gentle words might comfort me,
Thy speeches long ago had eas'd my sorrows ;
For kind and loving hast thou always been.

* A principal manor belonging to the Mortimers.

The griefs of private men are soon allay'd,
But not of kings. The forest deer being struck,
Runs to an herb that closeth up the wounds;
But when the imperial lion's flesh is gor'd,
He rends and tears it with his wrathful paw,
And highly scorning that the lowly earth
Should drink his blood, mounts up to th' air.
And so it fares with me, whose dauntless mind
Th' ambitious Mortimer would seek to curb,
And that unnatural queen, false Isabel,
That thus hath pent and mew'd me in a prison:
For such outrageous passions claw my soul,
As with the wings of rancor and disdain
Full oft am I soaring up to high heav'n,
To 'plain me to the gods against them both.
But when I call to mind I am a king,
Methinks I should revenge me of the wrongs.
That Mortimer and Isabel have done.
But what are kings, when regiment is gone,
But perfect shadows in a sunshine day?
My nobles rule, I bear the name of king;
I wear the crown, but am controll'd by them,
By Mortimer, and my unconstant queen,
Who spots my nuptial bed with infamy;
Whilst I am lodg'd within this cave of care,
Where sorrow at my elbow still attends,
To company my heart with sad laments,
That bleeds within me for this strange exchange.
But tell me, must I now resign my crown?
To make usurping Mortimer a king?
Bish. Your grace mistakes, it is for England's good,
And princely Edward's right, we crave the crown.
Edw. No, 'tis for Mortimer, not Edward's head;
For he 's a lamb, encompassed by wolves,
Which in a moment will abridge his life.
But if proud Mortimer do wear this crown,
Heav'ns turn it to a blaze of quenchless fire,
Or like the snaky wreath of Tisiphon,

Engirt the temples of his hateful head;
So shall not England's vines be perished,
But Edward's name survive, though Edward dies.
Lei. My lord, why waste you thus the time away?
They stay your answer, will you yield your crown?
Edw. Ah, Leister, weigh how hardly I can brook
To lose my crown and kingdom without cause;
To give ambitious Mortimer my right,
That like a mountain overwhelms my bliss,
In which extreme my mind here murther'd is.
But what the heav'ns appoint, I must obey.
Here, take my crown; the life of Edward too;
Two Kings in England cannot reign at once—
But stay awhile, let me be king till night,
That I may gaze upon this glittering crown;
So shall my eyes receive their last content,
My head the latest honor due to it,
And jointly both yield up their wished right.
Continue ever, thou celestial sun;
Let never silent night possess this clime;
Stand still, you watches of the element;
All times and seasons, rest you at a stay,
That Edward may be still fair England's king.
But day's bright beam doth vanish fast away,
And needs I must resign my wished crown;
Inhuman creatures! nurs'd with tiger's milk!
Why gape you for your sovereign's overthrow?
My diadem I mean, and guiltless life.
See, monsters, see, I'll wear my crown again.
What, fear you not the fury of your king?
But, hapless Edward, thou art fondly led,
They pass not for thy frowns as late they did,
But seek to make a new-elected king;
Which fills my mind with strange despairing thoughts,
Which thoughts are martyred with endless torments,
And in this torment comfort find I none,
But that I feel the crown upon my head;
And therefore let me wear it yet awhile.

Messenger. My lord, the parliament must have present news,
And therefore say, will you resign or no?
Edw. I'll not resign! but whilst I live be king.
Traitors be gone, and join with Mortimer.
Elect, conspire, install, do what you will;
Their blood and yours shall seal these treacheries!
Bish. This answer we 'll return, and so farewell.
Lei. Call them again, my lord, and speak them fair;
For if they go, the prince shall lose his right.
Edw. Call thou them back, I have no power to speak.
Lei. My lord, the king is willing to resign.
Bish. If he be not, let him choose.
Edw. O would I might! but heav'n and earth conspire
To make me miserable! here, receive my crown;
Receive it? no, these innocent hands of mine
Shall not be guilty of so foul a crime.
He of you all that most desires my blood,
And will be called the murtherer of a king,
Take it. What, are you mov'd? pity you me?
Then send for unrelenting Mortimer,
And Isabel, whose eyes, being turn'd to steel,
Will sooner sparkle fire than shed a tear.
Yet stay, for rather than I will look on them,
Here, here; now sweet God of heav'n,
Make me despise this transitory pomp,
And sit for ever inthroniz'd in heav'n!
Come death, and with thy fingers close my eyes,
Or, if I live, let me forget myself.

Berkley Castle. The King is left alone with Lightborn, a murderer.

Edw. Who's there? what light is that? wherefore com'st thou?
Light. To comfort you, and bring you joyful news.
Edw. Small comfort finds poor Edward in thy looks.
Villain, I know thou com'st to murder me.
Light. To murder you, my most gracious lord!
Far is it from my heart to do you harm.
The queen sent me to see how you were used,
For she relents at this your misery;
And what eyes can refrain from shedding tears,

To see a king in this most piteous state.
Edw. Weep'st thou already? list a while to me
And then thy heart, were it as Gurney's* is,
Or as Matrevis',* hewn from the Caucasus,
Yet will it melt, ere I have done my tale.
This dungeon where they keep me is a sink
Wherein the filth of all the castle falls.
Light. O villains!
Edw. And there, in mire and puddle have I stood
This ten days' space; and lest that I should sleep,
One plays continually upon a drum.
They give me bread and water, being a king;
So that, for want of sleep and sustenance,
My mind's distemper'd, and my body's numb'd,
And whether I have limbs or no, I know not.
O would my blood drop out from every vein,
As doth this water from my tattered robes.
Tell Isabel the queen, I look'd not thus,
When for her sake I ran at tilt in France,
And there unhors'd the duke of Cleremont.
Light. O speak no more, my lord! this breaks my heart.
Lie on this bed, and rest yourself awhile.
Edw. These looks of thine can harbor nought but death!
I see my tragedy written in thy brows.
Yet stay awhile, forbear thy bloody hand,
And let me see the stroke before it comes,
That even then when I shall lose my life,
My mind may be more stedfast on my God.
Light. What means your highness to mistrust me thus?
Edw. What mean'st thou to dissemble with me thus?
Light. These hands were never stained with innocent blood,
Nor shall they now be tainted with a king's.
Edw. Forgive my thought, for having such a thought.
One jewel have I left, receive thou this.
Still fear I, and I know not what's the cause,
But every joint shakes as I give it thee.
O if thou harbor'st murder in thy heart,

* His keepers.

Let the gift change thy mind, and save thy soul.
Know that I am a king ; Oh, at that name
I feel a hell of grief. Where is my crown?
Gone, gone, and do I still remain alive ?
Light. You're overwatch'd, my lord, lie down and rest.
Edw. But that grief keeps me waking, I should sleep;
For not these ten days have these eyelids closed.
Now as I speak they fall, and yet with fear
Open again. O wherefore sitt'st thou here ?
Light. If you mistrust me, I'll be gone, my lord.
Edw. No, no, for if thou mean'st to murder me,
Thou wilt return again; and therefore stay.
Light. He sleeps.
Edw. O let me not die ; yet stay, O stay awhile.
Light. How now, my lord ?
Edw. Something still buzzeth in mine ears,
And tells me if I sleep I never wake;
This fear is that which makes me tremble thus.
And therefore tell me, wherefore art thou come ?
Light. To rid thee of thy life ; Matrevis, come.
Edw. I am too weak and feeble to resist:
Assist me, sweet God, and receive my soul.

[This tragedy is in a very different style from "mighty Tamburlaine." The reluctant pangs of abdicating Royalty in Edward furnished hints which Shakspeare scarce improved in his Richard the Second; and the death-scene of Marlowe's king moves pity and terror beyond any scene, ancient or modern, with which I am acquainted.]

THE RICH JEW OF MALTA. A TRAGEDY, BY CHRISTOPHER MARLOWE.

Barabas, the Rich Jew, in his Counting-house, with heaps of gold before him; in contemplation of his wealth.

Bar. So that of thus much that return was made ;
And of the third part of the Persian ships
There was a venture summ'd and satisfied.

As to those Samnites, and the Men of Uzz,
That bought my Spanish oils and wines of Greece,
Here have I purst their paltry silverbings.
Fie, what a trouble 'tis to count this trash!
Well fare the Arabians, who so richly pay
The things they traffic for with wedge of gold,
Whereof a man may easily in a day
Tell that, which may maintain him all his life.
The needy groom, that never finger'd groat,
Would make a miracle of thus much coin:
But he whose steel-barr'd coffers are cramm'd full,
And all his life-time hath been tired,
Wearying his fingers' ends with telling it,
Would in his age be loth to labor so,
And for a pound to sweat himself to death.
Give me the merchants of the Indian mines,
That trade in metal of the purest mould;
The wealthy Moor, that in the eastern rocks
Without control can pick his riches up,
And in his house heap pearl like pebble-stones;
Receive them free and sell them by the weight,
Bags of fiery opals, sapphires, amethysts,
Jacinths, hard topas, grass-green emeralds,
Beauteous rubies, sparkling diamonds,
And seld-seen costly stones of so great price
As one of them, indifferently rated,
And of a caract of this quality,
May serve in peril of calamity
To ransome great kings from captivity.
This is the ware wherein consists my wealth:
And thus methinks should men of judgment frame
Their means of traffic from the vulgar trade,
And, as their wealth increaseth, so inclose
Infinite riches in a little room.
But now how stands the wind?
Into what corner peers my Halcyon's bill?
Ha! to the east? yes: see, how stand the vances?
East and by south: why then, I hope my ships,

I sent for Egypt and the bordering isles,
Are gotten up by Nilus' winding banks.
Mine argosies from Alexandria,
Loaden with spice and silks, now under sail,
Are smoothly gliding down by Candy shore
To Malta, through our Mediterranean sea.

Certain Merchants enter, and inform Barabas, that his ships from various ports are safe arrived, and riding in Malta roads.—He descants on the temporal condition of the Jews, how they thrive and attain to great worldly prosperity, in spite of the curse denounced against them.

Thus trolls our fortune in by land and sea,
And thus are we on every side enrich'd.
These are the blessings promis'd to the Jews,
And herein was old Abram's happiness.
What more may heaven do for earthly man,
Than thus to pour out plenty in their laps,
Ripping the bowels of the earth for them,
Making the sea their servants, and the winds
To drive their substance with successful blasts!
Who hateth me but for my happiness?
Or who is honor'd now but for his wealth?
Rather had I, a Jew, be hated thus,
Than pitied in a Christian poverty:
For I can see no fruits in all their faith,
But malice, falsehood, and excessive pride,
Which methinks fits not their profession.
Haply some hapless man hath conscience,
And for his conscience lives in beggary.
They say we are a scattered nation:
I cannot tell; but we have scrambled up
More wealth by far than those that brag of faith.
There's Kirriah Jairim, the great Jew of Greece,
Obed in Bairseth, Nones in Portugal,
Myself in Malta, some in Italy,
Many in France, and wealthy every one;
Aye, wealthier far than any Christian.
I must confess, we come not to be kings;

That's not our fault; alas! our number's few;
And crowns come either by succession,
Or urged by force; and nothing violent,
Oft have I heard tell, can be permanent.
Give us a peaceful rule; make Christians kings,
That thirst so much for principality.

[Marlowe's Jew does not approach so near to Shakspeare's as his Edward II. does to Richard II. Shylock, in the midst of his savage purpose, is a man. His motives, feelings, resentments, have something human in them. "If you wrong us, shall we not revenge?" Barabas is a mere monster, brought in with a large painted nose, to please the rabble. He kills in sport, poisons whole nunneries, invents infernal machines. He is just such an exhibition as a century or two earlier might have been played before the Londoners *by the Royal command*, when a general pillage and massacre of the Hebrews had been previously resolved on in the cabinet. It is curious to see a superstition wearing out. The idea of a Jew (which our pious ancestors contemplated with such horror) has nothing in it now revolting. We have tamed the claws of the beast, and pared its nails, and now we take it to our arms, fondle it, write plays to flatter it: it is visited by princes, affects a taste, patronises the arts, and is the only liberal and gentleman-like thing in Christendom.]

THE TRAGICAL HISTORY OF THE LIFE AND DEATH OF DOCTOR FAUSTUS. BY CHRISTOPHER MARLOWE.

How Faustus fell to the study of magic.

———— born of parents base of stock
In Germany, within a town called Rhodes:
At riper years to Wirtemberg he went,
Whereas his kinsmen chiefly brought him up.
So much he profits in Divinity,
That shortly he was graced with Doctor's name,
Excelling all, and sweetly can dispute
In the heavenly matters of theology:
Till swoln with cunning and a self-conceit,
His waxen wings did mount above his reach,
And melting, heaven conspired his overthrow;
For falling to a devilish exercise,

And glutted now with Learning's golden gifts,
He surfeits on the cursed necromancy.
Nothing so sweet as magic is to him,
Which he prefers before his chiefest bliss.

Faustus, in his study, runs through the circle of the sciences; and being satisfied with none of them, determines to addict himself to magic.

Faust. Settle thy studies, Faustus, and begin
To sound the depth of that thou wilt profess:
Having commenc'd, be a Divine in show,
Yet level at the end of every art,
And live and die in Aristotle's works.
Sweet Analytics, 'tis thou hast ravish'd me.
Bene disserere est finis Logices.
Is, to dispute well, Logic's chiefest end?
Affords this art no greater miracle?
Then read no more; thou hast attained that end.
A greater subject fitteth Faustus' wit.
Bid Economy farewell: and Galen come.
Be a physician, Faustus, heap up gold,
And be eterniz'd for some wond'rous cure.
Summum bonum medicinæ sanitas:
The end of physic is our bodies' health.
Why, Faustus: hast thou not attain'd that end?
Are not thy bills hung up as monuments,
Whereby whole cities have escap'd the plague,
And divers desperate maladies been cured?
Yet art thou still but Faustus, and a man.
Couldst thou make men but live eternally,
Or being dead raise men to life again,
Then this profession were to be esteem'd.
Physic, farewell. Where is Justinian?
Si una eademque res legatur duobus,
Alter rem, alter valorem, rei, &c.
A petty case of paltry legacies.
Exhereditari filium non potest pater, nisi, &c.
Such is the subject of the Institute,
And universal body of the Law.

This study fits a mercenary drudge,
Who aims at nothing but eternal trash,
Too servile and illiberal for me.
When all is done, Divinity is best.
Jerome's Bible, Faustus: view it well.
Stipendium peccati mors est: ha! *Stipendium, &c.*
The reward of sin is death: that's hard.
Si peccasse negamus, fallimur, et nulla est in nobis veritas.
If we say that we have no sin, we deceive ourselves, and there is no truth in us.
Why then belike we must sin, and so consequently die.
Aye, we must die an everlasting death.
What doctrine call you this? *Che sera sera:*
What will be shall be. Divinity adieu.
These Metaphysics of Magicians,
And necromantic books, are heavenly.
Lines, Circles, Letters, Characters:
Aye, these are those that Faustus most desires.
O what a world of profit and delight,
Of power, of honor, of omnipotence,
Is promised to the studious artizan!
All things that move between the quiet poles
Shall be at my command. Emperors and Kings
Are but obey'd in their several provinces;
But his dominion that exceeds in this,
Stretcheth as far as doth the mind of man:
A sound Magician is a Demigod.
Here tire my brains to gain a deity.
* * * * * * * *
How am I glutted with conceit of this!
Shall I make Spirits fetch me what I please?
Resolve me of all ambiguities?
Perform what desperate enterprises I will?
I'll have them fly to India for gold,
Ransack the ocean for orient pearl,
And search all corners of the new-found world
For pleasant fruits and princely delicates.
I 'll have them read me strange philosophy;

And tell the secrets of all foreign kings;
I'll have them wall all Germany with brass,
And with swift Rhine circle all Wirtemberg:
I 'll have them fill the public schools with skill,
Wherewith the students shall be bravely clad:
I 'll levy soldiers with the coin they bring,
And chase the Prince of Parma from our land;
And reign sole king of all the provinces;
Yea, stranger engines for the brunt of war,
Than was the fiery keel at Antwerp bridge,
I 'll make my servile Spirits to invent,
Come, German Valdes, and Cornelius,
And make me wise with your sage conference.

Enter VALDES *and* CORNELIUS.

Faust. Valdes, sweet Valdes, and Cornelius,
Know that your words have won me at the last
To practise magic and concealed Arts.
Philosophy is odious and obscure:
Both Law and Physic are for petty wits:
'Tis Magic, Magic, that hath ravish'd me.
Then gentle friends aid me in this attempt:
And I that have with subtil syllogisms
Gravell'd the Pastors of the German Church,
And made the flowering pride of Wirtemberg
Swarm to my problems, as th' infernal Spirits
On sweet Musæus when he came to hell,
Will be as cunning as Agrippa was,
Whose shadow made all Europe honor him.

Vald. Faustus, these books, thy wit, and our experience,
Shall make all nations canonize us.
As Indian Moors obey their Spanish Lords,
So shall the Spirits of every Element
Be always serviceable to us three:
Like Lions shall they guard us when we please;
Like Almain Rutters with their horsemen's staves,
Or Lapland Giants trotting by our sides:
Sometimes like Women, or unwedded Maids,

Shadowing more beauty in their airy brows
Than have the white breasts of the Queen of Love.
Corn. The miracles that magic will perform,
Will make thee vow to study nothing else.
He that is grounded in astrology,
Enricht with tongues, well seen in minerals,
Hath all the principles magic doth require.
Faust. Come, show me some demonstrations magical,
That I may conjure in some bushy grove,
And have these joys in full possession.
Vald. Then haste thee to some solitary grove,
And bear wise Bacon's and Albanus' works,
The Hebrew Psalter and New Testament;
And whatsoever else is requisite
We will inform thee, ere our conference cease.

Faustus being instructed in the elements of magic by his friends Valdes and Cornelius, sells his soul to the devil, to have an Evil Spirit at his command for twenty-four years.—When the years are expired, the devils claim his soul.

FAUSTUS—*the night of his death.* WAGNER, *his Servant.*

Faust. Say, Wagner, thou hast perused my Will,
How dost thou like it?
Wag. Sir, so wondrous well,
As in all humble duty I do yield
My life and lasting service for your love. [*Exit.*

Three Scholars enter.

Faust. Gramercy, Wagner,
Welcome, Gentlemen.
First Sch. Now, worthy Faustus, methinks your looks are chang'd.
Faust. Oh, Gentlemen.
Sec. Sch. What ails Faustus?
Faust. Ah, my sweet chamber-fellow, had I lived with thee, then had I lived still, but now must die eternally. Look, Sirs, comes he not? comes he not?
First Sch. Oh, my dear Faustus, what imports this fear?

Sec. Sch. Is all our pleasure turned to melancholy?

Third Sch. He is not well with being over solitary.

Sec. Sch. If it be so, we will have physicians, and Faustus shall be cured.

Third Sch. 'Tis but a surfeit, Sir; fear nothing.

Faust. A surfeit of a deadly sin that hath damn'd both body and soul.

Sec. Sch. Yet, Faustus, look up to heaven, and remember mercy is infinite.

Faust. But Faustus' offence can ne'er be pardoned. The serpent that tempted Eve may be saved, but not Faustus. O Gentlemen, hear me with patience, and tremble not at my speeches. Though my heart pant and quiver to remember that I have been a student here these thirty years. O would I had ne'er seen Wirtemberg, never read book! and what wonders have I done, all Germany can witness, yea, all the world: for which, Faustus hath lost both Germany and the world: yea, heaven itself, heaven the seat of God, the throne of the blessed, the kingdom of joy and must remain in hell for ever. Hell, O hell, for ever. Sweet friends, what shall become of Faustus being in hell for ever?

Sec. Sch. Yet Faustus call on God.

Faust. On God whom Faustus hath abjured? on God whom Faustus hath blasphemed? O my God, I would weep but the devil draws in my tears. Gush forth blood instead of tears, yea, life and soul. Oh, he stays my tongue: I would lift up my hands, but see, they hold 'em, they hold 'em.

Scholars. Who, Faustus?

Faust. Why, Lucifer and Mephostophilis. O gentlemen, I gave them my soul for cunning.

Scholars. O God forbid.

Faust. God forbid it indeed, but Faustus hath done it: for the vain pleasure of four-and-twenty years hath Faustus lost eternal joy and felicity. I writ them a bill with mine own blood, the date is expired: this is the time, and he will fetch me.

First Sch. Why did not Faustus tell us of this before, that Divines might have prayed for thee?

Faust. Oft have I thought to have done so; but the devil

threatened to tear me in pieces if I named God; to fetch me body and soul if I once gave ear to divinity; and now it is too late. Gentlemen, away, lest you perish with me.

Sec. Sch. O what may we do to save Faustus?

Faust. Talk not of me, but save yourselves and depart.

Third Sch. God will strengthen me, I will stay with Faustus.

First Sch. Tempt not God, sweet friend, but let us into the next room and pray for him.

Faust. Aye, pray for me, pray for me; and what noise soever you hear, come not unto me, for nothing can rescue me.

Sec. Sch. Pray thou, and we will pray, that God may have mercy upon thee.

Faust. Gentlemen, farewell; if I live till morning, I'll visit you: if not, Faustus is gone to hell.

Scholars. Faustus, farewell.

FAUSTUS *alone.—The clock strikes eleven.*

Faust. O Faustus,
Now hast thou but one bare hour to live,
And then thou must be damn'd perpetually.
Stand still you ever-moving spheres of heaven,
That time may cease, and midnight never come.
Fair Nature's eye, rise, rise again, and make
Perpetual day: or let this hour be but
A year, a month, a week, a natural day
That Faustus may repent and save his soul.
O lente lente currite noctis equi.
The stars move still, time runs, the clock will strike,
The devil will come, and Faustus must be damn'd.
O I will leap to heaven, who pulls me down?
See where Christ's blood streams in the firmament:
One drop of blood will save me; Oh, my Christ,
Rend not my heart for naming of my Christ.
Yet will I call on him: O spare me, Lucifer.
Where is it now? 'tis gone?
And see, a threat'ning arm, and angry brow.
Mountains and hills come, come, and fall on me,
And hide me from the heavy wrath of heaven.

No? then I will headlong run into the earth:
Gape earth. O no, it will not harbor me.
You stars that reigned at my nativity.
Whose influence have allotted death and hell,
Now draw up Faustus like a foggy mist
Into the entrails of yon laboring cloud;
That when you vomit forth into the air,
My limbs may issue from your smoaky mouths,
But let my soul mount, and ascend to heaven.

The watch strikes.

O half the hour is past: 'twill all be past anon.
O if my soul must suffer for my sin,
Impose some end to my incessant pain.
Let Faustus live in hell a thousand years,
A hundred thousand, and at the last be saved:
No end is limited to damned souls.
Why wert thou not a creature wanting soul?
Or why is this immortal that thou hast?
Oh, Pythagoras, Metempsychosis, were that true,
This soul should fly from me, and I be chang'd
Into some brutish beast.
All beasts are happy, for when they die,
Their souls are soon dissolv'd in elements;
But mine must live still to be plagued in hell.
Curst be the parents that engender'd me:
No, Faustus, curse thyself, curse Lucifer,
That hath depriv'd thee of the joys of heaven.

The clock strikes twelve.

It strikes, it strikes; now, body, turn to air,
Or Lucifer will bear thee quick to hell.
O soul, be chang'd into small water drops,
And fall into the ocean; ne'er be found.

Thunder, and enter the Devils.

O mercy heaven, look not so fierce on me.
Adders and serpents, let me breathe awhile:
Ugly hell gape not: come not Lucifer:

I'll burn my books: Oh Mephostophilis!
* * * * * *

Enter SCHOLARS.

First Sch. Come gentlemen, let us go visit Faustus,
For such a dreadful night was never seen
Since first the world's creation did begin;
Such fearful shrieks and cries were never heard.
Pray heaven the Doctor have escaped the danger.
Sec. Sch. O help us heavens! see here are Faustus' limbs
All torn asunder by the hand of death.
Third Sch. The devil whom Faustus serv'd hath torn him thus:
For 'twixt the hours of twelve and one, methought
I heard him shriek, and call aloud for help;
At which same time the house seem'd all on fire
With dreadful horror of these damned fiends.
Sec. Sch. Well, gentlemen, though Faustus' end be such
As every Christian heart laments to think on:
Yet, for he was a scholar once admired
For wondrous knowledge in our German schools,
We'll give his mangled limbs due burial:
And all the scholars, cloth'd in mourning black,
Shall wait upon his heavy funeral.
Chorus. Cut is the branch that might have grown full strait,
And burned is Apollo's laurel bough
That sometime grew within this learned man:
Faustus is gone! Regard his hellish fall,
Whose fiendful fortune may exhort the wise
Only to wonder at unlawful things:
Whose deepness doth entice such forward wits
To practise more than heavenly power permits.

[The growing horrors of Faustus are awfully marked by the hours and half hours as they expire and bring him nearer and nearer to the exactment of his dire compact. It is indeed an agony and bloody sweat.

Marlowe is said to have been tainted with atheistical positions, to have denied God and the Trinity. To such a genius the history of Faustus must have been delectable food: to wander in fields where curiosity is forbidden to go, to approach the dark gulf near enough to look in, to be busied in speculations which are the rottenest part of the core of the fruit that fell from the tree of knowledge. Barabas the Jew, and Faustus the conjuror, are offsprings of a mind which at least delighted to dally with interdicted subjects. They both talk a language which a believer would have been tender of putting into the mouth of a character though but in fiction. But the holiest minds have sometimes not thought it blameable to counterfeit impiety in the person of another, to bring Vice in upon the stage speaking her own dialect, and, themselves being armed with an Unction of self-confident impunity, have not scrupled to handle and touch that familiarly which would be death to others. Milton, in the person of Satan, has started speculations hardier than any which the feeble armory of the atheist ever furnished: and the precise, strait-laced Richardson has strengthened Vice, from the mouth of Lovelace, with entangling sophistries and abstruse pleas against her adversary Virtue, which Sedley, Villiers, and Rochester wanted depth of libertinism sufficient to have invented."]

THE HOG HATH LOST HIS PEARL; A COMEDY, BY ROBERT TAILOR.

Carracus appoints his friend Albert to meet him before the break of day at the house of the old Lord Wealthy, whose daughter Maria has consented to a stolen match with Carracus.—Albert, arriving before his friend, is mistaken by Maria for Carracus, and takes advantage of the night to wrong his friend.

Enter ALBERT, *solus.*

Alb. This is the green, and this the chamber-window ;
And see, the appointed light stands in the casement,
The ladder of ropes set orderly,
Yet he that should ascend, slow in his haste,
Is not as yet come hither.
Were it any friend that lives but Carracus,
I'd try the bliss which this fine time presents.
Appoint to carry hence so rare an heir,
And be so slack ! 'sfoot it doth move my patience.
Would any man that is not void of sense
Not have watch'd night by night for such a prize ?
Her beauty's so attractive, that by Heaven
My heart half grants to do my friend a wrong.
Forego these thoughts, Albert, be not a slave
To thy affection ; do not falsify

Thy faith to him whose only friendship's worth
A world of women. He is such a one,
Thou canst not live without his good,
He is and was ever as thine own heart's blood.

[*Maria beckons him from the window.*

'Sfoot, see, she beckons me for Carracus.
Shall my base purity cause me neglect
This present happiness! I will obtain it,
Spite of my timorous conscience. I am in person,
Habit and all, so like to Carracus,
It may be acted and ne'er call'd in question.
Mar. (*calls*) Hist! Carracus, ascend:
All is as clear as in our hearts we wish'd.

[*Albert ascends, and being on the top of the ladder puts out the candle.*

Mar. O love, why do you so?
Alb. I heard the steps of some coming this way.
Did you not hear Albert pass by as yet?
Mar. Not any creature pass this way this hour.
Alb. Then he intends just at the break of day
To lend his trusty help to our departure.
Mar. Come then, dear Carracus, thou now shalt rest
Upon that bed where fancy oft hath thought thee;
Which kindness until now I ne'er did grant thee,
Nor would I now but that thy loyal faith
I have so often tried! even now
Seeing thee come to that most honor'd end,
Through all the dangers which black night presents,
For to convey me hence and marry me. [*They go in.*

Enter CARRACUS, *to his appointment.*

Car. How pleasing are the steps we lovers make,
When in the paths of our content we pace,
To meet our longings! what happiness it is
For man to love! but oh, what greater bliss
To love and be belov'd! O what one virtue
E'er reign'd in me, that I should be enrich'd

With all earth's good at once? I have a friend,
Selected by the heavens as a gift
To make me happy whilst I live on earth;
A man so rare of goodness, firm of faith,
That earth's content must vanish in his death.
Then for my love and mistress of my soul,
A maid of rich endowments, beautified
With all the virtues nature could bestow
Upon mortality, who this happy night
Will make me gainer of her heavenly self.
And see, how suddenly I have attain'd
To the abode of my desired wishes!
This is the green; how dark the night appears!
I cannot hear the tread of my true friend.
Albert! hist, Albert!—he's not come as yet,
Nor is the appointed light set in the window.
What if I call Maria? it may be
She feared to set a light, and only heark'neth
To hear my steps; and yet I dare not call,
Lest I betray myself, and that my voice,
Thinking to enter in the ears of her,
Be of some other heard: no, I will stay
Until the coming of my dear friend Albert.
But now think, Carracus, what end will be
Of this thou dost determine: thou art come
Hither to rob a father of that wealth
That solely lengthens his now drooping years,
His virtuous daughter, and all (of that sex) left
To make him happy in his aged days.
The loss of her may cause him to despair,
Transport his near-decaying sense to frenzy,
Or to some such abhorred inconveniency
Whereto frail age is subject. I do ill in this,
And must not think but that a father's plaint
Will move the heavens to pour forth misery
Upon the head of disobediency.
Yet reason tells us, parents are o'erseen,
When with too strict a rein they do hold in

Their child's affections, and control that love
Which the high powers divine inspire them with;
When in their shallowest judgments they may know,
Affection crost brings misery and wo.
But whilst I run contemplating on this,
I softly pace to my desired bliss.
I'll go into the next field, where my friend
Told me the horses were in readiness. [*Exit.*

ALBERT *descending from* MARIA.

Mar. But do not stay. What if you find not Albert?
Alb. I'll then return alone to fetch you hence.
Mar. If you should now deceive me, having gain'd
What you men seek for——
Alb. Sooner I'll deceive
My soul—and so I fear I have. [*Aside.*
Mar. At your first call I will descend.
Alb. Till when, this touch of lips be the true pledge
Of Carracus' constant true devoted love.
Mar. Be sure you stay not long; farewell.
I cannot lend an ear to hear you part. [*Maria goes in.*
Alb. But you did lend a hand unto my entrance.
[*He descends.*
Alb. (*solus*) How have I wrong'd my friend, my faithful friend!
Robb'd him of what's more precious than his blood,
His earthly heaven, the unspotted honor
Of his soul-joying mistress! the fruition of whose bed
I yet am warm of; whilst dear Carracus
Wanders this cold night through the unshelt'ring field
Seeking me, treach'rous man, yet no man neither,
Though in an outward show of such appearance,
But am a dev'l indeed, for so this deed
Of wronged love and friendship rightly makes me.
I may compare my friend to one that's sick,
Who, lying on his death-bed, calls to him
His dearest-thought friend, and bids him go
To some rare-gifted man that can restore
His former health; this his friend sadly hears,

And vows with protestations to fulfil
His wish'd desires with his best performance;
But then no sooner seeing that the death
Of his sick friend would add to him some gain,
Goes not to seek a remedy to save,
But like a wretch hides him to dig his grave;
As I have done for virtuous Carracus.
Yet, Albert, be not reasonless to indanger
What thou may'st yet secure. Who can detect
The crime of thy licentious appetite?
I hear one's pace; 'tis surely Carracus.

Enter CARRACUS.

Car. Not find my friend! sure some malignant planet
Rules o'er this night, and envying the content
Which I in thought possess, debars me thus
From what is more than happy, the lov'd presence
Of a dear friend and love.

Alb. 'Tis wronged Carracus by Albert's baseness:
I have no power now to reveal myself.

Car. The horses stand at the appointed place,
And night's dark coverture makes firm our safety.
My friend is surely fall'n into a slumber
On some bank hereabouts; I will call him.
Friend, Albert, Albert.

Alb. Whate'er you are that call, you know my name.

Car. Aye, and thy heart, dear friend.

[*Maria appears above.*

Mar. My Carracus, are you so soon return'd?
I see, you'll keep your promise.

Car. Who would not do so having past it thee,
Cannot be fram'd of aught but treachery.
Fairest, descend, that by our hence departing
We may make firm the bliss of our content.

Mar. Is your friend Albert with you?

Alb. Yes, and your servant, honor'd Lady.

Mar. Hold me from falling, Carracus. [*She descends.*

Car. Come, fair Maria, the troubles of this night

Are as fore-runners to ensuing pleasures.
And, noble friend, although now Carracus
Seems, in the gaining of this beauteous prize,
To keep from you so much of his lov'd treasure,
Which ought not to be mixed; yet his heart
Shall so far strive in your wish'd happiness,
That if the loss and ruin of itself
Can but avail your good—
Alb. O friend, no more; come, you are slow in haste.
Friendship ought never be discuss'd in words,
Till all her deeds be finish'd. Who, looking in a book,
And reads but some part of it only, cannot judge
What praise the whole deserves, because his knowledge
Is grounded but on part—as thine, friend, is,
Ignorant of that black mischief I have done thee.
[*Aside.—Exeunt.*

Albert, after the marriage of Carracus, struck with remorse for the injury he has done to his friend, knocks at Carracus's door, but cannot summon resolution to see him, or to do more than inquire after his welfare.

Alb. Conscience, thou horror unto wicked men,
When wilt thou cease thy all-afflicting wrath,
And set my soul free from the labyrinth
Of thy tormenting terror? O but it fits not!
Should I desire redress, or wish for comfort,
That have committed an act so inhuman,
Able to fill Shame's spacious chronicle?
Who but a damn'd one could have done like me?
Robb'd my dear friend in a short moment's time
Of his love's high-priz'd gem of chastity:
That which so many years himself hath staid for.
How often hath he, as he lay in bed,
Sweetly discours'd to me of his Maria!
And with what pleasing passions did he suffer
Love's gentle war-siege: then he would relate
How he first came unto her fair eyes' view;
How long it was e'er she could brook affection;

And then how constant she did still abide.
I then at this would joy, as if my breast
Had sympathized in equal happiness
With my true friend, but now, when joy should be,
Who but a damn'd one would have done like me?
He hath been married now at least a month;
In all which time I have not once beheld him.
This is his house.
I'll call to know his health, but will not see him;
My looks would then betray me, for, should he ask
My cause of seeming sadness or the like,
I could not but reveal, and so pour on
Worse unto ill, which breeds confusion. [*He knocks.*

A Servant opens.

Alb. Is the master of the house within?
Serv Yes, marry, is he, sir: would you speak with him?
Alb. My business is not so troublesome:
Is he in health with his late espoused wife?
Serv. Both are exceeding well, sir.
Alb. I am truly glad on't: farewell, good friend.
Serv. I pray you, let's crave your name, sir; I may else have anger.
Alb. You may say, one Albert, riding by this way, only inquired their health.
Serv. I will acquaint so much. [*Exit Servant.*
Alb. How like a poisonous doctor have I come
To inquire their welfare, knowing that myself
Have giv'n the potion of their ne'er-recovery;
For which I will afflict myself with torture ever.
And since the earth yields not a remedy
Able to salve the sores my lust hath made,
I'll now take farewell of society,
And the abode of men, to entertain a life
Fitting my fellowship in desart woods,
Where beasts like me consort; there may I live,
Far off from wronging virtuous Carracus.
There's no Maria, that shall satisfy

My hateful lust: the trees shall shelter
This wretched trunk of mine, upon whose barks
I will engrave the story of my sin.
And there this short breath of mortality
I'll finish up in that repentant state,
Where not the allurements of earth's vanities
Can e'er o'ertake me: there's no baits for lust,
No friend to ruin; I shall then be free
From practising the art of treachery.
Thither then, steps, where such content abides,
Where penitency not disturb'd may grieve,
Where on each tree and springing plant I'll carve
This heavy motto of my misery,
Who but a damn'd one could have done like me?

THE TRAGEDY OF NERO. AUTHOR UNCERTAIN

Scenical Personation.

'Tis better in a play
Be Agamemnon, than himself indeed.
How oft, with danger of the field beset,
Or with home-mutinies, would he un-be
Himself; or, over cruel altars weeping,
Wish, that with putting off a vizard he
Might his true inward sorrow lay aside!
The shows of things are better than themselves,
How doth it stir this airy part of us
To hear our poets tell imagin'd fights
And the strange blows that feigned courage gives.
When I Achilles hear upon the Stage
Speak honor and the greatness of his soul,
Methinks I too could on a Phrygian spear
Run boldly, and make tales for after times:
But when we come to act it in the deed,
Death mars this bravery, and the ugly fears
Of th' other world sit on the proudest brow:
And boasting valor loseth his red cheek.

THE MERRY DEVIL OF EDMONTON.
AUTHOR UNCERTAIN.*

Millisent, the fair daughter of Clare, was betrothed, with the consent of her parents, to Raymond, son of Mounchensey; but the elder Mounchensey, being since fallen in his fortunes, Clare revokes his consent and plots a marriage for his daughter with the rich heir of Jerningham. Peter Fabel, a good magician, who had been Tutor to young Raymond Mounchensey at College, determines by the aid of his art to assist his pupil in obtaining fair Millisent.

PETER FABEL, *solus.*

Fab. Good old Mounchensey, is thy hap so ill,
That for thy bounty and thy royal parts,
Thy kind alliance should be held in scorn;
And after all these promises by Clare,
Refuse to give his daughter to thy son,
Only because thy revenues cannot reach
To make her dowage of so rich a jointure,
As can the heir of wealthy Jerningham?
And therefore is the false fox now in hand
To strike a match betwixt her and the other,
And the old grey-beards now are close together,
Plotting in the garden. Is it even so?
Raymond Mounchensey, boy, have thou and I
Thus long at Cambridge read the liberal arts,
The metaphysics, magic, and those parts
Of the most secret deep philosophy?
Have I so many melancholy nights
Watch'd on the top of Peter House highest tower?
And come we back unto our native home,
For want of skill to lose the wench thou lovest?
We'll first hang Envil† in such rings of mist,
As never rose from any dampish fen;
I'll make the brinish sea to rise at Ware,
And drown the marshes unto Stratford bridge;

* It has been ascribed without much proof to Shakspeare, and to Michael Drayton.

† Enfield.

I'll drive the deer from Waltham in their walks,
And scatter them like sheep in every field.
We may perhaps be crost; but if we be,
He shall cross the devil that but crosses me.
But here comes Raymond, disconsolate and sad;
And here comes the gallant must have his wench.

Enter RAYMOND MOUNCHENSEY, *young* JERNINGHAM, *ana young* CLARE.

Jern. I prithee, Raymond, leave these solemn dumps,
Revive thy spirits; thou that before hast been
More watchful than the day-proclaiming cock,
As sportive as a kid, as frank and merry
As mirth herself.—
If aught in me may thy content procure,
It is thy own, thou mayst thyself assure.

Raym. Ha! Jerningham, if any but thyself
Had spoke that word, it would have come as cold
As the bleak northern winds upon the face of winter,
From thee they have some power on my blood;
Yet being from thee, had but that hollow sound
Come from the lips of any living man,
It might have won the credit of mine ear,
From thee it cannot.

Jern. If I understand thee I am a villain:
What! dost thou speak in parables to thy friend;

Fab. (*to Jern.*) You are the man, sir, must have Millisent,
The match is making in the garden now;
Her jointure is agreed on, and the old men,
Your fathers, mean to launch their pursy bags,
But in mean time to thrust Mounchensey off,
For color of this new intended match.
Fair Millisent to Cheston* must be sent,
To take the approbation of a Nun.
Ne'er look upon me, lad, the match is done.

Jern. Raymond Mounchensey, now I touch thy grief
With the true feeling of a zealous friend.

* Cheshunt

And as for thy fair beauteous Millisent,
With my vain breath I will not seek to slubber
Her angel-like perfections. But thou know'st
That Essex hath the saint that I adore.
Where'er didst meet me, that we two were jovial,
But like a wag thou hast not laughed at me,
And with regardless jesting mock'd my love ?
How many a sad and weary summer's night
My sighs have drunk the dew from off the earth,
And I have taught the nightingale to wake,
And from the meadows sprung the early lark
An hour before she should have list to sing ?
I have loaded the poor minutes with my moans,
That I have made the heavy slow pac'd hours
To hang like heavy clogs upon the day.
But, dear Mounchensey, had not my affection
Seiz'd on the beauty of another dame,
Before I'd wrong the chase, and leave the love
Of one so worthy, and so true a friend,
I will abjure both beauty and her sight,
And will in love become a counterfeit.

Raym. Dear Jerningham, thou hast begot my life,
And from the mouth of hell, where now I sat,
I feel my spirit rebound against the stars;
Thou hast conquer'd me, dear friend, and my free soul
Nor time nor death can by their power control.

Fab. Frank Jerningham, thou art a gallant boy;
And were he not my pupil, I would say,
He were as fine a metal'd Gentleman,
Of as free a spirit, and as fine a temper,
As any in England; and he is a man,
That very richly may deserve thy love.
But, noble Clare, this while of our discourse,
What may Mounchensey's honor to thyself
Exact upon the measure of thy grace ?

Cla. Raymond Mounchensey, I would have thee know,
He does not breathe this air,
Whose love I cherish, and whose soul I love,

More than Mounchensey's:
Nor ever in my life did see the man,
Whom for his wit, and many virtuous parts,
I think more worthy of my sister's love.
But since the matter grows into this pass,
I must not seem to cross my father's will;
But when thou list to visit her by night,
My horse is saddled, and the stable door
Stands ready for thee; use them at thy pleasure.
In honest marriage wed her frankly, boy;
And if thou getst her, lad, God give thee joy.
Raym. Then care away! let fate my fall pretend,
Back'd with the favors of so true a friend.
Fab. Let us alone to bustle for the set;
For age and craft with wit and art hath met.
I'll make my Spirits dance such nightly jigs
Along the way 'twixt this and Tot'nam Cross,
The Carriers' Jades shall cast their heavy packs,
And the strong hedges scarce shall keep them in.
The milk-maids' cuts shall turn the wenches off,
And lay their dossers tumbling in the dust:
The frank and merry London Prentices,
That come for cream and lusty country cheer,
Shall lose their way, and scrambling in the ditches
All night, shall whoop and hollow, cry, and call,
And none to other find the way at all.
Raym. Pursue the project, scholar; what we can do
To help endeavor, join our lives thereto.*

* This scene has much of Shakspeare's manner in the sweetness and goodnaturedness of it. It seems written to make the reader happy. Few of our dramatists or novelists have attended enough to this. They torture and wound us abundantly. They are economists only in delight. Nothing can be finer, more gentlemanlike, and noble, than the conversation and compliments of these young men. How delicious is Raymond Mounchensey's forgetting, in his fears, that Jerningham has a "Saint in Essex:" and how sweetly his friend reminds him!—I wish it could be ascertained that Michael Drayton was the author of this piece: it would add a worthy appendage to the renown of that Panegyrist of my native Earth; who has gone over her soil (in his Polyolbion) with the fidelity of a herald, and the

The Prioress of Cheston's charge to fair Millisent.

Jesus' daughter, Mary's child,
Holy matron, woman mild,
For thee a Mass shall still be said,
Every sister drop a bead
And those again, succeeding them,
For you shall sing a Requiem.
To her Father. May your soul be blithe,
That so truly pay your tythe;
He, that many children gave,
'Tis fit that he one child should have.
To Millisent. Then, fair virgin, hear my spell,
For I must your duty tell.
First at mornings take your book,
The glass wherein yourself must look;
Your young thoughts so proud and jolly
Must be turn'd to motions holy;
For your busk, attires and toys,
Have your thoughts on heavenly joys:
And for all your follies past,
You must do penance, pray and fast.
You shall ring the sacring bell,
Keep your hours, and tell your knell.
Rise at midnight to your matins,
Read your psalter, sing your Latins;
And when your blood shall kindle pleasure,
Scourge yourself in plenteous measure.
You must read the morning mass,
You must creep unto the cross,
Put cold ashes on your head,
Have a hair-cloth for your bed,
Bind your beads and tell your needs,
Your holy Aves and your Creeds;
Holy maid, this must be done,
If you mean to live a Nun.

painful love of a son; who has not left a rivulet (so narrow that it may be stept over) without honorable mention; and has animated Hills and Streams with life and passion above the dreams of old mythology.

GREEN'S TU QUOQUE; OR, THE CITY GALLANT. A COMEDY. BY JOSEPH COOKE.

Men more niggardly of their love than women.

Thrice happy days they were, and too soon gone,
When as the heart was coupled with the tongue;
And no deceitful flattery, or guile
Hung on the lover's tear-commixed smile.
Could women learn but that imperiousness,
By which men use to stint our happiness
(When they have purchas'd us for to be theirs
By customary sighs and forced tears)
To give us bits of kindness, lest we faint,
But no abundance; that we ever want,
And still are begging: which too well they know
Endears affection, and doth make it grow.
Had we those sleights, how happy were we then
That we might glory over love-sick men!
But arts we know not, nor have any skill
To feign a sour look to a pleasing will;
Nor couch a secret love in show of hate:
But, if we like, must be compassionate.*

Adversity.

How ruthless men are to adversity!
My acquaintance scarce will know me; when we meet
They cannot stay to talk, they must be gone;
And shake me by the hand as if I burnt them.

Prodigality.

That which gilded over his imperfections,
Is wasted and consumed, even like ice,
Which by the vehemence of heat dissolves,
And glides to many rivers; so his wealth,
That felt a prodigal hand, hot in expense,
Melted within his gripe, and from his coffers
Ran like a violent stream to other men's.

* This is so like Shakspeare, that one seems almost to remember it as a speech of Desdemona's, upon perceiving an alteration in the behavior of the Moor.

THE COMEDY OF OLD FORTUNATUS. BY THOMAS DECKER.

The Goddess Fortune appears to Fortunatus, and offers him the choice of six things. He chooses Riches.

FORTUNE. FORTUNATUS.

Fortune. Before thy soul at this deep lottery
Draw forth her prize, ordain'd by destiny,
Know that here's no recanting a first choice.
Choose then discreetly : for the laws of fate,
Being grav'n in steel, must stand inviolate.
Fortunat. Daughters of Jove and the unblemish'd Night,
Most righteous Parcæ, guide my genius right:
Wisdom, Strength, Health, Beauty, Long Life, and Riches.
Fortune. Stay, Fortunatus ; once more hear me speak.
If thou kiss Wisdom's cheek and make her thine,
She'll breathe into thy lips divinity,
And thou (like Phœbus) shall speak oracle ;
Thy heav'n-inspired soul on Wisdom's wings
Shall fly up to the Parliament of Jove,
And read the Statutes of Eternity,
And see what's past and learn what is to come.
If thou lay claim to Strength, armies shall quake
To see thee frown: as Kings at mine do lie,
So shall thy feet trample on empery.
Make Health thine object, thou shalt be strong proof
'Gainst the deep searching darts of surfeiting,
Be ever merry, ever revelling.
Wish but for Beauty, and within thine eyes
Two naked Cupids amorously shall swim,
And on thy cheeks I'll mix such white and red,
That Jove shall turn away young Ganimede,
And with immortal arms shall circle thee.
Are thy desires Long Life ? thy vital thread
Shall be stretch'd out, thou shalt behold the change
Of monarchies, and see those children die
Whose great great grandsires now in cradles lie.
If through Gold's sacred hunger thou dost pine ;

Those gilded wantons which in swarms do run
To warm their slender bodies in the sun,
Shall stand for number of those golden piles
Which in rich pride shall swell before thy feet:
As those are, so shall these be infinite.
Fortunat. O whither am I wrapt beyond myself?
More violent conflicts fight in every thought
Than his whose fatal choice Troy's downfall wrought.
Shall I contract myself to Wisdom's love?
Then I lose Riches; and a wise man poor
Is like a sacred book that's never read;
To himself he lives and to all else seems dead.
This age thinks better of a gilded fool,
Than of a threadbare saint in Wisdom's school.
I will be Strong: then I refuse Long Life;
And though mine arm should conquer twenty worlds,
There's a lean fellow beats all conquerors:
The greatest Strength expires with loss of breath,
The mightiest in one minute stoop to death.
Then take Long Life, or Health; should I do so,
I might grow ugly, and that tedious scroll
Of months and years much misery might enroll:
Therefore I'll beg for Beauty; yet I will not:
The fairest cheek hath oftentimes a soul
Leprous as sin itself, than hell more foul.
The Wisdom of this world is idiotism;
Strength a week reed; Health Sickness' enemy,
And it at length will have the victory.
Beauty is but a painting; and Long Life
Is a long journey in December gone,
Tedious and full of tribulation,
Therefore dread sacred Empress, make me rich:
My choice is Store of Gold; the Rich are Wise,
He that upon his back rich garments wears
Is Wise, though on his head grow Midas' ears.
Gold is the Strength, the Sinews of the world,
The Health, the Soul, the Beauty most divine;
A mask of gold hides all deformities;

Gold is heaven's physic, life's restorative ;
Oh therefore make me Rich.

Fortune gives to Fortunatus a purse that is inexhaustible. With this he puts on costly attire, and visits all the Asian Courts, where he is caressed and made much of for his infinite wealth. At Babylon he is shown by the Soldan a wondrous hat, which in a wish transports the wearer whithersoever he pleases, over land and sea. Fortunatus puts it on, wishes himself at home in Cyprus ; where he arrives in a minute, as his sons Ampedo and Andelocia are talking of him ; and tells his Travels.

FORTUNATUS. AMPEDO. ANDELOCIA.

Fort. Touch me not, boys, I am nothing but air, let none speak to me till you have marked me well.—Am I as you are, or am I transformed ?

And. Methinks, father, you look as you did, only your face is more withered.

Fort. Boys, be proud ; your father hath the whole world in this compass. I am all felicity up to the brims. In a minute am I come from Babylon ; I have been this half hour in Farmagosta.

And. How ! in a minute, father ? I see travellers must lie.

Fort. I have cut through the air like a falcon. I would have it seem strange to you. But 'tis true. I would not have you believe it neither. But 'tis miraculous and true. Desire to see you brought me to Cyprus. I'll leave you more gold, and go to visit more countries.

Amp. The frosty hand of age now nips your blood,
And strews her snowy flowers upon your head,
And gives you warning that within few years
Death needs must marry you : those short lines, minutes,
That dribble out your life, must needs be spent
In peace, not travel ; rest in Cyprus then.
Could you survey ten worlds, yet you must die ;
And bitter is the sweet that's reaped thereby.

And. Faith, father, what pleasure have you met by walking your stations ?

Fort. What pleasure, boy ? I have revelled with Kings, danced with Queens, dallied with Ladies ; worn strange attires ;

seen Fantasticoes; conversed with Humorists; been ravished with divine raptures of Doric, Lydian and Phrygian harmonies; I have spent the day in triumphs and the night in banquetting.

And. O rare: this was heavenly.—He that would not be an Arabian Phœnix to burn in these sweet fires, let him live like an owl for the world to wonder at.

Amp. Why, brother, are not all these Vanities?

Fort. Vanities! Ampedo, thy soul is made of lead, too dull, too ponderous, to mount up to the incomprehensible glory that Travel lifts men to.

And. Sweeten mine ears, good father, with some more.

Fort. When in the warmth of mine own country's arms
We yawn'd like sluggards, when this small horizon
Imprison'd up my body, then mine eyes
Worshipp'd these clouds as brightest: but, my boys,
The glist'ring beams which do abroad appear
In other heavens, fire is not half so clear.
For still in all the regions I have seen,
I scorn'd to crowd among the muddy throng
Of the rank multitude, whose thicken'd breath
(Like to condensed fogs) do choke that beauty,
Which else would dwell in every Kingdom's cheek.
No; I still boldly stept into their Courts:
For there to live 'tis rare, O 'tis divine,
There shall you see faces angelical;
There shall you see troops of chaste Goddesses,
Whose star-like eyes have power (might they still shine)
To make night day, and day more crystalline.
Near these you shall behold great Heroes,
White-headed Councillors, and Jovial Spirits,
Standing like fiery Cherubim to guard
The monarch, who in godlike glory sits
In midst of these, as if this deity
Had with a look created a new world,
The standers by being the fair workmanship.

And. Oh how my soul is rapt to a Third Heaven!
I'll travel sure, and live with none but Kings.

Amp. But tell me, father, have you in all Courts

Beheld such glory, so majestical,
In all perfection, no way blemished?
  Fort. In some Courts shall you see Ambition
Sit, piecing Dædalus's old waxen wings;
But being clapt on, and they about to fly,
Even when their hopes are busied in the clouds,
They melt again the sun of Majesty,
And down they tumble to destruction.
By travel, boys, I have seen all these things.
Fantastic Compliment stalks up and down,
Trickt in outlandish feathers; all his words,
His looks, his oaths, are all ridiculous,
All apish, childish, and Italianate. * * *

Orleans to his friend Galloway defends the passion with which (being a prisoner in the English king's court) he is enamored to frenzy of the king's daughter Agripyna.

ORLEANS. GALLOWAY.

  Orl. This music makes me but more out of tune.
O Agripyna.
  Gall. Gentle friend, no more.
Thou say'st Love is a madness: hate it then,
Even for the name's sake.
  Orl. O I love that madness,
Even for the name's sake.
  Gall. Let me tame this frenzy,
By telling thee thou art a prisoner here,
By telling thee she's daughter to a King,
By telling thee the King of Cyprus' son
Shines like a sun between her looks and thine,
Whilst thou seem'st but a star to Agripyne.
He loves her.
  Orl. If he do, why so do I.
  Gall. Love is ambitious and loves Majesty.
  Orl. Dear friend, thou art deceiv'd: Love's voice doth sing
As sweetly in a beggar as a king.
  Gall. Dear friend, thou art deceiv'd: O bid thy soul
Lift up her intellectual eyes to heaven,

And in this ample book of wonders read,
Of what celestial mould, what sacred essence,
Her self is form'd: the search whereof will drive
Sounds musical among the jarring spirits,
And in sweet tune set that which none inherits.
Orl. I'll gaze on heaven if Agripyne be there.
If not: fa, la, la, Sol, la, &c.
Gall. O call this madness in: see, from the windows
Of every eye Derision thrusts out cheeks
Wrinkled with idiot laughter; every finger
Is like a dart shot from the hand of Scorn,
By which thy name is hurt, thy honor torn.
Orl. Laugh they at me, sweet Galloway?
Gall. Even at thee.
Orl. Ha, ha, I laugh at them: are they not mad,
That let my true true sorrow make them glad?
I dance and sing only to anger Grief,
That in his anger he might smite life down
With his iron fist: good heart! it seemeth then,
They laugh to see grief kill me: O fond Men,
You laugh at others' tears; when others smile,
You tear yourselves in pieces; vile, vile, vile.
Ha, ha, when I behold a swarm of Fools
Crowding together to be counted Wise,
I laugh because sweet Agripyne's not there,
But weep because she is not any where;
And weep because (whether she be or not)
My love was ever and is still forgot; forgot, forgot, forgot.
Gall. Draw back this stream: why should my Orleans mourn?
Orl. Look yonder, Galloway, dost thou see that sun?
Nay, good friend, stare upon it, mark it well:
Ere he be two hours elder, all that glory
Is banish'd heaven, and then, for grief, this sky
(That's now so jocund) will mourn all in black.
And shall not Orleans mourn? alack, alack:
O what a savage tyranny it were
To enforce Care laugh, and Wo not shed a tear!
Dead is my Love; I am buried in her scorn:

That is my sunset; and shall I not mourn!
Yes by my troth I will.
Gall. Dear friend forbear;
Beauty (like Sorrow) dwelleth every where.
Rase out this strong idea of her face:
As fair as her's shineth in any place.
Orl. Thou art a Traitor to that White and Red,
Which sitting on her cheeks (being Cupid's throne)
Is my heart's Soveraine: O when she is dead,
This wonder (beauty) shall be found in none.
Now Agripyne's not mine, I vow to be
In love with nothing but deformity.
O fair Deformity, I muse all eyes
Are not enamor'd of thee: thou didst never
Murder men's hearts, or let them pine like wax
Melting against the sun of thy destiny;
Thou art a faithful nurse to Chastity;
Thy beauty is not like to Agripyne's,
For cares, and age, and sickness her's deface,
But thine's eternal: O Deformity,
Thy fairness is not like to Agripyne's,
For (dead) her beauty will no beauty have,
But thy face looks most lovely in the grave.

[The humor of a frantic Lover is here done to the life. Orleans is as passionate an Inamorato as any which Shakspeare ever drew. He is just such another adept in Love's reasons. The sober people of the world are with him

a swarm of fools
Crowding together to be counted wise.

He talks "pure Biron and Romeo," he is almost as poetical as they, quite as philosophical, only a little madder. After all, Love's Sectaries are a "reason unto themselves." We have gone retrograde in the noble Heresy since the days when Sidney proselyted our nation to this mixed health and disease; the kindliest symptom yet the most alarming crisis in the ticklish state of youth; the nourisher and the destroyed of hopeful wits: the mother of twin-birds, wisdom and folly, valor and weakness; the servitude above freedom; the gentle mind's religion; the liberal superstition.]

SATIRO-MASTIX, OR THE UNTRUSSING OF THE HUMOROUS POET. BY THOMAS DECKER.

The King exacts an oath from Sir Walter Terill to send his Bride Cælestina to Court on the marriage night. Her Father, to save her honor, gives her a poisonous mixture which she swallows.

TERILL. CÆLESTINA. FATHER.

Cæl. Why didst thou swear?
Ter. The King
Sat heavy on my resolution,
Till (out of breath) it panted out an oath.
Cæl. An oath! why, what's an oath? 'tis but the smoke
Of flame and blood; the blister of the spirit
Which riseth from the steam of rage, the bubble
That shoots up to the tongue and scalds the voice
(For oaths are burning words). Thou swor'st but one,
'Tis frozen long ago: if one be number'd,
What countrymen are they, where do they dwell,
That speak nought else but oaths?
Ter. They 're Men of Hell.
An oath! why 'tis the traffic of the soul,
'Tis law within a man; the seal of faith,
The bond of every conscience; unto whom
We set our thoughts like hands; yea, such a one
I swore, and to the King; a King contains
A thousand thousand; when I swore to him,
I swore to them; the very hairs that guard
His head will rise up like sharp witnesses
Against my faith and loyalty: his eye
Would straight condemn me: argue oaths no more;
My oath is high, for to the King I swore.
Cæl. Must I betray my chastity, so long
Clean from the treason of rebelling lust?
O husband, O my father, if poor I
Must not live chaste, then let me chastely die.
Fath. Aye, here's a charm shall keep thee chaste, come, come.
Old time hath left us but an hour to play

Our parts; begin the scene; who shall speak first?
On I, I play the King, and Kings speak first:
Daughter, stand thou here, thou son Terill there;
We need no prologue, the King entering first
He 's a most gracious Prologue: marry, then
For the catastrophe or Epilogue,
There's one in cloth of silver, which no doubt
Will please the hearers well when he steps out;
His mouth is filled with words: see where he stands:
He 'll make them clap their eyes besides their hands.
But to my part: suppose who enters now,
A King whose eyes are set in silver; one
That blusheth gold, speaks music, dancing walks,
Now gathers nearer, takes thee by the hand,
When straight thou think'st the very orb of heaven,
Moves round about thy fingers; then he speaks,
Thus—thus—I know not how.

Cæl. Nor I to answer him.

Fath. No, girl, know'st thou not how to answer him?
Why, then, the field is lost, and he rides home
Like a great conqueror: not answer him!
Out of thy part already! foil'd the scene!
Disrank'd the lines! disarm'd the action!

Ter. Yes, yes, true chastity is tongued so weak
'Tis overcome ere it know how to speak.

Fath. Come, come, thou happy close of every wrong,
'Tis thou that canst dissolve the hardest doubt;
'Tis time for thee to speak, we all are out.
Daughter and you the man whom I call son,
I must confess I made a deed of gift
To heaven and you, and gave my child to both;
When on my blessing I did charm her soul
In the white circle of true chastity,
Still to run true till death: now, sir, if not,
She forfeits my rich blessing, and is fined
With an eternal curse; then I tell you,
She shall die now, now whilst her soul is true.

Ter. Die!

Cœl. Aye, I am death's echo.
Fath. O my son:
I am her father; every tear I shed
Is threescore ten years old; I weep and smile
Two kinds of tears; I weep that she must die,
I smile that she must die a virgin: thus
We joyful men mock tears, and tears mock us.
Ter. What speaks that cup?
Fath. White wine and poison.
Ter. Oh!
That very name of poison poisons me.
Thou winter of a man, thou walking grave,
Whose life is like a dying taper: how
Canst thou define a lover's laboring thoughts?
What scent hast thou but death! what taste but earth?
The breath that purls from thee is like the steam
Of a new-open'd vault: I know thy drift;
Because thou 'rt travelling to the land of graves,
Thou covet'st company, and hither bring'st
A health of poison to pledge death: a poison
For this sweet spring; this element is mine,
This is the air I breathe; corrupt it not;
This heaven is mine, I bought it with my soul
Of him that sells a heaven to buy a soul.
Fath. Well, let her go; she's thine, thou call'st her thine,
Thy element, the air thou breath'st; thou know'st
The air thou breath'st is common; make her so.
Perhaps thou 'lt say none but the King shall wear
Thy night-gown, she that laps thee warm with love;
And that Kings are not common: then to show
By consequence he cannot make her so.
Indeed she may promote her shame and thine,
And with your shames speak a good word for mine.
The King shining so clear, and we so dim,
Our dark disgraces will be seen through him.
Imagine her the cup of thy moist life,
What man would pledge a King in his own wife?
Ter. She dies: that sentence poisons her: O life!

What slave would pledge a King in his own Wife!
Cæl. Welcome O poison, physic against lust,
Thou wholesome medicine to a constant blood;
Thou rare apothecary that canst keep
My chastity preserv'd within this box
Of tempting dust, this painted earthen pot
That stands upon the stall of the white soul,
To set the shop out like a flatterer,
To draw the customers of sin: come, come,
Thou art no poison, but a diet drink
To moderate my blood: White-innocent Wine,
Art thou made guilty of my death? oh no,
For thou thyself art poison; take me hence,
For Innocence shall murder Innocence. [*Drinks.*
Ter. Hold, hold, thou shalt not die, my bride, my wife,
O stop that speedy messenger of death;
O let him not run down that narrow path
Which leads unto thy heart, nor carry news
To thy removing soul that thou must die.
Cæl. 'Tis done already, the Spiritual Court
Is breaking up, all Offices discharg'd
My Soul removes from this weak Standing-house
Of frail mortality: Dear father, bless
Me now and ever: Dearer man, farewell;
I jointly take my leave of thee and life;
Go tell the King thou hast a constant wife.
Fath. Smiles on my cheeks arise
To see how sweetly a true virgin dies.

[The beauty and force of this scene are much diminished to the reader of the entire play, when he comes to find that this solemn preparation is but a sham contrivance of the father's, and the potion which Cælestina swallows nothing more than a sleeping draught; from the effects of which she is to awake in due time, to the surprise of her husband, and the great mirth and edification of the King and his courtiers. As Hamlet says, they do but "poison in jest." The sentiments are worthy of a real martyrdom, and an Appian sacrifice in earnest.]

THE HONEST WHORE. A COMEDY. BY THOMAS DECKER

Hospital for Lunatics.

There are of mad men, as there are of tame,
All humor'd not alike. We have here some
So apish and fantastic, play with a feather;
And, though 'twould grieve a soul to see God's image
So blemish'd and defac'd, yet do they act
Such antick and such pretty lunacies,
That, spite of sorrow, they will make you smile.
Others again we have, like hungry lions,
Fierce as wild bulls, untameable as flies.—

Patience.

Patience! why, 'tis the soul of peace:
Of all the virtues, 'tis nearest kin to heaven;
It makes men look like gods.—The best of men
That e'er wore earth about him was a Sufferer,
A soft, meek, patient, humble, tranquil spirit;
The first true gentleman that ever breath'd.

THE SECOND PART OF THE HONEST WHORE. BY THOMAS DECKER.

Bellafront, a reclaimed Harlot, recounts some of the miseries of her profession.

Like an ill husband, though I knew the same
To be my undoing, follow'd I that game.
Oh when the work of lust had earn'd my bread,
To taste it how I trembled, lest each bit
Ere it went down should choke me chewing it.
My bed seemed like a cabin hung in hell,
The bawd hell's porter, and the liquorish wine
The pandar fetch'd was like an easy fine
For which methought I leas'd away my soul,
And oftentimes even in my quaffing-bowl
Thus said I to myself: I am a Whore,

And have drunk down thus much confusion more.
——— when in the street
A fair young modest damsel* I did meet,
She seem'd to all a Dove, when I pass'd by,
And I to all a Raven; every eye
That follow'd her, went with a bashful glance;
At me each bold and jeering countenance
Darted forth scorn: to her as if she had been
Some Tower unvanquished would they vail;
'Gainst me swoln rumor hoisted every sail;
She crown'd with reverend praises pass'd by them,
I though with face mask'd could not 'scape the Hem;
For, as if heaven had set strange marks on whores,
Because they should be pointing stocks to man,
Drest up in civilest shape a Courtezan;
Let her walk saint-like noteless and unknown,
Yet she's betray'd by some trick of her own.

The happy Man.

He that makes gold his wife, but not his whore,
He that at noon day walks by a prison door,
He that in the sun is neither beam nor moat,

* This simple picture of Honor and Shame, contrasted without violence, and expressed without immodesty, is worth all the *strong lines* against the Harlot's Profession, with which both Parts of this play are offensively crowded. A Satirist is always to be suspected, who, to make vice odious, dwells upon all its acts and minutest circumstances with a sort of relish and retrospective gust. But so near are the boundaries of panegyric and invective, that a worn-out Sinner is sometimes found to make the best Declaimer against Sin. The same high-seasoned descriptions which in his unregenerate state served to inflame his appetites, in his new province of a Moralist will serve him (a little turned) to expose the enormity of those appetites in other men. No one will doubt, who reads Marston's Satires, that the author in some part of his life must have been something more than a theorist in vice. Have we never heard an old preacher in the pulpit display such an insight into the mystery of ungodliness, as made us wonder with reason how a good man came by it? When Cervantes with such proficiency of fondness dwells upon the Don's library, who sees not that he has been a great reader of books of Knight-Errantry? perhaps was at some time of his life in danger of falling into those very extravagances which he ridicules so happily in his Hero?

He that's not mad after a petticoat,
He for whom poor men's curses dig no grave,
He that is neither Lord's nor Lawyer's slave,
He that makes This his sea and That his shore,
He that in 's coffin is richer than before,
He that counts Youth his sword and Age his staff,
He whose right hand carves his own epitaph,
He that upon his death-bed is a Swan,
And dead, no Crow ; he is a Happy Man.*

WESTWARD HOE. A COMEDY. BY THOMAS DECKER AND JOHN WEBSTER.

Pleasure, the general pursuit.

Sweet Pleasure !
Delicious Pleasure ! earth's supremest good,
The spring of blood, though it dry up our blood.
Rob me of that (though to be drunk with pleasure,
As rank excess even in best things is bad,
Turns man into a beast) yet, that being gone,
A horse, and this (the goodliest shape) all one.
We feed ; wear rich attires ; and strive to cleave
The stars with marble towers ; fight battles ; spend
Our blood, to buy us names ; and in iron hold
Will we eat roots to imprison fugitive gold :
But to do thus what spell can us excite ?
This ; the strong magic of our appetite :
To feast which richly, life itself undoes.
Who 'd not die thus ?
Why even those that starve in voluntary wants,
And, to advance the mind, keep the flesh poor,
The world enjoying them, they not the world ;
Would they do this, but that they are proud to suck
A sweetness from such sourness ?

* The turn of this is the same with Iago's definition of a Deserving Woman " She that was ever fair and never proud," &c. The matter is superior.

Music.

Let music
Charm with her excellent voice an awful silence
Through all this building, that her sphery soul
May (on the wings of air) in thousand forms
Invisibly fly, yet be enjoy'd.

LINGUA; A COMEDY. BY ANTHONY BREWER.

Languages.

The ancient Hebrew, clad with mysteries;
The learned Greek, rich in fit epithets,
Blest in the lovely marriage of pure words;
The Chaldee wise, the Arabian physical,
The Roman eloquent, and Tuscan grave,
The braving Spanish, and the smooth-tongued French—

Tragedy and Comedy.

—fellows both, both twins, but so unlike
As birth to death, wedding to funeral:
For this that rears himself in buskins quaint,
Is pleasant at the first, proud in the midst,
Stately in all, and bitter death at end.
That in the pumps doth frown at first acquaintance,
Trouble the midst, but in the end concludes
Closing up all with a sweet catastrophe.
This grave and sad, distained with brinish tears:
That light and quick, with wrinkled laughter painted:
This deals with nobles, kings, and emperors,
Full of great fears, great hopes, great enterprizes;
This other trades with men of mean condition,
His projects small, small hopes, and dangers little:
This gorgeous, broider'd with rich sentences:
That fair, and purfled round with merriments.
Both vice detect, and virtue beautify,
By being death's mirror, and life's looking-glass.

THE HISTORY OF ANTONIO AND MELLIDA. THE FIRST PART. BY JOHN MARSTON.

Andrugio, Duke of Genoa, banished his country, with the loss of a son, supposed drowned, is cast upon the territory of his mortal enemy the Duke of Venice with no attendants but Lucio, an old nobleman, and a Page.

Andr. Is not yon gleam the shudd'ring Morn that flakes
With silver tincture the east verge of heaven?
Luc. I think it is, so please your Excellence.
Andr. Away, I have no Excellence to please.
Prithee observe the custom of the world;
That only flatters greatness, states exalts.
And please my Excellence! O Lucio,
Thou hast been ever held respected, dear,
Even precious to Andrugio's inmost love:
Good, flatter not.
My thoughts are fixt in contemplation
Why this huge earth, this monstrous animal
That eats her children, should not have eyes and ears.
Philosophy maintains that Nature's wise,
And forms no useless nor unperfect thing.
Did Nature make the earth, or the earth Nature?
For earthly dirt makes all things, makes the man,
Moulds me up honor, and, like a cunning Dutchman,
Paints me a puppet even with seeming breath,
And gives a sot appearance of a soul.
Go to, go to; thou ly'st, Philosophy.
Nature forms things unperfect, useless, vain.
Why made she not the earth with eyes and ears?
That she might see desert and hear men's plaints;
That when a soul is splitted, sunk with grief,
He might fall thus upon the breast of Earth,
And in her ear halloo his misery,
Exclaiming thus: O thou all bearing Earth,
Which men do gape for till thou cramm'st their mouths
And choak'st their throats with dust: open thy breast,
And let me sink into thee: look who knocks;
Andrugio calls. But O she's deaf and blind.

A wretch but lean relief on earth can find.
Luc. Sweet Lord, abandon passion ; and disarm.
Since by the fortune of the tumbling sea
We are roll'd up upon the Venice marsh,
Let's clip all fortune, lest more low'ring fate—
Andr. More low'ring fate ! O Lucio, choke that breath.
Now I defy chance. Fortune's brow hath frown'd,
Even to the utmost wrinkle it can bend :
Her venom's spit. Alas ! what country rests,
What son, what comfort, that she can deprive ?
Triumphs not Venice in my overthrow ?
Gapes not my native country for my blood ?
Lies not my son tomb'd in the swelling main ?
And in more low'ring fate ? There's nothing left
Unto Andrugio but Andrugio :
And that
Nor mischief, force, distress, nor hell can take :
Fortune my fortunes not my mind shall shake.
Luc. Speak like yourself : but give me leave, my Lord,
To wish you safety. If you are but seen,
Your arms display you ; therefore put them off,
And take——
Andr. Would'st have me go unarm'd among my foes ?
Being besieg'd by Passion, entering lists
To combat with Despair and mighty Grief :
My soul beleaguer'd with the crushing strength
Of sharp Impatience. Ha, Lucio ; go unarm'd ?
Come, soul, resume the valor of thy birth ;
Myself myself will dare all opposites :
I'll muster forces, an unvanquish'd power :
Cornets of horse shall press th' ungrateful earth :
This hollow-wombed mass shall inly groan
And murmur to sustain the weight of arms :
Ghastly Amazement, with upstarted hair,
Shall hurry on before, and usher us,
Whilst trumpets clamor with a sound of death.
Luc. Peace, good my lord, your speech is all too light.
Alas, survey your fortunes, look what's left

Of all your forces and your utmost hopes;
A weak old man, a page, and your poor self.
Andr. Andrugio lives; and a Fair Cause of Arms,
Why, that's an army all invincible.
He who hath that, hath a battalion royal,
Armor of proof, huge troops of barbed steeds,
Main squares of pikes, millions of harquebush.
O, a Fair Cause stands firm, and will abide;
Legions of Angels fight upon her side.

[The situation of Andrugio and Lucio resembles that of Lear and Kent, in that King's distresses. Andrugio, like Lear, manifests a kind of royal impatience, a turbulent greatness, an affected resignation. The Enemies which he enters lists to combat, "Despair and mighty Grief, and sharp Impatience," and the Forces ("Cornets of Horse," &c.) which he brings to vanquish them, are in the boldest style of Allegory. They are such a "race of mourners" as "the infection of sorrows loud" in the intellect might beget on "some pregnant cloud" in the imagination.]

ANTONIO'S REVENGE. THE SECOND PART OF THE HISTORY OF ANTONIO AND MELLIDA. BY JOHN MARSTON.

*The Prologue.**

The rawish dank of clumsy winter ramps
The fluent summer's vein; and drizzling sleet
Chilleth the wan bleak cheek of the numb'd earth,
While snarling gusts nibble the juiceless leaves
From the nak'd shudd'ring branch, and pills† the skin
From off the soft and delicate aspects.
O now methinks a sullen tragic scene

* This prologue for its passionate earnestness, and for the tragic note of preparation which it sounds, might have preceded one of those old tales of Thebes, or Pelops' line, which Milton has so highly commended, as free from the common error of the poets in his days, "of intermixing comic stuff with tragic sadness and gravity, brought in without discretion corruptly to gratify the people." It is as solemn a preparative as the "warning voice which he who saw th' Apocalypse, heard cry."

† Peels.

Would suit the time with pleasing congruence.
May we be happy in our weak devoir,
And all part pleas'd in most wish'd content.
But sweat of Hercules can ne'er beget
So blest an issue. Therefore we proclaim,
If any spirit breathes within this round
Uncapable of weighty passion
(As from his birth being hugged in the arms,
And nuzled 'twixt the breasts of Happiness*),
Who winks and shuts his apprehension up
From common sense of what men were, and are;
Who would not know what men must be: let such
Hurry amain from our black visag'd shows;
We shall affright their eyes. But if a breast,
Nail'd to the earth with grief; if any heart,
Pierc'd through with anguish, pant within this ring;
If there be any blood, whose heat is choak'd
And stifled with true sense of misery:
If aught of these strains fill this consort up,
They arrive most welcome. O that our power
Could lacky or keep wing with our desires;
That with unused poize of stile and sense
We might weigh massy in judicious scale!
Yet here's the prop that doth support our hopes:
When our scenes falter, or invention halts,
Your favor will give crutches to our faults.

Antonio, son to Andrugio Duke of Genoa, whom Piero the Venetian Prince and father-in-law to Antonio has cruelly murdered, kills Piero's little son, Julio, as a sacrifice to the ghost of Andrugio.—The scene, a church-yard: the time, midnight.

JULIO. ANTONIO.

Jul. Brother Antonio, are you here i'faith?
Why do you frown? Indeed my sister said,
That I should call you brother, that she did,
When you were married to her. Buss me: good truth,
I love you better than my father, 'deed.

* "Sleek favorites of Fortune." Preface to Poems by S. T. Coleridge.

Ant. Thy father? gracious, O bounteous heaven,
I do adore thy justice. *Venit in nostras manus*
Tandem vindicta, venit et tota quidem.

Jul. Truth, since my mother died, I loved you best.
Something hath anger'd you: pray you, look merrily.

Ant. I will laugh, and dimple my thin cheek
With capering joy; chuck, my heart doth leap
To grasp thy bosom. Time, place, and blood,
How fit you close together! heaven's tones
Strike not such music to immortal souls,
As your accordance sweets my breast withal.
Methinks I pace upon the front of Jove,
And kick corruption with a scornful heel,
Griping this flesh, disdain mortality.
O that I knew which joint, which side, which limb
Were father all, and had no mother in it;
That I might rip it vein by vein, and carve revenge
In bleeding traces: but since 'tis mix'd together,
Have at adventure, pell-mell, no reverse.
Come hither, boy; this is Andrugio's hearse.

Jul. O God, you'll hurt me. For my sister's sake,
Pray you don't hurt me. And you kill me, 'deed
I'll tell my father.

Ant. Oh, for thy sister's sake I flag revenge.

Andrugio's Ghost cries "Revenge."

Ant. Stay, stay, dear father, fright mine eyes no more.
Revenge as swift as lightning, bursteth forth
And clears his heart. Come, pretty tender child,
It is not thee I hate, or thee I kill.
Thy father's blood that flows within thy veins,
Is it I lothe; is that, revenge must suck.
I love thy soul: and were thy heart lapt up
In any flesh but in Piero's blood,
I would thus kiss it: but, being his, thus, thus,
And thus I'll punch it. Abandon fears:
Whilst thy wounds bleed, my brows shall gush out tears.

Jul. So you will love me, do even what you will. [*Dies.*

Ant. Now barks the wolf against the full-cheekt moon;

Now lions' half-clam'd entrails roar for food ;
Now croaks the toad, and night-crows screech aloud,
Fluttering 'bout casements of departing souls!
Now gape the graves, and through their yawns let loose
Imprison'd spirits to revisit earth:
And now, swart Night, to swell thy hour out
Behold I spurt warm blood in thy black eyes.
(From under the earth a groan.)
Howl not, thou putry mould ; groan not, ye graves ;
Be dumb, all breath. Here stands Andrugio's son,
Worthy his father. So ; I feel no breath ;
His jaws are fall'n, his dislodged soul is fled.
And now there's nothing but Piero left.
He is all Piero, father all. This blood,
This breast, this heart, Piero all :
Whom thus I mangle Spright of Julio,
Forget this was thy trunk. I live thy friend.
Mayst thou be twined with the soft'st embrace
Of clear eternity ;* but thy father's blood
I thus make incense of to Vengeance. * *
* * * * * * *

Day breaking.

——see, the dapple grey coursers of the morn
Beat up the light with their bright silver hoofs
And chase it through the sky.

One who died, slandered.

Look on those lips,
Those now lawn pillows, on whose tender softness
Chaste modest Speech, stealing from out his breast,
Had wont to rest itself, as loth to post
From out so fair an Inn: look, look, they seem
To stir,
And breathe defiance to black obloquy.

Wherein fools are happy.

Even in that, note a fool's beatitude ;

* "To lie immortal in the arms of Fire." Browne's Religio Medici. Of the punishments in hell.

He is not capable of passion;
Wanting the power of distinction,
He bears an unturn'd sail with every wind:
Blow east, blow west, he steers his course alike.
I never saw a fool lean: the chub-faced fop
Shines sleek with full cram'd fat of happiness:
Whilst studious contemplation sucks the juice
From wisard's* cheeks, who making curious search
For nature's secrets, the First Innating Cause
Laughs them to scorn, as man doth busy Apes
When they will zany men.

Maria (the Duchess of Genoa) describes the death of Mellida, her daughter-in-law.

Being laid upon her bed she grasp'd my hand,
And kissing it, spake thus, Thou very poor,
Why dost not weep? the jewel of thy brow,
The rich adornment that inchas'd thy breast,
Is lost; thy son, my love, is lost, is dead.
And have I liv'd to see his virtues blurr'd
With guiltless blots? O world, thou art too subtil
For honest natures to converse withal:
Therefore I'll leave thee: farewell, mart of wo;
I fly to clip my love Antonio,—
With that, her head sunk down upon her breast;
Her cheek chang'd earth, her senses slept in rest:
Until my Fool,† that crept unto the bed,
Screech'd out so loud that he brought back her soul,
Call'd her again, that her bright eyes 'gan ope
And stared upon him: he audacious fool
Dared kiss her hand, wisht her *soft rest, lov'd Bride;*
She fumbled out, *thanks, good:* and so she died.

* Wise men's.

† Antonio, who is thought dead, but still lives in that disguise.

THE MALCONTENT. A TRAGI-COMEDY. BY JOHN MARSTON

The Malcontent describes himself.

I cannot sleep, my eyes' ill neighboring lids
Will hold no fellowship. O thou pale sober night,
Thou that in sluggish fumes all sense dost steep;
Thou that giv'st all the world full leave to play,
Unbend'st the feebled veins of sweaty labor:
The gally-slave, that all the toilsome day
Tugs at the oar against the stubborn wave,
Straining his rugged veins, snores fast;
The stooping scythe-man, that doth barb the field,
Thou mak'st wink sure; in night all creatures sleep,
Only the Malcontent, that 'gainst his fate
Repines and quarrels: alas he's Goodman Tell-clock;
His sallow jaw-bones sink with wasting moan;
Whilst others' beds are down, his pillow's stone.

Place for a Penitent.

My cell 'tis, lady; where, instead of masks,
Music, tilts, tournies, and such court-like shows,
The hollow murmur of the checkless winds
Shall groan again, whilst the unquiet sea
Shakes the whole rock with foamy battery.
There Usherless* the air come in and out;
The rheumy vault will force your eyes to weep,
Whilst you behold true desolation.
A rocky barrenness shall pierce your eyes;
Where all at once one reaches, where he stands,
With brows the roof, both walls with both his hands.

* *i. e.* without the ceremony of an Usher to give notice of its approach, as is usual in Courts. As fine as Shakspeare: "the bleak air thy boisterous Chamberlain."

THE WONDER OF WOMEN: OR THE TRAGEDY OF SOPHONISBA. BY JOHN MARSTON.

Description of the Witch Erictho.

Here in this desart, the great Soul of Charms
Dreadful Ericlho lives; whose dismal brow
Contemns all roofs, or civil coverture.
Forsaken graves and tombs (the ghosts forc'd out)
She joys to inhabit.
A loathsome yellow leanness spreads her face,
A heavy hell-like paleness loads her cheeks,
Unknown to a clear heaven. But if dark winds
Or black thick clouds drive back the blinded stars,
When her deep magic makes forc'd heaven quake,
And thunder, spite of Jove: Erictho then
From naked graves stalks out, heaves proud her head,
With long unkemb'd hair loaden, and strives to snatch
The night's quick sulphur; then she bursts up tombs
From half-rot sear-cloths; and she scrapes dry gums
For her black rites: but when she finds a corse
But newly grav'd, whose entrails are not turn'd
To slimy filth, with greedy havoc then
She makes fierce spoil, and swells with wicked triumph
To bury her lean knuckles in his eyes:
Then doth she gnaw the pale and o'er-grown nails
From his dry hand: but if she find some life
Yet lurking close, she bites his gelid lips,
And sticking her black tongue in his dry throat,
She breathes dire murmurs, which enforce him bear
Her baneful secrets to the spirits of horror.

Her Cave.

——Hard by the reverent ruins
Of a once glorious temple, rear'd to Jove,
Whose very rubbish (like the pitied fall
Of virtue much unfortunate) yet bears
A deathless majesty, though now quite ras'd,
Hurl'd down by wrath and lust of impious kings,

So that, where holy Flamens wont to sing
Sweet hymns to heaven, there the daw, and crow,
The ill-voic'd raven, and still chattering pye,
Send out ungrateful sounds and loathsome filth ;
Where statues and Jove's acts were vively* limn'd,
Boys with black coals draw the veil'd parts of nature
And lecherous actions of imagined lust ;
Where tombs and beauteous urns of well-dead men
Stood in assured rest, the shepherd now
Unloads his belly, corruption most abhorr'd
Mingling itself with their renowned ashes :
There once a charnel-house, now a vast cave,
Over whose brow a pale and untrod grove
Throws out her heavy shade, the mouth thick arms
Of darksome ewe, sun-proof, for ever choak ;
Within, rests barren darkness, fruitless drought
Pines in eternal night ; the steam of hell
Yields not so lazy air : there, that's her Cell.

WHAT YOU WILL: A COMEDY. BY JOHN MARSTON.

Venetian Merchant.

No knight,
But one (that title off) was even a prince,
A sultan Solyman : thrice was he made,
In dangerous arms, Venice' Providetore.
He was merchant, but so bounteous,
Valiant, wise, learned, all so absolute,
That nought was valued praiseful excellent,
But in 't was he most praiseful excellent.
O I shall ne'er forget how he went cloathed.
He would maintain it a base ill-used fashion,
To bind a merchant to the sullen habit
Of precise black, chiefly in Venice state,
Where merchants guilt the top.†

* Livelily. † " Her whose merchant Sons were Kings."—*Collins*

And therefore should you have him pass the bridge
Up the Rialto like a Soldier;
In a black bever belt, ash color plain,
A Florentine cloth-o'-silver jerkin, sleeves
White satin cut on tinsel, then long stock;
French panes embroider'd, goldsmith's work: O God,
Methinks I see him, how he would walk,
With what a jolly presence he would pace
Round the Rialto.*

Scholar and his Dog.

I was a scholar: seven useful springs
Did I deflower in quotations
Of cross'd opinions 'bout the soul of man;
The more I learnt, the more I learn to doubt.
Delight my spaniel slept, whilst I baus'd leaves,
Toss'd o'er the dunces, pored on the old print
Of titled words: and still my spaniel slept.
Whilst I wasted lamp-oil, baited my flesh,
Shrunk up my veins: and still my spaniel slept.
And still I held converse with Zabarell,
Aquinas, Scotus, and the musty saw
Of Antick Donate: still my spaniel slept.
Still on went I; first, *an sit anima;*
Then, an it were mortal. O hold, hold; at that
They 're at brain buffets, fell by the ears amain
Pell-mell together; still my spaniel slept.

* To judge of the liberality of these notions of dress, we must advert to the days of Gresham, and the consternation which a Phenomenon habited like the Merchant here described would have excited among the flat round caps, and cloth stockings, upon Change, when those "original arguments or tokens of a Citizen's vocation were in fashion not more for thrift and usefulness than for distinction and grace." The blank uniformity to which all professional distinctions in apparel have been long hastening, is one instance of the Decay of Symbols among us, which, whether it has contributed or not to make us a more intellectual, has certainly made us a less imaginative people. Shakspeare knew the force of signs:—"a malignant and turban'd Turk." "This meal-cap Miller," says the Author of God's Revenge against Murder, to express his indignation at an atrocious outrage committed by the miller Pierot upon the person of the fair Marieta.

Then, whether 'twere corporeal, local, fixt,
Ex traduce, but whether 't had free will
Or no, hot philosophers
Stood banding factions, all so strongly propt,
I stagger'd, knew not which was firmer part,
But thought, quoted, read, observ'd and pryed,
Stufft noting-books: and still my spaniel slept.
At length he wak'd, and yawned; and by yon sky,
For aught I know he knew as much as I.

Preparations for Second Nuptials.

Now is Albano's* marriage-bed new hung
With fresh rich curtains, now are my valence up,
Imbost with orient pearl, my grandsire's gift,
Now are the lawn sheets fum'd with violets
To fresh the pall'd lascivious appetite,
Now work the cooks, the pastry sweats with slaves,
The march-panes glitter, now, now the musicians
Hover with nimble sticks o'er squeaking crowds,†
Tickling the dried guts of a mewing cat:
The tailors, starchers, semsters, butchers, poulterers,
Mercers, all, all——none think on me.

THE INSATIATE COUNTESS: A TRAGEDY.
BY JOHN MARSTON.

Isabella (the Countess), after a long series of crimes of infidelity to her husband and of murder, is brought to suffer on a scaffold. Roberto, her husband, arrives to take a last leave of her.

Roberto. Bear record all you blessed saints in heaven
I come not to torment thee in thy death;
For of himself he 's terrible enough,
But call to mind a Lady like yourself,
And think how ill in such a beauteous soul,
Upon the instant morrow of her nuptials,

* Albano, the first husband speaks; supposed dead. † Fiddles

Apostacy and wild revolt would show.
Withal, imagine that she had a lord
Jealous, the air should ravish her chaste looks;
Doting, like the Creator in his models,
Who views them every minute, and with care
Mixt in his fear of their obedience to him.
Suppose he sung through famous Italy,
More common than the looser songs of Petrarch,
To every several Zany's instrument:
And he poor wretch, hoping some better fate
Might call her back from her adulterate purpose,
Lives in obscure and almost unknown life;
Till hearing that she is condemned to die,
For he once lov'd her, lends his pined corpse
Motion to bring him to her stage of honor,
Where, drown'd in wo at her so dismal chance,
He clasps her: thus he falls into a trance.
Isabella. O my offended lord, lift up your eyes;
But yet avert them from my lothed sight.
Had I with you enjoyed the lawful pleasure,
To which belongs nor fear nor public shame,
I might have lived in honor, died in fame.
Your pardon on my faltering knees I beg;
Which shall confirm more peace unto my death,
Than all the grave instructions of the Church.
Roberto. Freely thou hast it. Farewell, my Isabella;
Let thy death ransome thy soul, O die a rare example,
The kiss thou gav'st me in the church, here take:
As I leave thee, so thou the world forsake. [*Exit.*
Executioner. Madam, tie up your hair.
Isabella. O these golden nets,
That have insnared so many wanton youths!
Not one but has been held a thread of life,
And superstitiously depended on.
What else?
Executioner. Madam, I must intreat you blind your eyes.
Isabella. I have lived too long in darkness, my friend;
And yet mine eyes with their majestic light,

Have got new Muses in a Poet's spright.
They've been more gaz'd at than the God of day;
Their brightness never could be flattered;
Yet thou command'st a fixed cloud of lawn
To eclipse eternally these minutes of light.
I am prepared.—

Woman's Inconstancy.

Who would have thought it? She that could no more
Forsake my company, than can the day
Forsake the glorious presence of the sun,
When I was absent, then her galled eyes
Would have shed April showers, and outwept
The clouds in that same o'er-passionate mood
When they drown'd all the world: yet now forsakes me.
Women, your eyes shed glances like the sun;
Now shines your brightness, now your light is done,
On the sweet'st flowers you shine, 'tis but by chance,
And on the basest weed you'll waste a glance.

CÆSAR AND POMPEY. A TRAGEDY. BY GEORGE CHAPMAN

Sacrifice.

Imperial Cæsar, at your sacred charge
I drew a milk white ox into the Temple,
And turning there his face into the East
(Fearfully shaking at the shining light)
Down fell his horned forehead to his hoof.
When I began to greet him with the stroke
That should prepare him for the holy rites,
With hideous roars he laid out such a throat
As made the secret lurkings of the God
To answer, Echo-like, in threat'ning sounds:
I struck again at him, and then he slept;
His life-blood boiling out at every wound
In streams as clear as any liquid ruby,
———the beast cut up, and laid on the altar,
His limbs were all lickt up with instant flames;

Not like the elemental fire that burns
In household uses, lamely struggling up,
This way and that way winding as it rises,
But right and upright reacht his proper sphere
Where burns the fire eternal and sincere.

Joy unexpected, best.

Joys unexpected, and in desperate plight,
Are still most sweet, and prove from whence they come;
When earth's still moon-like confidence in joy
Is at her full: True Joy descending far
From past her sphere, and from the highest heaven
That moves and is not moved.

Inward help the best help.

——I will stand no more
On others' legs, nor build one joy without me.
If ever I be worth a house again,
I'll build all inward: not a light shall ope
The common out-way; no expense, no art,
No ornament, no door, will I use there;
But raise all plain and rudely like a rampire,
Against the false society of men,
That still batters
All reason piece-meal; and, for earthly greatness
All heavenly comforts rarifies the air.
I'll therefore live in dark; and all my light,
Like ancient Temples, let in at my top.
That where to turn one's back to all the world,
And only look at heaven.
———When our diseas'd affections
Harmful to human freedom, and storm-like
Inferring darkness to th' infected mind,
Oppress our comforts; 'tis but letting in
The light of reason, and a purer spirit
Take in another way; like rooms that fight
With windows 'gainst the wind, yet let in light.

BUSSY D'AMBOIS. A TRAGEDY. BY GEORGE CHAPMAN.

A Nuntius (or Messenger) in presence of King Henry the Third of France and his court tells the manner of a combat, to which he was witness, of three to three; in which D'Ambois remained sole survivor; begun upon an affront passed upon D'Ambois by some courtiers.

HENRY, GUISE, BEAUPRE, NUNTIUS, &c.

Nuntius. I saw fierce D'Ambois and his two brave friends
Enter the field, and at their heels their foes,
Which were the famous soldiers, Barrisor,
L'Anou, and Pyrrhot, great in deeds of arms:
All which arriv'd at the evenest piece of earth
The field afforded, the three challengers
Turn'd head, drew all their rapiers, and stood rank'd;
When face to face the three defendants met them,
Alike prepar'd, and resolute alike.
Like bonfires of contributory wood
Every man's look show'd, fed with other's spirit;
As one had been a mirror to another,
Like forms of life and death each took from other;
And so were life and death mix'd at their heights,
That you could see no fear of death (for life)
Nor love of life (for death): but in their brows
Pyrrho's opinion in great letters shone;
That "life and death in all respects are one."
Henry. Past there no sorts of words at their encounter!
Nuntius. As Hector twixt the hosts of Greece and Troy,
When Paris and the Spartan king should end
The nine years' war, held up his brazen lance
For signal that both hosts should cease from arms,
And hear him speak: so Barrisor (advis'd)
Advanced his naked rapier 'twixt both sides,
Ript up the quarrel, and compar'd six lives
Then laid in balance with six idle words;
Offer'd remission and contrition too:
Or else that he and D'Ambois might conclude
The others' danger. D'Ambois lik'd the last:
But Barrisor's friends (being equally engag'd

In the main quarrel), never would expose
His life alone to that they all deserv'd.
And (for the other offer of remission)
D'Ambois (that like a laurel put in fire
Sparkled and spit) did much much more than scorn
That his wrong should incense lim so like chaff
To go so soon out, and, like lighted paper,
Approve his spirit at once both fire and ashes;
So drew they lots, and in them fates appointed
That Barrisor should fight with fiery D'Ambois;
Pyrrhot with Melynell; with Brisac L'Anou:
And then like flame and powder they commixt,
So sprightly, that I wish'd they had been Spirits;
That the ne'er-shutting wounds, they needs must open,
Might as they open'd shut, and never kill.*
But D'Ambois' sword (that light'ned as it flew)
Shot like a pointed comet at the face
Of manly Barrisor; and there it stuck:
Thrice pluck'd he at it, and thrice drew on thrusts
From him, that of himself was free as fire;
Who thrust still, as he pluck'd, yet (past belief)
He with his subtil eye, hand, body, 'scap'd;
At last the deadly bitten point tugg'd off,
On fell his yet undaunted foe so fiercely
That (only made more horrid with his wound)
Great D'Ambois shrunk, and gave a little ground:
But soon return'd, redoubled in his danger,
And at the heart of Barrisor seal'd his anger.
Then, as in Arden I have seen an oak
Long shook with tempests, and his lofty top
Bent to his root, which being at length made loose
(Even groaning with his weight) he 'gan to nod
This way and that, as loth his curled brows
(Which he had oft wrapt in the sky with storms)
Should stoop; and yet, his radical fibres burst,

* One can hardly believe but that these lines were written after Milton had described his *warring angels*.

Storm-like he fell, and hid the fear-cold earth:
So fell stout Barrisor, that had stood the shocks
Of ten set battles in your highness' war
'Gainst the sole soldier of the world Navarre.
Guise. O piteous and horrid murder!
Beaupre. Such a life
Methinks had metal in it to survive
An age of men.
Henry. Such often soonest end.
Thy felt report calls on; we long to know
On what events the others have arrived.
Nuntius. Sorrow and fury, like two opposite fumes
Met in the upper region of a cloud,
At the report made by this worthy's fall,
Brake from the earth, and with them rose Revenge,
Ent'ring with fresh pow'rs his two noble friends:
And under that odds fell surcharg'd Brisac,
The friend of D'Ambois, before fierce L'Anou;
Which D'Ambois seeing: as I once did see,
In my young travels through Armenia,
An angry unicorn in his full career
Charge with too swift a foot a Jeweller
That watcht him for the treasure of his brow;
And, ere he could get shelter of a tree,
Nail him with his rich antler to the earth;
So D'Ambois ran upon reveng'd L'Anou,
Who eyeing th' eager point borne in his face,
And giving back, fell back, and in his fall
His foe's uncurb'd sword stopt in his heart:
By which time all the life-strings of th' two other
Were cut, and both fell (as their spirit flew)
Upwards: and still hunt honor at the view.
And now, of all the six, sole D'Ambois stood
Untouch't, save only with the others' blood.
Henry. All slain outright but he?
Nuntius. All slain outright but he:
Who kneeling in the warm life of his friends
(All freckled with the blood his rapier rain'd)

He kist their pale lips, and bade both farewell.

False Greatness.

As cedars beaten with continual storms,
So great men flourish; and do imitate
Unskilful statuaries, who suppose,
In forming a Colossus, if they make him
Straddle enough, strut, and look big, and gape,
Their work is goodly: so men merely great,
In their affected gravity of voice,
Sowerness of countenance, manners' cruelty,
Authority, wealth, and all the spawn of fortune,
Think they bear all the kingdom's worth before them;
Yet differ not from those Colossick statues,
Which, with heroic forms without o'erspread,
Within are nought but mortar, flint, and lead.

Virtue.—Policy.

—— as great seamen using all their wealth
And skills in Neptune's deep invisible paths,
In tall ships richly built and ribb'd with brass,
To put a girdle round about the world;
When they have done it, coming near the haven,
Are fain to give a warning piece, and call
A poor staid fisherman that never past
His country's sight, to waft and guide them in:
So when we wander furthest through the waves
Of glassy Glory, and the gulfs of State,
Topt with all titles, spreading all our reaches,
As if each private arm would sphere the earth,
We must to Virtue for her guide resort,
Or we shall shipwreck in our safest port.

Nick of Time

There is a deep nick in Time's restless wheel
For each man's good, when which nick comes, it strikes:
As Rhetorick yet works not persuasion,
But only is a mean to make it work:
So no man riseth by his real merit,

But when it tries clink in his Raiser's spirit.

Difference of the English and French Courts.

HENRY. GUISE. MONTSURRY.

Guise. I like not their Court* fashion, it is too crest-fall'n
In all observance, making demigods
Of their great Nobles, and of their old Queen†
An ever young and most immortal Goddess.
Mont. No question she's the rarest Queen in Europe.
Guise. But what's that to her immortality?
Henry. Assure you, cousin Guise; so great a Courtier,
So full of majesty and royal parts,
No Queen in Christendom may vaunt herself.
Her Court approves it. That's a Court indeed;
Not mix'd with clowneries us'd in common Houses:
But, as Courts should be, th' abstracts of their kingdoms,
In all the beauty, state, and worth they hold.
So is hers amply, and by her inform'd,
The world is not contracted in a Man,
With more proportion and expression,
Than in her Court her Kingdom. Our French Court
Is a mere mirror of confusion to it.
The King and Subject, Lord and every Slave,
Dance a continual hay. Our rooms of state
Kept like our stables: no place more observ'd
Than a rude market-place; and though our custom
Keep his assur'd confusion from our eyes,
'Tis ne'er the less essentially unsightly.

BYRON'S CONSPIRACY. BY GEO. CHAPMAN.

Byron described.

—— he is a man
Of matchless valor, and was ever happy
In all encounters, which were still made good

* The English. † Q. Elizabeth.

With an unwearied sense of any toil;
Having continued fourteen days together
Upon his horse; his blood is not voluptuous,
Nor much inclined to women; his desires
Are higher than his state; and his deserts
Not much short of the most he can desire,
If they be weigh'd with what France feels by them
He is past measure glorious: and that humor
Is fit to feed his spirit, whom it possesseth
With faith in any error; chiefly where
Men blow it up with praise of his perfections:
The taste whereof in him so soothes his palate,
And takes up all his appetite, that oft times
He will refuse his meat, and company,
To feast alone with their most strong conceit.
Ambition also cheek by cheek doth march
With that excess of glory, both sustain'd
With an unlimited fancy, that the king,
Nor France itself, without him can subsist.

Men's Glories eclipsed when they turn Traitors.

As when the moon hath comforted the night,
And set the world in silver of her light,
The planets, asterisms, and whole State of Heaven,
In beams of gold descending: all the winds
Bound up in caves, charg'd not to drive abroad
Their cloudy heads: an universal peace
(Proclaim'd in silence) of the quiet earth
Soon as her hot and dry fumes are let loose,
Storms and clouds mixing suddenly put out
The eyes of all those glories; the creation
Turn'd into Chaos; and we then desire,
For all our joy of life, the death of sleep.
So when the glories of our lives (men's loves,
Clear consciences, our fames and loyalties),
That did us worthy comfort, are eclips'd:
Grief and disgrace invade us; and for all
Our night of life besides, our misery craves
Dark earth would ope and hide us in our graves.

Opinion of the Scale of Good or Bad.

—— there is no truth of any good
To be discern'd on earth; and by conversion,
Nought therefore simply bad; but as the stuff
Prepar'd for Arras pictures, is no picture,
Till it be form'd, and man hath cast the beams
Of his imaginous fancy thorough it,
In forming ancient Kings and Conquerors
As he conceives they look'd and were attir'd,
Though they were nothing so: so all things here
Have all their price set down from men's Conceits;
Which make all terms and actions good or bad,
And are but pliant and well-color'd threads
Put into feigned images of Truth.

Insinuating Manners.

We must have these lures, when we hawk for friends:
And wind about them like a subtle River,
That, seeming only to run on his course,
Doth search yet, as he runs, and still finds out
The easiest parts of entry on the shore,
Gliding so slyly by, as scarce it touch'd,
Yet still eats something in it.

The Stars not able to foreshow anything.

I am a nobler substance than the stars:
And shall the baser over rule the better?
Or are they better since they are the bigger?
I have a will, and faculties of choice,
To do or not to do; and reason why
I do or not do this: the stars have none.
They know not why they shine, more than this Taper,
Nor how they work, nor what. I'll cnange my course:
I'll piece-meal pull the frame of all my thoughts:
And where are all your Caput Algols then?
Your planets all being underneath the earth
At my nativity: what can they do?
Malignant in aspects! in bloody houses!

The Master Spirit.

Give me a spirit that on life's rough sea
Loves to have his sails fill'd with a lusty wind,
Even till his sail-yards tremble, his masts crack,
And his rapt ship run on her side so low,
That she drinks water, and her keel ploughs air.
There is no danger to a man, that knows
What life and death is: there's not any law
Exceeds his knowledge; neither is it lawful
That he should stoop to any other law:
He goes before them, and commands them all,
That to himself is a law rational.

Vile Natures in High Places.

——————foolish Statuaries,
That under little Saints, suppose* great bases,
Make less (to sense) the saints: and so, where fortune
Advanceth vile minds to states great and noble,
She much the more exposeth them to shame;
Not able to make good, and fill their bases
With a conformed structure.

Innocence the Harmony of the Faculties.

——————Innocence, the sacred amulet
'Gainst all the poisons of infirmity,
Of all misfortune, injury and death:
That makes a man in tune still in himself;
Free from the hell to be his own accuser;
Ever in quiet, endless joy enjoying,
No strife nor no sedition in his powers;
No motion in his will against his reason;
No thought 'gainst thought; nor (as 'twere in the confines
Of whispering and repenting) both possess
Only a wayward and tumultuous peace;
But, all parts in him friendly and secure,
Fruitful of all best things in all worst seasons,
He can with every wish be in their plenty:

* Put under.

When the infectious guilt of one foul crime
Destroys the free content of all our time.

BYRON'S TRAGEDY. BY GEO. CHAPMAN.

King Henry the Fourth of France blesses the young Dauphin.

My royal blessing, and the King of Heaven,
Make thee an aged and a happy King
Help, nurse, to put my sword into his hand.
Hold, boy, by this ; and with it may thy arm
Cut from thy tree of rule all traitrous branches,
That strive to shadow and eclipse thy glories.
Have thy old father's Angel for thy guide,
Redoubled be his spirit in thy breast:
Who, when this State ran like a turbulent sea,
In civil hates and bloody enmity,
Their wraths and envies (like so many winds)
Settled and burst: and like the Halcyon's birth
Be thine, to bring a calm upon the shore :
In which the eyes of war may ever sleep,
As over-watch'd with former massacres,
When guilty mad Noblesse fed on Noblesse,
All the sweet plenty of the realm exhausted;
When the nak'd merchant was pursued for spoil :
When the poor peasants frighted neediest thieves
With their pale leanness, nothing left on them
But meagre carcases, sustained with air,
Wandering like ghosts affrighted from their graves ;
When with the often and incessant sounds
The very beasts knew the alarum-bell,
And hearing it ran bellowing to their home ;
From which unchristian broils and homicides
Let the religious sword of Justice free
Thee, and thy kingdoms govern'd after me ;
O Heaven ! Or if the unsettled blood of France,
With ease and wealth, renew her civil furies,

Let all my powers be emptied in my Son;
To curb and end them all as I have done.
Let him by virtue quite cut off from Fortune
Her feather'd shoulders, and her winged shoes,
And thrust from her light feet her turning stone;
That she may ever tarry by his throne.
And of his worth let after ages say
(He fighting for the land, and bringing home
Just conquests, loaden with his enemies' spoils),
His father past all France in martial deeds.
But he his father twenty times exceeds.

What we have, we slight; what we want, we think excellent.

——as a man, match'd with a lovely wife,
When his most heavenly theory of her beauties
Is dull'd and quite exhausted with his practice,
He brings her forth to feasts, where he, alas,
Falls to his viands with no thought like others,
That think him blest in her; and they, poor men,
Court, and make faces, offer service, sweat
With their desires' contention, break their brains
For jests and tales, sit mute, and loose their looks,
Far out of wit and out of countenance.
So all men else do, what they have, transplant;
And place their wealth in thirst of what they want.

Soliloquy of King Henry deliberating on the Death of a Traitor

O thou that governst the keen swords of Kings,
Direct my arm in this important stroke;
Or hold it, being advanc'd: the weight of blood.
Even in the basest subject, doth exact
Deep consultation in the highest King:
For in one subject, death's unjust affrights,
Passions, and pains, though he be ne'er so poor,
Ask more remorse than the voluptuous spleens
Of all Kings in the world deserve respect.
He should be born grey-headed that will bear
The weight of Empire. Judgment of the life,
Free state and reputation of a Man

(If it be just and worthy) dwells so dark,
That it denies access to sun and moon:
The soul's eye, sharpen'd with that sacred light
Of whom the sun itself is but a beam,
Must only give that judgment. O how much
Err those Kings then, that play with life and death;
And nothing put into their serious states
But humor and their lusts; for which alone
Men long for kingdoms; whose huge counterpoise
In cares and dangers could a fool comprise,
He would not be a King, but would be wise.

[The Selections which I have made from this poet are sufficient to give an idea of that "full and heightened style" which Webster makes characteristic of Chapman. Of all the English Play-writers, Chapman perhaps approaches nearest to Shakspeare in the descriptive and didactic, in passages which are less purel ydramatic. Dramatic imitation was not his talent. He could not go out of himself, as Shakspeare could shift at pleasure, to inform and animate other existences, but in himself he had an eye to perceive and a soul to embrace all forms. He would have made a great epic poet, if, indeed, he has not abundantly shown himself to be one; for his Homer is not so properly a Translation as the Stories of Achilles and Ulysses re-written. The earnestness and passion which he has put into every part of these poems would be incredible to a reader of mere modern translations. His almost Greek zeal for the honor of his heroes is only paralleled by that fierce spirit of Hebrew bigotry, with which Milton, as if personating one of the Zealots of the old law, clothed himself when he sate down to paint the acts of Sampson against the uncircumcised. The great obstacle to Chapman's Translations being read is their unconquerable quaintness. He pours out in the same breath the most just and natural and the most violent and forced expressions. He seems to grasp whatever words come first to hand during the impetus of inspiration, as if all other must be inadequate to the divine meaning. But passion (the all in all in Poetry) is everywhere present, raising the low, dignifying the mean, and putting sense into the absurd. He makes his readers glow, weep, tremble, take any affection which he pleases, be moved by words, or in spite of them, be disgusted and overcome their disgust. I have often thought that the vulgar misconception of Shakspeare, as of a wild irregular genius "in whom great faults are compensated by great beauties," would be really true applied to Chapman. But there is no scale by which to balance such disproportionate subjects as the faults and beauties of a great genius. To set off the former with any fairness against the latter, the pain which they give us should be in some proportion to the pleasure which we receive from the other. As these transport us to the highest heaven, those should steep us in agonies infernal.]

A CHALLENGE FOR BEAUTY. BY THOMAS HEYWOOD.

Petrocella a fair Spanish Lady loves Montferrers an English Sea Captain, who is Captive to Valladaura a noble Spaniard.—Valladaura loves the Lady; and employs Montferrers to be the Messenger of his love to her.

PETROCELLA. MONTFERRERS.

Pet. What art thou in thy country?
Mont. There, a man.
Pet. What here?
Mont. No better than you see: a slave.
Pet. Whose?
Mont. His that hath redeem'd me.
Pet. Valladaura's?
Mont. Yes, I proclaim 't; I that was once mine own,
Am now become his creature.
Pet. I perceive,
Your coming is to make me think you noble.
Would you persuade me deem your friend a God?
For only such make men. Are you a Gentleman?
Mont. Not here; for I am all dejectedness,
Captive to fortune, and a slave to want;
I cannot call these clothes I wear mine own,
I do not eat but at another's cost,
This air I breathe is borrowed; ne'er was man
So poor and abject. I have not so much
In all this universe as a thing to leave,
Or a country I can freely boast is mine.
My essence and my being is another's.
What should I say? I am not anything;
And I possess as little.
Pet. Tell me that?
Come, come, I know you to be no such man.
You are a soldier valiant and renown'd;
Your carriage tried by land, and prov'd at sea;
Of which I have heard such full expression,
No contradiction can persuade you less;
And in this faith I am constant.

Mont. A meer worm,
Trod on by every fate.
Pet. Rais'd by your merit
To be a common argument through Spain,
And speech at Princes' tables, for your worth;
Your presence when you please to expose 't abroad
Attracts all eyes, and draws them after you;
And those that understand you, call their friends,
And pointing through the street, say, This is he,
This is that brave and noble Englishman,
Whom soldiers strive to make their precedent,
And other men their wonder.
Mont. This your scorn
Makes me appear more abject to myself,
Than all diseases I have tasted yet
Had power to asperse upon me; and yet, lady,
I could say something, durst I.
Pet. Speak 't at once.
Mont. And yet ——
Pet. Nay, but we'll admit no pause.
Mont. I know not how my phrase may relish you,
And loth I were to offend; even in what's past
I must confess I was too bold. Farewell;
I shall no more distaste you.
Pet. Sir, you do not;
I do proclaim you do not. Stay, I charge you;
Or, as you say you have been fortune's scorn,
So ever prove to woman.
Mont. You charge deeply,
And yet now I bethink me ——
Pet. As you are a soldier,
And Englishman, have hope to be redeem'd
From this your scorned bondage you sustain,
Have comfort in ycur mother and fair sister,
Renown so blazed in the ears of Spain,
Hope to rebreathe that air you tasted first,
So tell me ——
Ment. What?

Pet. Your apprehension catch'd,
And almost was in sheaf ——
Mont. Lady, I shall.
Pet. And in a word.
Mont. I will.
Pet. Pronounce it then.
Mont. I love you.
Pet. Ha, ha, ha.
Mont. Still it is my misery
Thus to be mock'd in all things.
Pet. Pretty, faith.
Mont. I look'd thus to be laught at; my estate
And fortunes, I confess, deserve no less;
That made me so unwilling to denounce
Mine own derisions: but alas! I find
No nation, sex, complexion, birth, degree,
But jest at want, and mock at misery.
Pet. Love me?
Mont. I do, I do; and maugre Fate,
And spite of all sinister evil, shall.
And now I charge you, by that filial zeal
You owe your father, by the memory
Of your dear mother, by the joys you hope
In blessed marriage, by the fortunate issue
Stored in your womb, by these and all things else
That you can style with goodness; instantly
Without evasion, trick, or circumstance,
Nay, least premeditation, answer me,
Affect you me, or no?
Pet. How speak you that?
Mont. Without demur or pause.
Pet. Give me but time
To sleep upon 't.
Mont. I pardon you no minute: not so much,
As to apparel the least phrase you speak.
Speak in the shortest sentence.
Pet. You have vanquish'd me,
At mine own weapon: noble sir, I love you;

And what my heart durst never tell my tongue,
Lest it should blab my thoughts, at last I speak,
And iterate ; I love you.
Mont. Oh, my happiness!
What wilt thou feel me still ? art thou not weary
Of making me thy May-game, to possess me
Of such a treasure's mighty magazine,
Not suffer me to enjoy it ; tane with this hand,
With that to give 't another!
Pet. You are sad, Sir ;
Be so no more : if you have been dejected,
It lies in me to mount you to that height
You could not aim at greater. I am yours.
These lips, that only witness it in air,
Now with this truth confirm it. [*Kisses him*
Mont. I was born to 't ;
And it shall out at once.
Pet. Sir, you seem passionate ;
As if my answer pleas'd not.
Mont. Now my death ;
For mine own tongue must kill me : noble Lady,
You have endear'd me to you, but my vow
Was, ne'er to match with any, of what state
Or birth soever, till before the contract
Some one thing I impose her.
Pet. She to do it ?
Mont. Or, if she fail me in my first demand,
I to abjure her ever.
Pet. I am she,
That beg to be imploy'd so : name a danger,
Whose very face would fright all womanhood,
And manhood put in trance, nay, whose aspect
Would ague such as should but hear it told ;
But to the sad beholder, prove like those
That gazed upon Medusa's snaky locks,
And turn'd them into marble : these and more,
Should you but speak 't, Id do.
Mont. And swear to this ?

Pet. I vow it by my honor, my best hopes,
And all that I wish gracious: name it then,
For I am in a longing in my soul,
To show my love's expression.
Mont. You shall then ——
Pet. I'll do it, as I am a Virgin;
Lie it within mortality, I'll do it.
Mont. You shall ——
Pet. I will: that which appears in you
So terrible to speak, I'll joy to act;
And take pride in performance.
Mont. Then you shall——
Pet. What soldier, what?
Mont. — love noble Valladaura;
And at his soonest appointment marry him.
Pet. Then I am lost.——

Miracle of Beauty.

I remember,*
There lived a Spanish Princess of our name,
An Isabella too, and not long since,
Who from her palace windows stedfastly
Gazing upon the Sun, her hair took fire.
Some augurs held it as a prodigy:
I rather think that she was Latona's brood,
And that Apollo courted her bright hair;
Else, envying that her tresses put down his,
He scorcht them off in envy; nor dare I
(From her deriv'd) expose me to his beams;
Lest, as he burns the Phœnix in her nest,
Made of the sweetest aromatic wood,
Either in love, or envy, he agree
To use the like combustion upon me.

* A proud Spanish Princess relates this.

THE ROYAL KING AND THE LOYAL SUBJECT. BY THOMAS HEYWOOD.

Noble Traitor.

A Persian History
I read of late, how the great Sophy once
Flying a noble Falcon at the Herne,
In comes by chance an Eagle sousing by:
Which when the Hawk espies, leaves her first game,
And boldly ventures on the King of Birds;
Long tugg'd they in the air, till at the length
The Falcon (better breath'd) seiz'd on the Eagle,
And struck it dead. The Barons prais'd the Bird,
And for her courage she was peerless held.
The Emperor, after some deliberate thoughts,
Made her no less; he caus'd a crown of gold
To be new fram'd, and fitted to her head,
In honor of her courage: then the Bird,
With great applause, was to the market-place
In triumph borne; where, when her utmost worth
Had been proclaimed, the common executioner
First by the King's command took off her crown,
And after with a sword struck off her head,
As one no better than a noble Traitor
Unto the King of Birds.

A WOMAN KILL'D WITH KINDNESS: A TRAGEDY BY THOMAS HEYWOOD.

Mr. Frankford discovers that his Wife has been unfaithful to him.

Mrs. Fra. O by what words, what title, or what name
Shall I entreat your pardon? Pardon! oh!
I am as far from hoping such sweet grace,
As Lucifer from heaven. To call you husband!
(O me most wretched!) I have lost that name,
I am no more your wife.

Fran. Spare thou thy tears, for I will weep for thee,
And keep thy countenance, for I'll blush for thee.
Now, I protest, I think, 'tis I am tainted,
For I am most asham'd; and 'tis more hard
For me to look upon thy guilty face,
Than on the sun's clear brow: what wouldst thou speak?
Mrs. Fra. I would I had no tongue, no ears, no eyes,
No apprehension, no capacity.
When do you spurn me like a dog? when tread me
Under feet? when drag me by the hair?
Tho' I deserve a thousand thousand fold
More than you can inflict: yet, once my husband,
For womanhood, to which I am a shame,
Though once an ornament; even for his sake
That hath redeem'd our souls, mark not my face,
Nor hack me with your sword: but let me go
Perfect and undeformed to my tomb.
I am not worthy that I should prevail
In the least suit; no, not to speak to you,
Nor look on you, nor to be in your presence:
Yet as an abject this one suit I crave,
This granted, I am ready for my grave.
Fran. My God, with patience arm me! rise, nay rise,
And I'll debate with thee. Was it for want
Thou plaid'st the strumpet. Wast thou not supply'd
With every pleasure, fashion, and new toy;
Nay even beyond my calling?
Mrs. Fra. I was.
Fran. Was it then disability in me?
Or in thine eyes seem'd he a properer man?
Mrs. Fra. O no.
Fran. Did not I lodge thee in my bosom?
Wear thee in my heart?
Mrs. Fra. You did.
Fran. I did indeed, witness my tears I did.
Go bring my infants hither. O Nan, O Nan;
If neither fear of shame, regard of honor,
The blemish of my house, nor my dear love,

Could have withheld thee from so lewd a fact,
Yet for these infants, these young harmless souls,
On whose white brows thy shame is character'd,
And grows in greatness as they wax in years;
Look but on them, and melt away in tears.
Away with them: lest as her spotted body
Hath stained their names with stripe of bastardy,
So her adulterous breath may blast their spirits
With her infectious thoughts. Away with them.

Mrs. Fra. In this one life I die ten thousand deaths.

Fran. Stand up, stand up, I will do nothing rashly.
I will retire awhile into my study,
And thou shalt hear thy sentence presently. [*Exit.*

He returns with Cranwell *his friend. She falls on her knees.*

Fran. My words are register'd in heaven already.
With patience hear me. I'll not martyr thee,
Nor mark thee for a strumpet; but with usage
Of more humility torment thy soul,
And *kill* thee even with *kindness.*

Cran. Mr. Frankford.

Fran. Good Mr. Cranwell.—Woman, hear thy judgment;
Go make thee ready in thy best attire;
Take with thee all thy gowns, all thy apparel:
Leave nothing that did ever call thee mistress,
Or by whose sight, being left here in the house,
I may remember such a woman was.
Choose thee a bed and hangings for thy chamber;
Take with thee everything which hath thy mark,
And get thee to my manor seven miles off;
Where live; 'tis thine, I freely give it thee,
My tenants by shall furnish thee with wains
To carry all thy stuff within two hours;
No longer will I limit thee my sight.
Choose which of all my servants thou lik'st best,
And they are thine to attend thee.

Mrs. Fra. A mild sentence.

Fran. But as thou hop'st for heaven, as thou believ'st

Thy name's recorded in the book of life
I charge thee never after this sad day
To see me or to meet me; or to send
By word, or writing, gift, or otherwise,
To move me, by thyself, or by thy friends;
Nor challenge any part in my two children.
So farewell, Nan; for we will henceforth be
As we had never seen, ne'er more shall see.
Mrs. Fra. How full my heart is, in mine eyes appears;
What wants in words, I will supply in tears.
Fran. Come, take your coach, your stuff; all must along:
Servants and all make ready, all be gone.
It was thy hand cut two hearts out of one.

CRANWELL, FRANKFORD, *and* NICHOLAS, *a Servant.*

Cran. Why do you search each room about your house,
Now that you have dispatch'd your wife away?
Fran. O sir, to see that nothing may be left
That ever was my wife's; I lov'd her dearly,
And when I do but think of her unkindness,
My thoughts are all in hell; to avoid which torment,
I would not have a bodkin nor a cuff,
A bracelet, necklace, or rebato wire,
Nor anything that ever was call'd her's,
Left me, by which I might remember her.
Seek round about.
Nic. Here's her lute flung in a corner.
Fran. Her lute? Oh God! upon this instrument
Her fingers have ran quick division,
Swifter than that which now divides our hearts.
These frets have made me pleasant, that have now
Frets of my heart-strings made. O master Cranwell,
Oft hath she made this melancholy wood
(Now mute and dumb for her disastrous chance)
Speak sweetly many a note, sound many a strain
To her own ravishing voice, which being well strung,
What pleasant strange airs have they jointly rung!

Post with it after her ; now nothing's left ;
Of her and her's I am at once bereft.

NICHOLAS *overtakes* MRS. FRANKFORD *on her journey, and delivers the lute.*

Mrs. Fra. I know the lute ; oft have I sung to thee:
We both are out of tune, both out of time.
Nic. My master commends him unto ye ;
There's all he can find that was ever yours.
He prays you to forget him, and so he bids you farewell.
Mrs. Fra. I thank him, he is kind, and ever was.
All you that have true feeling of my grief,
That know my loss, and have relenting hearts,
Gird me about ; and help me with your tears
To wash my spotted sins: my lute shall groan ;
It cannot weep, but shall lament my moan.
If you return unto your master, say
(Tho' not from me, for I am unworthy
To blast his name so with a strumpet's tongue)
That you have seen me weep, wish myself dead.
Nay you may say too (for my vow is past)
Last night you saw me eat and drink my last.
This to your master you may say and swear:
For it is writ in heaven, and decreed here.
Go break this lute on my coach's wheel,
As the last music that I e'er shall make ;
Not as my husband's gift, but my farewell
To all earth's joy ; and so your master tell.
Nic. I'll do your commendations.
Mrs. Fra. O no :
I dare not so presume ; nor to my children :
I am disclaim'd in both, alas, I am.
O never teach them, when they come to speak,
To name the name of mother ; chide their tongue
If they by chance light on that hated word ;
Tell them 'tis naught, for when that word they name
(Poor pretty souls) they harp on their own shame.
So, now unto my coach, then to my home,

So to my death-bed ; for from this sad hour,
I never will nor eat, nor drink, nor taste
Of any cates that may preserve my life :
I never will nor smile, nor sleep, nor rest.
But when my tears have wash'd my black soul white,
Sweet Saviour to thy hands I yield my sprite.

Mrs. FRANKFORD (*dying*). *Sir* FRANCIS ACTON (*her brother*). *Sir* CHARLES MOUNTFORD. *Mr.* MALBY, *and other of her husband's friends.*

Mal. How fare you, Mrs. Frankford ?
Mrs. Fra. Sick, sick, O sick : give me some air. I pray
Tell me, oh tell me, where is Mr. Frankford.
Will he not deign to see me ere I die ?
Mal. Yes, Mrs. Frankford : divers gentlemen,
Your loving neighbors, with that just request
Have mov'd and told him of your weak estate :
Who, tho' with much ado to get belief,
Examining of the general circumstance,
Seeing your sorrow and your penitence,
And hearing therewithal the great desire
You have to see him ere you left the world,
He gave to us his faith to follow us ;
And sure he will be here immediately.
Mrs. Fra. You have half reviv'd me with the pleasing news :
Raise me a little higher in my bed.
Blush I not, brother Acton ? blush I not, sir Charles ?
Can you not read my fault writ in my cheek ?
Is not my crime there ? tell me, gentlemen.
Char. Alas ! good mistress, sickness hath not left you
Blood in your face enough to make you blush.
Mrs. Fra. Then sickness like a friend my fault would hide.
Is my husband come ? my soul but tarries
His arrival, then I am fit for heaven.
Acton. I came to chide you, but my words of hate
Are turn'd to pity and compassionate grief.
I came to rate you, but my brawls, you see,

Melt into tears, and I must weep by thee.
Here's Mr. Frankford now.

MR. FRANKFORD *enters.*

Fran. Good-morrow, brother; morrow, gentlemen:
God, that hath laid this cross upon our heads,
Might (had he pleas'd) have made our cause of meeting
On a more fair and more contented ground:
But he that made us, made us to his wo.
Mrs. Fra. And is he come? methinks that voice I know.
Fran. How do you, woman?
Mrs. Fra. Well, Mr. Frankford, well; but shall be better
I hope within this hour. Will you vouchsafe
(Out of your grace, and your humanity)
To take a spotted strumpet by the hand?
Fran. This hand once held my heart in faster bonds
Than now 'tis grip'd by me. God pardon them
That made us first break hold.
Mrs. Fra. Amen, amen.
Out of my zeal to heaven, whither I'm now bound,
I was so impudent to wish you here;
And once more beg your pardon. O! good man,
And father to my children, pardon me.
Pardon, O pardon me: my fault so heinous is,
That if you in this world forgive it not,
Heaven will not clear it in the world to come.
Faintness hath so usurp'd upon my knees
That kneel I cannot: but on my heart's knees
My prostrate soul lies thrown down at your feet
To beg your gracious pardon. Pardon, O pardon me!
Fran. As freely from the low depth of my soul
As my Redeemer hath for us given his death,
I pardon thee; I will shed tears for thee;
Pray with thee:
And, in mere pity of thy weak estate,
I'll wish to die with thee.
All. So do we all.
Fran. Even as I hope for pardon at that day,

When the great judge of heaven in scarlet sits,
So be thou pardon'd. Tho' thy rash offence
Divorc'd our bodies, thy repentant tears
Unite our souls.

Char. Then comfort, mistress Frankford;
You see your husband hath forgiven your fall;
Then rouse your spirits, and cheer your fainting soul.

Susan. How is it with you?

Acton. How d'ye feel yourself?

Mrs. Fra. Not of this world.

Fran. I see you are not, and I weep to see it.
My wife, the mother to my pretty babes;
Both those lost names I do restore thee back,
And with this kiss I wed thee once again:
Tho' thou art wounded in thy honor'd name,
And with that grief upon thy death-bed liest;
Honest in heart, upon my soul, thou diest.

Mrs. Fra. Pardon'd on earth, soul, thou in heaven art free
Once more. Thy wife dies thus embracing thee.

[Heywood is a sort of *prose* Shakspeare. His scenes are to the full as natural and affecting. But we miss *the Poet*, that which in Shakspeare always appears out and above the surface of *the nature*. Heywood's characters, his Country Gentlemen, &c., are exactly what we see (but of the best kind of what we see) in life. Shakspeare makes us believe, while we are among his lovely creations, that they are nothing but what we are familiar with, as in dreams new things seem old: but we awake, and sigh for the difference.]

THE ENGLISH TRAVELLER. BY THOMAS HEYWOOD.

Young Geraldine comes home from his Travels, and finds his Playfellow, that should have been his Wife, married to old Wincott. The old Gentleman receives him hospitably, as a Friend of his Father's: takes delight to hear him tell of his Travels, and treats him in all respects like a second Father; his house being always open to him. Young Geraldine and the Wife agree not to wrong the old Gentleman.

WIFE. GERALDINE.

Ger. We now are left alone.

Wife. Why, say we be; who should be jealous of us?

This is not first of many hundred nights,
That we two have been private, from the first
Of our acquaintance ; when our tongues but clipt
Our mother's tongue, and could not speak it plain,
We knew each other : as in stature, so
Increast our sweet society. Since your travel,
And my late marriage, through my husband's love,
Mid-night has been as mid-day, and my bed-chamber
As free to you, as your own father's house,
And you as welcome to it.
Ger. I must confess,
It is in you, your noble courtesy ;
In him, a more than common confidence,
And, in his age, can scarce find precedent.
Wife. Most true : it is withal an argument,
That both our virtues are so deep imprest
In his good thoughts, he knows we cannot err.
Ger. A villain were he, to deceive such trust,
Or (were there one) a much worse character.
Wife. And she no less, whom either beauty, youth,
Time, place, or opportunity could tempt
To injure such a husband.
Ger. You deserve,
Even for his sake, to be for ever young ;
And he, for yours, to have his youth renew'd :
So mutual is your true conjugal love.
Yet had the fates so pleas'd—
Wife. I know your meaning.
It was once voic'd, that we two should have matcht ;
The world so thought and many tongues so spake ;
But heaven hath now dispos'd us other ways :
And being as it is (a thing in me
Which I protest was never wisht nor sought)
Now done, I not repent it.
Ger. In those times
Of all the treasures of my hopes and love
You were th' Exchequer, they were stored in you ;
And had not my unfortunate Travel crost them,

They had been here reserv'd still.
Wife. Troth they had,
I should have been your trusty Treasurer.
Ger. However, let us love still, I entreat;
That, neighborhood and breeding will allow;
So much, the laws divine and humble both
Twixt brother and a sister will approve:
.Heaven then forbid that they should limit us
Wish well to one another.
Wife. If they should not,
We might proclaim they were not charitable,
Which were a deadly sin but to conceive.
Ger. Will you resolve me one thing?
Wife. As to one,
That in my bosom hath a second place,
Next my dear husband.
Ger. That's the thing I crave,
And only that; to have a place next him.
Wife. Presume on that already, but perhaps
You mean to stretch it further.
Ger. Only thus far:
Your husband's old; to whom my soul does wish
A Nestor's age, so much he merits from me;
Yet if (as proof and nature daily teach,
Men cannot always live, especially
Such as are old and crazed) he be called hence,
Fairly, in full maturity of time,
And we two be reserv'd to after life;
Will you confer your widow-hood on me?
Wife. You ask the thing I was about to beg;
Your tongue hath spoke mine own thoughts.
Ger. 'Tis enough, that word
Alone instates me happy: now, so please you,
We will divide; you to your private chamber,
I to find out my friend.
Wife. You are now my brother;
But then, my second husband. [*They part.*

Young Geraldine absents himself from the house of Mr. Wincott longer than is usual to him The old Gentleman sends for him, to find out the reason. He pleads his Father's commands.

WINCOTT. GERALDINE.

Ger. With due acknowledgment
Of all your more than many courtesies:
You have been my second father, and your wife
My noble and chaste mistress; all your servants
At my command; and this your bounteous table
As free and common as my father's house:
Neither 'gainst any or the least of these
Can I commence this quarrel.
Win. What might then be
The cause of this constraint, in thus absenting
Yourself from such as love you?
Ger. Out of many,
I will propose some few: the care I have
Of your (as yet unblemished) renown;
The untoucht honor of your virtuous wife;
And (which I value least, yet dearly too)
My own fair reputation.
Win. How can these
In any way be question'd?
Ger. Oh, dear sir,
Bad tongues have been too busy with us all;
Of which I never yet had time to think,
But with sad thoughts and griefs unspeakable.
It hath been whisper'd by some wicked ones,
But loudly thunder'd in my father's ears,
By some that have maligned our happiness
(Heaven, if it can brook slander, pardon them),
That this my customary coming hither,
Hath been to base and sordid purposes;
To wrong your bed, injure her chastity,
And be mine own undoer: which, how false—
Win. As heaven is true, I know it—
Ger. Now this calumny

Arriving first ùnto my father's ears,
His easy nature was induced to think
That these things might perhaps be possible:
I answer'd him, as I would do to heaven,
And clear'd myself in his suspicious thoughts
As truly, as the high all-knowing judge
Shall of these stains acquit me; which are merely
Aspersions and untruths. The good old man
Possessed with my sincerity, and yet careful
Of your renown, her honor, and my fame,
To stop the worst that scandal could inflict
And to prevent false rumors, charges me
The cause remov'd, to take away th' effect;
Which only could be, to forbear your house:
And this upon his blessing. You hear all.
Win. And I of all acquit you: this your absence,
With which my love most cavill'd, orators
In your behalf. Had such things pass'd betwixt you,
Not threats nor chidings could have driv'n you hence;
It pleads in your behalf, and speaks in her's;
And arms me with a double confidence
Both of your friendship and her loyalty.
I am happy in you both, and only doubtful
Which of you two doth most impart my love.
You shall not hence to-night.
Ger. Pray, pardon, sir.
Win. You are in your lodging.
Ger. But my father's charge.
Win. My conjuration shall dispense with that;
You may be up as early as you please,
But hence to-night you shall not.
Ger. You are powerful.

Traveller's Stories.

Sir, my husband
Hath took much pleasure in your strange discourse
About Jerusalem and the Holy Land;
How the new city differs from the old;

What ruins of the Temple yet remain;
And whether Sion, and those hills about,
With these adjacent towns and villages,
Keep that proportioned distance as we read:
And then in Rome, of that great Pyramis
Rear'd in the front, on four lions mounted;
How many of those Idol temples stand,
First dedicated to their heathen gods,
Which ruin'd, which to better use repair'd;
Of their Pantheon, and their Capitol;
What structures are demolish'd, what remain.
—— And what more pleasure to an old man's ear,
That never drew save his own country's air,
Than hear such things related?

Shipwreck by Drink.

This Gentleman and I
Passt but just now by your next neighbor's house,
Where, as they say, dwells one young Lionel,
An unthrift youth: his father now at sea.
——— There this night
Was a great feast.
In the height of their carousing, all their brains
Warm'd with the heat of wine, discourse was offer'd
Of ships and storms at sea: when suddenly,
Out of his giddy wildness, one conceives
The room wherein they quaff'd to be a Pinnace,
Moving and floating, and the confus'd noise
To be the murmuring winds, gusts, mariners;
That their unsteadfast footing did proceed
From rocking of the vessel: this conceiv'd,
Each one begins to apprehend the danger,
And to look out for safety. Fly, saith one,
Up to the main top, and discover. He
Climbs up the bed-post to the tester there,
Reports a turbulent sea and tempest towards;
And wills them, if they'll save their ship and lives,
To cast their lading over-board. At this

All fall to work, and hoist into the street,
As to the sea, what next came to their hand,
Stools, tables, tressels, trenchers, bed-steds, cups,
Pots, plate, and glasses. Here a fellow whistles;
They take him for the boatswain: one lies struggling
Upon the floor, as if he swam for life:
A third takes the base-viol for the cock-boat,
Sits in the belly on't, labors, and rows;
His oar, the stick with which the fiddler played:
A fourth bestrides his fellow, thinking to scape
(As did Arion) on the dolphin's back,
Still fumbling on a gittern.——The rude multitude,
Watching without, and gaping for the spoil
Cast from the windows, went by th' ears about it;
The Constable is call'd to atone the broil;
Which done, and hearing such a noise within
Of eminent ship-wreck, enters th' house, and finds them
In this confusion: they adore his Staff,
And think it Neptune's Trident; and that he
Comes with his Tritons (so they call'd his watch)
To calm the tempest and appease the waves:
And at this point we left them.

[This piece of pleasant exaggeration (which, for its life and humor, might have been told or acted by Petruchio himself,) gave rise to the title of Cowley's Latin Play, Naufragium Joculare, and furnished the idea of the best scene in it. Heywood's Preface to this Play is interesting, as it shows the heroic indifference about posterity, which some of these great writers seem to have felt. There is a magnanimity in Authorship as in everything else.

"If Reader thou hast of this play been an Auditor, there is less apology to be used by entreating thy patience. This Tragi-comedy (being one reserved amongst 220 in which I had either an entire hand, or at the least a main finger) coming accidentally to the press, and I having intelligence thereof, thought it not fit that it should pass as filius populi, a Bastard without a father to acknowledge it: true it is that my plays are not exposed to the world in volumes, to bear the title of works (as others*): one reason is, that many of them, by shifting and change of companies, have been negligently lost. Others of them are still retained in the hands of some actors, who think it against their peculiar profit to have them come in print

* He seems to glance at Ben Jonson.

and a third that it never was any great ambition in me to be in this kind voluminously read. All that I have further to say at this time is only this: censure I entreat as favorably as it is exposed to thy view freely.

"Ever
"Studious of thy Pleasure and Profit,
"TH. HEYWOOD."

Of the 220 pieces which he here speaks of having been concerned in, only 25, as enumerated by Dodsley, have come down to us, for the reasons assigned in the preface. The rest have perished, exposed to the casualties of a theatre. Heywood's ambition seems to have been confined to the pleasure of hearing the Players speak his lines while he lived. It does not appear that he ever contemplated the possibility of being read by after ages. What a slender pittance of fame was motive sufficient to the production of such Plays as the English Traveller, the Challenge for Beauty, and the Woman Killed with Kindness! Posterity is bound to take care that a Writer loses nothing by such a noble modesty.]

THE LATE LANCASHIRE WITCHES: A COMEDY. BY THOMAS HEYWOOD AND RICHARD BROOME.

Mr. Generous, by taking off a Bridle from a seeming Horse in his Stable, discovers it to be his Wife, who has transformed herself by Magical Practices, and is a Witch.

MR. GENEROUS. WIFE. ROBIN, *a groom.*

Gen. My blood is turned to ice, and all my vitals
Have ceas'd their working. Dull stupidity
Surpriseth me at once, and hath arrested
That vigorous agitation, which till now
Exprest a life within me. I, methinks,
Am a meer marble statue, and no man.
Unweave my age, O time, to my first thread;
Let me lose fifty years, in ignorance spent;
That, being made an infant once again,
I may begin to know. What, or where am I,
To be thus lost in wonder?
Wife. Sir.
Gen. Amazement still pursues me, how am I chang'd,
Or brought ere I can understand myself
Into this new world!

Rob. You will believe no witches ?
Gen. This makes me believe all, aye, anything;
And that myself am nothing. Prithee, Robin,
Lay me to myself open; what art thou,
Or this new transform'd creature ?
Rob. I am Robin;
And this your wife, my mistress.
Gen. Tell me, the earth
Shall leave its seat, and mount to kiss the moon;
Or that the moon, enamor'd of the earth,
Shall leave her sphere, to stoop to us thus low.
What, what's this in my hand, that at an instant
Can from a four-legg'd creature make a thing
So like a wife ?
Rob. A bridle; a jugling bridle, Sir.
Gen. A bridle! Hence, enchantment.
A viper were more safe within my hand,
Than this charm'd engine.—
A witch! my wife a witch!
The more I strive to unwind
Myself from this meander, I the more
Therein am intricated. Prithee, woman,
Art thou a witch ?
Wife. It cannot be denied,
I am such a curst creature.
Gen. Keep aloof:
And do not come too near me. O my trust;
Have I, since first I understood myself,
Been of my soul so chary, still to study
What best was for its health, to renounce all
The works of that black fiend with my best force;
And hath that serpent twined me so about,
That I must lie so often and so long
With a devil in my bosom ?
Wife. Pardon, Sir. [*She looks down.*]
Gen. Pardon! can such a thing as that be hoped ?
Lift up thine eyes, lost woman, to yon hills;
It must be thence expected: look not down

Into that horrid dwelling, which thou hast sought
At such dear rate to purchase. Prithee, tell me
For now I can believe) art thou a witch?
Wife. I am.
Gen. With that word I am thunderstruck,
And know not what to answer; yet resolve me,
Hast thou made any contract with that fiend,
The enemy of mankind?
Wife. O I have.
Gen. What? and how far?
Wife. I have promis'd him my soul.
Gen. Ten thousand times better thy body had
Been promis'd to the stake; aye, and mine too,
To have suffer'd with thee in a hedge of flames,
Than such a compact ever had been made. Oh——
Resolve me, how far doth that contract stretch?
Wife. What interest in this Soul myself could claim,
I freely gave him; but his part that made it
I still reserve, not being mine to give.
Gen. O cunning devil: foolish woman, know,
Where he can claim but the least little part,
He will usurp the whole. Thou'rt a lost woman.
Wife. I hope not so.
Gen. Why, hast thou any hope?
Wife. Yes, sir, I have.
Gen. Make it appear to me.
Wife. I hope I never bargain'd for that fire,
Further than penitent tears have power to quench.
Gen. I would see some of them.
Wife. You behold them now
(If you look on me with charitable eyes)
Tinctur'd in blood, blood issuing from the heart.
Sir, I am sorry; when I look towards heaven,
I beg a gracious pardon; when on you,
Methinks your native goodness should not be
Less pitiful than they; 'gainst both I have err'd;
From both I beg atonement.
Gen. May I presume 't?

Wife. I kneel to both your mercies.
Gen. Knowest thou what
A witch is ?
Wife. Alas, none better ;
Or after mature recollection can be
More sad to think on't.
Gen. Tell me, are those tears
As full of true hearted penitence,
As mine of sorrow to behold what state,
What desperate state, thou'rt faln in ?
Wife. Sir, they are.
Gen. Rise ; and, as I do you, so heaven pardon me ;
We all offend, but from such falling off
Defend us ! Well, I do remember, wife,
When I first took thee, 'twas *for good and bad :*
O change thy bad to good, that I may keep thee
(As then we past our faiths) 'till Death us sever.
O woman, thou hast need to weep thyself
Into a fountain, such a penitent spring
As may have power to quench invisible flames ;
In which my eyes shall aid : too little, all.*

Frank Hospitality.

Gentlemen, welcome ; 'tis a word I use ;
From me expect no further compliment ;
Nor do I name it often at one meeting ;
Once spoke, to those that understand me best,
And know I always purpose as I speak,
Hath ever yet sufficed : so let it you.
Nor do I love that common phrase of guests,
As, we make bold, or, we are troublesome,
We take you unprovided, and the like ;
I know you understanding Gentlemen,
And knowing me, cannot persuade yourselves
With me you shall be troublesome or bold.——
Nor shall you find

* Compare this with a story in the Arabian Nights, where a man discov ers his wife to be a *goul.*

Being set to meat, that I 'll excuse your fare,
Or say, I am sorry it falls out so poor,
And, had I known your coming, we 'd have had
Such things and such ; nor blame my Cook, to say
This dish or that hath not been sauc't with care:
Words fitting best a common hostess' mouth,
When there's perhaps some just cause of dislike;
But not the table of a Gentleman.

A FAIR QUARREL: A COMEDY. BY THOMAS MIDDLETON AND WILLIAM ROWLEY.

Captain Ager, in a dispute with a Colonel his friend, receives from the Colonel the appellation of Son of a Whore. A challenge is given and accepted: but the Captain, before he goes to the field, is willing to be confirmed of his mother's honor from her own lips. Lady Ager being questioned by her Son, to prevent a duel, falsely slanders herself of unchastity. The Captain, thinking that he has a bad cause, refuses to fight. But being reproached by the Colonel with cowardice, he esteems that he has now sufficient cause for a quarrel, in the vindicating of his honor from that aspersion; and draws, and disarms his opponent.

LADY. CAPTAIN, *her Son.*

La. Where left you your dear friend the Colonel ?
Cap. Oh the dear Colonel, I should meet him soon.
La. Oh fail him not then, he 's a Gentleman
The fame and reputation of your time
Is much engag'd to.
Cap. Yes, and you knew all, mother,
La. I thought I 'd known so much of his fair goodness,
More could not have been look'd for.
Cap. O yes, yes, Madam:
And this his last exceeded all the rest.
La. For gratitude's sake let me know this I prithee.
Cap. Then thus; and I desire your censure freely,
Whether it appear'd not a strange noble kindness in him.
La. Trust me, I long to hear't.

Cap. You know he's hasty ;
That by the way.
La. So are the best conditions :
Your father was the like.
Cap. I begin now
To doubt me more : why am not I so too then ?
Blood follows blood through forty generations ;
And I 've a slow-pac'd wrath : a shrewd dilemma.— [*Aside.*
La. Well, as you were saying, Sir.
Cap. Marry, thus, good Madam.
There was in company a foul-mouth'd villain——.
Stay, stay——
Who should I liken him to that you have seen ?
He comes so near one that I would not match him with,
Faith, just o' the Colonel's pitch ; he's never the worse man ;
Usurers have been compar'd to magistrates,
Extortioners to lawyers, and the like,
But they all prove ne'er the worse men for that.
La. That's bad enough, they need not.
Cap. This rude fellow,
A shame to all humanity and manners,
Breathes from the rottenness of his gall and malice,
The foulest stain that ever man's fame blemish'd,
Part of which fell upon your honor, madam,
Which heighten'd my affliction.
La. Mine, my honor, Sir ?
Cap. The Colonel soon enrag'd (as he's all touchwood)
Takes fire before me, makes the quarrel his,
Appoints the field ; my wrath could not be heard,
His was so high picht, so gloriously mounted.
Now what's the friendly fear that fights within me,
Should his brave noble fury undertake
A cause that were unjust in our defence,
And so to lose him everlastingly,
In that dark depth where all bad quarrels sink
Never to rise again, what pity 'twere,
First to die here, and never to die there ?
La. Why what's the quarrel, speak, Sir, that should rise

Such fearful doubt, my honor bearing part on 't?
The words, whate'er they were——
Cap. *Son of a whore.*
La. Thou liest:
And were my love ten thousand times more to thee,
Which is as much now as e'er mother's was,
So thou shouldst feel my anger. Dost thou call
That quarrel doubtful? where are all my merits? [*Strikes him.*
Not one stand up to tell this man his error?
Thou might'st as well call the Sun's truth in question,
As thy birth or my honor.
Cap. Now blessings crown you for 't;
It is the joyfull'st blow that e'er flesh felt.
La. Nay, stay, stay, Sir; thou art not left so soon:
This is no question to be slighted off,
And at your pleasure closed up fair again.
As though you'd never touch'd it, no; honor doubted,
Is honor deeply wounded; and it rages
More than a common smart, being of thy making.
For thee to fear my truth it kills my comfort.
Where should fame seek for her reward, when he
That is her own by the great tye of blood
Is farthest off in bounty: O poor Goodness,
That only pay'st thyself with thy own works;
For nothing else looks towards thee. Tell me, pray,
Which of my loving cares dost thou requite
With this vile thought? which of my prayers or wishes?
Many thou ow'st me for. This seven year hast thou known me
A widow, only married to my vow;
That's no small witness of my faith and love
To him that in life was thy honor'd father:
And live I now to know that good mistrusted?
Cap. No, it shall appear that my grief is chearful!
For never was a mother's reputation
Noblier defended; 'tis my joy and pride
I have a firmness to bestow upon it.
La. What 's that you said, Sir?
Cap. 'Twere too bold and soon yet

To crave forgiveness of you. I will earn it first.
Dead or alive I know I shall enjoy it.
La. What 's all this, Sir ?
Cap. My joy 's beyond expression :
I do but think how wretched I had been,
Were this another's quarrel and not mine.
La. Why, is it your's ?
Cap. Mine ? think me not so miserable,
Not to be mine : then were I worse than abject,
More to be loath'd than vileness, or sin's dunghill :
Nor did I fear your goodness, faithful Madam,
But came with greedy joy to be confirm'd in 't,
To give the nobler onset : then shines valor,
And admiration from her fix'd sphere draws,
When it comes burnish'd with a righteous cause ;
Without which I'm ten fathoms under coward,
That now am ten degrees above a man.
Which is but one of virtue's easiest wonders.
La. But pray stay : all this while I understand you
The Colonel was the man.
Cap. Yes, he's the man,
The man of injury, reproach, and slander,
Which I must turn into his soul again.
La. The Colonel do 't ! that 's strange.
Cap. The villain did it :
That 's not so strange. Your blessing, and your leave—
La. Come, come, you shall not go.
Cap. Not go ? were death
Sent now to summon me to my eternity,
I 'd put him off an hour : why, the whole world,
Has not chains strong enough to bind me from it :
The strongest is my Reverence for you,
Which if you force upon me in this case,
I must be forced to break it.
La. Stay, I say.
Cap. In anything command me but in this, Madam.
La. 'Las, I shall lose him. You will hear me first ?
Cap. At my return I will.

La. You 'll never hear me more then.
Cap. How !
La. Come back, I say !
You may well think there 's cause, I call so often.
Cap. Ha ! cause ? what cause ?
La. So much, you must not go.
Cap. Must not, why ?
La. I know a reason for 't ;
Which I could wish you 'd yield to, and not know :
If not, it must come forth. Faith, do not know ;
And yet obey my will.
Cap. Why, I desire
To know no other than the cause I have,
Nor should you wish it, if you take your injury ;
For one more great I know the world includes not.
La. Yes ; one that makes this nothing :—yet be ruled,
And if you understand not, seek no farther.
Cap. I must, for this is nothing.
La. Then take all ;
And if amongst it you receive that secret
That will offend you, though you condemn me,
Yet blame yourself a little, for perhaps
I would have made my reputation sound
Upon another's hazard with less pity ;
But upon yours I dare not.
Cap. How ?
La. I dare not :
'Twas your own seeking, this.
Cap. If you mean evilly,
I cannot understand you, nor for all the riches
This life has, would I.
La. Would you never might !
Cap. Why, your goodness, that I joy to fight for.
La. In that you neither right your joy nor me.
Cap. What an ill orator has virtue got here !
Why, shall I dare to think it a thing possible,
That you were ever false ?
La. Oh, fearfully ;

As much as *you* come to.
Cap. Oh silence cover me;
I 've felt a deadlier wound than man can give me.
False ?
La. I was betray'd to a most sinful hour
By a corrupted soul I put in trust once,
A kinswoman.
Cap. Where is she ? let me pay her.
La. Oh dead long since.
Cap. Say then, she has all her wages.
False ? do not say 't; for honor's goodness do not;
You never could be so: he I call'd father
Deserv'd you at your best; when youth and merit
Could boast at highest in you, you 'd no grace
Or virtue that he match'd not; no delight
That you invented, but he sent it crown'd
To your full wishing soul.
La. That heaps my guiltiness.
Cap. O were you so unhappy to be false
Both to yourself and me, but to me chiefly ?
What a day's hope is here lost, and with it
The joys of a just cause! Had you but thought
On such a noble quarrel, you 'd ha' died
Ere you 'd ha' yielded, for the sin's hate first.
Next for the hate of this hour's cowardice.
Curst be the heat that lost me such a cause,
A work that I was made for. Quench, my spirit,
And out with honor's flaming lights within thee:
Be dark and dead to all respects of manhood;
I never shall have use of valor more.
Put off your vow for shame: why should you hoard up
Such justice for a barren widowhood;
That was so injurious to the faith of wedlock ?
I should be dead: for all my life's work 's ended.
I dare not fight a stroke now, nor engage [*Exit Lady.*
The noble resolution of my friends;

Enter two Friends of Captain AGER'S.

That were more vile. They 're here. Kill me, my shame.
I am not for the fellowship of honor.
1. *Friend.* Captain, fie, come, Sir: we 've been seeking for you
Very late to-day; this was not wont to be,
Your enemy 's in the field.
Cap. Truth enters chearfully.
2. *Friend.* Good faith, Sir, you 've a royal quarrel on 't.
Cap. Yes, in some other country, Spain or Italy,
It would be held so.
1. *Friend.* How! and is 't not here so?
Cap. 'Tis not so contumeliously receiv'd
In these parts, and you mark it.
1. *Friend.* Not in these?
Why prithee what is more, or can be?
Cap. Yes:
That ordinary Commotioner *the lye*
Is father of most quarrels in this climate,
And held here capital, and you go to that.
2. *Friend.* But, Sir, I hope you will not go to that,
Or change your own for it; *son of a whore!*
Why there 's the lye down to posterity;
The lye to birth, the lye to honesty.
Why would you cozen yourself so and beguile
So brave a cause, Manhood's best masterpiece?
Do you ever hope for one so brave again?
Cap. Consider then the man, the Colonel,
Exactly worthy, absolutely noble,
However spleen and rage abuses him:
And 'tis not well nor manly to pursue
A man's infirmity.
1. *Friend.* O miracle!
So hopeful valiant and complete a Captain
Possest with a tame devil: come out, thou spoilest
The most improv'd young soldier of seven kingdoms,
Made Captain at nineteen; which was deserv'd
The year before, but honor comes behind still:

Come out, I say: this was not wont to be,
That spirit ne'er stood in need of provocation,
Nor shall it now. Away, Sir.
Cap. Urge me not.
1. *Friend.* By Manhood's reverend honor but we must.
Cap. I will not fight a stroke.
1. *Friend.* O blasphemy
To sacred valor.
Cap. Lead me where you list.
1. *Friend.* Pardon this traiterous slumber, clog'd with evils:
Give Captains rather wives than such tame devils.

The Field.

Enter Captain Ager *with his two Friends.*

Cap. Well, your wills now.
1. *Friend.* Our wills? our loves, our duties
To honor'd fortitude: what wills have we
But our desires to nobleness and merit,
Valor's advancement, and the sacred rectitude
Due to a valorous cause?
Cap. Oh, that 's not mine.
2. *Friend.* War has his Court of Justice, that 's the field,
Where all cases of Manhood are determined,
And your case is no mean one.
Cap. True, then 't were virtuous;
But mine is in extremes, foul and unjust.
Well, now ye 've got me hither, ye are as far
To seek in your desire as at first minute:
For by the strength and honor of a vow
I will not lift a finger in this quarrel.
1. *Friend.* How! not in this! be not so rash a sinner.
Why, Sir, do you ever hope to fight again then?
Take heed on 't, you must never look for that.
Why, the universal stock of the World's injury
Will be too poor to find a quarrel for you.
Give up your right and title to desert, Sir;
If you fail virtue here, she needs you not
All your time after; let her take this wrong,

And never presume then to serve her more:
Bid farewell to the integrity of Arms,
And let that honorable name of soldier
Fall from you like a shiver'd wreath of laurel,
By thunder struck from a desertless forehead
That wears another's right by usurpation.
Good Captain, do not wilfully cast away
At one hour all the fame your life has won.
This is your native seat. Here you should seek
Most to preserve it; or if you will doat
So much on life, poor life, which in respect
Of life in honor is but death and darkness,
That you will prove neglectful of yourself
(Which is to me too fearful to imagine)
Yet for that virtuous Lady's cause, your Mother,
Her reputation, dear to nobleness,
As grace to penitence; whose fair memory
E'en crowns fame in your issue; for that blessedness,
Give not this ill place, but in spite of hell
And all her base fears be exactly valiant.

Cap. Oh! oh!——

2. *Friend.* Why, well said; there's fair hope in that.
Another such a one.

Cap. Came they in thousands,
'Tis all against you.

1. *Friend.* Then poor friendless Merit,
Heav'n be good to thee, thy Professor leaves thee.

Enter COLONEL *and his two friends.*

He 's come; do you but draw; we 'll fight it for you.

Cap. I know too much to grant that.

1. *Friend.* O dead manhood!
Had ever such a cause so faint a servant?
Shame brand me if I do not suffer for him.

Col. I 've heard, Sir, you 've been guilty of much boasting
For your brave earliness at such a meeting,
You 've lost the glory of that way this morning:
I was the first to-day.

Cap. So were you ever
In my respect, Sir.
1. *Friend.* O most base præludium!
Cap. I never thought on victory our mistress
With greater reverence than I have your worth,
Nor ever lov'd her better.
Success in you has been my absolute joy,
And when I 've wish'd content I 've wish'd your friendship.
Col. I come not hither, Sir, for an encomium.
I came provided
For storms and tempests, and the foulest season
That ever rage let forth, or blew in wildness
From the incensed prison of man's blood.
Cap. Tis otherwise with me: I come with mildness,
Peace, constant amity, and calm forgiveness,
The weather of a Christian and a friend.
1. *Friend.* Give me a valiant Turk, though not worth ten-pence.
Cap. Yet, Sir, the world will judge the injury mine,
Insufferably mine, mine beyond injury,
Thousands have made a less wrong reach to hell,
Aye and rejoic'd in his most endless vengeance
(A miserable triumph though a just one);
But when I call to memory our long friendship,
Methinks it cannot be too great a wrong
That then I should not pardon. Why should Man
For a poor hasty syllable or two
(And vented only in forgetful fury)
Chain all the hopes and riches of his soul
To the revenge of that? die lost for ever?
For he that makes his last peace with his Maker
In anger, anger is his peace eternally:
He must expect the same return again,
Whose venture is deceitful. Must he not, Sir?
Col. I see what I must do, fairly put up again,
For here 'll be nothing done, I perceive that.
Cap. What shall be done in such a worthless business
But to be sorry and to be forgiven?
You, Sir, to bring repentance; and I pardon.

Col. I bring repentance, Sir?
Cap. If 't be too much
To say, repentance; call it what you please, Sir;
Choose your own word, I know you 're sorry for it,
And that 's as good.
Col. I sorry? by fame's honor, I am wrong'd:
Do you seek for peace and draw the quarrel larger?
Cap. Then 'tis I 'm sorry that I thought you so.
1. *Friend.* A Captain! I could gnaw his title off.
Cap. Nor is it any misbecoming virtue, Sir,
In the best manliness, to repent a wrong:
Which made me bold with you.
1. *Friend.* I could cuff his head off.
2. *Friend.* Nay, pish.
Col. So once again take thou thy peaceful rest then;
[*To his sword.*
But as I put thee up, I must proclaim
This Captain here, both to his friends and mine,
That only came to see fair valor righted,
A base submissive Coward: so I leave him.
Cap. Oh, heaven has pitied my excessive patience,
And sent me a Cause: now I have a Cause:
A Coward I was never.———Come you back, Sir.
Col. How!
Cap. You left a Coward here.
Col. Yes, Sir, with you.
Cap. 'Tis such base metal, Sir, 't will not be taken,
It must home again with you.
2. *Friend.* Should this be true now——
1. *Friend.* Impossible! Coward do more than Bastard!
Col. I prithee mock me not, take heed you do not,
For if I draw once more I shall grow terrible,
And rage will force me do what will grieve honor.
Cap. Ha, ha, ha.
Col. He smiles, dare it be he? what think ye, Gentlemen
Your judgments; shall I not be cozen'd in him?
This cannot be the man; why he was bookish,
Made an invective lately against fighting,

A thing in truth that mov'd a little with me;
Put up a fouler contumely far
Than thousand Cowards came to, and grew thankful.

Cap. Blessed remembrance in time of need;
I 'd lost my honor else.

2. *Friend.* Do you note his joy?

Cap. I never felt a more severe necessity:
Then came thy excellent pity. Not yet ready!
Have you such confidence in my just manhood
That you dare so long trust me, and yet tempt me
Beyond the toleration of man's virtue?
Why, would you be more cruel than your injury?
Do you first take pride to wrong me, and then think me
Not worth your fury? do not use me so:
I shall deceive you then: Sir, either draw,
And that not slightingly, but with the care
Of your best preservation, with that watchfulness
As you 'd defend yourself from circular fire,
Your sin's rage, or her Lord (this will require it)
Or you 'll be too soon lost: for I 've an anger,
Has gather'd mighty strength against you: mighty,
Yet you shall find it honest to the last,
Noble and fair.

Col. I 'll venture it once again,
And if 't be but as true as it is wondrous
I shall have that I come for. Your leave, Gentlemen.

[*They fight.*

1. *Friend.* If he should do 't indeed, and deceive us all now——
Stay, by this hand he offers; fights i'faith;
Fights: by this light, he fights, Sir.

2. *Friend.* So methinks, Sir.

1. *Friend.* An absolute Punto, ha?

2. *Friend.* 'Twas a Passado, Sir.

1. *Friend.* Why, let it pass, and 'twas: I 'm sure 'twas somewhat.
What 's that now?

2. *Friend.* That 's a Punto.

1. *Friend.* O go to then,
I knew 'twas not far off: What a world's this!
Is Coward a more stirring meat than Bastard?
——ho! I honor thee:
'Tis right and fair, and he that breathes against it,
He breathes against the justice of a man;
And man to cut him off, 'tis no injustice.
Thanks, thanks, for this most unexpected nobleness.
[*The Colonel is disarmed.*

Cap. Truth never fails her servant, Sir, nor leaves him
With the day's shame upon him.

1. *Friend.* Thou 'st redeemed
Thy worth to the same height, 'twas first esteemed.

[The insipid levelling morality to which the modern stage is tied down would not admit of such admirable passions as these scenes are filled with. A puritanical obtuseness of sentiment, a stupid infantile goodness, is creeping among us, instead of the vigorous passions, and virtues clad in flesh and blood, with which the old dramatists present us. These noble and liberal casuists could discern in the differences, the quarrels, the animosities of man, a beauty and truth of moral feeling, no less than in the iterately inculcated duties of forgiveness and atonement. With us all is hypocritical meekness. A reconciliation scene (let the occasion be never so absurd or unnatural) is always sure of applause. Our audiences come to the theatre to be complimented on their goodness. They compare notes with the amiable characters in the play, and find a wonderful similarity of disposition between them. We have a common stock of dramatic morality out of which a writer may be supplied without the trouble of copying it from originals within his own breast. To know the boundaries of honor, to be judiciously valiant, to have a temperance which shall beget a smoothness in the angry swellings of youth, to esteem life as nothing when the sacred reputation of a parent is to be defended, yet to shake and tremble under a pious cowardice when that ark of an honest confidence is found to be frail and tottering, to feel the true blows of a real disgrace blunting that sword which the imaginary strokes of a supposed false imputation had put so keen an edge upon but lately: to do, or to imagine this done in a feigned story, asks something more of a moral sense, somewhat a greater delicacy of perception in questions of right and wrong, than goes to the writing of two or three hackneyed sentences about the laws of honor as opposed to the laws of the land, or a common-place against duelling. Yet such things would stand a writer now a days in far better stead than Captain Ager and his conscientious honor; and he would be considered as a far better teacher of morality than old Rowley or Middleton if they were living.]

ALL'S LOST BY LUST. A TRAGEDY. BY WILLIAM ROWLEY.

Roderigo, King of Spain, takes the opportunity to violate the Daughter of Julianus, while that old General is fighting his battles against the Moors. Jacinta seeks her Father in the Camp, at the moment of Victory.

JULIANUS. *Servant.*

Ser. Sir, here's a Woman (forced by some tide of sorrow)
With tears intreats your pity, and to see you.
Jul. If any Soldier has done violence to her,
Beyond our military discipline,
Death shall divide him from us: fetch her in.
I have myself a Daughter, on whose face
But thinking, I must needs be pitiful:
And when I ha' told my conquest to my King,
My poor girl then shall know, how for her sake
I did one pious act:

Servant returns with JACINTA *veiled.*

Is this the creature?
Serv. Yes, my Lord, and a sad one.
Jul. Leave us. A sad one!
The down-cast look calls up compassion in me,
A corse going to the grave looks not more deadly.
Why kneel'st thou? art thou wrong'd by any Soldier?
Rise: for this honor is not due to me.
Hast not a tongue to read thy sorrows out?
This book I understand not.
Jacin. O my dear father!
Jul. Thy father, who has wrong'd him?
Jacin. A great Commander.
Jul. Under me?
Jacin. Above you.
Jul. Above me! who's above a general?
None but the general of all Spain's armies;
And that's the king, king Roderick: he's all goodness,
He cannot wrong thy father.
Jacin. What was Tarquin?

Jul. A king, and yet a ravisher.
Jacin. Such a sin
Was in those days a monster; now 'tis common.
Jul. Prithee be plain.
Jacin. Have not you, Sir, a daughter?
Jul. If I have not, I am the wretched'st man
That this day lives; for all the wealth I have
Lives in that child.
Jacin. O for your daughter's sake then hear my woes.
Jul. Rise then, and speak 'em.
Jacin. No, let me kneel still:
Such a resemblance of a daughter's duty
Will make you mindful of a father's love:
For such my injuries must exact from you,
As you would for your own.
Jul. And so they do;
For whilst I see thee kneeling, I think of my Jacinta
Jacin. Say your Jacinta then, chaste as the rose
Coming on sweetly in the springing bud,
And ne'er felt heat, to spread the summer sweet;
But, to increase and multiply it more,
Did to itself keep in its own perfume;
Say that some rapine hand had pluck'd the bloom,*
Jacinta, like that flower, and ravish'd her,
Defiling her white lawn of chastity
With ugly blacks of lust: what would you do?
Jul. O 'tis too hard a question to resolve,
Without a solemn council held within
Of man's best understanding faculties:
There must be love, and fatherhood, and grief,
And rage, and many passions: and they must all
Beget a thing call'd vengeance: but they must sit upon 't.
Jacin. Say this were done by him that carried
The fairest seeming face of friendship to yourself.
Jul. We should fall out.
Jacin. Would you in such a case respect degrees?
Jul. I know not that.

* "Cropt this fair Rose," &c.—*Otway.*

Jacin. Say he were noble.

Jul. Impossible: the act's ignoble. The Bee can breed
No poison, though it suck the juice of hemlock.

Jacin. Say a king should do it; were the act less done,
By the greater power? does majesty
Extenuate a crime?

Jul. Augment it rather.

Jacin. Say then that Roderick, your king and master,
To quit the honors you are bringing home,
Had ravish'd your Jacinta.

Jul. Who has sent
A Fury in this foul-fair shape to vex me?
I ha' seen that face methinks yet know it not:
How darest thou speak this treason 'gainst my king?
Durst any man in the world bring me this lie,
By this, he had been in hell: Roderick a Tarquin!

Jacin. Yes, and thy daughter (had she done her part)
Should be the second Lucrece. View me well:
I am Jacinta.

Jul. Ha!

Jacin. The king my ravisher.

Jul. The king thy ravisher! oh, unkingly sound.
He dares not sure; yet in thy sullied eyes
I read a tragic story.

ANTONIO, ALONZO, *and other Officers, enter.*

Jul. O noble friends,
Our wars are ended, are they not?

All. They are, Sir.

Jul. But Spain has now begun a civil war,
And to confound me only. See you my daughter?
She sounds the trumpet which draws forth my sword
To be revenged.

Alon. On whom? speak loud your wrongs;
Digest your choler into temperance;
Give your considerate thoughts the upper hand
In your hot passions, 'twill assuage the swelling
Of your big heart: if you have injuries done you,

Revenge them, and we second you.
Jacin. Father, dear father.
Jul. Daughter, dear daughter.
Jacin. Why do you kneel to me, Sir!
Jul. To ask thee pardon that I did beget thee.
I brought thee to a shame, stains all the way
'Twixt earth and Acheron: not all the clouds
(The skies' large canopy) could they drown the seas
With a perpetual inundation,
Can wash it ever out: leave me, I pray. [*Falls down.*
Alon. His fighting passion will be o'er anon,
And all will be at peace.
Ant. Best in my judgment
We wake him with the sight of his won honors.
Call up the army, and let them present
His prisoners to him: such a sight as that
Will brook no sorrow near it.
Jul. 'Twas a good doctor that prescrib'd that physic.
I'll be your patient, Sir; show me my soldiers,
And my new honors won: I will truly weigh them
With my full griefs, they may perhaps o'ercome.
Alon. Why now there's hopes of his recovery.
Jul. Jacinta, welcome, thou art my child still:
No forced stain of lust can alienate
Our consanguinity.
Jacin. Dear father,
Recollect your noble spirits: conquer grief,
The manly way: you have brave foes subdued,
Then let no female passions thus o'erwhelm you.
Jul. Mistake me not, my child, I am not mad,
Nor must be idle; for it were more fit
(If I could purchase more) I had more wit,
To help in these designs: I am grown old:
Yet I have found more strength within this arm,
Than (without proof) I durst ha' boasted on.
Roderick, thou king of monsters, couldst thou do this,
And for thy lust confine me from the court?
There's reason in thy shame, thou shouldst not see me.

Ha! they come, Jacinta, they come, hark, hark;
Now thou shalt see what cause I have given my king.

Vanquished Moors' address to the Sun.

Descend thy sphere, thou burning Deity.
Haste from our shame, go blushing to thy bed;
Thy sons* we are, thou everlasting Ball,
Yet never shamed these our impressive brows
Till now: we that are stampt with thine own seal,
Which the whole ocean cannot wash away,
Shall those cold ague cheeks that Nature moulds
Within her winter shop, those smooth white skins,
That with a palsy hand she paints the limbs,
Make us recoil?

Man's Heart.

I would fain know what kind thing a man's heart is.
——— were you never
At Barber Surgeons' Hall to see a dissection?
I will report it to you: 'tis a thing framed
With divers corners, and into every corner
A man may entertain a friend: (there came
The proverb, A man may love one well, and yet
Retain a friend in a corner.)——
————— tush, 'tis not
The real heart; but the unseen faculties.——
———Those I'll decipher unto you: (for surely
The most part are but ciphers.) The heart indeed
For the most part doth keep a better guest
Than himself in him; that is, the soul. Now the soul
Being a tree, there are divers branches spreading out of it,
As loving-affection, suffering-sorrows, and the like.
Then, Sir, these affections or sorrows being but branches,
Are sometimes lopt off, or of themselves wither;
And new shoot in their rooms: as for example;
Your friend dies, there appears sorrow, but it quickly
Withers; then is that branch gone. Again, you love a friend;

* "Children of the Sun."—*Zanga in the Revenge.*

There affection springs forth; at last you distaste;
Then that branch withers again, and another buds
In his room.

A NEW WONDER: A WOMAN NEVER VEXT. A COMEDY BY WILLIAM ROWLEY.

The Woman never Vext states her Case to a Divine.

WIDOW. DOCTOR.

Doc. You sent for me, gentlewoman?
Wid. Sir, I did, and to this end.
I have some scruples in my conscience;
Some doubtful problems which I cannot answer,
Nor reconcile; I'd have you make them plain.
Doc. This is my duty; pray speak your mind.
Wid. And as I speak, I must remember heaven
That gave those blessings which I must relate:
Sir, you now behold a wondrous woman;
You only wonder at the epithet;
I can approve it good: guess at mine age.
Doc. At the half-way 'twixt thirty and forty.
Wid. 'Twas not much amiss; yet nearest to the last.
How think you then, is not this a Wonder,
That a Woman lives full seven-and-thirty years,
Maid to a wife, and wife unto a widow,
Now widow'd, and mine own; yet all this while,
From the extremest verge of my remembrance,
Even from my weaning hour unto this minute,
Did never taste what was calamity.
I know not yet what grief is, yet have sought
A hundred ways for his acquaintance: with me
Prosperity hath kept so close a watch,
That even those things that I have meant a cross,
Have that way turn'd a blessing. Is it not strange?
Doc. Unparallel'd; this gift is singular,
And to you alone belonging: you are the moon,

For there 's but one, all women else are stars,
For there are none of like condition.
Full oft and many have I heard complain
Of discontents, thwarts, and adversities;
But a second to yourself I never knew,
To groan under the superflux of blessings,
To have ever been alien unto sorrow.
No trip of fate ? sure it is wonderful.
Wid. Aye, Sir, 'tis wonderful, but is it well ?
For it is now my chief affliction.
I have heard you say that the Child of Heaven
Shall suffer many tribulations;
Nay, kings and princes share them with their subjects:
Then I that know not any chastisement,
How may I know my part of childhood ?
Doc. 'Tis a good doubt; but make it not extreme.
'Tis some affliction that you are afflicted
For want of affliction: cherish that:
Yet wrest it not to misconstruction;
For all your blessings are free gifts from heaven,
Health, wealth, and peace; nor can they turn into
Curses, but by abuse. Pray, let me question you:
You lost a husband, was it no grief to you ?
Wid. It was, but very small: no sooner I
Had given it entertainment as a sorrow,
But straight it turn'd unto my treble joy:
A comfortable revelation prompts me then,
That husband (whom in life I held so dear)
Had chang'd a frailty to unchanging joys:
Methought I saw him stellified in heaven,
And singing hallelujahs 'mongst a quire
Of white sainted souls: then again it spake,
And said, it was a sin for me to grieve
At his best good, that I esteemed best:
And thus this slender shadow of a grief
Vanish'd again.
Doc. All this was happy, nor
Can you wrest it from a heavenly blessing. Do not

Appoint the rod: leave still the stroke unto
The magistrate: the time is not past, but
You may feel enough.—
Wid. One taste more I had, although but little,
Yet I would aggravate to make the most on 't:
'Twas thus: the other day it was my hap,
In crossing of the Thames,
To drop that wedlock ring from off my finger,
That once conjoined me and my dear husband:
It sunk; I prized it dear; the dearer, 'cause it kept
Still in mine eye the memory of my loss:
Yet I grieved the loss; and did joy withal,
That I had found a grief. And this is all
The sorrow I can boast of.
Doc. This is but small.
Wid. Nay, sure, I am of this opinion,
That had I suffer'd a draught to be made for it,
The bottom would have sent it up again;
I am so wondrously fortunate.

Foster, a wealthy Merchant, has a profligate Brother, Stephen, whom Robert, Son to Foster, relieves out of Prison with some of his Father's money intrusted to him. For this, his Father turns him out of doors and disinherits him. Meantime, by a reverse of fortune, Stephen becomes rich; and Foster by losses in trade is thrown into the same Prison (Ludgate) from which his brother had been relieved. Stephen adopts his Nephew, on the condition that he shall not assist or go near his Father: but filial piety prevails, above the consideration either of his Uncle's displeasure, or of his Father's late unkindness; and he visits his father in Prison.

FOSTER. ROBERT.

Fos. O torment to my soul, what mak'st thou here?
Cannot the picture of my misery
Be drawn, and hung out to the eyes of men,
But thou must come to scorn and laugh at it?
Rob. Dear Sir, I come to thrust my back under your load,
To make the burthen lighter.
Fos. Hence from my sight, dissembling villain, go:
Thine uncle sends defiance to my wo,

And thou must bring it: hence, thou Basilisk,
That killst me with thine eyes. Nay, never kneel;
These scornful mocks more than my woes I feel.
Rob. Alas, I mock ye not, but come in love
And natural duty, Sir, to beg your blessing;
And for mine uncle ——
Fos. Him and thee I curse.
I'll starve ere I eat bread from his purse,
Or from thy hand: out, villain; tell that cur,
Thy barking uncle, that I lie not here
Upon my bed of riot, as he did,
Cover'd with all the villainies which man
Had ever woven; tell him I lie not so;
It was the hand of heaven struck me thus low,
And I do thank it. Get thee gone, I say,
Or I shall curse thee, strike thee; prithee away:
Or if thou'lt laugh thy fill at my poor state,
Then stay, and listen to the prison grate,
And hear thy father, an old wretched man,
That yesterday had thousands, beg and cry
To get a penny: Oh, my misery.
Rob. Dear Sir, for pity hear me.
Fos. Upon my curse I charge, no nearer come;
I'll be no father to so vile a son.
Rob. O my abortive fate,
Why for my good am I thus paid with hate?
From this sad place of Ludgate here I freed
An uncle, and I lost a father for it;
Now is my father here, whom if I succor,
I then must lose my uncle's love and favor.
My father once being rich, and uncle poor,
I him relieving was thrust forth of doors,
Baffled, reviled, and disinherited.
Now mine own father here must beg for bread,
Mine uncle being rich; and yet, if I
Feed him, myself must beg. Oh misery;
How bitter is thy taste; yet I will drink
Thy strongest poison; fret what mischief can,

I'll feed my father; though like the Pelican,
I peck mine own breast for him.

His Father appears above at the Grate, a Box hanging down.

Fos. Bread, bread, one penny to buy a loaf of bread, for the tender mercy.

Rob. O me my shame! I know that voice full well;
I'll help thy wants although thou curse me still.

He stands where he is unseen by his Father.

Fos. Bread, bread, some christian man send back
Your charity to a number of poor prisoners.
One penny for the tender mercy—
[ROBERT *puts in Money.*
The hand of heaven reward you, gentle Sir,
Never may you want, never feel misery;
Let blessings in unnumber'd measure grow,
And fall upon your head, where'er you go.

Rob. O happy comfort: curses to the ground
First struck me: now with blessings am I crown'd.*

Fos. Bread, bread, for the tender mercy, one penny for a loaf of bread.

Rob. I'll buy more blessings: take thou all my store;
I'll keep no coin and see my Father poor.

Fos. Good angels guard you, Sir, my prayers shall be
That heaven may bless you for this charity.

Rob. If he knew me, sure he would not say so:
Yet I have comfort, if by any means
I get a blessing from my father's hands.
How cheap are good prayers! a poor penny buys
That, by which man up in a minute flies
And mounts to heaven.

Enter STEPHEN.

Oh me, mine uncle sees me.

Step. Now, Sir, what makes you here
So near the prison?

* A blessing stolen at least as fairly as Jacob's was.

Rob. I was going, Sir,
To buy meat for a poor bird I have,
That sits so sadly in the cage of late,
I think he'll die for sorrow.
Step. So, Sir:
Your pity will not quit your pains, I fear me.
I shall find that bird (I think) to be that churlish wretch
Your father, that now has taken
Shelter here in Ludgate. Go to, Sir; urge me not,
You'd best; I have giv'n you warning: fawn not on him,
Nor come not near him if you'll have my love.
Rob. 'Las, Sir; that lamb
Were most unnatural that should hate the dam.
Step. Lamb me no lambs, Sir.
Rob. Good uncle, 'las, you know, when you lay here,
I succor'd you: so let me now help him.
Step. Yes, as he did me;
To laugh and triumph at my misery.
You freed me with his gold, but 'gainst his will:
For him I might have rotted, and lain still.
So shall he now.
Rob. Alack the day!
Step. If him thou pity, 'tis thine own decay.
Fos. Bread, bread, some charitable man remember the poor
Prisoners, bread for the tender mercy, one penny.
Rob. O listen, uncle, that's my poor father's voice.
Step. There let him howl. Get you gone, and come not near him.
Rob. Oh my soul,
What tortures dost thou feel! earth ne'er shall find
A son so true, yet forc'd to be unkind.

Robert disobeys his Uncle's Injunctions, and again visits his Father

FOSTER. WIFE. ROBERT.

Fos. Ha! what art thou? Call for the keeper there,
And thrust him out of doors, or lock me up.
Wife. O 'tis your son.
Fos. I know him not.

I am no king, unless of scorn and wo,
Why kneel'st thou then, why dost thou mock me so?
Rob. O my dear father, hither am I come,
Not like a threatening storm to increase your wrack,
For I would take all sorrows from your back,
To lay them all on my own.
Fos. Rise, mischief, rise; away, and get thee gone.
Rob. O if I be thus hateful to your eye,
I will depart, and wish I soon may die;
Yet let your blessing, Sir, but fall on me.
Fos. My heart still hates thee.
Wife. Sweet husband.
Fos. Get you both gone;
That misery takes some rest that dwells alone.
Away, thou villain.
Rob. Heaven can tell;
Ake but your finger, I to make it well
Would cut my hand off.
Fos. Hang thee, hang thee.
Wife. Husband.
Fos. Destruction meet thee. Turn the key there, ho.
Rob. Good Sir, I'm gone, I will not stay to grieve you.
Oh, knew you, for your woes what pains I feel,
You would not scorn me so. See, Sir, to cool,
Your heat of burning sorrow, I have got
Two hundred pounds, and glad it is my lot
To lay it down with reverence at your feet;
No comfort in the world to me is sweet,
Whilst thus you live in moan.
Fos. Stay.
Rob. Good truth, Sir, I'll have none of it back,
Could but one penny of it save my life.
Wife. Yet stay, and hear him: Oh unnatural strife
In a hard father's bosom.
Fos. I see mine error now: Oh, can there grow
A rose upon a bramble? did there e'er flow
Poison and health together in one tide?
I'm born a man: reason may step aside,

And lead a father's love out of the way:
Forgive me, my good boy, I went astray;
Look, on my knees I beg it: no: for joy,
Thou bring'st this golden rubbish; which I spurn:
But glad in this, the heavens mine eye-balls turn,
And fix them right to look upon that face,
Where love remains with pity, duty, grace.
Oh my dear wronged boy.
Rob. Gladness o'erwhelms
My heart with joy: I cannot speak.
Wife. Crosses of this foolish world
Did never grieve my heart with torments more
Than it is now grown light
With joy and comfort of this happy sight.

[The old play-writers are distinguished by an honest boldness of exhibition, they show everything without being ashamed. If a reverse in fortune be the thing to be personified, they fairly bring us to the prison-gate and the alms-basket. A poor man on our stage is always a gentleman, he may be known by a peculiar neatness of apparel, and by wearing black. Our delicacy, in fact, forbids the dramatizing of Distress at all. It is never shown in its essential properties;* it appears but as the adjunct to some virtue, as some-

* Guzman de Alfarache in that good old book, "The Spanish Rogue," has summed up a few of the properties of poverty—" that poverty, which is not the daughter of the spirit, is but the mother of shame and reproach; it is a disreputation that drowns all the other good parts that are in man; it is a disposition to all kind of evil; it is man's most foe; it is a leprosy full of anguish; it is a way that leads unto hell; it is a sea wherein our patience is overwhelmed, our honor is consumed, our lives are ended, and our souls are utterly lost and cast away for ever. The poor man is a kind of money that is not current; the subject of every idle huswife's chat; the offscum of the people; the dust of the street, first trampled under foot and then thrown on the dunghill; in conclusion, the poor man is the rich man's ass. He dineth with the last, fareth of the worst, and payeth dearest: his sixpence will not go so far as a rich man's threepence; his opinion is ignorance; his discretion, foolishness; his suffrage, scorn; his stock upon the common, abused by many and abhorred of all. If he come in company, he is not heard; if any chance to meet him, they seek to shun him; if he advise, though never so wisely, they grudge and murmur at him; if he work miracles, they say he is a witch: if virtuous, that he goeth about to deceive; his venial sin is a blasphemy his thought is made treason; his cause, be it

thing which is to be relieved, from the approbation of which relief the spectators are to derive a certain soothing of self-referred satisfaction. We turn away from the real essences of things to hunt after their relative shadows, moral duties: whereas if the truth of things were fairly represented, the relative duties might be safely trusted to themselves, and moral philosophy lose the name of a science.]

WOMEN BEWARE WOMEN; A TRAGEDY. BY THOMAS MIDDLETON.

Livia, the Duke's creature, cajoles a poor Widow with the appearance of Hospitality and neighborly Attentions, that she may get her Daughter in-Law (who is left in the Mother's care in the Son's absence) into her trains, to serve the Duke's pleasure.

LIVIA. WIDOW. *A Gentleman, Livia's Guest.*

Liv. Widow, come, come, I have a great quarrel to you,
Faith I must chide you that you must be sent for;
You make yourself so strange, never come at us,
And yet so near a neighbor, and so unkind;
Troth, you 're to blame; you cannot be more welcome
To any house in Florence, that I 'll tell you.
Wid. My thanks must needs acknowledge so much, madam.
Liv. How can you be so strange then? I sit here
Sometimes whole days together without company,
When business draws this gentleman from home,
And should be happy in society
Which I so well affect as that of yours.
I know you 're alone too; why should not we
Like two kind neighbors then supply the wants

never so just, it is not regarded; and, to have his wrongs righted, he must appeal to that other life. All men crush him; no man favoreth him; there is no man that will relieve his wants; no man that will comfort him in his miseries; nor no man that will bear him company, when he is all alone, and oppressed with grief. None help him; all hinder him; none give him, all take from him; he is debtor to none, and yet must make payment to all. O the unfortunate and poor condition of him that is poor, to whom even the very hours are sold, which the clock striketh, and pays custom for the sunshine in August."

Of one another, having tongue-discourse,
Experience in the world, and such kind helps,
To laugh down time and meet age merrily ?
Wid. Age, madam! you speak mirth: 'tis at my door,
But a long journey from your Ladyship yet.
Liv. My faith, I 'm nine and thirty, every stroke, wench ;
And 'tis a general observation
'Mongst knights ; wives, or widows, we account ourselves
Then old, when young men's eyes leave looking at us.
Come, now I have thy company, I 'll not part with it
Till after supper.
Wid. Yes, I must crave pardon, madam.
Liv. I swear you shall stay supper ; we have no strangers, woman,
None but my sojourners and I, this gentleman
And the young heir his ward ; you know your company.
Wid. Some other time I will make bold with you, madam.
Liv. Faith she shall not go.
Do you think I'll be forsworn ?
Wid. 'Tis a great while
Till supper time ; I'll take my leave then now, madam,
And come again in the evening, since your ladyship
Will have it so.
Liv. In the evening ! by my troth, wench,
I'll keep you while I have you ; you've great business sure,
To sit alone at home ; I wonder strangely
What pleasure you take in 't. Were 't to me now,
I should be ever at one neighbor's house
Or other all day long ; having no charge,
Or none to chide you, if you go, or stay,
Who may live merrier, aye, or more at heart's ease ?
Come, we'll to chess or draughts, there are a hundred tricks
To drive out time till supper, never fear 't, wench.
[*A Chess-board is set.*
Wid. I'll but make one step home, and return straight, madam.
Liv. Come, I'll not trust you, you make more excuses
To your kind friends than ever I knew any.
What business can you have, if you be sure

You've lock'd the doors? and, that being all you have,
I know you're careful on 't: one afternoon
So much to spend here! say I should entreat you now
To lie a night or two, or a week, with me,
Or leave your own house for a month together;
It were a kindness that long neighborhood
And friendship might well hope to prevail in:
Would you deny such a request? i'faith
Speak truly and freely.

Wid. I were then uncivil, madam.

Liv. Go to then, set your men: we'll have whole nights
Of mirth together, ere we be much older, wench.

Wid. As good now tell her then, for she will know it;
I've always found her a most friendly lady. [*Aside.*

Liv. Why, widow, where's your mind?

Wid. Troth, even at home, madam.
To tell you truth, I left a gentlewoman
Even sitting all alone, which is uncomfortable,
Especially to young bloods.

Liv. Another excuse.

Wid. No, as I hope for health, madam, that's a truth;
Please you to send and see.

Liv. What gentlewoman? pish.

Wid. Wife to my son indeed.

Liv. Now I beshrew you.
Could you be so unkind to her and me,
To come and not bring her? faith, 'tis not friendly.

Wid. I fear'd to be too bold.

Liv. Too bold! Oh what's become
Of the true hearty love was wont to be
'Mongst neighbors in old time?

Wid. And she's a stranger, madam.

Liv. The more should be her welcome: when is courtesy
In better practice, than when 'tis employ'd
In entertaining strangers. I could chide ye in faith.
Leave her behind, poor gentlewoman, alone too!
Make some amends, and send for her betimes, go.

Wid. Please you command one of your servants, madam.

Liv. Within there.—
Attend the gentlewoman. ———*

Brancha resists the Duke's attempt.

Bran. Oh treachery to honor!
Duke. Prithee tremble not.
I feel thy breast shake like a turtle panting
Under a loving hand that makes much on't.
Why art so fearful?
Bran. Oh my extremity!
My Lord, what seek you?
Duke. Love.
Bran. 'Tis gone already:
I have a husband.
Duke. That's a single comfort;
Take a friend to him.
Bran. That's a double mischief;
Or else there's no religion.
Duke. Do not tremble
At fears of thy own making.
Bran. Nor, great lord,
Make me not bold with death and deeds of ruin,
Because they fear not you; me they must fright;
Then am I best in health: should thunder speak
And none regard it, it had lost the name,
And were as good be still. I'm not like those
That take their soundest sleeps in greatest tempests;
Then wake I most, the weather fearfullest,
And call for strength to virtue. ———

Winding Sheet.

—— to have a being, and to live 'mongst men,
Is a fearful living and a poor one; let a man truly think on 't.
To have the toil and griefs of fourscore years

* This is one of those scenes which has the air of being an immediate transcript from life. Livia the "good neighbor" is as real a creature as one of Chaucer's characters She is such another jolly Housewife as the Wife of Bath.

Put up in a white sheet, tied with two knots:
Methinks it should strike earthquakes in adulterers,
When even the very sheets they commit sin in
May prove for aught they know all their last garments.

Great Men's looks.

Did not the duke look up? methought he saw us.—
——That's every one's conceit that sees a duke,
If he look steadfastly, he looks straight at them:
When he perhaps, good careful gentleman,
Never minds any, but the look he casts
Is at his own intentions, and his object
Only the public good. ——

Weeping in Love.

Why should those tears be fetch'd forth! cannot love
Be even as well expressed in a good look,
But it must see her face still in a fountain?
It shows like a country maid dressing her head
By a dish of water: come, 'tis an old custom
To weep for love.

Lover's Chidings.

—prithee forgive me,
I did but chide in jest: the best loves use it
Sometimes; it sets an edge upon affection.
When we invite our best friends to a feast,
'Tis not all sweetmeats that we set before 'em;
There's something sharp and salt, both to whet appetite,
And make 'em taste their wine well: so methinks,
After a friendly sharp and savory chiding,
A kiss tastes wondrous well, and full o' the grape.

Wedlock.

O thou the ripe time of man's misery, wedlock;
When all his thoughts like over-laden trees
Crack with the fruits they bear, in cares, in jealousies.
O that's a fruit that ripens hastily,

After 'tis knit to marriage; it begins,
As soon as the sun shines upon the bride,
A little to show color. ——

Marrying the Adulteress, the Husband dead.

Is not sin sure enough to wretched man,
But he must bind himself in chains to 't? worse!
Must marriage, that immaculate robe of honor,
That renders Virtue glorious, fair, and fruitful,
To her great master, be now made the garment
Of leprosy and foulness? is this penitence,
To sanctify hot lust? what is it otherways
Than worship done to devils? is this the best
Amends that sin can make after her riots!
As if a drunkard, to appease heaven's wrath,
Should offer up his surfeit for a sacrifice:
If that be comely, then lust's offerings are
On wedlock's sacred altar.

MORE DISSEMBLERS BESIDES WOMEN: A COMEDY. BY THOMAS MIDDLETON.

Death.

———when the heart's above, the body walks here
But like an idle servingman below,
Gaping and waiting for his master's coming.
He that lives fourscore years, is but like one
That stays here for a friend: when death comes, then
Away he goes, and is ne'er seen again.

Loving a Woman.

——of all the frenzies
That follow flesh and blood,
The most ridiculous is to fawn on women;
There's no excuse for that: 'tis such a madness,
There is no cure set down for 't; no physician
Ever spent hour about it, for they guess'd

'Twas all in vain, when they first lov'd, themselves,
And never since durst practise: cry *heu mihi;*
That's all the help they have for 't. I'd rather meet
A witch far north than a fine fool in love;
The sight would less afflict me. But for modesty,
I should fall foul in words upon fond man,
That can forget his excellence and honor,
His serious meditations, being the end
Of his creation, to learn well to die;
And live a prisoner to a woman's eye.

Widow's Vow.

Lord Cardinal. Increase of health and a redoubled courage
To chastity's great soldier: what, so sad, Madam?
The memory of her seven years deceas'd Lord
Springs yet into her eyes, as fresh and full
As at the seventh hour after his departure.
What a perpetual fountain is her virtue!
Too much to afflict yourself with ancient sorrow
Is not so strictly for your strength required:
Your vow is charge enough, believe me 'tis, Madam;
You need no weightier task.
Duch. Religious Sir,
You heard the last words of my dying Lord.
Lord Card. Which I shall ne'er forget.
Duch. May I entreat
Your goodness but to speak 'em over to me,
As near as memory can befriend your utterance:
That I may think awhile I stand in presence
Of my departing Husband.
Lord Card. What's your meaning
In this, most virtuous Madam?
Duch. 'Tis a courtesy
I stand in need of, Sir, at this time especially;
Urge it no farther yet: as it proves to me,
You shall hear from me; only I desire it
Effectually from you, Sir, that's my request.
Lord Card. I wonder; yet I'll spare to question farther;

You shall have your desire.

Duch. I thank you, Sir:
A blessing come along with it.

Lord Card. [*repeats*] "You see, my Lords, what all earth's glory is,
"Rightly defined in me, uncertain breath:
"A dream of threescore years to the long sleeper,
"To most not half the time. Beware ambition;
"Heaven is not reach'd with pride, but with submission.
"And you Lord Cardinal labor to perfect
"Good purposes begun, be what you seem,
"Stedfast and uncorrupt, your actions noble,
"Your goodness simple, without gain or art;
"And not in vesture holier than in heart.
"But 'tis a pain more than the pangs of death
"To think that we must part, fellows of life.—
"Thou richness of my joys, kind and dear Princess,
"Death had no sting, but for our separation;
"'Twould come more calm than an evening's peace,
"That brings on rest to labors: Thou art so precious,
"I should depart in everlasting envy
"Unto the man, that ever should enjoy thee.
"Oh a new torment strikes his face into me,
"When I but think on 't, I am rack'd and torn
"(Pity me) in thy virtues."

Duch. "My lov'd Lord,
"Let your confirm'd opinion of my life,
"My love, my faithful love, seal an assurance
"Of quiet to your spirit, that no forgetfulness
"Can cast a sleep so deadly on my senses,
"To draw my affections to a second liking."

Lord Card. "It has ever been the promise, and the spring
"Of my great love to thee. For, once to marry
"Is honorable in woman, and her ignorance
"Stands for a virtue, coming new and fresh;
"But second marriage shows desires in flesh;
"Thence lust, and heat, and common custom grows:
"But she's part virgin, who but one man knows.

"I here expect a work of thy great faith:
"At my last parting I can crave no more;
"And with thy vow, I rest myself for ever;
"My soul and it shall fly to heaven together:
"Seal to my spirit that quiet satisfaction,
"And I go hence in peace."
Duch. "Then here I vow, never——"
Lord Card. Why, Madam——
Duch. I can go no further.
Lord Card. What, have you forgot your vow?
Duch. I have, too certainly.
Lord Card. Your vow? that cannot be; it follows now,
Just where I left.
Duch. My frailty gets before it;
Nothing prevails but ill.
Lord Card. What ail you, Madam?
Duch. Sir, *I'm in love.*

NO WIT / HELP LIKE A WOMAN'S.

A COMEDY. BY THOMAS MIDDLETON.

Virtuous Poverty.

'Life, had he not his answer? what strange impudence
Governs in man, when lust is lord of him!
Thinks he me mad? 'cause I have no monies on earth,
That I'll go forfeit my estate in heaven,
And live eternal beggar? he shall pardon me;
That's my soul's jointure; I'll starve ere I sell that.

Comfort.

——husband,
Wake, wake, and let not patience keep thee poor,
Rouse up thy spirit from this falling slumber:
Make thy distress seem but a weeping dream,
And this the opening morning of thy comforts.

Wipe the salt dew from off thy careful eyes,
And drink a draught of gladness next thy heart
To expel the infection of all poisonous sorrows.

Good and Ill Fortune.

O my blessing!
I feel a hand of mercy lift me up
Out of a world of waters, and now sets me
Upon a mountain, where the sun plays most,
To cheer my heart even as it dries my limbs.
What deeps I see beneath me! in whose falls
Many a nimble mortal toils,
And scarce can feed himself: the streams of fortune,
'Gainst which he tugs in vain, still beat him down,
And will not suffer him (past hand to mouth)
To lift his arm to his posterities' blessing.
I see a careful sweat run in a ring
About his temples, but all will not do:
For till some happy means relieve his state,
There he must stick and bide the wrath of fate.

Parting in Amity.

Let our Parting
Be full as charitable as our meeting was;
That the pale envious world, glad of the food
Of others' miseries, civil dissensions,
And nuptial strifes, may not feed fat with ours.

Meeting with a Wife supposed Dead.

O my reviving joy! thy quickening presence
Makes the sad night of threescore and ten years
Sit like a youthful spring upon my blood.
I cannot make thy welcome rich enough
With all the wealth of words.

Mother's Forgiveness.

Moth. Why do your words start back? are they afraid
Of her that ever lov'd them?
Philip. I have a suit to you, Madam.

Moth. You have told me that already; pray, what is 't?
If 't be so great, my present state refuse it,
I shall be abler, then command and use it.
Whatever 't be, let me have warning to provide for 't.
Philip. Provide forgiveness then, for that's the want
My conscience feels. O, my wild youth has led me
Into unnatural wrongs against your freedom once.
I spent the ransom which my father sent,
To set my pleasures free; while you lay captive.
Moth. And is this all now?
You use me like a stranger: pray, stand up.
Philip. Rather fall flat: I shall deserve yet worse.
Moth. Whate'er your faults are, esteem me still a friend;
Or else you wrong me more in asking pardon
Than when you did the wrong you ask'd it for:
And since you have prepar'd me to forgive you.
Pray let me know for what; the first fault's nothing.
Philip. Here comes the wrong then that drives home the rest.
I saw a face at Antwerp, that drew me
From conscience and obedience; in that fray
I lost my heart, I must needs lose my way.
There went the ransome, to redeem my mind;
Stead of the money, I brought over her;
And to cast mists before my father's eyes,
Told him it was my sister (lost so long)
And that yourself was dead.—You see the wrong.
Moth. This is but youthful still—
I forgive thee
As freely as thou didst it. For alas,
This may be call'd good dealing, to some parts
That love and youth plays daily among sons.

THE WITCH; A TRAGI-COMEDY BY THOMAS MIDDLETON

HECATE, *and the other Witches, at their Charms.*

Hec. Titty and Tiffin, Suckin
And Pidgen, Liard and Robin!

White spirits, black spirits, grey spirits, red spirits,
Devil-toad, devil-ram, devil-cat, and devil-dam,
Why Hoppo and Stadlin, Hellwain and Puckle!
Stad. Here, sweating at the vessel.
Hec. Boil it well.
Hop. It gallops now.
Hec. Are the flames blue enough,
Or shall I use a little seeten* more?
Stad. The nips of Fairies upon maids' white hips
Are not more perfect azure.
Hec. Tend it carefully.
Send Stadlin to me with a brazen dish,
That I may fall to work upon these serpents,
And squeeze 'em ready for the second hour.
Why, when?
Stad. Here's Stadlin and the dish.
Hec. Here take this unbaptized brat:
Boil it well—preserve the fat:
You know 'tis precious to transfer
Our 'nointed flesh into the air,
In moonlight nights, o'er steeple tops,
Mountains, and pine trees, that like pricks, or stops,
Seem to our height: high towers, and roofs of princes,
Like wrinkles in the earth: whole provinces
Appear to our sight then even like
A russet mole upon some lady's cheek.
When hundred leagues in air, we feast and sing,
Dance, kiss, and coll, use everything:
What young man can we wish to pleasure us,
But we enjoy him in an Incubus?
Thou know'st it, Stadlin?
Stad. Usually that's done.
Hec. Away, in.
Go feed the vessel for the second hour.
Stad. Where be the magical herbs?
Hec. They 're down his throat,†
His mouth cramm'd full; his ears and nostrils stuft.

* Seething. † The dead Child's.

I thrust in Eleaselinum, lately
Aconitum, frondes populeas, and soot.
You may see that, he looks so black i' th' mouth.
Then Sium, Acharum, Vulgaro too,
Dentaphillon, the blood of a flitter-mouse,
Solanum somnificum et oleum.
Stad. Then there's all, Hecate.
Hec. Is the heart of wax
Stuck full of magic needles ?
Stad. 'Tis done, Hecate.
Hec. And is the farmer's picture, and his wife's,
Laid down to the fire yet ?
Stad. They are a roasting both too.
Hec. Good ;
Then their marrows are a melting subtilly,
And three months' sickness sucks up life in 'em.
They denied me often flour, barm, and milk,
Goose-grease and tar, when I ne'er hurt their churnings,
Their brew-locks nor their batches, nor forespoke
Any of their breedings. Now I'll be meet with 'em.
Seven of their young pigs I have bewitch'd already
Of the last litter, nine ducklings, thirteen goslings and a hog
Fell lame last Sunday, after even-song too.
And mark how their sheep prosper; or what soup
Each milch-kine gives to th' pail : I'll send these snakes
Shall milk 'em all before hand : the dew'd skirted dairy wench
Shall stroke dry dugs for this, and go home cursing :
I'll mar their sillabubs, and swarthy feastings
Under cows' bellies, with the parish youths.

SEBASTIAN *consults the* WITCH *for a Charm to be revenged on his successful Rival.*

Hec. Urchins, elves, hags, satires, pans, fawns, silence.
Kit with the candlestick; tritons, centaurs, dwarfs, imps.
The spoon, the mare, the man i' th' oak, the hellwain, the fire drake, the puckle. A. ab. hur. hus.
Seb. Heaven knows with what unwillingness and hate
I enter this damn'd place: but such extremes

Of wrongs in love fight 'gainst religion's knowledge,
That were I led by this disease to deaths
As numberless as creatures that must die,
I could not shun the way.—I know what 'tis
To pity mad men now: they're wretched things
That ever were created, if they be
Of woman's making and her faithless vows.
I fear they're now a kissing: what's a clock?
'Tis now but supper time: but night will come,
And all new-married couples make short suppers.
Whate'er thou art, I have no spare time to fear thee;
My horrors are so strong and great already
That thou seem'st nothing: Up and laze not;
Hadst thou my business, thou couldst ne'er sit so;
'Twould firk thee into air a thousand mile,
Beyond thy ointments: I would I were read
So much in thy black pow'r, as mine own griefs.
I'm in great need of help: wilt give me any?
Hec. Thy boldness takes me bravely; we are all sworn
To sweat for such a spirit; see; I regard thee,
I rise, and bid thee welcome. What's thy wish now?
Seb. Oh my heart swells with 't. I must take breath first.
Hec. Is 't to confound some enemy on the seas?
It may be done to-night. Stadlin's within;
She raises all your sudden ruinous storms
That shipwreck barks; and tears up growing oaks;
Flies over houses, and takes Anno Domini
Out of a rich man's chimney (a sweet place for 't,
He would be hang'd ere he would set his own years there;
They must be chamber'd in a five pound picture,
A green silk curtain drawn before the eyes on 't,
His rotten diseas'd years)! Or dost thou envy
The fat prosperity of any neighbor?
I'll call forth Hoppo, and her incantation
Can straight destroy the young of all his cattle:
Blast vine-yards, orchards, meadows; or in one night
Transport his dung, hay, corn, by reeks, whole stacks,
Into thine own ground.

Seb. This would come most richly now
To many a country grazier: But my envy
Lies not so low as cattle, corn, or wines:
'Twill trouble your best pow'rs to give me ease.
Hec. Is it to starve up generation?
To strike a barrenness in man or woman?
Seb. Hah!
Hec. Hah! Did you feel me there? I knew your grief.
Seb. Can there be such things done?
Hec. Are these the skins
Of serpents? these of snakes?
Seb. I see they are.
Hec. So sure into what house these are convey'd
Knit with these charms, and retentive knots,
Neither the man begets, nor woman breeds,
No, nor performs the least desire of wedlock,
Being then a mutual duty; I could give thee
Chiroconita, Adincantida,
Archimadon, Marmaritin, Calicia,
Which I could sort to villainous barren ends;
But this leads the same way: More I could instance:
As the same needles thrust into their pillows
That sow and sock up dead men in their sheets:
A privy grissel of a man that hangs
After sun set: Good, excellent: yet all's there, Sir.
Seb. You could not do a man that special kindness
To part them utterly, now? Could you do that?
Hec. No: time must do 't: we cannot disjoin wedlock;
'Tis of heaven's fastening: well may we raise jars,
Jealousies, strifes, and heart-burning disagreements,
Like a thick scurf o'er life, as did our master
Upon that patient* miracle; but the work itself
Our power cannot disjoin.
Seb. I depart happy
In what I have then, being constrain'd to this:
And grant, you greater powers that dispose men

* Job.

That I may never need this hag again. [*Exit.*
Hec. I know he loves me not, nor there's no hope on 't;
'Tis for the love of mischief I do this:
And that we are sworn to the first oath we take.

HECATE, STADLIN, HOPPO, *with the other Witches, preparing for their midnight journey through the Air.* FIRESTONE, HECATE'S *Son.*

Hec. The moon's a gallant: see how brisk she rides.
Stad. Here's a rich evening, Hecate.
Hec. Ay, is 't not, wenches,
To take a journey of five thousand mile?
Hop. Ours will be more to-night.
Hec. Oh 'twill be precious.
Heard you the owl yet!
Stad. Briefly in the copse,
As we came through now.
Hec. 'Tis high time for us then.
Stad. There was a bat hung at my lips three times
As we came through the woods, and drank her fill.
Old Puckle saw her.
Hec. You are fortunate still:
The very screech owl lights upon your shoulder,
And wooes you like a pigeon. Are you furnish'd?
Have you your ointments?
Stad. All.
Hec. Prepare to flight then:
I 'll overtake you swiftly.
Stad. Hie thee, Hecate:
We shall be up betimes.
Hec. I'll reach you quickly. [*The other Witches mount.*
Fire. They are all going a birding to-night. They talk of fowls in the air, that fly by day; I am sure, they 'll be a company of foul sluts there to-night. If we have not mortality offer'd,* I 'll be hanged; for they are able to putrify it, to infect a whole region. She spies me now.

* Probably the true reading is *after 't.*

Hec. What, Firestone, our sweet son?

Fire. A little sweeter than some of you; or a dunghill were too good for me.

Hec. How much hast here?

Fire. Nineteen, and all brave plump ones; besides six lizards, and three serpentine eggs.

Hec. Dear and sweet boy: what herbs hast thou?

Fire. I have some Marmartin and Mandragon.

Hec. Marmaritin and Mandragora thou wouldst say.

Fire. Here 's Pannax too: I thank thee, my pan akes I am sure
With kneeling down to cut 'em.

Hec. And Selago,
Hedge hysop too: how near he goes my cuttings!
Were they all cropt by moon-light?

Fire. Every blade of 'em, or I am a moon-calf, mother.

Hec. Hie thee home with 'em.
Look well to the house to-night; I am for aloft.

Fire. Aloft, quoth you? I would you would break your neck once, that I might have all quickly. Hark, hark, mother; they are above the Steeple already, flying over your head with a noise of musicians.

Hec. They are indeed. Help me, help me; I'm too late else.

Song in the Air.

Come away, come away;
Hecate, Hecate, come away.
Hec. I come, I come, I come, I come,
With all the speed I may,
With all the speed I may.
Where's Stadlin?
[*Above.*] Here.
Hec. Where's Puckle?
[*Above.*]——Here:
And Hoppo too, and Hellwain too:
We lack but you; we lack but you:
Come away, make up the count.
Hec. I will but 'noint, and then I mount.

[*A spirit like a Cat descends.*

[*Above.*]——There's one come down to fetch his dues;
A kiss, a coll, a slip of blood:
And why thou stay'st so long, I muse, I muse,
Since the air's so sweet and good.
Hec. Oh art thou come?
What news, what news?
Spirit. All goes still to our delight:
Either come, or else
Refuse, refuse.
Hec. Now I am furnish'd for the flight.
Fire. Hark, hark, the Cat sings a brave treble in her own language.
Hec. [*Going up.*] Now I go, now I fly,
Malkin my sweet Spirit and I.
Oh what a dainty pleasure 'tis
To ride in the air
When the moon shines fair,
And sing, and dance, and toy, and kiss:
Over woods, high rocks, and mountains,
Over seas (our mistress' fountains),
Over steep towers and turrets,
We fly by night 'mongst troops of Spirits.
No ring of bells to our ears sounds,
No howls of wolves, no yelps of hounds;
No, not the noise of water's-breach,
Or cannon's throat, our height can reach.
[*Above.*]——No ring of bells, &c.
Fire. Well, mother, I thank your kindness; you must be
Gamboling in the air, and leave me to walk here like a fool and a mortal. * * * * * * *

A Duchess consults the Witch about inflicting a sudden Death.

DUCHESS. HECATE. FIRESTONE.

Hec. What death is 't you desire for Almachildes?
Duch. A sudden and a subtle.
Hec. Then I 've fitted you.
Here lie the gifts of both; sudden and subtle:
His picture made in wax, and gently molten

By a blue fire, kindled with dead men's eyes,
Will waste him by degrees.
Duch. In what time prithee ?
Hec. Perhaps in a moon's progress.
Duch. What, a month ?
Out upon pictures, if they be so tedious :
Give me things with some life.
Hec. Then seek no farther.
Duch. This must be done with speed, dispatch'd this night,
If it be possible.
Hec. I have it for you :
Here 's that will do 't : stay but perfection's time,
And that' s not five hours hence.
Duch. Canst thou do this ?
Hec. Can I ?
Duch. I mean, so closely ?
Hec. So closely do you mean too ?
Duch. So artfully, so cunningly ?
Hec. Worse and worse. Doubts and incredulities,
They make me mad. Let scrupulous creatures know :
Cum volui, ripis ipsis mirantibus, amnes
In fontes rediere suos ; concussaque sisto,
Stantia concutio cantu freta ; nubila pello,
Nubilaque induco : ventos abigoque, vocoque.
Vipereas rumpo verbis et carmine fauces ;
Et sylvas moveo, jubeoque tremiscere montes,
Et mugiere solum, manesque exire sepulchris.
Te quoque, Luna, traho.
Can you doubt me then, daughter ;
That can make mountains tremble, miles of woods walk :
Whole earth's foundations bellow, and the spirits
Of the entomb'd to burst out from their marbles ;
Nay, draw yon Moon to my involv'd designs ?
Fire. I know as well as can be when my mother 's mad, and our
Great cat angry ; for one spits French then, and the other spits Latin.
Duch. I did not doubt you, mother.

Hec. No! what, did you?
My power 's so firm, it is not to be question'd.
Duch. Forgive what 's past; and now I know th' offensiveness
That vexes art, I 'll shun the occasion ever.
Hec. Leave all to me and my five sisters, daughter.
It shall be convey'd in at howlet-time.
Take you no care. My spirits know their moments:
Raven or screech-owl never fly by the door
But they call in (I thank 'em) and they lose not by 't.
I give 'em barley soak'd in infant's blood:
They shall have semina cum sanguine,
Their gorge cramm'd full, if they come once to our house:
We are no niggard.——
Fire. They fare but too well when they come hither: they ate up as much the other night as would have made me a good conscionable pudding.
Hec. Give me some lizard's brain, quickly, Firestone.
Where 's grannam Stadlin, and all the rest of the sisters?
Fire. All at hand, forsooth.
[*The other Witches appear.*
Hec. Give me Marmaritin; some Bear-breech: when?
Fire. Here 's Bear-breech and lizard's brain, forsooth.
Hec. Into the vessel;
And fetch three ounces of the red-hair'd girl
I kill'd last midnight.
Fire. Whereabout, sweet mother?
Hec. Hip; hip, or flank. Where 's the Acopus?
Fire. You shall have Acopus, forsooth.
Hec. Stir, stir about; whilst I begin the charm.

A Charm Song about a Vessel.

Hec. Black spirits and white, red spirits and grey;
Mingle, mingle, mingle, you that mingle may.
Titty, Tiffin, keep it stiff in;
Fire-drake, Puckey, make it lucky;
Liard, Robin, you must bob in.
Round, around, around, about, about;
All Ill come running in, all Good keep out.

First Witch. Here 's the blood of a bat.
Hec. Put in that, oh, put in that.
Sec. Witch. Here 's libbard's bane.
Hec. Put in again.
First Witch. The juice of toad ; the oil of adder.
Sec. Witch. Those will make the younker madder.
Hec. Put in, there 's all, and rid the stench.
Fire. Nay, here 's three ounces of the red-hair'd wench.
All. Round, around, around, &c.
Hec. So, so, enough : into the vessel with it.
There ; 't hath the true perfection : I am so light*
At any mischief, there's no villainy
But is a tune methinks.
Fire. A tune ! 'tis to the tune of damnation then, I warrant you,
And that song hath a villainous burthen.
Hec. Come my sweet sisters, let the air strike our tune ;
Whilst we show reverence to yon peeping moon.
[*The Witches dance, et Exeunt.*

[Though some resemblance may be traced between the Charms in Macbeth, and the incantations in this Play, which is supposed to have preceded it, this coincidence will not detract much from the originality of Shakspeare. His witches are distinguished from the Witches of Middleton by essential differences. These are creatures to whom man or woman plotting some dire mischief might resort for occasional consultation. Those originate deeds of blood, and begin bad impulses to men. From the moment that their eyes first meet with Macbeth's, he is spell bound. That meeting sways his destiny. He can never break the fascination. These Witches can hurt the body : those have power over the soul.—Hecate in Middleton has a Son, a low buffoon : the hags of Shakspeare have neither child of their own, nor seem to be descended from any parent. They are foul Anomalies, of whom we know not whence they are sprung, nor whether they have beginning or ending. As they are without human passions, so they seem to be without human relations. They come with thunder and lightning, and vanish to airy music. This is all we know of them.—Except Hecate, they have no names ; which heightens their mysteriousness. Their names, and some of the properties, which Middleton has given to his hags, excite smiles. The Weird Sisters are serious things. Their presence cannot co-exist with mirth. But, in a lesser degree, the Witches of Middleton are fine creations. Their power too is, in some measure, over the mind. They raise jars, jealousies, strifes, *like a thick scurf o'er life.*]

* Light-hearted.

THE WITCH OF EDMONTON; A TRAGI-COMEDY. BY WILLIAM ROWLEY, THOMAS DECKER, JOHN FORD, &c.

MOTHER SAWYER (*before she turns Witch*) *alone.*

Saw. And why on me? why should the envious world
Throw all their scandalous malice upon me?
'Cause I am poor, deform'd, and ignorant,
And like a bow buckled and bent together
By some more strong in mischiefs than myself;
Must I for that be made a common sink
For all the filth and rubbish of men's tongues
To fall and run into? Some call me Witch,
And being ignorant, of myself, they go
About to teach me how to be one: urging
That my bad tongue (by their bad usage made so)
Forespeaks their cattle, doth bewitch their corn,
Themselves, their servants, and their babes at nurse:
This they enforce upon me; and in part
Make me to credit it.*

BANKS, *a Farmer, enters.*

Banks. Out, out upon thee, Witch.
Saw. Dost call me Witch?
Banks. I do, Witch, I do:
And worse I would, knew I a name more hateful.
What makest thou upon my ground?
Saw. Gather a few rotten sticks to warm me.
Banks. Down with them when I bid thee, quickly;
I'll make thy bones rattle in thy skin else.
Saw. You won't? churl, cut-throat, miser: there they be. Would they stuck cross thy throat, thy bowels, thy maw, thy midriff——
Banks. Say'st thou me so? Hag, out of my ground.
Saw. Dost strike me, slave, curmudgeon? Now thy bones aches, thy joints cramps,
And convulsions stretch and crack thy sinews.

* This Soliloquy anticipates all that Addison has said in the conclusion of the 117th Spectator.

Banks. Cursing, thou hag? take that, and that. [*Exit.*

Saw. Strike, do: and wither'd may that hand and arm
Whose blows have lam'd me, drop from the rotten trunk.
Abuse me! beat me! call me hag and witch!
What is the name, where, and by what art learn'd?
What spells, or charms, or invocations,
May the thing call'd Familiar be purchased?
——————————I am shunn'd
And hated like a sickness: made a scorn
To all degrees and sexes. I have heard old beldams
Talk of Familiars in the shape of mice,
Rats, ferrets, weasels, and I wot not what,
That have appear'd: and suck'd, some say, their blood.
But by what means they came acquainted with them,
I'm now ignorant. Would some power good or bad
Instruct me which way I might be reveng'd
Upon this churl, I'd go out of myself,
And give this fury leave to dwell within
This ruined cottage, ready to fall with age:
Abjure all goodness, be at hate with prayer,
And study curses, imprecations,
Blasphemous speeches, oaths, detested oaths,
Or anything that's ill; so I might work
Revenge upon this miser, this black cur,
That barks, and bites, and sucks the very blood
Of me, and of my credit. 'Tis all one
To be a witch as to be counted one.

She gets a familiar which serves her in the likeness of a Black Dog

MOTHER SAWYER. *Familiar.*

Saw. I am dried up
With cursing and with madness; and have yet
No blood to moisten these sweet lips of thine.
Stand on thine hind-legs up. Kiss me, my Tommy;
And rub away some wrinkles on my brow,
By making my old ribs to shrug for joy
Of thy fine tricks. What hast thou done? Let's tickle.
Hast thou struck the horse lame as I bid thee?

Famil. Yes, and nipt the sucking-child.
Saw. Ho, ho, my dainty,
My little pearl. No lady loves her hound,
Monkey, or parakeet, as I do thee.
Famil. The maid has been churning butter nine hours, but it shall not come.
Saw. Let 'em eat cheese and choak.
Famil. I had rare sport
Among the clowns in the morrice.
Saw. I could dance
Out of my skin to hear thee. But, my curl-pate,
That jade, that foul-tongued——Nan Ratcliff,
Who, for a little soap lick'd by my sow,
Struck, and had almost lamed it: did not I charge thee
To pinch that quean to the heart? * * * *

Her Familiar absents himself: she invokes him.

Saw. ————————Not see me in three days?
I'm lost without my Tomalin; prithee come;
Revenge to me is sweeter far than life;
Thou art my raven, on whose coal-black wings
Revenge comes flying to me: Oh, my best love,
I am on fire (even in the midst of ice)
Raking my blood up, till my shrunk knees feel
Thy curl'd head leaning on them. Come then, my darling,
If in the air thou hover'st, fall upon me
In some dark cloud; and, as I oft have seen
Dragons and serpents in the elements,
Appear thou now so to me. Art thou i' the sea!
Muster up all the monsters from the deep,
And be the ugliest of them: so that my bulch
Show but his swarth cheek to me, let earth cleave,
And break from hell, I care not; could I run
Like a swift powder-mine beneath the world,
Up would I blow it, all to find out thee,
Though I lay ruin'd in it.—Not yet come?
I must then fall to my old prayer: *sanctibiceter nomen tuum.*

He comes in White.

Saw. Why dost thou thus appear to me in white,
As if thou wert the ghost of my dear love?
Famil. I am dogged list not to tell thee, yet to torment thee,
My whiteness puts thee in mind of thy winding sheet.
Saw. Am I near death?
Famil. Be blasted with the news.
Whiteness is day's footboy, a forerunner to light, which shows thy old rivel'd face: villainies are stript naked, the witch must be beaten out of her cockpit.
Saw. Why to mine eyes art thou a flag of truce?
I am at peace with none; 'tis the black color,
Or none, which I fight under: I do not like
Thy puritan-paleness.——

[Mother Sawyer differs from the hags of Middleton or Shakspeare. She is the plain traditional old woman Witch of our ancestors; poor, deformed and ignorant; the terror of villages, herself amenable to a justice. That should be a hardy sheriff, with the power of a county at his heels, that would lay hands on the Weird Sisters. They are of another jurisdiction. But upon the common and received opinion the author (or authors) have engrafted strong fancy There is something frightfully earnest in her invocations to the Familiar.]

THE ATHEIST'S TRAGEDY; OR, THE HONEST MAN'S REVENGE. BY CYRIL TOURNEUR.

D'Amville (the Atheist) with the aid of his wicked instrument, Borachio, murders his Brother, Montferrers, for his Estate. After the deed is done, Borachio and he talk together of the circumstances which attended the murder.

D'Am. Here's a sweet comedy, begins with *O dolentis,* and concludes with ha, ha, he.

Bor. Ha, ha, he.

D'Am. O my echo! I could stand reverberating this sweet musical air of joy, till I had perished my sound lungs with violent laughter. Lovely nigh raven, thou hast seized a carcase?

Bor. Put him out on's pain. I lay so fitly underneath the bank from whence he fell, that ere his faltering tongue could utter double O, I knocked out his brains with this fair ruby; and had another stone just of this form and bigness ready, that I had laid in the broken scull upon the ground for his pillow, against the which they thought he fell and perished.

D'Am. Upon this ground I'll build my manor house,
And this shall be chiefest corner stone.

Bor. This crown'd the most judicious murder, that
The brain of man was e'er deliver'd of.

D'Am. Aye, mark the plot. Not any circumstance
That stood within the reach of the design,
Of persons, dispositions, matter, time,
Or place but by this brain of mine was made
An instrumental help; yet nothing from
The induction to the accomplishment seem'd forced,
Or done o' purpose, but by accident.

[*Here they reckon up the several circumstances.*

Bor. Then darkness did
Protect the execution of the work
Both from prevention and discovery.

D'Am. Here was a murder bravely carried through
The eye of observation, unobserved.

Bor. And those that saw the passage of it, made
The instruments; yet knew not what they did.

D'Am. That power of rule, philosophers ascribe
To him they call the Supreme of the Stars,
Making their influences governors
Of sublunary creatures, when theirselves
Are senseless of their operations. [*Thunder and lightning.*
What! dost start at thunder? Credit my belief, 'tis a mere effect of nature, an exhalation hot and dry, involved within a watry vapor in the middle region of the air, whose coldness congealing that thick moisture to a cloud, the angry exhalation shut within a prison of contrary quality, strives to be free; and with the violent

eruption through the grossness of that cloud, makes this noise we hear.

Bor. 'Tis a fearful noise.

D'Am. 'Tis a brave noise; and, methinks, graces our accomplished project, as a peal of ordnance does a triumph. It speaks encouragement. Now nature shows thee how it favor'd our performance: to forbear this noise when we set forth, because it should not terrify my brother's going home, which would have dashed our purpose: to forbear this lightning in our passage, lest it should ha' warned him of the pitfall. Then propitious nature winked at our proceeding; now, it doth express how that forbearance favor'd our success. * * * * *

Drowned Soldier.

——— walking upon the fatal shore,
Among the slaughter'd bodies of their men,
Which the full-stomach'd sea had cast upon
The sands, it was my unhappy chance to light
Upon a face, whose favor when it lived
My astonish'd mind inform'd me I had seen.
He lay in his armor, as if that had been
His coffin; and the weeping sea (like one
Whose milder temper doth lament the death
Of him whom in his rage he slew) runs up
The shore, embraces him, kisses his cheek;
Goes back again, and forces up the sands
To bury him; and every time it parts,
Sheds tears upon him; till at last (as if
It could no longer endure to see the man
Whom it had slain, yet loath to leave him) with
A kind of unresolv'd unwilling pace,
Winding her waves one in another (like
A man that folds his arms, or wrings his hands
For grief) ebb'd from the body, and descends;
As if it would sink down into the earth,
Aud hide itself for shame of such a deed.*

* This way of description, which seems unwilling ever to leave off

Match Refused.

I entertain the offer of this match,
With purpose to confirm it presently.
I have already mov'd it to my daughter;
Her soft excuses savor'd at the first
Methought but of a modest innocence
Of blood, whose unmov'd stream was never drawn
Into the current of affection. But when I
Replied with more familiar arguments,
Thinking to make her apprehension bold;
Her modest blush fell to a pale dislike,
And she refus'd it with such confidence,
As if she had been prompted by a love
Inclining firmly to some other man;
And in that obstinacy she remains.

Love and Courage.

O do not wrong him. 'Tis a generous mind
That led his disposition to the war;
For gentle love and noble courage are
So near allied, that one begets another:
Or love is sister, and courage is the brother.
Could I affect him better than before,
His soldier's heart would make me love him more.

THE REVENGER'S TRAGEDY. BY CYRIL TOURNEUR.

Vindici addresses the Scull of his dead Lady.

Thou sallow picture of my poison'd love,
My study's ornament, thou shell of death,
Once the bright face of my betroth'd lady,
When life and beauty naturally fill'd out
These ragged imperfections:

weaving parenthesis within parenthesis, was brought to its height by Sir Philip Sidney. He seems to have set the example to Shakspeare. Many beautiful instances may be found all over the Arcadia. These bountiful Wits always give full measure, pressed down and running over

When two heav'n-pointed diamonds were set
In those unsightly rings —— then 'twas a face
So far beyond the artificial shine
Of any woman's bought complexion,
That the uprightest man (if such there be
That sin but seven times a day) broke custom,
And made up eight with looking after her.
O she was able to ha' made a usurer's son
Melt all his patrimony in a kiss;
And what his father fifty years told,
To have consum'd, and yet his suit been cold.

Again.

Here 's an eye,
Able to tempt a great man—to serve God;
A pretty hanging lip, that has forgot now to dissemble.
Methinks this mouth should make a swearer tremble;
A drunkard clasp his teeth, and not undo 'em,
To suffer wet damnation to run thro' 'em,
Here 's a cheek keeps her color let the wind go whistle:
Spout rain, we fear thee not: be hot or cold,
All 's one with us: and is not he absurd,
Whose fortunes are upon their faces set,
That fear no other God but wind and wet?
Does the silk-worm expend her yellow labors
For thee? for thee does she undo herself?
Are lordships sold to maintain ladyships,
For the poor benefit of a bewitching minute?
Why does yon fellow falsify highways,
And put his life between the judge's lips,
To refine such a thing? keep his horse and men,
To beat their valors for her?
Surely we 're all mad people, and they
Whom we think are, are not.
Does every proud and self-affecting dame
Camphire her face for this? and grieve her maker
In sinful baths of milk, when many an infant starves,
For her superfluous outside, for all this?

Who now bids twenty pound a night? prepares
Music, perfumes, and sweet meats? all are hush'd.
Thou may'st lie chaste now! it were fine, methinks,
To have thee seen at revels, forgetful feasts,
And unclean brothels: sure 'twould fright the sinner,
And make him a good coward: put a reveller
Out of his antick amble,
And cloy an epicure with empty dishes,
Here might a scornful and ambitious woman
Look through and through herself.—See ladies, with false forms,
You deceive men, but cannot deceive worms.*

Vindici, having disguised himself, makes trial of his Sister Castiza's virtue; and afterwards of his Mother's.

VINDICI. CASTIZA.

Vin. Lady, the best of wishes to your sex,
Fair skins and new gowns. [*Offers her a letter.*
Cast. Oh, they shall thank you, Sir.
Whence this?
Vin. Oh, from a dear and worthy friend.
Cast. From whom?
Vin. The duke's son.
Cast. Receive that. [*A Box o' the Ear to her Brother.*
I swore I would put anger in my hand.
And pass the virgin limits of myself,
To him that next appear'd in that base office,
To be his sin's attorney. Bear to him
That figure of my hate upon thy cheek,
Whilst 'tis yet hot, and I'll reward thee for 't:
Tell him my honor shall have a rich name,

* The male and female Skeleton in Gondibert is the finest lecture of mortification which has been read from bones.

This dismal gallery, lofty, long and wide,
Was hung with Skeletons of every kind;
Human, and all that learned human pride
Thinks made to obey man's high immortal mind.
Yet on that wall hangs He, too, who so thought:
And she, dried by Him, who that He obey'd.

When several harlots shall share his with shame.
Farewell; commend me to him in my hate. [*Exit.*

Vin. It is the sweetest box
That e'er my nose came nigh;
The finest draw-work cuff that e'er was worn;
I 'll love this blow for ever, and this cheek
Shall still henceforward take the wall of this.
Oh, I 'm above my tongue: most constant sister,
In this thou hast right honorable shown;
Many are call'd by their honor, that have none.
Thou art approv'd for ever in my thoughts.
It is not in the power of words to taint thee.
And yet for the salvation of my oath,
As my resolve in that point, I will lay
Hard siege unto my mother, tho' I know,
A siren's tongue could not bewitch her so.
Mass, fitly here she comes! thanks, my disguise—

The Mother enters.

Madam, good afternoon.

Moth. Y 'are welcome, Sir.

Vin. The next of Italy commends him to you,
Our mighty expectation, the duke's son.

Moth. I think myself much honor'd, that he pleases
To rank me in his thoughts.

Vin. So may you, lady:
One that is like to be our sudden duke;
The crown gapes for him every tide; and then
Commander o'er us all, do but think on him,
How blest were they now that could pleasure him
E'en with anything almost!

Moth. Ay, save their honor.

Vin. Tut, one would let a little of that go too,
And ne'er be seen in 't, ne'er be seen in 't, mark you,
I 'd wink and let it go.

Moth. Marry but I would not.

Vin. Marry but I would, I hope, I know you would too.
If you'd that blood now which you gave your daughter.

To her indeed 'tis, this wheel comes about;
That man that must be all this, perhaps ere morning
(For his white father does but mould away)
Has long desir'd your daughter.
Moth. Desir'd?
Vin. Nay, but hear me,
He desires now, that will command hereafter;
Therefore be wise, I speak as more a friend
To you than him; madam, I know you 're poor.
And (lack the day!) there are too many poor ladies already;
Why should you wax the number? 'tis despised.
Live wealthy, rightly understand the world,
And chide away that foolish country girl
Keeps company with your daughter, Chastity.
Moth. O fie, fie! the riches of the world cannot hire a mother
To such a most unnatural task.
Vin. No, but a thousand angels can;
Men have no power, angels must work you to 't:
The world descends into such base-born evils,
That forty angels can make fourscore devils.
There will be fools still I perceive—still fool?
Would I be poor, dejected, scorn'd of greatness,
Swept from the palace, and see others' daughters
Spring with the dew of the court, having mine own
So much desir'd and lov'd—by the duke's son?
No, I would raise my state upon her breast,
And call her eyes my tenants; I would count
My yearly maintenance upon her cheeks;
Take coach upon her lip; and all her parts
Should keep men after men; and I would ride
In pleasure upon pleasure.
You took great pains for her, once when it was,
Let her requite it now, tho' it be but some;
You brought her forth, she may well bring you home.
Moth. O heavens! this o'ercomes me!
Vin. Not I hope already? [*Aside.*
Moth. It is too strong for me; men know that know us,
We are so weak their words can overthrow us:

He touch'd me nearly, made my virtues bate,
When his tongue struck upon my poor estate. [*Aside.*
Vin. I even quake to proceed, my spirit turns edge.
I fear me she 's unmother'd, yet I'll venture. [*Aside.*
What think you now, lady ? speak, are you wiser ?
What said advancement to you ? thus it said,
The daughter's fall lifts up the mother's head:
Did it not, Madam ? but I 'll swear it does
In many places ; but this age fears no man,
'Tis no shame to be bad, because 'tis common.
Moth. Aye, that 's the comfort on 't.
Vin. The comfort on 't !—
I keep the best for last. Can these persuade you
To forget heaven—and— [*Offers her money.*
Moth. Ay, these are they—
Vin. Oh!
Moth. That enchant our sex;
These are the means that govern our affections,—
That woman
Will not be troubled with the mother long,
That sees the comfortable shine of you :
I blush to think what for your sakes I 'll do.
Vin. O suffering heaven ! with thy invisible finger,
E'en at this instant turn the precious side
Of both mine eye-balls inward, not to see myself.
[*Aside.*
Moth. Look you, Sir.
Vin. Hollo.
Moth. Let us thank your pains.
Vin. O you are a kind Madam.
Moth. I 'll see how I can move.
Vin. Your words will sting.
Moth. If she be still chaste, I 'll ne'er call her mine.
Vin. Spoke truer than you meant it!
Moth. Daughter Castiza——
Cast. [*within.*] Madam!
Vin. O she 's yonder, meet her.
Troops of celestial soldiers guard her heart.

Your dam nas devils enough to take her part.
[CASTIZA *returns*

Cast. Madam, what makes yon evil-offic'd man
In presence of you ?

Moth. Why ?

Cast. He lately brought
Immodest writing sent from the duke's son,
To tempt me to dishonorable act.

Moth. Dishonorable act ?—good honorable fool.
That wouldst be honest, 'cause thou wouldst be so,
Producing no one reason but thy will;
And it has a good report, prettily commended,
But pray by whom ? poor people : ignorant people;
The better sort, I 'm sure, cannot abide it.
And by what rule should we square out our lives
But by our betters' actions ? oh, if thou knew'st
What 'twere to lose it, thou wouldst never keep it;
But there 's a cold curse laid upon all maids,
Whilst others clip the sun, they clasp the shades.
Deny advancement ! treasure ! the duke's son !

Cast. I cry you mercy, lady, I mistook you;
Pray did you see my mother? which way went you ?
Pray God I have not lost her.

Vin. Prettily put by. [*Aside.*

Moth. Are you as proud to me, as coy to him ?
Do you not know me now ?

Cast. Why, are you she ?
The world 's so chang'd, one shape into another,
It is a wise child now that knows her mother.

Vin. Most right, i' faith. [*Aside.*

Moth. I owe your cheek my hand
For that presumption now, but I 'll forget it;
Come, you shall leave those childish 'haviors,
And understand your time. Fortunes flow to you.
What will you be a girl ?
If all fear'd drowning that spy waves ashore,
Gold would grow rich, and all the merchants poor.

Cast. It is a pretty saying of a wicked one, but methinks now

It does not show so well out of your mouth;
Better in his.
Vin. Faith, bad enough in both,
Were I in earnest, as I 'll seem no less. [*Aside.*
I wonder, lady, your own mother's words
Cannot be taken, nor stand in full force.
'Tis honesty you urge; what 's honesty?
'Tis but heaven's beggar; and what woman is so foolish to keep honesty,
And be not able to keep herself? no,
Times are grown wiser, and will keep less charge.
A maid that has small portion now, intends
To break up house, and live upon her friends.
How blest are you! you have happiness alone;
Others must fall to thousands, you to one;
Sufficient in himself to make your forehead
Dazzle the world with jewels, and petitionary people
Start at your presence.
O think upon the pleasure of the palace!
Secured ease and state! the stirring meats,
Ready to move out of the dishes, that e'en now quicken when they're eaten!
Banquets abroad by torch-light! music! sports!
Bare-headed vassals, that had ne'er the fortune
To keep on their own hats, but let horns wear 'em!
Nine coaches waiting—hurry, hurry, hurry—
Cast. Aye, to the devil—
Vin. Aye, to the devil! to the duke, by my faith.
Moth. Aye, to the duke. Daughter, you'd scorn to think
Of the devil, and you were there once.
Vin. Who'd sit at home in a neglected room,
Dealing her short-liv'd beauty to the pictures,
That are as useless as old men, when those
Poorer in face and fortune than herself
Walk with a hundred acres on their backs,
Fair meadows cut into green fore-parts?—
Fair trees, those comely foretops of the field,
Are cut to maintain head-tires:—much untold—

All thrives but chastity, she lies cold.
Nay, shall I come near to you? mark but this:
Why are there so few honest women, but because 'tis the poorer profession? that's accounted best, that's best followed; least in trade, least in fashion; and that's not honesty, believe it; and do but note the low and dejected price of it:
Lose but a pearl, we search and cannot brook it:
But that once gone, who is so mad to look it?
Moth. Troth, he says true.
Cast. False: I defy you both.
I have endur'd you with an ear of fire;
Your tongues have struck hot irons on my face.
Mother, come from that poisonous woman there.
Moth. Where?
Cast. Do you not see her? she's too inward then.
Slave, perish in thy office. You heavens please,
Henceforth to make the mother a disease,
Which first begins with me; yet I've outgone you. [*Exit.*
Vin. O angels, clap your wings upon the skies,
And give this virgin crystal plaudities! [*Aside.*
Moth. Peevish, coy, foolish!—but return this answer,
My lord shall be most welcome, when his pleasure
Conducts him this way; I will sway mine own;
Women with women can work best alone. [*Exit.*
Vin. Forgive me, heaven, to call my mother wicked!
O lessen not my days upon the earth.
I cannot honor her.

The Brothers, Vindici and Hippolito, threaten their Mother with Death for consenting to the Dishonor of their Sister

Vin. O thou for whom no name is bad enough.
Moth. What mean my sons? what, will you murther me?
Vin. Wicked unnatural parent!
Hip. Friend of women!
Moth. Oh! are sons turn'd monsters! help!
Vin. In vain.
Moth. Are ye so barbarous to set iron nipples
Upon the breast that gave you suck?

Vin. That breast
Is turn'd to quarled poison.
Moth. Cut not your days for 't. Am not I your mother?
Vin. Thou dost usurp that title now by fraud,
For in that shell of mother breeds a bawd.
Moth. A bawd! O name far loathsomer than hell!
Hip. It should be so, knew'st thou thy office well.
Moth. I hate it.
Vin. Ah, is it possible, you powers on high,
That women should dissemble when they die?
Moth. Dissemble!
Vin. Did not the duke's son direct
A fellow of the world's condition hither,
That did corrupt all that was good in thee?
Made thee uncivilly forget thyself,
And work our sister to his purpose?
Moth. Who, I?
That had been monstrous. I defy that man
For any such intent. None lives so pure,
But shall be soil'd with slander.
Good son, believe it not.
Vin. Oh, I'm in doubt
Whether I am myself or no—
Stay, let me look again upon this face.
Who shall be saved when mothers have no grace?
[*Resumes his Disguise.*
Hip. 'Twould make one half despair.
Vin. I was the man.
Defy me now, let's see, do 't modestly.
Moth. O hell unto my soul!
Vin. In that disguise, I, sent from the duke's son,
Tried you, and found you base metal,
As any villain might have done.
Moth. O no,
No tongue but yours could have bewitched me so.
Vin. O nimble in damnation, quick in turn!
There is no devil could strike fire so soon.
I am confuted in a word.

Moth. Oh sons,
Forgive me, to myself I'll prove more true;
You that should honor me, I kneel to you.
Vin. A mother to give aim to her own daughter!
Hip. True, brother; how far beyond nature 'tis,
Though many mothers do it.
Vin. Nay, and you draw tears once, go you to bed.
Wet will make iron blush and change to red.
Brother it rains, 'twill spoil your dagger, house it.
Hip. 'Tis done.
Vin. I' faith 'tis a sweet shower, it does much good.
The fruitful grounds and meadows of her soul
Have been long dry; pour down, thou blessed dew.
Rise, mother; troth, this shower has made you higher.
Moth. O you heavens!
Take this infectious spot out of my soul;
I'll rince it in seven waters of mine eyes.
Make my tears salt enough to taste of grace.
To weep is to our sex naturally given;
But to weep truly, that's a gift from heaven.
Vin. Nay, I'll kiss you now. Kiss her, brother·
Let's marry her to our souls, wherein's no lust,
And honorably love her.
Hip. Let it be.
Vin. For honest women are so seld and rare
'Tis good to cherish those poor few that are.
O you of easy wax! do but imagine
Now the disease has left you, how leprously
That office would have cling'd unto your forehead,
All mothers that had any graceful hue,
Would have worn masks to hide their face at you.
It would have grown to this, at your foul name
Green-color'd maids would have turn'd red with shame.
Hip. And then our sister, full of hire and baseness—
Vin. There had been boiling lead again!
The duke's son's great concubine!
A drab of state, a cloth-o'-silver slut,
To have her train borne up, and her soul trail in the dirt

Hip. To be great, miserable ; to be rich, eternally wretched.
Vin. O common madness !
Ask but the thriving'st harlot in cold blood,
She'd give the world to make her honor good.
Perhaps you'll say, but only to the duke's son
In private ; why, she first begins with one
Who afterwards to thousands proves a whore :
Break ice in one place, it will crack in more.
Moth. Most certainly applied.
Hip. O brother, you forget our business.
Vin. And well remember'd ; joy's a subtil elf;
I think man's happiest when he forgets himself.
Farewell, once dry, now holy-water'd mead ;
Our hearts wear feathers that before wore lead.
Moth. I'll give you this, that one I never knew
Plead better for, and 'gainst the devil than you.
Vin. You make me proud on 't.
Hip. Commend us in all virtue to our sister.
Vin. Ay, for the love of heaven, to that true maid.
Moth. With my best words.
Vin. Why that was motherly said.*

Castiza seems to consent to her Mother's wicked motion.

CASTIZA. MOTHER.

Cast. Now, mother, you have wrought with me so strongly,
That, what for my advancement, as to calm
The trouble of your tongue, I am content.
Moth. Content, to what ?
Cast. To do as you have wish'd me :
To prostitute my breast to the duke's son,
And put myself to common usury.

* The reality and life of this Dialogue passes any scenical illusion I ever felt. I never read it but my ears tingle, and I feel a hot blush spread my cheeks, as if I were presently about to " proclaim " some such " malefactions" of myself, as the Brothers here rebuke in their unnatural parent; in words more keen and dagger-like than those which Hamlet speaks to his mother. Such power has the passion of shame truly personated, not only to " strike guilty creatures unto the soul," but to " appal " even those that are " free."

Moth. I hope you will not so.
Cast. Hope you I will not?
That's not the hope you look to be saved in.
Moth. Truth, but it is.
Cast. Do not deceive yourself.
I am as you, e'en out of marble wrought.
What would you now: are ye not pleas'd yet with me?
You shall not wish me to be more lascivious,
Than I intend to be.
Moth. Strike not me cold.
Cast. How often have you charg'd me on your blessing
To be a cursed woman! when you knew
Your blessing had no force to make me lewd,
You laid your curse upon me; that did more:
The mother's curse is heavy; where that fights,
Sons set in storm and daughters lose their lights.
Moth. Good child, dear maid, if there be any spark
Of heavenly intellectual light within thee,
O let my breath revive it to a flame.
Put not all out with woman's wilful follies.
I am recover'd of that foul disease
That haunts too many mothers; kind, forgive me,
Make me not sick in health! if then
My words prevail'd, when they were wickedness,
How much more now, when they are just and good!
Cast. I wonder what you mean; are not you she,
For whose infect persuasions, I could scarce
Kneel out my prayers; and had much ado,
In three hours' reading, to untwist so much
Of the black serpent, as you wound about me!
Moth. 'Tis unfruitful held, tedious, to repeat what's past.
I'm now your present mother.
Cast. Pish, now 'tis too late.
Moth. Bethink again, thou know'st not what thou say'st.
Cast. No! deny advancement! treasure! the duke's son!
Moth. O see, I spoke those words, and now they poison me.
What will the deed do then?
Advancement! true; as high as shame can pitch!

For treasure: who e'er knew a Harlot rich?
Or could build by the purchase of her sin
An hospital to keep their bastards in?
The duke's son! oh; when women are young courtiers,
They are sure to be old beggars.
To know the miseries most harlots taste,
Thou'dst wish thyself unborn when thou'rt unchaste.
Cast. O mother, let me twine about your neck,
And kiss you till my soul melt on your lips;
I did but this to try you.
Moth. O speak truth.
Cast. Indeed I did not; for no tongue hath force
To alter me from honest:
If maidens would, men's words could have no power;
A virgin's honor is a crystal tower,
Which being weak is guarded with good spirits;
Until she basely yields, no ill inherits.
Moth. O happy child! faith, and thy birth, hath saved me,
'Mongst thousand daughters, happiest of all others;
Buy thou a glass for maids, and I for mothers.

Evil Report after Death.

What is it to have
A flattering false insculption on a tomb,
And in men's hearts reproach? the 'bowel'd corps
May be sear'd in, but (with free tongue I speak)
The faults of great men through their sear-clothes break.

Bastards.

Oh what a grief 'tis that a man should live
But once in the world, and then to live a Bastard?
The curse of the womb, the thief of nature,
Begot against the seventh commandment,
Half damn'd in the conception by the justice
Of that unbribed everlasting law.

Too nice respects in Courtship.

Ceremony has made many fools.
It is as easy way unto a duchess

As to a hatted dame, if her love answer:
But that by timorous honors, pale respects,
Idle degrees of fear, men make their ways
Hard of themselves.

THE DEVIL'S LAW CASE; OR, WHEN WOMEN GO TO LAW, THE DEVIL IS FULL OF BUSINESS. A TRAGI-COMEDY. BY JOHN WEBSTER.

Contarino challenges Ercole to fight him for the possession of Jolenta, whom they both love.

Con. Sir; my love to you has proclaim'd you one,
Whose word was still led by a noble thought,
And that thought follow'd by as fair a deed:
Deceive not that opinion: we were students
At Padua together, and have long
To the world's eye shown like friends.
Was it hearty on your part to me?
Erc. Unfained.
Con. You are false
To the good thought I held of you; and now,
Join the worst part of man to you, your malice,
To uphold that falsehood. Sacred innocence
Is fled your bosom. Signor, I must tell you;
To draw the picture of unkindness truly,
Is to express two that have dearly loved,
And fall'n at variance. 'Tis a wonder to me,
Knowing my interest in the fair Jolenta,
That you should love her.
Erc. Compare her beauty and my youth together
And you will find the fair effects of love
No miracle at all.
Con. Yes, it will prove
Prodigious to you: I must stay your voyage.
Erc. Your warrant must be mighty.
Con. 'Tis a seal

From heaven to do it, since you'd ravish from me
What's there intitled mine ; and yet I vow,
By the essential front of spotless virtue,
I have compassion of both our youths :
To approve which, I have not tane the way
Like an Italian, to cut your throat
By practice that had giv'n you now for dead
And never frown'd upon you.
You must fight with me.
Erc. I will, Sir.
Con. And instantly.
Ere. I will haste before you. Point whither.
Con. Why, you speak nobly ; and, for this fair dealing,
Were the rich jewel (which we vary for)
A thing to be divided, by my life,
I would be well content to give you half:
But since 'tis vain to think we can be friends,
Tis needful one of us be tane away
From being the other's enemy.
Erc. Yet, methinks,
This looks not like a quarrel.
Con. Not a quarrel !
Erc. You have not apparelled your fury well ;
It goes too plain, like a scholar.
Con. It is an ornament,
Makes it more terrible ; and you shall find it
A weighty injury, and attended on
By discreet valor ; because I do not strike you,
Or give you the lie (such foul preparatives
Would show like the stale injury of wine)
I reserve my rage to sit on my sword's piont ;
Which a great quantity of your best blood
Can't satisfy.
Erc. You promise well to yourself.
Shall 's have no seconds ?
Con. None, for fear of prevention.
Erc. The length of our weapons——
Con. We'll fit them by the way :

So whether our time calls us to live or die,
Let us do both like noble gentlemen,
And true Italians.
Erc. For that, let me embrace you.
Con. Methinks, being an Italian, I trust you
To come somewhat too near me:
But your jealousy gave that embrace, to try
If I were arm'd; did it not?
Erc. No, believe me.
I take your heart to be sufficient proof
Without a privy coat: and, for my part,
A taffaty is all the shirt of mail
I am arm'd with.
Con. You deal equally.*

Sitting for a picture.

Must you have my Picture?
You will enjoin me to a strange punishment.
With what a compell'd face a woman sits
While she is drawing? I have noted divers
Either to fain smiles, or suck in the lips,
To have a little mouth; ruffle the cheeks,
To have the dimple seen; and so disorder
The face with affectation, at next sitting
It has not been the same: I have known others
Have lost the entire fashion of their face
In half an hour's sitting—in hot weather—
The painting on their face has been so mellow,
They have left the poor man harder work by half
To mend the copy he wrought by: But indeed,
If ever I would have mine drawn to the life,
I would have a painter steal it at such a time
I were devoutly kneeling at my prayers;
There is then a heavenly beauty in 't, the soul
Moves in the superficies.

* I have selected this scene as the model of a well managed and gentlemanlike difference.

Honorable Employment.

Oh, my lord, lie not idle :
The chiefest action for a man of great spirit
Is never to be out of action. We should think ;
The soul was never put into the body,
Which has so many rare and curious pieces
Of mathematical motion, to stand still.
Virtue is ever sowing of her seeds :
In the trenches for the soldier ; in the wakeful study
For the scholar ; in the furrows of the sea
For men of our profession : of all which
Arise and spring up honor.

Selling of Land.

I could wish
That noblemen would ever live in the country,
Rather than make their visits up to the city
About such business. Noble houses
Have no such goodly prospects any way
As into their own land : the decay of that
(Next to their begging church-land) is a ruin
Worth all men's pity.

Dirge in a Funeral Pageant.

All the flowers of the spring
Meet to perfume our burying :
These have but their growing prime,
And man does flourish but his time.
Survey our progress from our birth ;
We are set, we grow, we turn to earth
Courts adieu, and all delights,
All bewitching appetites.
Sweetest breath and clearest eye
(Like perfumes) go out and die ;
And consequently this is done,
As shadows wait upon the sun.
Vain the ambition of kings,
Who seek by trophies and dead things

To leave a living name behind,
And weave but nets to catch the wind.

APPIUS AND VIRGINIA: A TRAGEDY. BY JOHN WEBSTER.

Appius, the Roman Decemvir, not being able to corrupt the Innocence of Virginia, Daughter to Virginius the Roman General, and newly married to Icilius, a young and noble Gentleman; to get possession of her person, suborns one Clodius to claim her as the Daughter of a deceased bondwoman of his, on the testimony of certain forged writings, pretended to be the Deposition of that Woman, on her deathbed, confessing that the Child had been spuriously passed upon Virginius for his own: the Cause is tried at Rome before Appius.

APPIUS. VIRGINIA. VIRGINIUS, *her Father.* ICILIUS, *her Husband. Senators of Rome. Nurse and other Witnesses.*

Virginius. My Lords, believe not this spruce orator.*
Had I but fee'd him first, he would have told
As smooth a tale on our side.
Appius. Give us leave.
Virginius. He deals in formal glosses, cunning shows,
And cares not greatly which way the case goes.
Examine I beseech you this old woman,
Who is the truest witness of her birth.
Appius. Soft you, is she your only witness?
Virginius. She is, my Lord.
Appius. Why, is it possible,
Such a great Lady in her time of child birth
Should have no other witness but a nurse?
Virginius. For aught I know, the rest are dead, my Lord.
Appius. Dead? no, my Lord, belike they were of counsel
With your deceased Lady, and so shamed
Twice to give color to so vile an act.
Thou nurse, observe me, thy offence already
Doth merit punishment above our censure;
Pull not more whips upon thee.

* Counsel for Clodius.

Nurse. I defy your whips, my Lord.
Appius. Command her silence, Lictors.
Virginius. O injustice! you frown away my witness,
Is this law, is this uprightness?
Appius. Have you view'd the writings?
This is a trick to make our slaves our heirs
Beyond prevention.
Virginius. Appius, wilt thou hear me?
You have slander'd a sweet Lady that now sleeps
In a most noble monument. Observe me;
I would have tane her simple word to gage
Before his soul or thine.
Appius. That makes thee wretched.
Old man, I am sorry for thee; that thy love
By custom is grown natural, which by nature
Should be an absolute lothing. Note the sparrow;
That having hatch'd a cuckow, when it sees
Her brood a monster to her proper kind,
Forsakes it, and with more fear shuns the nest
Than she had care i' the spring to have it drest.
Here's witness, most sufficient witness.
Think you, my Lord, our laws are writ in snow,
And that your breath can melt them?
Virginius. No, my Lord,
We have not such hot livers: mark you that?
Virginia. Remember yet the gods, O Appius;
Who have no part in this. Thy violent lust
Shall like the biting of th' invenom'd aspick,
Steal thee to hell. So subtle are thy evils;
In life they'll seem good angels, in death devils.
Appius. Observe you not this scandal?
Icilius. Sir, 'tis none.
I'll show thy letters full of violent lust
Sent to this Lady.
Appius. My Lords, these are but dilatory shifts.
Sirrah, I know you to the very heart,
And I 'll observe you.
Icilius. Do, but do it with justice.

Clear thyself first, O Appius, ere thou judge
Our imperfections rashly, for we wot
The office of a justice is perverted quite
When one thief hangs another.

1. *Senator*. You are too bold.

Appius. Lictor, take charge of him.

Icilius. 'Tis very good.
Will no man view these papers,* what not one?
Jove, thou hast found a rival upon earth,
His nod strikes all men dumb.
My duty to you.
The ass that carried Isis on his back,
Thought that the superstitious people kneel'd
To give his dulness humble reverence
If thou thinkst so, proud judge, I let thee see
I bend low to thy gown but not to thee.

Virginius. There's one in hold already. Noble youth;
Fetters grace one, being worn for speaking truth.
I'll lie with thee, I swear, though in a dungeon.
The injuries you do us we shall pardon:
But it is just, the wrongs which we forgive
The gods are charg'd therewith to see revenged.

Appius. Your madness wrongs you: by my soul, I love you.

Virginius. Thy soul!
O thy opinion, old Pythagoras:
Whither, O whither should thy black soul fly,
Into what ravenous bird, or beast most vile?
Only into a weeping crocodile.
Love me!
Thou lov'st me, Appius, as the earth loves rain,
Only to swallow it.

Appius. Know you the place you stand in?

Virginius. I'll speak freely.
Good men, too much trusting their innocence,
Do not betake them to that just defence
Which gods and nature gave them; but even wink
In the black tempest, and so fondly sink.

* The Forgery.

Appius. Let us proceed to sentence.
Virginius. Ere you speak,
One parting farewell let me borrow of you
To take of my Virginia.
Appius. Pray, take your course.
Virginius. Farewell, my sweet Virginia: never, never
Shall I taste fruit of the most blessed hope
I had in thee. Let me forget the thought
Of thy most pretty infancy: when first,
Returning from the wars, I took delight
To rock thee in my target; when my girl
Would kiss her father in his burganet
Of glittering steel hung 'bout his armed neck,
And, viewing the bright metal, smile to see
Another fair Virginia smile on thee;
When I first taught thee how to go, to speak;
And, when my wounds have smarted) I have sung,
With an unskilful yet a willing voice,
To bring my girl asleep. O my Virginia;
When we begun to be, begun our woes;
Increasing still, as dying life still grows.
Thus I surrender her into the court
Of all the gods. [*Kills her*
And see, proud Appius, see;
Although not justly, I have made her free.
And if thy lust with this act be not fed,
Bury her in thy bowels now she's dead.

THE TRAGEDY OF THE DUCHESS OF MALFY. BY JOHN WEBSTER.

The Duchess of Malfy marries Antonio, her Steward.

DUCHESS. CARIOLA, *her Maid.*

Duchess. Is Antonio come?
Cariola. He attends you.
Duch. Good dear soul,

Leave me: but place thyself behind the arras,
Where thou mayst overhear us: wish me good speed,
For I am going into a wilderness,
Where I shall find nor path nor friendly clue
To be my guide. [*Cariola withdraws.*

Antonio enters.

I sent for you, sit down.
Take pen and ink and write. Are you ready ?
Ant. Yes.
Duch. What did I say ?
Ant. That I should write somewhat.
Duch. Oh, I remember.
After these triumphs and this large expense
It's fit, like thrifty husbands, we inquire
What's laid up for to-morrow.
Ant. So please your beauteous excellence.
Duch. Beauteous indeed! I thank you; I look young
For your sake. You have tane my cares upon you.
Ant. I'll fetch your grace the particulars of your revenue and expense.
Duch. Oh, you're an upright treasurer: but you mistook,
For when I said I meant to make inquiry
What's laid up for to-morrow, I did mean
What's laid up yonder for me.
Ant. Where ?
Duch. In heaven.
I'm making my will (as 'tis fit princes should)
In perfect memory; and I pray, sir, tell me,
Were not one better make it smiling, thus,
Than in deep groans and terrible ghastly looks,
As if the gifts we parted with procur'd
That violent distraction ?
Ant. Oh, much better.
Duch. If I had a husband now, this care were quit.
But I intend to make you overseer;
What good deed shall we first remember, say ?
Ant. Begin with that first good deed, began in the world

After man's creation, the sacrament of marriage.
I'd have you first provide for a good husband;
Give him all.
Duch. All!
Ant. Yes, your excellent self.
Duch. In a winding sheet?
Ant. In a couple.
Duch. St. Winifred, that were a strange will.
Ant. 'Twere stranger if there were no will in you
To marry again.
Duch. What do you think of marriage?
Ant. I take it, as those that deny purgatory;
It locally contains or heaven or hell,
There's no third place in 't.
Duch. How do you affect it?
Ant. My banishment feeding my melancholy,
Would often reason thus.
Duch. Pray, let us hear it.
Ant. Say a man never marry, nor have children,
What takes that from him? only the bare name
Of being a father, or the weak delight
To see the little wanton ride a cock-horse
Upon a painted stick, or hear him chatter
Like a taught starling.
Duch. Fie, fie, what's all this?
One of your eyes is blood-shot; use my Ring to 't.
They say 'tis very sovran, 'twas my wedding ring,
And I did vow never to part with it
But to my second husband.
Ant. You have parted with it now.
Duch. Yes, to help your eye-sight.
Ant. You have made me stark blind.
Duch. How?
Ant. There is a saucy and ambitious devil,
Is dancing in this circle.
Duch. Remove him.
Ant. How?
Duch. There needs small conjuration, when your finger

May do it; thus: is it fit?

[*She puts the ring on his finger.*

Ant. What said you? [*He kneels.*

Duch. Sir!

This goodly roof of yours is too low built;
I cannot stand upright in 't nor discourse,
Without I raise it higher: raise yourself;
Or, if you please my hand to help you: so.

Ant. Ambition, Madam, is a great man's madness,
That is not kept in chains and close-pent rooms,
But in fair lightsome lodgings, and is girt
With the wild noise of prattling visitants,
Which makes it lunatick beyond all cure.
Conceive not I'm so stupid, but I aim
Whereto your favors tend: but he's a fool
That, being a cold, would thrust his hands in the fire
To warm them.

Duch. So, now the ground 's broke,
You may discover what a wealthy mine
I make you Lord of.

Ant. O my unworthiness.

Duch. You were ill to sell yourself.
This darkning of your worth is not like that
Which tradesmen use in the city; their false lights
Are to rid bad wares off: and I must tell you,
If you will know where breathes a complete man
(I speak it without flattery) turn your eyes,
And progress through yourself.

Ant. Were there nor heaven nor hell,
I should be honest: I have long serv'd virtue
And never tane wages of her.—

Duch. Now she pays it.
The misery of us that are born great!
We are forc'd to woo, because none dare woo us:
And as a tyrant doubles with his words,
And fearfully equivocates: so we
Are forced to express our violent passions
In riddles and in dreams, and leave the path

Of simple virtue, which was never made
To seem the thing it is not. Go, go, brag
You have left me heartless ; mine is in your bosom ;
I hope 'twill multiply love there ; you do tremble ;
Make not your heart so dead a piece of flesh,
To fear more than to love me ; Sir, be confident.
What is it distracts you ? This is flesh and blood, Sir
'Tis not the figure cut in alabaster,
Kneels at my husband's tomb. Awake, awake, man.
I do here put off all vain ceremony,
And only do appear to you a young widow :
I use but half a blush in 't.
Ant. Truth speak for me ;
I will remain the constant sanctuary
Of your good name.
Duch. I thank you, gentle love ;
And 'cause you shall not come to me in debt
(Being now my Steward) here upon your lips
I sign your *quietus est :* this you should have begg'd now
I have seen children oft eat sweetmeats thus,
As fearful to devour them too soon.
Ant. But, for your brothers—
Duch. Do not think of them.
All discord, without this circumference,
Is only to be pitied, and not fear'd :
Yet, should they know it, time will easily
Scatter the tempest.
Ant. These words should be mine,
And all the parts you have spoke ; if some part of it
Would not have savor'd flattery.
[Cariola *comes forward.*
Duch. Kneel.
Ant. Hah !
Duch. Be not amaz'd ; this woman's of my council.
I have heard lawyers say, a contract in a chamber
Per verba præsenti is absolute marriage ;
Bless heaven this sacred Gordian, which let violence
Never untwine.

Ant. And may our sweet affections, like the spheres,
Be still in motion.
Duch. Quickening, and make
The like soft music.
Car. Whether the spirit of greatness, or of woman,
Reign most in her, I know not; but it shows
A fearful madness: I owe her much of pity.

The Duchess's marriage with Antonio being discovered, her brother Ferdinand shuts her up in a Prison, and torments her with various trials of studied Cruelty. By his command Bosola, the instrument of his Devices, shows her the Bodies of her Husband and Children counterfeited in Wax, as dead.

Bos. He doth present you this sad spectacle,
That now you know directly they are dead,
Hereafter you may wisely cease to grieve
For that which cannot be recovered.
Duch. There is not between heaven and earth one wish
I stay for after this: it wastes me more
Than were 't my picture fashion'd out of wax,
Stuck with a magical needle, and then buried
In some foul dunghill; and yond's an excellent property
For a tyrant, which I would account mercy.
Bos. What's that?
Duch. If they would bind me to that lifeless trunk,
And let me freeze to death.
Bos. Come, you must live.
Leave this vain sorrow.
Things being at the worst begin to mend.
The Bee,
When he hath shot his sting into your hand,
May then play with your eye-lid.
Duch. Good comfortable fellow,
Persuade a wretch that's broke upon the wheel
To have all his bones new set; intreat him live
To be executed again. Who must dispatch me?
I account this world a tedious theatre,
For I do play a part in 't 'gainst my will.
Bos. Come, be of comfort, I will save your life.

Duch. Indeed I have not leisure to attend
So small a business.
I will go pray.—No: I'll go curse.
Bos. O fie.
Duch. I could curse the stars:
Bos. O fearful.
Duch. And those three smiling seasons of the year
Into a Russian winter: nay, the world
To its first chaos.
Plagues (that make lanes through largest families)
Consume them.*
Let them like tyrants
Ne'er be remember'd but for the ill they've done.
Let all the zealous prayers of mortified
Churchmen forget them.
Let heaven a little while cease crowning martyrs,
To punish them: go, howl them this; and say, I long to bleed
It is some mercy when men kill with speed. [*Exit.*

Ferdinand enters.

Ferd. Excellent, as I would wish: she's plagued in art.
These presentations are but fram'd in wax,
By the curious master in that quality
Vincentio Lauriola, and she takes them
For true substantial bodies.
Bos. Why do you do this?
Ferd. To bring her to despair.
Bos. Faith, end here;
And go no further in your cruelty.
Send her a penitential garment to put on
Next to her delicate skin, and furnish her
With beads and prayer books.
Ferd. Damn her; that body of her's,
While that my blood ran pure in 't, was more worth
Than that, which thou would'st comfort, call'd a soul.
I'll send her masques of common courtezans,
Have her meat served up by bawds and ruffians,

* Her Brothers.

And ('cause she'll need be mad) I am resolv'd
To remove forth the common hospital
All the mad folk, and place them near her lodging:
There let 'em practise together, sing, and dance,
And act their gambols to the full o' the moon.

She is kept waking with noises of Madmen; and, at last, is strangled by common Executioners.

DUCHESS. CARIOLA.

Duch. What hideous noise was that?
Car. 'Tis the wild consort
Of madmen, Lady: which your tyrant brother
Hath placed about your lodging: this tyranny
I think was never practis'd till this hour.
Duch. Indeed I thank him; nothing but noise and folly
Can keep me in my right wits, whereas reason
And silence make me stark mad; sit down,
Discourse to me some dismal tragedy.
Car. O 'twill increase your melancholy.
Duch. Thou art deceived.
To hear of greater grief would lessen mine.
This is a prison?
Car. Yes: but thou shalt live
To shake this durance off.
Duch. Thou art a fool.
The Robin-red-breast and the Nightingale
Never live long in cages.
Car. Pray, dry your eyes.
What think you of, Madam?
Duch. Of nothing:
When I muse thus, I sleep.
Car. Like a madman, with your eyes open?
Duch. Dost thou think we shall know one anothe
In the other world?
Car. Yes, out of question.
Duch. O that it were possible we might
But hold some two days conference with the dead,
From them I should learn somewhat I am sure

I never shall know here. I'll tell thee a miracle;
I am not mad yet, to my cause of sorrow.
Th' heaven o'er my head seems made of molten brass,
The earth of flaming sulphur, yet I am not mad:
I am acquainted with sad misery,
As the tann'd galley-slave is with his oar;
Necessity makes me suffer constantly,
And custom makes it easy. Who do I look like now?

Car. Like to your picture in the gallery;
A deal of life in show, but none in practice:
Or rather, like some reverend monument
Whose ruins are even pitied.

Duch. Very proper:
And Fortune seems only to have her eyesight,
To behold my tragedy: how now,
What noise is that?

A Servant enters.

Serv. I am come to tell you,
Your brother hath intended you some sport.
A great physician when the Pope was sick
Of a deep melancholy, presented him
With several sorts of madmen, which wild object
(Being full of change and sport) forc'd him to laugh,
And so th' imposthume broke: the selfsame cure
The duke intends on you.

Duch. Let them come in.

Here follows a Dance of Madmen, with Music answerable thereto: after which Bosola (like an old Man) enters.

Duch. Is he mad too?

Bos. I am come to make thy tomb.

Duch. Ha: my tomb?
Thou speak'st as if I lay upon my deathbed:
Gasping for breath: dost thou perceive me sick?

Bos. Yes, and the more dangerously, since thy sickness is insensible.

Duch. Thou art not mad sure: dost know me?

Bos. Yes.

Duch. Who am I?

Bos. Thou art a box of wormseed; at best but a salvatory of green mummy. What's this flesh? a little crudded milk, fantastical puff-paste. Our bodies are weaker than those paper-prisons boys use to keep flies in, more contemptible; since ours is to preserve earth-worms. Didst thou ever see a lark in a cage? Such is the soul in the body: this world is like her little turf of grass; and the heaven o'er our heads like her looking-glass, only gives us a miserable knowledge of the small compass of our prison.

Duch. Am not I thy duchess?

Bos. Thou art some great woman sure, for riot begins to sit on thy forehead (clad in grey hairs) twenty years sooner than on a merry milk-maid's. Thou sleepest worse, than if a mouse should be forced to take up her lodging in a cat's ear: a little infant that breeds its teeth, should it lie with thee would cry out, as if thou wert the more unquiet bedfellow.

Duch. I am Duchess of Malfy still.

Bos. That makes thy sleeps so broken:
Glories, like glow-worms, afar off shine bright;
But, look'd too near, have neither heat nor light.

Duch. Thou art very plain.

Bos. My trade is to flatter the dead, not the living. I am a tomb-maker.

Duch. And thou comest to make my tomb?

Bos. Yes.

Duch. Let me be a little merry.
Of what stuff wilt thou make it?

Bos. Nay, resolve me first; of what fashion?

Duch. Why, do we grow fantastical in our death-bed?
Do we affect fashion in the grave?

Bos. Most ambitiously. Princes' images on their tombs do not lie as they were wont, seeming to pray up to heaven: but with their hands under their cheeks (as if they died of the tooth-ache): they are not carved with their eyes fixed upon the stars; but, as their minds were wholly bent upon the world, the same way they seem to turn their faces.

Duch. Let me know fully therefore the effect
Of this thy dismal preparation,
This talk, fit for a charnel.

Bos. Now I shall. [*A Coffin, Cords, and a Bell, produced.*
Here is a present from your princely brothers;
And may it arrive welcome, for it brings
Last benefit, last sorrow.

Duch. Let me see it,
I have so much obedience in my blood,
I wish it in their veins to do them good.

Bos. This is your last presence chamber.

Car. O my sweet lady.

Duch. Peace, it affrights not me.

Bos. I am the common bell-man,
That usually is sent to condemn'd persons
The night before they suffer.

Duch. Even now thou saidst,
Thou wast a tomb-maker.

Bos. 'Twas to bring you
By degrees to mortification: Listen.

Dirge.

Hark, now everything is still;
This screech-owl, and the whistler shrill,
Call upon our dame aloud,
And bid her quickly d'on her shroud.
Much you had of land and rent;
Your length in clay's now competent.
A long war disturb'd your mind;
Here your perfect peace is sign'd.
Of what is 't fools make such vain keeping?
Sin, their conception; their birth, weeping:
Their life, a general mist of error,
Their death, a hideous storm of terror.
Strew your hair with powders sweet,
D'on clean linen, bathe your feet:

And (the foul fiend more to check)
A crucifix let bless your neck.
'Tis now full tide 'tween night and day:
End your groan, and come away.
Car. Hence, villains, tyrants, murderers: alas!
What will you do with my lady? Call for help.
Duch. To whom; to our next neighbors? They are mad folks.
Farewell, Cariola.
I pray thee look thou giv'st my little boy
Some syrup for his cold; and let the girl
Say her pray'rs ere she sleep.—Now what you please;
What death?
Bos. Strangling. Here are your executioners.
Duch. I forgive them.
The apoplexy, catarrh, or cough o' the lungs,
Would do as much as they do.
Bos. Doth not death fright you?
Duch. Who would be afraid on 't,
Knowing to meet such excellent company
In th' other world.
Bos. Yet methinks,
The manner of your death should much afflict you;
This cord should terrify you.
Duch. Not a whit.
What would it pleasure me to have my throat cut
With diamonds? or to be smothered
With cassia? or to be shot to death with pearls?
I know, death hath ten thousand several doors
For men to take their exits; and 'tis found
They go on such strange geometrical hinges,
You may open them both ways: any way: (for heav'n sake)
So I were out of your whispering: tell my brothers,
That I perceive, death (now I'm well awake)
Best gift is, they can give or I can take.
I would fain put off my last woman's fault;
I'd not be tedious to you.
Pull, and pull strongly, for your able strength
Must pull down heaven upon me.

Yet stay, heaven gates are not so highly arch'd
As princes' palaces ; they that enter there
Must go upon their knees. Come, violent death,
Serve for Mandragora to make me sleep,
Go tell my brothers ; when I am laid out,
They then may feed in quiet. [*They strangle her kneeling.*

FERDINAND *enters.*

Ferd. Is she dead ?
Bos. She is what you would have her.
Fix your eye here.
Ferd. Constantly.
Bos. Do you not weep ?
Other sins only speak ; murder shrieks out.
The element of water moistens the earth,
But blood flies upwards and bedews the heavens.
Ferd. Cover her face : mine eyes dazzle : she died young.
Bos. I think not so : her infelicity
Seem'd to have years too many.
Ferd. She and I were twins ;
And should I die this instant, I had lived
Her time to a minute.*

* * * * * * * *

* All the several parts of the dreadful apparatus with which the Duchess's death is usher'd in, are not more remote from the conceptions of ordinary vengeance, than the strange character of suffering which they seem to bring upon their victims, is beyond the imagination of ordinary poets. As they are not like inflictions *of this life*, so her language seems *not of this world.* She has lived among horrors till she is become " native and endowed unto that element." She speaks the dialect of despair, her tongue has a snatch of Tartarus and the souls in bale.—What are " Luke's iron crown," the brazen bull of Perillus, Procrustes' bed, to the waxen images which counterfeit death, to the wild masque of madmen, the tomb-maker, the bellman, the living person's dirge, the mortification by degrees ! To move a horror skilfully, to touch a soul to the quick, to lay upon fear as much as it can bear, to wean and weary a life till it is ready to drop, and then step in with mortal instruments to take its last forfeit : this only a Webster can do. Writers of an inferior genius may " upon horror's head horrors accumulate," but they cannot do this. They mistake quantity for quality ; they " terrify babes with painted devils," but they know not how a soul is capable of being moved ; their terrors want dignity, their affrightments are without decorum.

Single Life.

O fie upon this single life: forego it.
We read how Daphne, for her peevish flight,
Became a fruitless bay-tree: Syrinx turn'd
To the pale empty reed: Anaxarate
Was frozen into marble; whereas those
Which married, or prov'd kind unto their friends,
Were, by a gracious influence, trans-shap'd
Into the olive, pomgranate, mulberry;
Became flowers, precious stones, or eminent stars.

Fable.

Upon a time, Reputation, Love, and Death,
Would travel o'er the world: and 'twas concluded
That they should part, and take three several ways.
Death told them, they should find him in great battles,
Or cities plagued with plagues: Love gives them counsel
To inquire for him 'mongst unambitious shepherds,
Where dowries were not talked of; and sometimes,
'Mongst quiet kindred that had nothing left
By their dead parents: stay, quoth Reputation;
Do not forsake me, for it is my nature,
If once I part from any man I meet,
I am never found again.

Another.

A Salmon, as she swam unto the sea,
Met with a Dog-fish; who encounters her
With his rough language; why art thou so bold
To mix thyself with our high state of floods?
Being no eminent courtier, but one
That for the calmest and fresh time of the year
Dost live in shallow rivers, rank'st thyself
With silly Smelts and Shrimps:—and darest thou
Pass by our Dog-ship without reverence?
O (quoth the Salmon) sister, be at peace,
Thank Jupiter we both have past the net.
Our value never can be truly known,
Till in the fisher's basket we be shown:

In the market then my price may be the higher;
Even when I am nearest to the cook and fire.
So to great men the moral may be stretched:
Men oft are valued high when they are most wretched.

THE WHITE DEVIL: OR, VITTORIA COROMBONA, A LADY OF VENICE. A TRAGEDY. BY JOHN WEBSTER.*

The arraignment of Vittoria.—Paulo Giordano Ursini, Duke of Brachiano, for the love of Vittoria Corombona, a Venetian Lady, and at her suggestion, causes her husband Camillo to be murdered. Suspicion falls upon Vittoria, who is tried at Rome, on a double charge of Murder and Incontinence, in the presence of Cardinal Monticelso, Cousin to the deceased Camillo; Francisco de Medicis, Brother-in-Law to Brachiano; the Ambassadors of France, Spain, England, &c. As the arraignment is beginning, the Duke confidently enters the Court.

Mon. Forbear, my Lord, here is no place assign'd you:
This business, by his holiness, is left
To our examination.

* The Author's Dedication to this Play is so modest, yet so conscious of self-merit withal, he speaks so frankly of the deservings of others, and by implication insinuates his own deserts so ingenuously, that I cannot forbear inserting it, as a specimen how a man may praise himself gracefully and commend others without suspicion of envy.

"To the Reader.

"In publishing this Tragedy, I do but challenge to myself that liberty which other men have taken before me; not that I affect praise by it, for *nos hæc novimus esse nihil;* only since it was acted in so open and black a theatre, that it wanted (that which is the only grace and setting out of a tragedy) a full and understanding auditory; and that, since that time I have noted most of the people that come to that play-house resemble those ignorant asses (who, visiting stationers' shops, their use is not to inquire for good books, but new books) I present it to the general view with this confidence,

Nec rhoncos metues malignorum
Nec scombris tunicas dabis molestas.

If it be objected this is no true dramatic poem, I shall easily confess it, *non potes in nugas dicere plura meas, ipse ego quam dixi;* willingly, and not ignorantly, have I faulted. For should a man present, to such an auditory, the most sententious tragedy that ever was written, observing all the critical

Bra. May it thrive with you.
Fra. A chair there for his lordship. [*Lays a rich gown under him*
Bra. Forbear your kindness; an unbidden guest
Should travel as Dutch women go to church,
Bear their stool with them.
Mon. At your pleasure, Sir,
Stand to the table, gentlewoman.—Now, Signior,
Fall to your plea.
Lawyer. *Domine judex converte oculos in hanc pestem mulierum corruptissimam.*
Vit. What 's he?
Fra. A lawyer, that pleads against you.
Vit. Pray, my Lord, let him speak his usual tongue,
I 'll make no answer else.
Fra. Why, you understand Latin.

laws, as height of style, and gravity of person, enrich it with the sententious chorus, and, as it were, enliven death, in the passionate and weighty Nuntius: yet after all this divine rapture, *O dura messorum ilia*, the breath that comes from the uncapable multitude is able to poison it; and ere it be acted, let the author resolve to fix to every scene this of Horace:

—— *Hæc hodie porcis comedenda relinques.*

"To those who report I was a long time in finishing this Tragedy, I confess, I do not write with a goose-quill wing'd with two feathers: and if they will needs make it my fault, I must answer them with that of Euripides to Alcestides, a tragic writer: Alcestides objecting that Euripides had only, in three days, composed three verses, whereas himself had written three hundred: Thou tell'st truth (quoth he); but here's the difference, thine shall only be read for three days, whereas mine shall continue three ages.

"Detraction is the sworn friend to ignorance: for mine own part, I have ever truly cherish'd my good opinion of other men's worthy labors, especially of that full and heighten'd stile of Master Chapman, the labor'd and understanding works of Master Jonson, the no less worthy composures of the both worthily excellent Master Beaumont and Master Fletcher; and lastly (without wrong last to be named), the right happy and copious industry of Master Shakspeare, Master Decker, and Master Heywood, wishing what I write may be read by their light; protesting, that in the strength of mine own judgment, I know them so worthy, that tho' I rest silent in my own work, yet to most of theirs, I dare (without flattery) to fix that of Martial: *non norunt hæc monumenta mori.*"

Vit. I do, Sir, but amongst this auditory
Which come to hear my cause, the half or more
May be ignorant in 't.
Mon. Go on, Sir.
Vit. By your favor,
I will not have my accusation clouded
In a strange tongue: all this assembly
Shall hear what you can charge me with.
Fra. Signior,
You need not stand on 't much; pray, change your language.
Mon. Oh, for God's sake! gentlewoman, your credit
Shall be more famous by it.
Law. Well then have at you.
Vit. I am the mark, Sir, I 'll give aim to you,
And tell you how near you shoot.
Law. Most literated judges, please your lordships
So to connive your judgments to the view
Of this debauch'd and diversivolent woman:
Who such a concatenation
Of mischief hath effected, that to extirp
The memory of it, must be the consummation
Of her and her projections.
Vit. What 's all this?
Law. Hold your peace!
Exorbitant sins must have exulceration.
Vit. Surely, my Lords, this lawyer hath swallowed
Some apothecaries bills, or proclamations;
And now the hard and undigestible words
Come up like stones we use give hawks for physic.
Why, this is Welch to Latin.
Law. My Lords, the woman
Knows not her tropes, nor is perfect
In the academick derivation
Of grammatical elocution
Fra. Sir, your pains
Shall be well spared, and your deep eloquence
Be worthily applauded among those
Which understand you.

Law. My good Lord.

Fra. Sir,
Put up your papers in your fustian bag;
[FRANCISCO *speaks this as in scorn.*
Cry mercy, Sir, 'tis buckram, and accept
My notion of your learn'd verbosity.

Law. I most graduatically thank your lordship;
I shall have use for them elsewhere.

Mon. (*to* VITTORIA.) I shall be plainer with you, and paint out
Your follies in more natural red and white,
Than that upon your cheek.

Vit. O you mistake,
You raise a blood as noble in this cheek
As ever was your mother's.

Mon. I must spare you, till proof cry whore to that.
Observe this creature here, my honor'd Lords,
A woman of a most prodigious spirit.

Vit. My honorable Lord,
It doth not suit a reverend Cardinal
To play the Lawyer thus.

Mon. Oh your trade instructs your language.
You see, my Lords, what goodly fruit she seems,
Yet like those apples travellers report
To grow where Sodom and Gomorrah stood,
I will but touch her, and you straight shall see
She'll fall to soot and ashes.

Vit. Your invenom'd apothecary should do 't.

Mon. I am resolved,
Were there a second paradise to lose,
This devil would betray it.

Vit. O poor charity,
Thou art seldom found in scarlet.

Mon. Who knows not how, when several night by night
Her gates were choakt with coaches, and her rooms
Outbrav'd the stars with several kinds of lights;
When she did counterfeit a Prince's court
In music, banquets, and most riotous surfeits;
This whore forsooth was holy.

Vit. Ha! whore? what's that?

Mon. Shall I expound whore to you? sure I shall.
I'll give their perfect character. They are first,
Sweetmeats which rot the eater: In man's nostrils
Poison'd perfumes. They are cozening alchymy;
Shipwrecks in calmest weather. What are whores?
Cold Russian winters, that appear so barren,
As if that nature had forgot the spring.
They are the true material fire of hell.
Worse than those tributes i' th' low countries paid,
Exactions upon meat, drink, garments, sleep;
Ay even on man's perdition, his sin.
They are those brittle evidences of law,
Which forfeit all a wretched man's estate
For leaving out one syllable. What are whores?
They are those flattering bells have all one tune,
At weddings and at funerals. Your rich whores
Are only treasuries by extortion fill'd,
And empty'd by curs'd riot. They are worse,
Worse than dead bodies, which are begg'd at th' gallows,
And wrought upon by surgeons, to teach man
Wherein he is imperfect. What's a whore?
She's like the guilt counterfeited coin,
Which, whosoe'er first stamps it, brings in trouble
All that receive it.

Vit. This character 'scapes me.

Mon. You, gentlewoman?
Take from all beasts and from all minerals
Their deadly poison—

Vit. Well, what then?

Mon. I'll tell thee;
I'll find in thee an apothecary's shop,
To sample them all.

Fr. Emb. She hath lived ill.

En. Emb. True, but the Cardinal's too bitter,

Mon. You know what whore is. Next the devil adult'ry,
Enters the devil murder.

Fra. Your unhappy husband
Is dead.
Vit. O he 's a happy husband,
Now he owes Nature nothing.
Fra. And by a vaulting engine.
Mon. An active plot:
He jumpt into his grave.
Fra. What a prodigy was 't,
That from some two yards high, a slender man
Should break his neck?
Mon. I' th' rushes!
Fra. And what 's more,
Upon the instant lose all use of speech,
All vital motion, like a man had lain
Wound up three days. Now mark each circumstance.
Mon. And look upon this creature was his wife.
She comes not like a widow: she comes arm'd
With scorn and impudence: is this a mourning-habit?
Vit. Had I foreknown his death as you suggest,
I would have bespoke my mourning.
Mon. O you are cunning!
Vit. You shame your wit and judgment,
To call it so; what, is my just defence
By him that is my judge call'd impudence?
Let me appeal then from this christian court
To the uncivil Tartar.
Mon. See, my lords,
She scandals our proceedings.
Vit. Humbly thus,
Thus low, to the most worthy and respected
Leiger embassadors, my modesty
And woman-hood I tender; but withall,
So entangled in a cursed accusation,
That my defence, of force, like Perseus,
Must personate masculine virtue. To the point.
Find me but guilty, sever head from body,
We 'll part good friends: I scorn to hold my life
At yours, or any man's intreaty, Sir.

En. Emb. She hath a brave spirit.
Mon. Well, well, such counterfeit jewels
Make true ones oft suspected.
Vit. You are deceived;
For know, that all your strict combined heads,
Which strike against this mine of diamonds,
Shall prove but glassen hammers, they shall break.
These are but feigned shadows of my evils.
Terrify babes, my Lord, with painted devils;
I am past such needless palsy. For your names
Of whore and murdress, they proceed from you,
As if a man should spit against the wind
The filth returns in 's face.
Mon. Pray you, mistress, satisfy me one question:
Who lodg'd beneath your roof that fatal night
Your husband brake his neck?
Bra. That question
Inforceth me break silence; I was there.
Mon. Your business?
Bra. Why, I came to comfort her,
And take some course for settling her estate,
Because I heard her husband was in debt
To you, my Lord.
Mon. He was.
Bra. And 'twas strangely fear'd
That you would cozen her.
Mon. Who made you overseer?
Bra. Why, my charity, my charity, which should flow
From every generous and noble spirit,
To orphans and to widows.
Mon. Your lust.
Bra. Cowardly dogs bark loudest! sirrah, priest,
I'll talk with you hereafter.——Do you hear?
The sword you frame of such an excellent temper,
I'll sheath in your own bowels.
There are a number of thy coat resemble
Your common post-boys.
Mon. Ha!

Bra. Your mercenary post-boys.
Your letters carry truth, but 'tis your guise
To fill your mouths with gross and impudent lies.
Servant. My Lord, your gown.
Bra. Thou liest, 'twas my stool.
Bestow 't upon thy master, that will challenge
The rest o' th' household stuff, for Brachiano
Was ne'er so beggarly to take a stool
Out of another's lodging: let him make
Vallance for his bed on't, or demy foot-cloth
For his most reverend moile. Monticelso, *nemo me impune lacessit.* [*Exit* BRACHIANO.
Mon. Your champion's gone.
Vit. The wolf may prey the better.
Fra. My Lord, there's great suspicion of the murder,
But no sound proof who did it. For my part,
I do not think she hath a soul so black
To act a deed so bloody: if she have,
As in cold countries husband-men plant vines,
And with warm blood manure them, even so
One summer she will bear unsavory fruit,
And ere next spring wither both branch and root.
The act of blood let pass, only descend
To matter of incontinence.
Vit. I discern poison
Under your gilded pills.
Mon. Now the Duke's gone I will produce a letter,
Wherein twas plotted, he and you shall meet,
At an apothecary's summer-house,
Down by the river Tiber. View 't, my Lords;
Where after wanton bathing and the heat
Of a lascivious banquet.—I pray read it.—
I shame to speak the rest.
Vit. Grant I was tempted;
Temptation proves not the act:
Casta est quam nemo rogavit.
You read his hot love to me, but you want
My frosty answer.

Mon. Frost i' th' dog-days! strange!
Vit. Condemn you me for that the Duke did love me;
So may you blame some fair and crystal river
For that some melancholic distracted man
Hath drown'd himself in 't.
Mon. Truly drown'd, indeed.
Vit. Sum up my faults, I pray, and you shall find,
That beauty and gay clothes, a merry heart,
And a good stomach to feast, are all,
All the poor crimes that you can charge me with.
In faith, my Lord, you might go pistol flies,
The sport would be more noble.
Mon. Very good.
Vit. But take you your course, it seems you've begg'd me first,
And now would fain undo me. I have houses,
Jewels, and a poor remnant of crusadoes;
Would these would make you charitable.
Mon. If the devil
Did ever take good shape, behold his picture.
Vit. You have one virtue left,
You will not flatter me.
Fra. Who brought this letter?
Vit. I am not compell'd to tell you.
Mon. My Lord Duke sent to you a thousand ducats,
The twelfth of August.
Vit. 'Twas to keep your cousin*
From prison, I paid use for 't.
Mon. I rather think,
'Twas interest for his lust.
Vit. Who says so but yourself? if you be my accuser,
Pray cease to be my judge; come from the bench,
Give in your evidence against me, and let these
Be moderators. My Lord Cardinal,
Were your intelligencing ears as loving,
As to my thoughts, had you an honest tongue,
I would not care though you proclaim'd them all.
Mon. Go to, go to.

* Her husband Camillo, who was cousin to Monticelso.

After your goodly and vain-glorious banquet,
I 'll give you a choak-pear.
Vit. Of your own grafting?
Mon. You were born in Venice, honorably descended
From the Vittelli; 'twas my cousin's fate,
Ill may I name the hour, to marry you;
He bought you of your father.
Vit. Ha!
Mon. He spent there in six months
Twelve thousand ducats, and (to my knowledge)
Receiv'd in dowry with you not one julio.
'Twas a hard penny-worth, the ware being so light.
I yet but draw the curtain, now to your picture:
You came from thence a most notorious strumpet,
And so you have continued.
Vit. My Lord!
Mon. Nay hear me,
You shall have time to prate. My Lord Brachiano——
Alas! I make but repetition,
Of what is ordinary and Ryalto talk,
And ballated, and would be plaid o' th' stage
But that vice many times finds such loud friends,
That preachers are charm'd silent.
Your public fault,
Join'd to th' condition of the present time,
Takes from you all the fruits of noble pity,
Such a corrupted trial have you made
Both of your life and beauty, and been styl'd
No less an ominous fate, than blazing stars
To Princes. Hear your sentence; you are confin
Unto a house of converts.
Vit. A house of converts! what's that?
Mon. A house of penitent whores.
Vit. Do the Noblemen in Rome
Erect it for their wives, that I am sent
To lodge there?
Fra. You must have patience.
Vit. I must first have vengeance.

I fain would know if you have your salvation
By patent, that you proceed thus.
Mon. Away with her,
Take her hence.
Vit. A rape! a rape!
Mon. How?
Vit. Yes, you have ravish'd justice;
Forc'd her to do your pleasure.
Mon. Fie, she 's mad!
Vit. Die with those pills in your most cursed maw,
Should bring you health! or while you set o' th' bench,
Let your own spittle choak you!
Mon. She's turn'd fury.
Vit. That the last day of judgment may so find you,
And leave you the same Devil you were before!
Instruct me some good horse-leach to speak treason,
For since you cannot take my life for deeds,
Take it for words: O woman's poor revenge!
Which dwells but in the tongue. I will not weep.
No; I do scorn to call up one poor tear
To fawn on your injustice; bear me hence
Unto this house of —— what's your mitigating title?
Mon. Of converts.
Vit. It shall not be a house of converts;
My mind shall make it honester to me
Than the Pope's palace, and more peaceable
Than thy soul, though thou art a Cardinal,
Know this, and let it somewhat raise your spight,
Through darkness diamonds spread their richest light.*

* This White Devil of Italy sets off a bad cause so speciously, and pleads with such an innocence-resembling boldness, that we seem to see that matchless beauty of her face which inspires such gay confidence into her; and are ready to expect, when she has done her pleadings, that her very judges, her accusers, the grave ambassadors who sit as spectators, and all the court, will rise and make proffer to defend her in spite of the utmost conviction of her guilt; as the shepherds in Don Quixote make proffer to follow the beautiful shepherdess Marcela "without reaping any profi out of her manifest resolution made there in their hearing."—

So sweet and lovely does she make the shame,
Which, like a canker in the fragrant rose,
Does spot the beauty of her budding name!

Marcello and Flamineo, Sons to Cornelia, having quarrelled; Flamineo slays his brother Marcello, their mother being present.

CORNELIA. MARCELLO.

Cor. I hear a whispering all about the court,
You are to fight: who is your opposite?
What is the quarrel?
Mar. 'Tis an idle rumor.
Cor. Will you dissemble? sure you do not well
To fright me thus: you never look thus pale,
But when you are most angry. I do charge you,
Upon my blessing; nay I'll call the Duke,
And he shall school you.
Mar. Publish not a fear,
Which would convert to laughter: 'tis not so.
Was not this crucifix my father's?
Cor. Yes.
Mar. I have heard you say, giving my brother suck,
He took the crucifix between his hands,
And broke a limb off.
Cor. Yes; but 'tis mended.

FLAMINEO *enters.*

Fla. I have brought your weapon back.
[FLAMINEO *runs* MARCELLO *through.*
Cor. Ha, oh my horror!
Mar. You have brought it home, indeed.
Cor. Help, oh he's murder'd!
Fla. Do you turn your gall up? I'll to the sanctuary,
And send a surgeon to you. [*Exit* FLAM.

HORTENSIUS (*an Officer*) *enters.*

Hor. How, o' th' ground?
Mar. O mother, now remember what I told
Of breaking off the crucifix. Farewell.
There are some sins, which heaven doth duly punish
In a whole family. This it is to rise
By all dishonest means. Let all men know,

That tree shall long time keep a steady foot,
Whose branches spread no wider than the root.

Cor. O my perpetual sorrow!

Hor. Virtuous Marcello!
He's dead. Pray leave him, lady: come, you shall.

Cor. Alas! he is not dead; he's in a trance.
Why, here's nobody shall get anything by his death.
Let me call him again, for God's sake!

Hor. I would you were deceived.

Cor. O you abuse me, you abuse me, you abuse me!
How many have gone away thus, for lack of 'tendance!
Rear up 's head, rear up 's head; his bleeding inward will kill him.

Hor. You see he is departed.

Cor. Let me come to him; give me him as he is; if he be turn'd to earth, let me but give him one hearty kiss, and you shall put us both into one coffin. Fetch a looking-glass, see if his breath will not stain it; or pull out some feathers from my pillow, and lay them to his lips. will you lose him for a little pains taking?

Hor. Your kindest office is to pray for him.

Cor. Alas! I would not pray for him yet. He may live to lay me i' th' ground, and pray for me, if you'll let me come to him.

The Duke *enters with* Flamineo, *and* Page.

Bra. Was this your handy-work?

Fla. It was my misfortune.

Cor. He lies, he lies; he did not kill him: these have kill'd him, that would not let him be better look'd to.

Bra. Have comfort, my griev'd mother.

Cor. O yon' screech-owl!

Hor. Forbear, good Madam.

Cor. Let me go, let me go.

[*She runs to* Flamineo *with her knife drawn, and coming to him, lets it fall.*

The God of heaven forgive thee. Dost not wonder
I pray for thee? I'll tell thee what's the reason;

I have scarce breath to number twenty minutes;
I'd not spend that in cursing. Fare thee well:
Half of thyself lies there: and may'st thou live
To fill an hour-glass with his moulder'd ashes,
To tell how thou should'st spend the time to come
In blest repentance.
Bra. Mother, pray tell me
How came he by his death? what was the quarrel?
Cor. Indeed, my younger boy presum'd too much
Upon his manhood, gave him bitter words,
Drew his sword first; and so, I know not how,
For I was out of my wits, he fell with 's head
Just in my bosom.
Page. This is not true, Madam.
Cor. I pr'ythee peace.
One arrow 's graz'd already: it were vain
To lose this, for that will ne'er be found again.

* * * * * *
* * * * * *

FRANCISCO *describes to* FLAMINEO *the grief of* CORNELIA *at the funeral of* MARCELLO.

Your reverend Mother
Is grown a very old woman in two hours.
I found them winding of Marcello's corse;
And there is such a solemn melody,
'Tween doleful songs, tears, and sad elegies:
Such as old grandames, watching by the dead,
Were wont to outwear the nights with; that, believe me,
I had no eyes to guide me forth the room,
They were so o'ercharg'd with water.

Funeral Dirge for Marcello.

[*His mother sings it.*

Call for the Robin-red-breast and the Wren,
Since o'er shady groves they hover,
And with leaves and flowers do cover
The friendless bodies of unburied men.

Call unto his funeral dole
The Ant, the Field-mouse, and the Mole,
To raise him hillocks that shall keep him warm,
And (when gay tombs are robb'd) sustain no harm;
But keep the wolf far thence, that's foe to men,
For with his nails he'll dig them up again.*

Folded Thoughts.

Come, come, my Lord, unite your folded thoughts,
And let them dangle loose as a bride's hair.
Your sister 's poison'd.

Dying Princes.

To see what solitariness is about dying Princes! As heretofore they have unpeopled towns, divorced friends, and made great houses unhospitable! so now, O justice! where are their flatterers now? flatterers are but the shadows of princes' bodies, the least thick cloud makes them invisible.

Natural Death.

O thou soft natural death! that art joint twin
To sweetest slumber!—no rough-bearded Comet
Stares on thy mild departure; the dull Owl
Beats not against thy casement; the hoarse Wolf
Scents not thy carrion. Pity winds thy corse,
Whilst horror waits on princes' ——

Vow of Murder rebuked.

Miserable creature,
If thou persist in this 'tis damnable.
Dost thou imagine thou canst slide on blood,
And not be tainted with a shameful fall?
Or like the black and melancholic yew-tree,
Dost think to root thyself in dead men's graves
And yet to prosper! ——

* I never saw anything like this Dirge, except the Ditty which reminds Ferdinand of his drowned father in the Tempest. As that is of the water, watery; so this is of the earth, earthy. Both have that intenseness of feeling, which seems to resolve itself into the elements which it contemplates.

Dying Man.

See see how firmly he doth fix his eyes
Upon the crucifix.
Oh hold it constant.
It settles his wild spirits: and so his eyes
Melt into tears.

Despair.

O the cursed Devil,
Which doth present us with all other sins
Thrice candied o'er; despair, with gall and stibium,
Yet we carouse it off.

END OF PART I.

TABLE OF REFERENCE TO THE EXTRACTS.

FRANCIS BEAUMONT AND JOHN FLETCHER.

JOHN FLETCHER.

PHILIP MASSINGER.

PHILIP MASSINGER AND THOMAS DECKER.

PHILIP MASSINGER AND NATHANIEL FIELD.

PHILIP MASSINGER, THOMAS MIDDLETON, AND WILLIAM ROWLEY.

GEORGE CHAPMAN AND JAMES SHIRLEY.

JAMES SHIRLEY.

SPECIMENS

OF

ENGLISH DRAMATIC POETS.

THE LOVER'S MELANCHOLY. BY JOHN FORD.

Contention of a Bird and a Musician.

Passing from Italy to Greece, the tales
Which poets of an elder time have feign'd
To glorify their Tempe, bred in me
Desire of visiting that paradise.
To Thessaly I came, and living private,
Without acquaintance of more sweet companions
Than the old inmates to my love, my thoughts,
I day by day frequented silent groves,
And solitary walks. One morning early
This accident encounter'd me: I heard
The sweetest and most ravishing contention
That art or nature ever were at strife in.
A sound of music touch'd mine ears, or rather
Indeed entranc'd my soul: as I stole nearer,
Invited by the melody, I saw
This youth, this fair fac'd youth, upon his lute
With strains of strange variety and harmony
Proclaiming (as it seem'd) so bold a challenge
To the clear quiristers of the woods, the birds,
That as they flocked about him, all stood silent
Wond'ring at what they heard. I wonder'd too.
A Nightingale,

Nature's best skill'd musician, undertakes
The challenge; and, for every several strain
The well-shap'd youth could touch, she sung her down;
He could not run division with more art
Upon his quaking instrument, than she
The nightingale did with her various notes
Reply to.
Some time thus spent, the young man grew at last
Into a pretty anger; that a bird,
Whom art had never taught cliffs, moods, or notes,
Should vie with him for mastery, whose study
Had busied many hours to perfect practice:
To end the controversy, in a rapture,
Upon his instrument he plays so swiftly,
So many voluntaries, and so quick,
That there was curiosity and cunning,
Concord in discord, lines of diff'ring method
Meeting in one full centre of delight.
The bird (ordained to be
Music's first martyr) strove to imitate
These several sounds: which when her warbling throat
Fail'd in, for grief down dropt she on his lute
And brake her heart. It was the quaintest sadness,
To see the conqueror upon her hearse
To weep a funeral elegy of tears.
He looks upon the trophies of his art,
Then sigh'd, then wiped his eyes, then sigh'd, and cried.
" Alas, poor creature, I will soon revenge
This cruelty upon the author of it.
Henceforth this lute, guilty of innocent blood,
Shall never more betray a harmless peace
To an untimely end;" and in that sorrow,
As he was pashing it against a tree,
I suddenly stept in.

[This Story, which is originally to be met with in Strada's Prolusions, has been paraphrased in rhyme by Crashaw, Ambrose Phillips, and others. but none of those versions can at all compare for harmony and grace with this blank verse of Ford's; It is as fine as anything in Beaumont and Fletcher; and almost equals the strife which it celebrates.]

THE LADIES TRIAL. BY JOHN FORD.

Auria, in the possession of Honors, Preferment, Fame, can find no peace in his mind while he thinks his Wife unchaste.

AURIA. AURELIO.

Auria. Count of Savona, Genoa's Admiral,
Lord Governor of Corsica, enroll'd
A Worthy of my country, sought and sued to,
Prais'd, courted, flatter'd !—
—————————— My triumphs
Are echoed under every roof, the air
Is streightned with the sound, there is not room
Enough to brace them in ; but not a thought
Doth pierce into the grief that cabins here :
Here through a creek, a little inlet, crawls
A flake no bigger than a sister's thread,
Which sets the region of my heart a fire.
I had a kingdom once, but am depos'd
From all that royalty of blest content,
By a confed'racy 'twixt love and frailty.
Aurelio. Glories in public view but add to misery,
Which travails in unrest at home.
Auria. At home !
That home, Aurelio speaks of, I have lost :
And which is worse, when I have roll'd about,
Toil'd like a pilgrim, round this globe of earth,
Wearied with care, and over-worn with age,
Lodg'd in the grave, I am not yet at home.
There rots but half of me : the other part
Sleeps, heaven knows where. Would she and I, my wife
I mean, but what, alas, talk I of wife ?
The woman, would we had together fed
On any out-cast parings coarse and mouldy,
Not liv'd divided thus !

LOVE'S SACRIFICE; A TRAGEDY. BY JOHN FORD.

Biancha, Wife to Caraffa, Duke of Pavia, loves and is loved by Fernando the Duke's favorite. She long resists his importunate suit; at length she enters the room where he is sleeping and awakens him, to hear her confession of her love for him.

BIANCHA. FERDINAND, *sleeping*.

Bian. Resolve, and do; 'tis done. What, are those eyes,
Which lately were so over-drown'd in tears,
So easy to take rest? O happy man,
How sweetly sleep hath seal'd up sorrows here!
But I will call him: what, my Lord, my Lord,
My Lord Fernando ——
Fer. Who calls?
Bian. My Lord:
Sleeping, or waking?
Fer. Ha, who is 't?
Bian. 'Tis I:
Have you forgot my voice? or is your ear
But useful to your eye?
Fer. Madam the Duchess!
Bian. She, 'tis she; sit up:
Sit up and wonder, whiles my sorrow swell:
The nights are short and I have much to say.
Fer. Is 't possible 'tis you?
Bian. 'Tis possible:
Why do you think I come?
Fer. Why? to crown joys,
And make me master of my best desires.
Bian. 'Tis true, you guess aright; sit up and listen.
With shame and passion now I must confess,
Since first mine eyes beheld you, in my heart
You have been only king. If there can be
A violence in love, then I have felt
That tyranny; be record to my soul
The justice which I for this folly fear.
Fernando, in short words, howe'er my tongue
Did often chide thy love, each word thou spak'st

Was music to my ear : was never poor
Poor wretched woman liv'd, that lov'd like me ;
So truly, so unfeignedly.
Fer. Oh Madam——
Bian. To witness that I speak is truth, look here ;
Thus singly I adventure to thy bed,
And do confess my weakness : if thou tempt'st
My bosom to thy pleasures, I will yield.
Fer. Perpetual happiness !
Bian. Now hear me out :
When first Caraffa, Pavy's Duke, my Lord
Saw me, he lov'd me, and (without respect
Of dower) took me to his bed and bosom,
Advanc'd me to the titles I possess,
Not mov'd by counsel, or remov'd by greatness
Which to requite, betwixt my soul and heaven
I vow'd a vow to live a constant wife.
I have done so : nor was there in the world
A man created, could have broke that truth,
For all the glories of the earth, but thou,
But thou, Fernando. Do I love thee now ?
Fer. Beyond imagination.
Bian. True, I do,
Beyond imagination : if no pledge
Of love can instance what I speak is true,
But loss of my best joys, here, here, Fernando,
Be satisfied and ruin me.
Fer. What do you mean ?
Bian. To give my body up to thy embraces ;
A pleasure that I never wish'd to thrive in
Before this fatal minute : mark me now ;
If thou dost spoil me of this robe of shame,
By my best comforts here, I vow again,
To thee, to heaven, to the world, to time,
Ere yet the morning shall new christen day,
I 'll kill myself.
Fer. How, Madam, how ?
Bian. I will :

Do what thou wilt, 'tis in thy choice; what say ye?
Fer. Pish, do you come to try me? tell me first,
Will you but grant a kiss?
Bian. Yes, take it; that,
Or what thy heart can wish: I am all thine.
Fer. Oh me——come, come, how many women, pray,
Were ever heard or read of, granted love,
And did as you protest you will?
Bian. Fernando! [*Kneels.*
Jest not at my calamity: I kneel:
By these dishevel'd hairs, these wretched tears,
By all that 's good, if what I speak, my heart
Vows not eternally; then think, my Lord,
Was never man sued to me I denied,
Think me a common and most cunning whore,
And let my sins be written on my grave,
My name rest in reproof. Do as you list.
Fer. I must believe ye; yet I hope anon,
When you are parted from me, you will say
I was a good cold easy-spirited man,
Nay, laugh at my simplicity: say, will ye?
Bian. No; by the faith I owe my bridal vows:
But ever hold thee much much dearer far
Than all my joys on earth; by this chaste kiss.
Fer. You have prevailed: and heaven forbid that I
Should by a wanton appetite profane
This sacred temple. 'Tis enough for me,
You'll please to call me servant.
Bian. Nay, be thine:
Command my power, my bosom, and I'll write
This love within the tables of my heart.
Fer. Enough: I'll master passion, and triumph
In being conquer'd, adding to it this,
In you my love as it begun shall end.
Bian. The latter I new vow——but day comes on:
What now we leave unfinish'd of content,
Each hour shall perfect up. Sweet, let us part.
Fer. Best Life, good rest.

THE CHRONICLE HISTORY OF PERKIN WARBECK. BY JOHN FORD.

Perkin Warbeck and his Followers are by Lord Dawbney presented to King Henry as Prisoners.

Dawb. Life to the King, and safety fix his throne.
I here present you, royal Sir, a shadow
Of majesty, but in effect a substance
Of pity; a young man, in nothing grown
To ripeness, but th' ambition of your mercy:
Perkin; the christian world's strange wonder!
King H. Dawbney,
We observe no wonder; I behold ('tis true)
An ornament of nature, fine, and polisht,
A handsome youth indeed, but not admire him.
How came he to thy hands?
Dawb. From sanctuary
At Bewley, near Southampton; registred,
With these few followers, for persons privileged.
King H. I must not thank you, Sir; you were to blame
To infringe the liberty of houses sacred:
Dare we be irreligious?
Dawb. Gracious Lord,
They voluntarily resign'd themselves,
Without compulsion.
King H. So? 'twas very well;
'Twas very well. Turn now thine eyes,
Young man, upon thyself and thy past actions.
What revels in combustion through our kingdom
A frenzy of aspiring youth hath danced:
Till wanting breath, thy feet of pride have slipt
To break thy neck.
Warb. But not my heart: my heart
Will mount, till every drop of blood be frozen
By death's perpetual winter. If the sun
Of majesty be darkned, let the sun
Of life be hid from me, in an eclipse
Lasting, and universal. Sir; remember,

There was a shooting in of light, when Richmond
(Not aiming at the crown) retired, and gladly,
For comfort to the Duke of Bretagne's Court.
Richard, who sway'd the sceptre, was reputed
A tyrant then; yet then, a dawning glimmer'd
To some few wand'ring remnants, promising day,
When first they ventur'd on a frightful shore,
At Milford Haven.
Dawb. Whither speeds his boldness?
Check his rude tongue, great Sir.
King H. O let him range:
The player 's on the stage still; 'tis his part:
He does but act.——What follow'd?
Warb. Bosworth field:
Where at an instant, to the world's amazement,
A morn to Richmond and a night to Richard
Appear'd at once. The tale is soon applied:
Fate which crown'd these attempts, when least assured,
Might have befriended others, like resolved.
King H. A pretty gallant! thus your Aunt of Burgundy,
Your Duchess Aunt, inform'd her nephew; so
The lesson prompted, and well conn'd, was moulded
Into familiar dialogue, oft rehears'd,
Till, learnt by heart, 'tis now received for truth.
Warb. Truth in her pure simplicity wants art
To put a feigned blush on; scorn wears only
Such fashion, as commends to gazers' eyes
Sad ulcerated novelty, far beneath
The sphere of majesty: in such a court
Wisdom and gravity are proper robes,
By which the sovereign is best distinguish'd
From zanies to his greatness.
King H. Sirrah, shift
Your antick pageantry, and now appear
In your own nature; or you 'll taste the danger
Of fooling out of season.
Warb. I expect
No less than what severity calls justice,

And politicians safety ; let such beg,
As feed on alms : but if there can be mercy
In a protested enemy, then may it
Descend to these poor creatures,* whose engagements
To the bettering of their fortunes, have incurr'd
A loss of all : to them if any charity
Flow from some noble orator, in death
I owe the fee of thankfulness.
King H. So brave ?
What a bold knave is this !
We trifle time with follies.
Urswick, command the Dukeling, and these fellows,
To Digby, the Lieutenant of the Tower :
With safety let them be convey'd to London.
It is our pleasure, no uncivil outrage,
Taunts, or abuse, be suffer'd to their persons :
They shall meet fairer law than they deserve.
Time may restore their wits, whom vain ambition
Hath many years distracted.
Warb. Noble thoughts
Meet freedom in captivity. The Tower :
Our childhood's dreadful nursery !
King H. Was ever so much impudence in forgery ?
The custom sure of being styl'd a King,
Hath fast'ned in his thoughts that he is such.

Warbeck is led to his Death.

Oxford. Look ye, behold your followers, appointed
To wait on ye in death.
Warb. Why, Peers of England,
We 'll lead 'em on courageously. I read
A triumph over tyranny upon
Their several foreheads. Faint not in the moment
Of victory ! our ends, and Warwick's head,
Innocent Warwick's head (for we are prologue
But to his tragedy), conclude the wonder
Of Henry's fears : and then the glorious race

* His Followers.

Of fourteen kings Plantagenets, determines
In this last issue male. Heaven be obey'd.
Impoverish time of its amazement, friends:
And we will prove as trusty in our payments,
As prodigal to nature in our debts.
Death! pish, 'tis but a sound; a name of air;
A minute's storm; or not so much; to tumble
From bed to bed, be massacred alive
By some physicians for a month or two,
In hope of freedom from a fever's torments,
Might stagger manhood; here, the pain is past
Ere sensibly 'tis felt. Be men of spirit;
Spurn coward passion: so illustrious mention
Shall blaze our names, and style us Kings o'er Death.

'TIS PITY SHE'S A WHORE: A TRAGEDY, BY JOHN FORD.

*Giovanni, a Young Gentleman of Parma, entertains an illicit love for his Sister. He asks counsel of Bonaventura, a Friar.**

FRIAR. GIOVANNI.

Friar. Dispute no more in this, for know, young man,
These are no school-points; nice philosophy
May tolerate unlikely arguments,
But heaven admits no jests! wits that presumed
On wit too much, by striving how to prove
There was no God, with foolish grounds of art,
Discover'd first the nearest way to hell;
And fill'd the world with devilish atheism.
Such questions, youth, are fond; far better 'tis
To bless the sun, than reason why it shines;
Yet he thou talk'st of is above the sun.
No more; I may not hear it.
Gio. Gentle father,

* The good Friar in this Play is evidently a Copy of Friar Lawrence in Romeo and Juliet. He is the same kind Physician to the Souls of his young Charges; but he has more desperate Patients to deal with.

To you have I unclasp'd my burthen'd soul,
Emptied the store-house of my thoughts and heart,
Made myself poor of secrets; have not left
Another word untold, which hath not spoke
All what I ever durst, or think, or know;
And yet is here the comfort I shall have?
Must I not do what all men else may, love?

Friar. Yes, you may love, fair son.

Gio. Must I not praise
That beauty which, if framed anew, the Gods
Would make a God of, if they had it there;
And kneel to it, as I do kneel to them?

Friar. Why, foolish madman!

Gio. Shall a peevish sound,
A customary form, from man to man,
Of brother and of sister, be a bar
'Twixt my perpetual happiness and me?

Friar. Have done, unhappy youth, for thou art lost.

Gio. No, father: in your eyes I see the change
Of pity and compassion: from your age,
As from a sacred oracle, distils
The life of counsel. Tell me, holy man,
What cure shall give me ease in these extremes?

Friar. Repentance, son, and sorrow for this sin:
For thou hast moved a majesty above
With thy unguarded almost blasphemy.

Gio. O do not speak of that, dear confessor.

Friar. Art thou, my son, that miracle of wit,
Who once within these three months wert esteem'd
A wonder of thine age throughout Bononia?
How did the university applaud
Thy government, behavior, learning, speech,
Sweetness, and all that could make up a man!
I was proud of my tutelage, and chose
Rather to leave my books than part with thee.
I did so; but the fruits of all my hopes
Are lost in thee, as thou art in thyself.
O Giovanni, hast thou left the schools

Of knowledge, to converse with lust and death ?
For death waits on thy lust.——Look through the world,
And thou shalt see a thousand faces shine
More glorious than this idol thou adorest.
Leave her and take thy choice ; 'tis much less sin :
Though in such games as those they lose that win.
Gio. It were more ease to stop the ocean
From flows and ebbs, than to dissuade my vows.
Friar. Then I have done, and in thy wilful flames
Already see thy ruin ! heaven is just.
Yet hear my counsel !
Gio. As a voice of life.
Friar. Hie to thy father's house, there lock thee fast
Alone within thy chamber, then fall down
On both thy knees, and grovel on the ground ;
Cry to thy heart, wash every word thou utter'st
In tears, and (if 't be possible) of blood :
Beg heaven to cleanse the leprosy of lust
That rots thy soul ; acknowledge what thou art,
A wretch, a worm, a nothing : weep, sigh, pray
Three times a day, and three times every night ;
For seven days' space do this, then, if thou find'st
No change in thy desires, return to me ;
I 'll think on remedy. Pray for thyself
At home, whilst I pray for thee here ; away.——
My blessing with thee——we have need to pray.

Giovanni discloses his Passion to his Sister Annabella.—They compare their unhappy Loves.

Anna. Do you mock me, or flatter me ?
[*He has been praising her beauty.*
Gio. If you would see a beauty more exact
Than art can counterfeit, or nature frame,
Look in your glass and there behold your own.
Anna. O you are a trim youth.
Gio. Here. [*Offers his dagger to her.*
Anna. What to do ?
Gio. And here 's my breast. Strike home,
Rip up my bosom ; there thou shalt behold

A heart, in which is writ the truth I speak.
Why stand you ?
Anna. Are you in earnest ?
Gio. Yes, most earnest.
You cannot love.
Anna. Whom ?
Gio. Me.——My tortur'd soul
Hath felt affliction in the heat of death.
O Annabella, I am quite undone.
The love of thee, my sister, and the view
Of thy immortal beauty, have untuned
All harmony both of my rest and life.
Why do you not strike ?
Anna. Forbid it, my just fears.
If this be true 'twere fitter I were dead.
Gio. True, Annabella ! 'tis no time to jest ;
I have too long suppress'd my hidden flames,
That almost have consum'd me : I have spent
Many a silent night in sighs and groans,
Ran over all my thoughts, despis'd my fate,
Reason'd against the reasons of my love,
Done all that smooth-cheek'd virtue could advise.
But found all bootless : 'tis my destiny
That you must either love, or I must die.
Anna. Comes this in sadness from you ?
Gio. Let some mischief
Befall me soon, if I dissemble aught.
Anna. You are my brother, Giovanni.
Gio. You
My sister, Annabella, I know this :
And could afford you instance why to love
So much the more for this.—

He gives some sophistical Reasons and resumes.

Must I now live or die ?
Anna. Live : thou hast won
The field, and never fought. What thou hast urg'd,
My captive heart had long ago resolv'd.

I blush to tell thee (but I tell thee now)
For every sigh that thou hast spent for me,
I have sigh'd ten ; for every tear shed twenty :
And not so much for that I lov'd, as that
I durst not say I lov'd, nor scarcely think it.
Gio. Let not this music be a dream, ye gods,
For pity's sake I beg ye.
Anna. On my knees, [*She kneels.*
Brother, even by our mother's dust, I charge you,
Do not betray me to your mirth or hate ;
Love me, or kill me, brother.
Gio. On my knees, [*He kneels.*
Sister, even by my mother's dust, I charge you,
Do not betray me to your mirth or hate ;
Love me, or kill me, sister.
Anna. You mean good sooth, then ?
Gio. In good truth I do ;
And so do you, I hope: say, I'm in earnest.
Anna. I'll swear it ; and I.
Gio. And I.
I would not change this minute for Elysium.

Annabella proves pregnant by her Brother. Sorano, her Husband, to whom she is newly married, discovers that she is pregnant, but cannot make her confess by whom. At length by means of Vasques, his servant, he comes to the truth of it. He feigns forgiveness and reconcile ment with his Wife: and makes a sumptuous Feast to which are invited Annabella's old Father, with Giovanni, and all the chief Citizens in Parma; meaning to entrap Giovanni by that bait to his death.- Annabella suspects his drift.

GIOVANNI. ANNABELLA.

Gio. What, chang'd so soon ?
——does the fit come on you, to prove treacherous
To your past vows and oaths ?
Anna. Why should you jest
At my calamity, without all sense
Of the approaching dangers you are in ?
Gio. What danger's half so great as thy revolt ?

Thou art a faithless sister, else thou know'st,
Malice or any treachery beside
Would stoop to my bent brows: why, I hold fate
Clasp'd in my fist, and could command the course
Of time's eternal motion, had'st thou been
One thought more steady than an ebbing sea.
Anna. Brother, dear brother, know what I have been;
And know that now there's but a dining time
'Twixt us and our confusion: let's not waste
These precious hours in vain and useless speech.
Alas, these gay attires were not put on
But to some end; this sudden solemn feast
Was not ordain'd to riot and expense;
I that have now been chamber'd here alone,
Barr'd of my guardian, or of any else,
Am not for nothing at an instant freed
To fresh access. Be not deceiv'd, my brother;
This banquet is a harbinger of death
To you and me; resolve yourself it is,
And be prepar'd to welcome it.
Gio. Well then,
The schoolmen teach that all this globe of earth
Shall be consumed to ashes in a minute.
Anna So I have read too.
Gio But 'twere somewhat strange
To see the waters burn. Could I believe
This might be true, I could believe as well
There might be hell or heaven.
Anna. That's most certain.——But
Good brother, for the present, how do you mean
To free yourself from danger? some way think
How to escape. I'm sure the guests are come.
Gio. Look up, look here: what see you in my face?
Anna. Distraction and a troubled conscience.
Gio. Death and a swift repining wrath——yet look,
What see you in mine eyes?
Anna. Methinks you weep.
Gio. I do indeed; these are the funeral tears

Shed on your grave: these furrow'd up my cheeks,
When first I lov'd and knew not how to woo.
Fair Annabella, should I here repeat
The story of my life, we might lose time.
Be record all the spirits of the air,
And all things else that are, that day and night,
Early and late, the tribute which my heart
Hath paid to Annabella's sacred love,
Hath been these tears which are her mourners now.
Never till now did Nature do her best,
To show a matchless beauty to the world,
Which in an instant, ere it scarce was seen,
The jealous destinies requir'd again.
Pray, Annabella, pray; since we must part,
Go thou, white in thy soul, to fill a throne
Of innocence and sanctity in heaven.
Pray, pray, my sister.
Anna. Then I see your drift.
Ye blessed angels, guard me!
Gio. Give me your hand. How sweetly life doth run
In these well-color'd veins! how constantly
This pulse doth promise health! But I could chide
With Nature for this cunning flattery!
Forgive me.
Anna. With my heart.
Gio. Farewell.
Anna. Will you be gone?——
Gio. Be dark, bright sun,
And make this mid-day night, that thy gilt rays
May not behold a deed, will turn their splendor
More sooty than the poets feign their Styx.
Anna. What means this? [*Stabs her.*
Gio. To save thy fame.——
Thus die, and die by me, and by my hand;
Revenge is mine, honor doth love command.
Anna. Forgive him, heaven, and me my sins. Farewell.
Brother unkind, unkind—— [*Dies.*

[Sir Thomas Browne, in the last Chapter of his Enquiries into Vulgar and Common Errors, rebukes such Authors as have chosen to relate prodigious and nameless Sins. The Chapter is entitled, *Of some Relations whose Truth we fear.* His reasoning is solemn and fine.—" Lastly, as there are many Relations whereto we cannot assent, and make some doubt thereof, so there are divers others whose verities we fear, and heartily wish there were no truth therein. Many other accounts like these we meet sometimes in History, scandalous unto Christianity, and even unto humanity; whose not only verities but relations honest minds do deprecate. For of sins heteroclital, and such as want either name or precedent, there is oft-times a sin even in their histories. We desire no records of such enormities; sins should be accounted new, that so they may be esteemed monstrous. They omit of monstrosity, as they fall from their rarity; for men count it venial to err with their forefathers, and foolishly conceive they divide a sin in its society. The pens of men may sufficiently expatiate without these singularities of villainy: for, as they increase the hatred of vice in some, so do they enlarge the theory of wickedness in all. And this is one thing that may make latter ages worse than were the former: for the vicious example of ages past, poison the curiosity of these present, affording a hint of sin unto seduceable spirits, and soliciting those unto the imitation of them, whose heads were never so perversely principled as to invent them. In things of this nature silence commendeth History; 'tis the veniable part of things lost, wherein there must never rise a Pancirollus* nor remain any register but that of Hell."]

THE BROKEN HEART. A TRAGEDY. BY JOHN FORD.

Ithocles loves Calantha, Princess of Sparta; and would have his sister Penthea plead for him with the Princess. She objects to him her own wretched condition, made miserable by a Match, into which he forced her with Bassanes, when she was precontracted by her dead Father's Will, and by inclination, to Orgilus; but at last she consents.

ITHOCLES. PENTHEA.

Ith. Sit nearer, sister, to me, nearer yet;
We had one father, in one womb took life,
Were brought up twins together, yet have liv'd
At distance like two strangers. I could wish,
That the first pillow whereon I was cradled
Had proved to me a grave.

* Who wrote *De Antiquis Deperditis*, or the Lost Inventions of Antiquity.

Pen. You had been happy:
Then had you never known that sin of life
Which blots all following glories with a vengeance;
For forfeiting the last will of the dead,
From whom you had your being.
Ith. Sad Penthea,
Thou canst not be too cruel; my rash spleen
Hath with a violent hand pluck'd from thy bosom
A lover-blest heart, to grind it into dust;
For which mine's now a breaking.
Pen. Not yet, heaven,
I do beseech thee: first let some wild fires
Scorch, not consume it; may the heat be cherish'd
With desires infinite but hopes impossible.
Ith. Wrong'd soul, thy prayers are heard.
Pen. Here, lo, I breathe,
A miserable creature, led to ruin
By an unnatural brother.
Ith. I consume
In languishing affections for that trespass,
Yet cannot die.
Pen. The handmaid to the wages,
The untroubled* of country toil, drinks streams,
With leaping kids, and with the bleating lambs,
And so allays her thirst secure; while I
Quench my hot sighs with fleetings of my tears.
Ith. The laborer doth eat his coarsest bread,
Earn'd with his sweat, and lies him down to sleep;
While every bit I touch turns in digestion
To gall, as bitter as Penthea's curse.
Put me to any penance for my tyranny,
And I will call thee merciful.
Pen. Pray kill me;
Rid me from living with a jealous husband;
Then we will join in friendship, be again
Brother and sister——

* A word seems defective here.

Ith. After my victories abroad, at home
I meet despair; ingratitude of nature
Hath made my actions monstrous: Thou shalt stand
A deity, my sister, and be worshipp'd
For thy resolved martyrdom; wrong'd maids
And married wives shall to thy hallow'd shrine
Offer their orisons, and sacrifice
Pure turtles crown'd with mirtle, if thy pity
Unto a yielding brother's pressure lend
One finger but to ease it.
Pen. O no more.
Ith. Death waits to waft me to the Stygian banks,
And free me from this chaos of my bondage;
And till thou wilt forgive, I must endure.
Pen. Who is the saint you serve?
Ith. Friendship, or nearness
Of birth, to any but my sister, durst not
Have mov'd that question: as a secret, sister,
I dare not murmur to myself.
Pen. Let me,
By your new protestations I conjure ye,
Partake her name.
Ith. Her name——'tis——'tis—I dare not—
Pen. All your respects are forg'd.
Ith. They are not—Peace.—
Calantha is the princess, the king's daughter,
Sole heir of Sparta. Me most miserable
Do I now love thee? For my injuries,
Revenge thyself with bravery, and gossip
My treasons to the king's ears. Do; Calantha
Knows it not yet, nor Prophilus my nearest.
Pen. Suppose you were contracted to her, would it not
Split even your very soul to see her father
Snatch her out of your arms against her will,
And force her on the Prince of Argos?
Ith. Trouble not
The fountains of mine eyes with thine own story:
I sweat in blood for 't.

Pen. We are reconciled.
Alas, Sir, being children, but two branches
Of one stock, 'tis not fit we should divide.
Have comfort, you may find it.
Ith. Yes, in thee,
Only in thee, Penthea mine.
Pen. If sorrows
Have not too much dull'd my infected brain,
I'll cheer invention for an active strain.

Penthea recommends her Brother as a dying bequest to the Princess.

CALANTHA. PENTHEA.

Cal. Being alone, Penthea, you have granted
The opportunity you sought, and might
At all times have commanded.
Pen. 'Tis a benefit
Which I shall owe your goodness even in death for.
My glass of life, sweet princess, hath few minutes
Remaining to run down; the sands are spent;
For by an inward messenger I feel
The summons of departure short and certain.
Cal. You feed too much your melancholy.
Pen. Glories
Of human greatness are but pleasing dreams
And shadows soon decaying: on the stage
Of my mortality my youth hath acted
Some scenes of vanity, drawn out at length;
By varied pleasures sweetened in the mixture,
But tragical in issue.
Cal. Contemn not your condition, for the proof
Of bare opinion only: to what end
Reach all these moral texts?
Pen. To place before ye
A perfect mirror, wherein you may see
How weary I am of a lingering life,
Who count the best a misery.
Cal. Indeed

You have no little cause; yet none so great,
As to distrust a remedy.
Pen. That remedy
Must be a winding sheet, a fold of lead,
And some untrod on corner in the earth.
Not to detain your expectation, Princess;
I have an humble suit.
Cal. Speak, and enjoy it.
Pen. Vouchsafe then to be my Executrix;
And take that trouble on ye, to dispose
Such legacies as I bequeath impartially:
I have not much to give, the pains are easy;
Heaven will reward your piety and thank it,
When I am dead; for sure I must not live;
I hope I cannot.
Cal. Now beshrew thy sadness;
Thou turnst me too much woman.
Pen. Her fair eyes
Melt into passion: then I have assurance
Encouraging my boldness. In this paper
My will was character'd; which you, with pardon,
Shall now know from mine own mouth.
Cal. Talk on, prithee;
It is a pretty earnest.
Pen. I have left me
But three poor jewels to bequeath. The first is
My youth; for though I am much old in griefs,
In years I am a child.
Cal. To whom that?
Pen. To virgin wives; such as abuse not wedlock
By freedom of desires, but covet chiefly
The pledges of chaste beds, for ties of love
Rather than ranging of their blood: and next
To married maids; such as prefer the number
Of honorable issue in their virtues,
Before the flattery of delights by marriage;
May those be ever young.
Cal. A second jewel

You mean to part with ?
Pen. 'Tis my fame ; I trust,
By scandal yet untouch'd : this I bequeath
To Memory and Time's old daughter, Truth.
If ever my unhappy name find mention,
When I am fall'n to dust, may it deserve
Beseeming charity without dishonor.
Cal. How handsomely thou play'st with harmless sport
Of mere imagination ! Speak the last.
I strangely like thy will.
Pen. This jewel, Madam,
Is dearly precious to me ; you must use
The best of your discretion, to employ
This gift as I intend it.
Cal. Do not doubt me.
Pen. 'Tis long ago, since first I lost my heart ;
Long I have liv'd without it : but in stead
Of it, to great Calantha, Sparta's heir,
By service bound, and by affection vow'd,
I do bequeath in holiest rites of love
Mine only brother Ithocles.
Cal. What saidst thou ?
Pen. Impute not, heav'n-blest lady, to ambition,
A faith as humbly perfect as the prayers
Of a devoted suppliant can endow it :
Look on him, Princess, with an eye of pity ;
How like the ghost of what he late appear'd
He moves before you.
Cal. Shall I answer here,
Or lend my ear too grossly ?
Pen. First his heart
Shall fall in cinders, scorch'd by your disdain,
Ere he will dare, poor man, to ope an eye
On these divine looks, but with low-bent thoughts
Accusing such presumption : as for words,
He dares not utter any but of service ;
Yet this lost creature loves you. Be a Princess
In sweetness as in blood ; give him his doom,

Or raise him up to comfort.
Cal. What new change
Appears in my behavior, that thou darest
Tempt my displeasure?
Pen. I must leave the world,
To revel in Elysium; and 'tis just
To wish my brother some advantage here.
Yet by my best hopes, Ithocles is ignorant
Of this pursuit. But, if you please to kill him,
Lend him one angry look, or one harsh word,
And you shall soon conclude how strong a power
Your absolute authority holds over
His life and end.
Cal. You have forgot, Penthea,
How still I have a father.
Pen. But remember
I am sister: though to me this brother
Hath been, you know, unkind, O most unkind.
Cal. Christalla, Philema, where are ye?—Lady,
Your check lies in my silence.*

While Calantha (Princess of Sparta) is celebrating the Nuptials of Prophilus and Euphranea at Court with Music and Dancing, one enters to inform her that the King her Father is dead; a second brings the News that Penthea (Sister to Ithocles) is starved; and a third comes to tell that Ithocles himself (to whom the Princess is contracted) is cruelly murdered.

CALANTHA. PROPHILUS. EUPHRANEA. NEARCHUS. CROTOLON. CHRISTALLA. PHILEMA, *and others.*

Cal. We miss our servant Ithocles, and Orgilus;
On whom attend they?
Crot. My son, gracious princess,
Whisper'd some new device, to which these revels
Should be but usher: wherein, I conceive,
Lord Ithocles and he himself are actors.

* It is necessary to the understanding of the Scene which follows, to know that the Princess is won by these solicitations of Penthea, and by the real deserts of Ithocles, to requite his love, and that they are contracted with the consent of the King her Father.

Cal. A fair excuse for absence : as for Bassanes,
Delights to him are troublesome ; Armostes
Is with the King.
Crot. He is.
Cal. On to the dance :
(*To* NEARCHUS.) Dear cousin, hand you the bride ; the bride-groom must be
Intrusted to my courtship : be not jealous,
Euphranea ; I shall scarcely prove a temptress.
Fall to our dance.

They dance the first Change, during which ARMOSTES *enters.*

Arm. The King your Father 's dead.
Cal. To the other change.
Arm. Is it possible ?

They dance again : BASSANES *enters.*

Bass. O Madam.
Penthea, poor Penthea 's starv'd.
Cal. Beshrew thee. ——
Lead to the next.
Bass. Amazement dulls my senses.

They dance again : ORGILUS *enters.*

Org. Brave Ithocles is murder'd, murder'd cruelly.
Cal. How dull this music sounds ! Strike up more sprightly :
Our footings are not active like our heart,
Which treads the nimbler measure.
Org. I am thunder-struck.

They dance the last Change. The Music ceases.

Cal. So let us breathe awhile : hath not this motion
Rais'd fresher color on your cheeks ? [*To Nearchus.*
Near. Sweet Princess,
A perfect purity of blood enamels
The beauty of your white.
Cal. We all look cheerfully ;
And, cousin, 'tis methinks a rare presumption

In any, who prefers our lawful pleasures
Before their own sour censure, to interrupt
The custom of this ceremony bluntly.

Near. None dares, Lady.

Cal. Yes, yes; some hollow voice deliver'd to me
How that the King was dead.

Arm. The King is dead:
That fatal news was mine; for in mine arms
He breath'd his last, and with his crown bequeath'd you
Your Mother's wedding-ring, which here I tender.

Crot. Most strange.

Cal. Peace crown his ashes: we are Queen then.

Near. Long live Calantha, Sparta's sovereign Queen.

All. Long live the Queen.

Cal. What whisper'd Bassanes?

Bass. That my Penthea,* miserable soul,
Was starv'd to death.

Cal. She 's happy; she hath finish'd
A long and painful progress.—A third murmur
Pierc'd mine unwilling ears.

Org. That Ithocles
Was murder'd.

Cal. By whose hand?

Org. By mine: this weapon
Was instrument to my revenge. The reasons†
Are just and known. Quit him of these, and then
Never liv'd gentleman of greater merit,
Hope, or abiliment to steer a kingdom.

Cal. We begin our reign
With a first act of justice; thy confession,
Unhappy Orgilus, dooms thee a sentence;
But yet thy father's or thy sister's presence
Shall be excus'd: give Crotolon,‡ a blessing
To thy lost son: Euphranea,§ take a farewell:

* Wife to Bassanes.

† Penthea (sister to Ithocles) was betrothed at first to Orgilus, but compelled by her brother to marry Bassanes: by which forced match she becoming miserable, refused to take food, and died.

‡ His Father

§ His Sister.

And both begone.
(*To* ORGILUS.) Bloody relater of thy stains in blood
For that thou hast reported him (whose fortunes
And life by thee are both at once snatch'd from him)
With honorable mention, make thy choice
Of what death likes thee best; there's all our bounty.
But to excuse delays, let me, dear cousin,
Intreat you and these lords see execution.
Instant, before ye part.
Near. Your will commands us.
Org. One suit, just Queen; my last. Vouchsafe your clemency,
That by no common hand I be divided
From this my humble frailty.
Cal. To their wisdoms,
Who are to be spectators of thine end,
I make the reference. Those that are dead,
Are dead; had they not now died, of necessity
They must have paid the debt they owed to nature
One time or other. Use dispatch, my lords.—
We 'll suddenly prepare our Coronation. [*Exit.*
Arm. 'Tis strange these tragedies should never touch on
Her female pity.
Bass. She has a masculine spirit.

The Coronation of the Princess takes place after the execution of Orgilus.—She enters the Temple, dressed in White, having a Crown on her Head. She kneels at the Altar. The dead body of Ithocles (whom she should have married) is borne on a hearse, in rich Robes, having a Crown on his Head: and placed by the side of the Altar, where she kneels. Her devotions ended, she rises.—

CALANTHA. NEARCHUS. PROPHILUS. CROTOLON. BASSANES. ARMOSTES. EUPHANEA. AMELUS. CHRISTALLA. PHILEMA, *and others.*

Cal. Our orisons are heard, the gods are merciful.
Now tell me, you, whose loyalties pay tribute
To us your lawful sovereign, how unskilful
Your duties, or obedience is, to render

Subjection to the sceptre of a virgin;
Who have been ever fortunate in princes
Of masculine and stirring composition.
A woman has enough to govern wisely
Her own demeanors, passions, and divisions.
A nation warlike, and inured to practice
Of policy and labor, cannot brook
A feminate authority: we therefore
Command your counsel, how you may advise us
In choosing of a husband, whose abilities
Can better guide this kingdom.
Near. Royal Lady
Your law is in your will.
Arm. We have seen tokens
Of constancy too lately to mistrust it.
Crot. Yet if your Highness settle on a choice
By your own judgment both allow'd and liked of,
Sparta may grow in power and proceed
To an increasing height.
Cal. Cousin of Argos.
Near. Madam.
Cal. Were I presently
To choose you for my Lord, I 'll open freely
What articles I would propose to treat on,
Before our marriage.
Near. Name them, virtuous Lady.
Cal. I would presume you would retain the royalty
Of Sparta in her own bounds: then in Argos
Armostes might be viceroy; in Messene
Might Crotolon bear sway; and Bessanes
Be Sparta's marshall:
The multitudes of high employments could not
But set a peace to private griefs. These gentlemen,
Groneas and Lemophil, with worthy pensions,
Should wait upon your person in your chamber.
I would bestow Christalla on Amelus;
She 'll prove a constant wife: and Philema
Should into Vesta's Temple.

Bass. This is a testament;
It sounds not like conditions on a marriage.
Near. All this should be perform'd.
Cal. Lastly for Prophilus,
He should be (cousin) solemnly invested
In all those honors, titles, and preferments,
Which his dear friend and my neglected husband
Too short a time enjoy'd.
Proph. I am unworthy
To live in your remembrance.
Euph. Excellent Lady.
Near. Madam, what means that word, neglected husband?
Cal. Forgive me: Now I turn to thee, thou shadow
[*To the dead body of* ITHOCLES
Of my contracted Lord: bear witness all,
I put my mother's wedding-ring upon
His finger; 'twas my father's last bequest:
Thus I new marry him, whose wife I am;
Death shall not separate us. O my lords,
I but deceiv'd your eyes with antick gesture,
When one news straight came huddling on another,
Of death, and death, and death, still I danc'd forward;
But it struck home, and here, and in an instant.
Be such mere women, who with shrieks and outcries
Can vow a present end to all their sorrows:
Yet live to vow new pleasures, and out-live them.
They are the silent griefs which cut the heart-strings:
Let me die smiling.
Near. 'Tis a truth too ominous.
Cal. One kiss on these cold lips; my last. Crack, crack.
Argos now 's Sparta's King. [*Dies.*

[I do not know where to find in any Play a catastrophe so grand, so solemn, and so surprising as this. This is indeed, according to Milton, to "describe high passions and high actions." The fortitude of the Spartan Boy who let a beast gnaw out his bowels till he died without expressing a groan, is a faint bodily image of this dilaceration of the spirit, and exenteration of the inmost mind, which Calantha with a holy violence against her nature keeps closely covered, till the last duties of a Wife and a Queen are fulfilled. Stories of martyrdom are but of chains and the stake; a little bodily suffering; these torments

On the purest spirits prey
As on entrails, joints, and limbs,
With answerable pains, but more intense.

What a noble thing is the soul in its strengths and its weaknesses! who would be less weak than Calantha? who can be so strong? the expression of this transcendant scene almost bears me in imagination to Calvary and the Cross; and I seem to perceive some analogy between the scenical sufferings which I am here contemplating, and the real agonies of that final completion to which I dare no more than hint a reference.

Ford was of the first order of Poets. He sought for sublimity not by parcels in metaphors or visible images, but directly where she has her full residence in the heart of man; in the actions and sufferings of the greatest minds. There is a grandeur of the soul above mountains, seas, and the elements. Even in the poor perverted reason of Giovanni and Annabella (in the play which precedes this) we discern traces of that fiery particle, which in the irregular starting from out of the road of beaten action, discovers something of a right line even in obliquity, and shows hints of an improvable greatness in the lowest descents and degradations of our nature.]

HYMEN'S TRIUMPH: A PASTORAL TRAGI-COMEDY. BY SAMUEL DANIEL.

Love in Infancy.

Ah, I remember well (and how can I
But evermore remember well) when first
Our flame began, when scarce we knew what was
The flame we felt: when as we sat and sigh'd
And look'd upon each other, and conceiv'd
Not what we ail'd, yet something we did ail;
And yet were well, and yet we were not well
And what was our disease we could not tell.
Then would we kiss, then sigh, then look: And thus
In that first garden of our simpleness
We spent our childhood: But when years began
To reap the fruit of knowledge: ah, how then
Would she with graver looks, with sweet stern brow,
Check my presumption and my forwardness;
Yet still would give me flowers, still would me show
What she would have me, yet not have me know.

Love after Death.

Palæmon. Fie, Thirsis, with what fond remembrances
Dost thou these idle passions entertain!
For shame leave off to waste your youth in vain,
And feed on shadows: make your choice anew;
You other nymphs shall find, no doubt will be
As lovely, and as fair, and sweet as she.
Thirsis. As fair and sweet as she! Palæmon, peace:
Ah, what can pictures be unto the life?
What sweetness can be found in images?
Which all nymphs else besides her seem to me.
She only was a real creature, she,
Whose memory must take up all of me.
Should I another love, then must I have
Another heart, for this is full of her,
And evermore shall be: here is she drawn
At length, and whole: and more, this table is
A story, and is all of her; and all
Wrought in the liveliest colors of my blood;
And can there be a room for others here?
Should I disfigure such a piece, and blot
The perfect'st workmanship that love e'er wrought?
Palæmon, no, ah no, it cost too dear;
It must remain entire whilst life remains,
The monument of her and of my pains.

The Story of Isulia.

There was sometimes a nymph,
Isulia named, and an Arcadian born,
Whose mother dying left her very young
Unto her father's charge, who carefully
Did breed her up until she came to years
Of womanhood, and then provides a match
Both rich and young, and fit enough for her.
But she, who to another shepherd had,
Call'd Sirthis, vow'd her love, as unto one
Her heart esteem'd more worthy of her love,
Could not by all her father's means be wrought

To leave her choice, and to forget her vow.
This nymph one day, surcharg'd with love and grief,
Which commonly (the more the pity) dwell
As inmates both together, walking forth
With other maids to fish upon the shore;
Estrays apart, and leaves her company,
To entertain herself with her own thoughts:
And wanders on so far, and out of sight,
As she at length was suddenly surpris'd
By pirates, who lay lurking underneath
Those hollow rocks, expecting there some prize.
And notwithstanding all her piteous cries,
Intreaties, tears, and prayers, those fierce men
Rent hair and veil, and carried her by force
Into their ship, which in a little creek
Hard by at anchor lay,
And presently hoisted sail and so away.
When she was thus inshipp'd and wofully
Had cast her eyes about to view that hell
Of horror, whereinto she was so suddenly emplung'd,
She spies a woman sitting with a child
Sucking her breast, which was the captain's wife.
To her she creeps, down at her feet she lies;
"O woman, if that name of a woman may
"Move you to pity, pity a poor maid:
"The most distressed soul that ever breath'd;
"And save me from the hands of those fierce men.
"Let me not be defil'd and made unclean,
"Dear woman, now, and I will be to you
"The faithfull'st slave that ever mistress serv'd;
"Never poor soul shall be more dutiful,
"To do whatever you command, than I.
"No toil will I refuse; so that I may
"Keep this poor body clean and undeflower'd,
"Which is all I will ever seek. For know
"It is not fear of death lays me thus low,
"But of that stain will make my death to blush."
All this would nothing move the woman's heart,

Whom yet she would not leave, but still besought;
" O woman, by that infant at your breast,
" And by the pains it cost you in the birth,
" Save me, as ever you desire to have
" Your babe to joy and prosper in the world:
" Which will the better prosper sure, if you
" Shall mercy show, which is with mercy paid!"
Then kisses she her feet, then kisses too
The infant's feet; and, " Oh, sweet babe" (said she),
" Could'st thou but to thy mother speak for me,
" And crave her to have pity on my case,
" Thou might'st perhaps prevail with her so much
" Although I cannot; child, ha, could'st thou speak."
The infant, whether by her touching it,
Or by instinct of nature, seeing her weep,
Looks earnestly upon her, and then looks
Upon the mother, then on her again,
And then it cries, and then on either looks;
Which she perceiving; " Blessed child" (said she),
" Although thou canst not speak, yet dost thou cry
" Unto thy mother for me. Hear thy child,
" Dear mother, it 's for me it cries,
" It 's all the speech it hath. Accept those cries,
" Save me at his request from being defil'd:
" Let pity move thee, that thus moves the child."
The woman, tho' by birth and custom rude,
Yet having veins of nature, could not be
But pierceable, did feel at length the point
Of pity enter so, as out gush'd tears
(Not usual to stern eyes), and she besought
Her husband to bestow on her that prize,
With safeguard of her body at her will.
The captain seeing his wife, the child the nymph,
All crying to him in this piteous sort,
Felt his rough nature shaken too, and grants
His wife's request, and seals his grant with tears;
And so they wept all four for company:
And some beholders stood not with dry eyes;

Such passion wrought the passion of their prize.
Never was there pardon, that did take
Condemned from the block more joyful than
This grant to her. For all her misery
Seem'd nothing to the comfort she receiv'd,
By being thus saved from impurity :
And from the woman's feet she would not part,
Nor trust her hand to be without some hold
Of her, or of the child, so long as she remain'd
Within the ship, which in few days arrives
At Alexandria, whence these pirates were ;
And there this woful maid for two years space
Did serve, and truly serve this captain's wife
(Who would not lose the benefit of her
Attendance, for her profit otherwise),
But daring not in such a place as that
To trust herself in woman's habit, crav'd
That she might be apparel'd like a boy ;
And so she was, and as a boy she served.
At two years end her mistress sends her forth
Unto the port for some commodities,
Which whilst she sought for, going up and down,
She heard some merchantmen of Corinth talk,
Who spake that language the Arcadians did,
And were next neighbors of one continent,
To them, all wrapt with passion, down she kneels,
Tells them she was a poor distressed boy,
Born in Arcadia, and by pirates took,
And made a slave in Egypt ; and besought
Them, as they fathers were of children, or
Did hold their native country dear, they would
Take pity on her, and relieve her youth
From that sad servitude wherein she liv'd :
For which she hop'd that she had friends alive
Would thank them one day, and reward them too ;
If not, yet that she knew the heav'ns would do.
The merchants moved with pity of her case,
Being ready to depart, took her with them,

And landed her upon her country coast:
Where when she found herself, she prostrate falls,
Kisses the ground, thanks gives unto the gods,
Thanks them who had been her deliverers,
And on she trudges through the desart woods,
Climbs over craggy rocks, and mountains steep,
Wades thorough rivers, struggles thorough bogs,
Sustained only by the force of love;
Until she came unto the native plains,
Unto the fields where first she drew her breath.
There she lifts up her eyes, salutes the air,
Salutes the trees, the bushes, flow'rs and all:
And, "Oh, dear Sirthis, here I am," said she,
"Here, notwithstanding all my miseries,
"I am the same I was to thee; a pure,
"A chaste, and spotless maid."

ALAHAM: A TRAGEDY. BY FULKE GREVILLE, LORD BROOKE.

Alaham, second son to the King of Ormus, deposes his father; whose eyes, and the eyes of his elder brother Zophi (acting upon a maxim of Oriental Policy), he causes to be put out. They, blind, and fearing for their lives, wander about. In this extremity they are separately met by the King's daughter Cælica, who conducts them to a place of refuge; hiding her father amid the vaults of a temple, and guiding her brother to take sanctuary at the altar.

KING. CÆLICA.

King. Cælica; thou only child, whom I repent
Not yet to have begot, thy work is vain:
Thou run'st against my destiny's intent.
Fear not my fall; the steep is fairest plain;
And error safest guide unto his end,
Who nothing but mischance can have to friend.
We parents are but nature's nursery;
When our succession springs, then ripe to fall.
Privation unto age is natural.
Age there is also in a prince's state,

Which is contempt, grown of misgovernment;
Where love of change begetteth princes' hate:
For hopes must wither, or grow violent,
If fortune bind desires to one estate.
Then mark! Blind, as a man: scorn'd, as a king,
A father's kindness loath'd, and desolate:
Life without joy, or light: what can it bring,
But inward horror unto outward hate?
O safety! thou art then a hateful thing,
When children's death assures the father's state.
No, safe I am not, though my son were slain,
My frailty would beget such sons again.
Besides, if fatal be the heavens' will,
Repining adds more force to destiny;
Whose iron wheels stay not on fleshly wit,
But headlong run down steep necessity.
And as in danger, we do catch at it.
That comes to help; and unadvisedly
Oft do our friends to our misfortune knit:
So with the harm of those who would us good
Is destiny impossibly withstood.
Cælica, then cease; importune me no more:
My son, my age, the state where things are now,
Require my death. Who would consent to live
Where love cannot revenge, nor truth forgive?
Cælica. Though fear see nothing but extremity,
Yet danger is no deep sea, but a ford,
Where they that yield can only drowned be.
In wrongs, and wounds, Sir, you are too remiss.
To thrones a passive nature fatal is.
King. Occasion to my son hath turn'd her face;
My inward wants all outward strengths betray;
And so make that impossible I may.
Cælica. Yet live:
Live for the state.
King. Whose ruins glasses are,
Wherein see errors of myself I must,
And hold my life of danger, shame, and care.

Cælica. When fear propounds, with loss men ever choose.
King. Nothing is left me but myself to lose.
Cælica. And is it nothing then to lose the state?
King. Where chance is ripe, there counsel comes too late,
Cælica, by all thou ow'st the gods and me,
I do conjure thee, leave me to my chance.
What's past was error's way; the truth it is,
Wherein I wretch can only go amiss.
If nature saw no cause of sudden ends,
She, that but one way made to draw our breath,
Would not have left so many doors to death.
Cælica. Yet, Sir, if weakness be not such a sand
As neither wrong nor counsel can manure;
Choose and resolve what death you will endure.
King. This sword, thy hands, may offer up my breath
And plague my life's remissness in my death.
Cælica. Unto that duty if these hands be born,
I must think God, and truth, were names of scorn.
Again, this justice were if life were loved,
Now merely grace; since death doth but forgive
A life to you, which is a death to live.
Pain must displease that satisfies offence.
King. Chance hath left death no more to spoil but sense.
Cælica. Then sword, do justice' office thorough me:
I offer more than that he hates to thee.
[*Offers to kill herself.*
King. Ah! stay thy hand. My state no equal hath,
And much more matchless my strange vices be:
One kind of death becomes not thee and me.
Kings' plagues by chance or destiny should fall;
Headlong he perish must that ruins all.
Cælica. No cliff or rock is so precipitate,
But down it eyes can lead the blind away;
Without me live, or with me die you may.
King. Cælica, and wilt thou Alaham exceed?
His cruelty is death, you torments use;
He takes my crown, you take myself from me;
A prince of this fall'n empire let me be.

Cælica. Then be a king, no tyrant of thyself:
Be: and be what you will: what nature lent
Is still in hers, and not our government.
King. If disobedience, and obedience both,
Still do me hurt; in what strange state am I?
But hold thy course: it well becomes my blood,
To do their parents mischief with their good.
Cælica. Yet, Sir, hark to the poor oppressed tears
The just men's moan, that suffer by your fall;
A prince's charge is to protect them all.
And shall it nothing be that I am yours?
The world without, my heart within, doth know,
I never had unkind, unreverent powers.
If thus you yield to Alaham's treachery,
He ruins you: 'tis you, Sir, ruin me.
King. Cælica, call up the dead; awake the blind;
Turn back the time; bid winds tell whence they come:
As vainly strength speaks to a broken mind.
Fly from me, Cælica, hate all I do:
Misfortunes have in blood successions too.
Cælica. Will you do that which Alaham cannot?
He hath no good; you have no ill, but he:
This mar-right yielding 's honor's tyranny.
King. Have I not done amiss? am I not ill,
That ruin'd have a king's authority?
And not one king alone: since princes all
Feel part of those scorns, whereby one doth fall.
Treason against me cannot treason be:
All laws have lost authority in me.
Cælica. The laws of power chain'd to men's humors be.
The good have conscience; the ill (like instruments)
Are, in the hands of wise authority,
Moved, divided, used, or laid down;
Still, with desire, kept subject to a crown.
Stir up all states, all spirits: hope and fear,
Wrong and revenge, are current everywhere.
King. Put down my son: for that must be the way:
A father's shame; a prince's tyranny:

The sceptre ever shall misjudged be.
Cœlica. Let them fear rumor that do work amiss;
Blood, torments, death, horrors of cruelty,
Have time, and place. Look through these skins of fear,
Which still persuade the better side to bear.
And since thy son thus trait'rously conspires,
Let him not prey on all thy race, and thee:
Keep ill example from posterity.
King. Danger is come, and must I now unarm,
And let in hope to weaken resolution?
Passion! be thou my legacy and will;
To thee I give my life, crown, reputation;
My pomps to cloud; and (as forlorn with men)
My strength to women; hoping this alone,
Though fear'd, sought, and a king, to live unknown.
Cælica, all these to thee; do thou bestow
This living darkness, wherein I do go.
Cœlica. My soul now joys. Doing breathes horror out
Absence must be our first step. Let us fly:
A pause in rage makes Alaham to doubt;
Which doubt may stir in people hope, and fear,
With love, or hate, to seek you everywhere.
For princes' lives are fortune's misery:
As dainty sparks, which till men dead do know,
To kindle for himself each man doth blow.
But hark! what's this? Malice doth never sleep:
I hear the spies of power drawing near.
Sir, follow me: Misfortune's worst is come;
Her strength is changed: and change yields better doom.
Choice now is past. Hard by there is a pile,
Built under color of a sacrifice;
If God do grant, it is a place to save;
If God denies, it is a ready grave.

ZOPHI *appears.*

Cœlica. What see I here? more spectacles of woe!
And are my kindred only made to be
Agents and patients in iniquity?

Ah forlorn wretch! ruin's example right!
Lost to thyself, not to thy enemy,
Whose hand even while thou fliest thou fall'st into;
And with thy fall thy father dost undo.
Save one I may: Nature would save them both;
But Chance hath many wheels, Rage many eyes.
What, shall I then abandon Innocents?*
Not help a helpless brother thrown on me?
Is nature narrow to adversity?
No, no. Our God left duty for a law;
Pity, at large; love, in authority;
Despair, in bonds; fear, of itself in awe:
That rage of time, and power's strange liberty,
Oppressing good men, might resistance find:
Nor can I to a brother be less kind.
Dost thou, that canst not see, hope to escape?
Disgrace can have no friend; contempt no guide;
Right is thy guilt; thy judge iniquity;
Which desolation casts on them that see.
Zophi. Make calm thy rage: pity a ghost distrest:
My right, my liberty, I freely give:
Give him, that never harm'd thee, leave to live.
Cælica. Nay, God, the world, thy parents it deny;
A brother's jealous heart; usurped might
Grows friends with all the world, except thy right.
Zophi. Secure thyself. Exile me from this coast:
My fault, suspicion is; my judge, is fear;
Occasion, with myself, away I bear.
Cælica. Fly unto God: for in humanity
Hope there is none. Reach me thy fearful hand:
I am thy sister; neither fiend, nor spy
Of tyrant's rage; but one that feels despair
Of thy estate, which thou dost only fear.
Kneel down; embrace this holy mystery;
A refuge to the worst for rape and blood,
And yet, I fear, not hallow'd for the good.

* Zophi is represented as a prince of weak understanding.

Zophi. Help, God! defend thine altar! since thy might,
In earth, leaves innocents no other right.
Cælica. Eternal God! that see'st thyself in us,
If vows be more than sacrifice of lust,
Rais'd from the smokes of hope and fear in us,
Protect this Innocent, calm Alaham's rage;
By miracles faith goes from age to age.
Affection trembles; reason is opprest;
Nature, methinks, doth her own entrails tear;
In resolution ominous is fear.

Alaham causes Search to be made after his Father and Brother. Zophi is discovered, and Cælica; who, being questioned by Alaham where she has hid her Father, dissembles as though she thought that the King was dead; but being threatened with the rack, her Exclamations call her Father from his hiding-place; who, together with her, and her Brother Zophi, aresentenced by Alaham to the Flames

ALAHAM. *Attendants.*

Alaham. Sirs, seek the city, examine, torture, rack;
Sanctuaries none let there be; make darkness known;
Pull down the roofs, dig, burn, put all to wrack;
And let the guiltless for the guilty groan.
Change, shame, misfortune, in their 'scaping lie,
And in their finding our prosperity.

He sees Cælica.

Good fortune welcome! We have lost our care,
And found our loss: Cælica distract I see.
The king is near: She is her father's eyes.

He sees Zophi.

Behold! the forlorn wretch, half of my fear,
Takes sanctuary at holy altar's feet:
Lead him apart, examine, force, and try;
These bind the subject not the monarchy.
Cælica! awake: that God of whom you crave
Is deaf, and only gives men what they have.
Cælica. Ah cruel wretch! guilty of parent's blood!
Might I, poor innocent, my father free,

My murther yet were less impiety.
But on ; devour : fear only to be good :
Let us not scape : thy glory then doth rise,
When thou at once thy house dost sacrifice.
Alaham. Tell me where thy father is.
Cælica. O bloody scorn.
Must he be kill'd again that gave thee breath ?
Is duty nothing else in thee but death ?
Alaham. Leave off this mask ; deceit is never wise ;
Though he be blind, a king hath many eyes.
Cælica. O twofold scorn ! God be reveng'd for me.
Yet since my father is destroy'd by thee,
Add still more scorn, it sorrow multiplies.
Alaham. Passions are learn'd, not born within the heart,
That method keep : Order is quiet's art.
Tell where he is : for look what love conceals,
Pain out of nature's labyrinths reveals.
Cælica. This is reward which thou dost threaten me
If terror thou wilt threaten, promise joys
Alaham. Smart cools these boiling styles of vanity.
Cælica. And if my father I no more shall see,
Help me unto the place where he remains :
To hell below, or to the sky above,
The way is easy where the guide is love.
Alaham. Confess ; where is he hid ?
Cælica. Rack not my woe.
Thy glorious pride of this unglorious deed
Doth mischief ripe, and therefore falling, show.
Alaham. Bodies have place, and blindness must be led,
Graves be the thrones of kings when they be dead.
Cælica. He was (unhappy) cause that thou art now ;
Thou art, ah wicked ! cause that he is not,
And fear'st thou parricide can be forgot ?
Bear witness, though Almighty God on high,
And you black powers inhabiting below,
That for his life myself would yield to die.
Alaham. Well, Sirs, go seek the dark and secret caves,
The holy temples, sanctified cells,

All parts wherein a living corpse may dwell.
Cælica. Seek him amongst the dead, you placed him there:
Yet lose no pains, good souls, go not to hell;
And, but to heaven, you may go everywhere.
Guilty, with you, of his blood let me be,
If any more I of my father know,
Than that he is where you would have him go.
Alaham. Tear up the vaults. Behold her agonies!
Sorrow subtracts, and multiplies, the spirits;
Care, and desire, do under anguish cease;
Doubt curious is, affecting piety;
Woe loves itself; fear from itself would fly.
Do not these trembling motions witness bear,
That all these protestations be of fear?
Cælica. If aught be quick in me, move it with scorn;
Nothing can come amiss to thoughts forlorn.
Alaham. Confess in time. Revenge is merciless.
Cælica. Reward and pain, fear and desire too,
Are vain in things impossible to do.
Alaham. Tell yet where thou thy father last did see.
Cælica. Even where he by his loss of eyes hath won
That he no more shall see his monstrous son.
First in perpetual night thou mad'st him go;
His flesh the grave; his life the stage, where sense
Plays all the tragedies of pain and woe.
And wouldst thou trait'rously thyself exceed,
By seeking thus to make his ghost to bleed?
Alaham. Bear her away: devise; add to the rack
Torments, that both call death and turn it back.
Cælica. The flattering glass of power is others' pain.
Perfect thy work; that heaven and hell may know,
To worse I cannot, going from thee, go.
Eternal life, that ever liv'st above!
If sense there be with thee of hate, or love;
Revenge my king and father's overthrow.
O father! if that name reach up so high,
And be more than a proper word of art,
To teach respects in our humanity;

Accept these pains, whereof you feel no smart.

The King comes forth.

King. What sound is this of Cælica's distress?
Alaham, wrong not a silly sister's faith.
'Tis plague enough that she is innocent;
My child, thy sister; born (by thee and me)
With shame and sin to have affinity.
Break me; I am the prison of thy thought:
Crowns dear enough with father's blood are bought.
Alaham. Now feel thou shalt, thou ghost unnatural,
Those wounds which thou to my heart did'st give,
When, in despite of God, this state and me,
Thou did'st from death mine elder brother free.
The smart of king's oppression doth not die:
Time rusteth malice; rust wounds cruelly.
King. Flatter thy wickedness; adorn thy rage;
To wear a crown, tear up thy father's age.
Kill not thy sister: it is lack of wit
To do an ill that brings no good with it.
Alaham. Go, lead them hence. Prepare the funeral.
Hasten the sacrifice and pomp of woe.
Where she did hide him, thither let them go.

A Nuntius (or Messenger) relates to Alaham the manner of his Father's, Brother's, and Sister's deaths; and the popular discontents which followed. Alaham by the sudden working of Remorse is distracted, and imagines that he sees their Ghosts.

ALAHAM. NUNTIUS.

Nuntius. The first which burnt, as Cain* his next of kin,
In blood your brother, and your prince in state,
Drew wonder from men's hearts, brought horror in.
This innocent, this soul too meek for sin,
Yet made for others to do harm withal,
With his self-pity tears drew tears from us;

* The execution, to make it plausible to the people, is colored with the pretext, that the being burnt is a voluntary sacrifice of themselves by the victims at the funeral of Cain a bashaw and relative.

His blood compassion had: his wrong stirr'd hate:
Deceit is odious in a king's estate.
Repiningly he goes unto his end:
Strange visions rise; strange furies haunt the flame;
People cry out, Echo repeats, his name.
These words he spake, even breathing out his breath:
"Unhappy weakness! never innocent!
"If in a crown, yet but an instrument.
"People! observe; this fact may make you see,
"Excess hath ruin'd what itself did build:
"But ah! the more opprest the more you yield."
The next was He whose age had reverence,
His gesture something more than privateness;
Guided by One, whose stately grace did move
Compassion, even in hearts that could not love.
As soon as these approached near the flame,
The wind, the steam, or furies, rais'd their veils;
And in their looks this image did appear:
Each unto other, life to neither, dear.
These words he spake. "Behold one that hath lost
"Himself within; and so the world without;
"A king, that brings authority in doubt:
"This is the fruit of power's misgovernment.
"People! my fall is just; yet strange your fate,
"That, under worst, will hope for better state."
Grief roars aloud. Your sister yet remain'd;
Helping in death to him in whom she died;
Then going to her own, as if she gain'd,
These mild words spake with looks to heaven bent.
"O God! 'Tis thou that suff'rest here, not we:
"Wrong doth but like itself in working thus:
"At thy will, Lord! revenge thyself, not us."
The fire straight upward bears the souls in breath:
Visions of horror circle in the flame
With shapes and figures like to that of Death,
But lighter-tongued and nimbler wing'd than Fame:
Some to the church; some to the people fly:
A voice cries out; "revenge and liberty.

" Princes, take heed ; your glory is your care ;
" And power's foundations, strengths, not vices, are."
Alaham. What change is this, that now I feel within ?
Is it disease that works this fall of spirits ?
Or works this fall of spirits my disease ?
Things seem not as they did ; horror appears.
What Sin embodied, what strange sight is this ?
Doth sense bring back but what within me is ?
Or do I see those shapes which haunt the flame ?
What summons up remorse ? Shall conscience rate
Kings' deeds, to make them less than their estate ?
Ah silly ghost ! is 't you that swarm about ?
Would'st thou, that art not now, a father be ?
These body laws do with the life go out,
What thoughts be these that do my entrails tear ?
You wand'ring spirits frame in me your hell ;
I feel my brother and my sister there.

MUSTAPHA: A TRAGEDY. BY FULKE GREVILLE, LORD BROOKE.

Rossa, Wife to Solyman, the Turkish Emperor, persuades her Husband, that Mustapha, his Son by a former Marriage, and Heir to his Crown, seeks his life: that she may make way, by the death of Mustapha, for the advancement of her own children, Zanger and Camena. Camena, the virtuous Daughter of Rossa, defends the Innocence of Mustapha, in a Conference which she holds with the Emperor.

CAMENA. SOLYMAN.

Cam. They that from youth do suck at fortune's breast
And nurse their empty hearts with seeking higher,
Like dropsy-fed, their thirst doth never rest ;
For still, by getting, they beget desire :
Till thoughts, like wood, while they maintain the flame
Of high desires, grow ashes in the same.
But virtue ! those that can behold thy beauties,

Those that suck, from their youth, thy milk of goodness,
Their minds grow strong against the storms of fortune,
And stand, like rocks in winter-gusts, unshaken;
Not with the blindness of desire mistaken.
O virtue therefore! whose thrall I think fortune,
Thou who despisest not the sex of women,
Help me out of these riddles of my fortune,
Wherein (methinks) you with yourself do pose me;
Let fates go on: sweet virtue! do not lose me.
My mother and my husband have conspired,
For brother's good, the ruin of my brother:
My father by my mother is inspired,
For one child to seek ruin of another.
I that to help by nature am required.
While I do help, must needs still hurt a brother.
While I see who conspire, I seem conspired
Against a husband, father and a mother.
Truth bids me run, by truth I am retired;
Shame leads me both the one way, and the other.
In what a labyrinth is honor cast,
Drawn divers ways with sex, with time, with state,
In all which, error's course is infinite.
By hope, by fear, by spite, by love, and hate;
And but one only way unto the right,
A thorny way, where pain must be the guide,
Danger the light, offence of power the praise:
Such are the golden hopes of iron days.
Yet virtue, I am thine, for thy sake grieved
(Since basest thoughts, for their ill-plac'd desires,
In shame, in danger, death, and torment, glory)
That I cannot with more pains write thy story.
Chance, therefore, if thou scornest those that scorn thee;
Fame, if thou hatest those that force thy trumpet
To sound aloud, and yet despise thy sounding;
Laws, if you love not those that be examples
Of nature's laws, whence you are fall'n corrupted;
Conspire that I, against you all conspired,
Joined with tyrant virtue, as you call her,

That I, by your revenges may be named,
For virtue, to be ruin'd, and defamed.
My mother oft and diversly I warned,
What fortunes were upon such courses builded :
That fortune still must be with ill maintained,
Which at the first with any ill is gained.
I Rosten* warn'd, that man's self-loving thought
Still creepeth to the rude-embracing might
Of princes' grace : a lease of glories let,
Which shining burns ; breeds serenes when tis set.
And, by this creature of my mother's making,
This messenger, I Mustapha have warn'd,
That innocence is not enough to save,
Where good and greatness, fear and envy have.
Till now, in reverence I have forborn
To ask, or to presume to guess, or know
My father's thoughts ; whereof he might think scorn :
For dreadful is that power that all may do ;
Yet they, that all men fear, are fearful too.
Lo where he sits ! Virtue, work thou in me,
That what thou seekest may accomplish'd be.
Solym. Ah death ! is not thyself sufficient anguish,
But thou must borrow fear, that threatning glass,
Which, while it goodness hides, and mischief shows,
Doth lighten wit to honor's overthrows ?
But hush ! methinks away Camena steals ;
Murther, belike, in me itself reveals.
Camena ! whither now ? why haste you from me ?
Is it so strange a thing to be a father ?
Or is it I that am so strange a father ?
Cam. My lord, methought, nay, sure I saw you busy :
Your child presumes, uncall'd, that comes unto you.
Solym. Who may presume with fathers, but their own,
Whom nature's law hath ever in protection,
And gilds in good belief of dear affection ?
Cam. Nay, reverence, Sir, so children's worth doth hide,

* Her Husband.

As of the fathers it is least espy'd.
Solym. I think 'tis true, who know their children least,
Have greatest reason to esteem them best.
Cam. How so, my lord? since love in knowledge lives,
Which unto strangers therefore no man gives.
Solym. The life we gave them soon they do forget,
While they think our lives do their fortunes let.
Cam. The tenderness of life it is so great,
As any sign of death we hate too much;
And unto parents sons, perchance, are such.
Yet nature meant her strongest unity
Twixt sons and fathers; making parents cause
Unto the sons, of their humanity;
And children pledge of their eternity.
Fathers should love this image in their sons.
Solym. But streams back to their springs do never run.
Cam. Pardon, my lord, doubt is succession's foe:
Let not her mists poor children overthrow.
Though streams from springs do seem to run away,
Tis nature leads them to their mother sea.
Solym. Doth nature teach them, in ambition's strife,
To seek his death, by whom they have their life?
Cam. Things easy, to desire impossible do seem:
Why should fear make impossible seem easy?
Solym. Monsters yet be, and being are believed.
Cam. Incredible hath some inordinate progression:
Blood, doctrine, age, corrupting liberty,
Do all concur, where men such monsters be.
Pardon me, Sir, if duty do seem angry:
Affection must breathe out afflicted breath,
Where imputation hath such easy faith.
Solym. Mustapha is he that hath defil'd his nest;
The wrong the greater for I loved him best.
He hath devised that all at once should die.
Rosten, and Rossa, Zanger, thou and I.
Cam. Fall none but angels suddenly to hell?
Are kind and order grown precipitate?
Did ever any other man but he

In instant lose the use of doing well?
Sir, these be mists of greatness. Look again:
For kings that, in their fearful icy state,
Behold their children as their winding-sheet,
Do easily doubt; and what they doubt, they hate.
Solym. Camena! thy sweet youth, that knows no ill,
Cannot believe thine elders, when they say,
That good belief is great estates' decay.
Let it suffice, that I, and Rossa too,
Are privy what your brother means to do.
Cam. Sir, pardon me, and nobly, as a father,
What I shall say, and say of holy mother;
Know I shall say it, but to right a brother.
My mother is your wife: duty in her
Is love: she loves: which not well govern'd, bears
The evil angel of misgiving fears;
Whose many eyes, whilst but itself they see,
Still makes the worst of possibility:
Out of this fear she Mustapha accuseth:
Unto this fear, perchance, she joins the love
Which doth in mothers for their children move.
Perchance, when fear hath show'd her yours must fall,
In love she sees that hers must rise withall.
Sir, fear a frailty is, and may have grace,
And over-care of you cannot be blamed;
Care of our own in nature hath a place;
Passions are oft mistaken and misnamed;
Things simply good grow evil with misplacing.
Though laws cut off, and do not care to fashion,
Humanity of error hath compassion.
Yet God forbid, that either fear, or care,
Should ruin those that true and faultless are.
Solym. Is it no fault, or fault I may forgive,
For son to seek the father should not live?
Cam. Is it a fault, or fault for you to know,
My mother doubts a thing that is not so?
These ugly works of monstrous parricide,
Mark from what hearts they rise, and where they bide.

Violent, despair'd, where honor broken is;
Fear lord, time death ; where hope is misery ;
Doubt having stopt all honest ways to bliss ;
And custom shut the windows up of shame,
That craft may take upon her wisdom's name.
Compare now Mustapha with this despair :
Sweet youth, sure hopes, honor, a father's love,
No infamy to move, or banish fear,
Honor to stay, hazard to hasten fate : ——
Can horrors work in such a child's estate ?
Besides, the gods, whom kings should imitate,
Have placed you high to rule, not overthrow ;
For us, not for yourselves, is your estate :
Mercy must hand in hand with power go.
Your sceptre should not strike with arms of fear,
Which fathoms all men's imbecility,
And mischief doth, lest it should mischief bear.
As reason deals within with frailty,
Which kills not passions that rebellious are,
But adds, subtracts, keeps down ambitious spirits.
So must power form, not ruin instruments :
For flesh and blood, the means 'twixt heav'n and hell,
Unto extremes extremely racked be ;
Which kings in art of government should see :
Else they, which circle in themselves with death,
Poison the air wherein they draw their breath.
Pardon, my lord, pity becomes my sex :
Grace with delay grows weak, and fury wise.
Remember Theseus' wish, and Neptune's haste,
Kill'd innocence, and left succession waste.
Solym. If what were best for them that do offend,
Laws did inquire, the answer must be grace.
If mercy be so large, where 's justice' place ?
Cam. Where love despairs, and where God's promise ends.
For mercy is the highest reach of wit,
A safety unto them that save with it :
Born out of God, and unto human eyes,
Like God, not seen, till fleshly passion dies.

Solym. God may forgive, whose being, and whose harms
Are far removed from reach of fleshly arms:
But if God equals or successors had,
Even God of safe revenges would be glad.
Cam. While he is yet alive, he may be slain;
But from the dead no flesh comes back again.
Solym. While he remains alive, I live in fear.
Cam. Though he were dead, that doubt still living were.
Solym. None hath the power to end what he begun.
Cam. The same occasion follows every son.
Solym. Their greatness, or their worth, is not so much.
Cam. And shall the best be slain for being such?
Solym. Thy mother, or thy brother, are amiss;
I am betray'd, and one of them it is.
Cam. My mother if she errs, errs virtuously;
And let her err, ere Mustapha should die.
Solym. Kings for their safety must not blame mistrust.
Cam. Nor for surmises sacrifice the just.
Solym. Well, dear Camena, keep this secretly:
I will be well advised before he die.

Heli a Priest acquaints Mustapha with the intentions of his Father towards him, and counsels him to seek his safety in the Destruction of Rossa and her Faction. Mustapha refuses to save his Life at the Expense of the Public Peace: and being sent for by his Father, obeys the Mandate to his Destruction.

Priest. Thy father purposeth thy death.
Must. What have I to my father done amiss?
Priest. That wicked Rossa thy step-mother is.
Must. Wherein have I of Rossa ill-deserved?
Priest. In that the empire is for thee reserved.
Must. Is it a fault to be my father's son?
Ah foul ambition! which like water floods
Not channel-bound dost neighbors over-run,
And growest nothing when thy rage is done.
Must Rossa's heirs out of my ashes rise?
Yet, Zanger, I acquit thee of my blood;
For I believe, thy heart hath no impression
To ruin Mustapha for his succession.

But tell what colors they against me use,
And how my father's love they first did wound ?
Priest. Of treason towards him they thee accuse:
Thy fame and greatness gives their malice ground.
Must. Good world, where it is danger to be good!
Yet grudge I not power of myself to power:
This baseness only in mankind I blame,
That indignation should give laws to fame.
Show me the truth.——To what rules am I bound?
Priest. No man commanded is by God to die,
As long as he may persecution fly.
Must. To fly, hath scorn,——it argues guiltiness,
Inherits fear, weakly abandons friends,
Gives tyrants fame, takes honor from distress——
Death do thy worst! thy greatest pains have end.
Priest. Mischief is like the cockatrice's eyes,
Sees first, and kills; or is seen first, and dies.
Fly to thy strength, which makes misfortune vain.
Rossa intends thy ruin. What is she?
Seek in her bowels for thy father lost:
Who can redeem a king with viler cost?
Must. O false and wicked colors of desire!
Eternal bondage unto him that seeks
To be possest of all things that he likes!
Shall I, a son and subject, seem to dare,
For any selfness, to set realms on fire;
Which golden titles to rebellions are?
Heli, even you have told me, wealth was given
The wicked, to corrupt themselves and others;
Greatness and health to make flesh proud and cruel,
Where in the good, sickness mows down desire,
Death glorifies, misfortune humbles.
Since therefore life is but the throne of woe,
Which sickness, pain, desire, and fear inherit,
Ever most worth to men of weakest spirit;
Shall we, to languish in this brittle jail,
Seek, by ill deeds, to shun ill destiny;
And so, for toys, lose immortality?

Priest. Fatal necessity is never known
Until it strike ; and till that blow be come,
Who falls is by false visions overthrown.
Must. Blasphemous love ! safe conduct of the ill !
What power hath given man's wickedness such skill ?
Priest. Ah servile man ! how are your thoughts bewitch'd
With hopes and fears, the price of your subjection,
That neither sense nor time can make you see,
The art of power will leave you nothing free !
Must. Is it in us to rule a Sultan's will ?
Priest. We made them first for good, and not for ill.
Must. Our Gods they are, their God remains above.
To think against anointed power is death.
Priest. To worship tyrants is no work of faith.
Must. 'Tis rage of folly that contends with fate.
Priest. Yet hazard something to preserve the state.
Must. Sedition wounds what should preserved be.
Priest. To wound power's humors, keeps their honors free.
Must. Admit this true : what sacrifice prevails ?
Priest. Force the petition is that never fails.
Must. Where then is nature's place for innocence ?
Priest. Prosperity, that never makes offence.
Must. Hath destiny no wheels but mere occasion ?
Priest. Could east upon the west else make invasion ?
Must. Confusion follows where obedience leaves.
Priest. The tyrant only that event deceives.
Must. And are the ways of truth and honor such ?
Priest. Weakness doth ever think it owes too much.
Must. Hath fame her glorious colors out of fear ?
Priest. What is the world to him that is not there ?
Must. Tempt me no more. Good-will is then a pain,
When her words beat the heart and cannot enter.
I constant in my counsel do remain,
And more lives for my own life will not venture.
My fellows, rest : our Alcoran doth bind,
That I alone should firs; my father find.

A Messenger enters.

Messenger. Sire, by our lord's commandment, here I wait,
To guide you to his presence,
Where, like a king and father, he intends
To honor and acquaint you with his ends.
Must. Heli, farewell, all fates are from above
Chain'd unto humors that must rise or fall.
Think what we will: men do but what they shall.

Achmat describes the manner of Mustapha's Execution to Zanger

ACHMAT. ZANGER.

Achm. When Solyman, by cunning spite
Of Rossa's witchcrafts, from his heart had banish'd
Justice of kings, and lovingness of fathers,
To wage and lodge such camps of heady passions,
As that sect's cunning practices could gather;
Envy took hold of worth: doubt did misconstrue;
Renown was made a lie, and yet a terror:
Nothing could calm his rage, or move compassion:
Mustapha must die. To which end fetch'd he was,
Laden with hopes and promises of favor.
So vile a thing is craft in every heart,
As it makes power itself descend to art.
While Mustapha, that neither hoped nor feared,
Seeing the storms of rage and danger coming,
Yet came; and came accompanied with power.
But neither power, which warranted his safety,
Nor safety, that makes violence a justice,
Could hold him from obedience to this throne:
A gulph, which hath devoured many a one.
Zang. Alas! could neither truth appease his fury,
Nor his unlook'd humility of coming,
Nor any secret-witnessing remorses?
Can nature from herself make such divorces?
Tell on, that all the world may rue and wonder.
Achm. There is a place environed with trees,
Upon whose shadow'd centre there is pitch'd

A large embroider'd sumptuous pavilion ;
The stately throne of tyranny and murder ;
Where mighty men are slain, before they know
That they to other than to honor go.
Mustapha no sooner to the port did come
But hither he is sent for and conducted
By six slave eunuchs, either taught to color
Mischief with reverence, or forced, by nature,
To revérence true virtue in misfortune.
While Mustapha, whose heart was now resolved,
Not fearing death, which he might have prevented ;
Nor craving life, which he might well have gotten,
If he would other duties have forgotten ;
Yet glad to speak his last thoughts to his father,
Desired the eunuchs to entreat it for him.
They did ; wept they, and kneeled to his father.
But bloody rage that glories to be cruel,
And jealousy that fears she is not fearful,
Made Solyman refuse to hear, or pity.
He bids them haste their charge : and bloody-eyed
Behold his son, while he obeying died.

Zang. How did that doing heart endure to suffer ?
Tell on.
Quicken my powers, harden'd and dull to good,
Which, yet unmoved, hear tell of brother's blood.

Achm. While these six eunuchs to this charge appointed
(Whose hearts had never used their hands to pity,
Whose hands, now only, trembled to do murder)
With reverence and fear stood still amazed ;
Loth to cut off such worth, afraid to save it :
Mustapha, with thoughts resolved and united,
Bids them fulfil their charge and look no further.
Their hearts afraid to let their hands be doing,
The cord, that hateful instrument of murder,
They lifting up let fall, and falling lift it :
Each sought to help, and helping hinder'd other.
Till Mustapha, in haste to be an angel,
With heavenly smiles, and quiet words, foreshows

The joy and peace of those souls where he goes.
His last words were; "O father now forgive me;
"Forgive them too that wrought my overthrow:
"Let my grave never minister offences.
"For since my father coveteth my death,
"Behold with joy I offer him my breath."
The eunuchs roar: Solyman his rage is glutted:
His thoughts divine of vengeance for this murder:
Rumor flies up and down: the people murmur:
Sorrow gives laws before men know the truth:
Fear prophecieth aloud, and threatens ruth.

Rosten describes to Achmat the popular Fury which followed upon the Execution of Mustapha.

ROSTEN. ACHMAT.

Ros. When Mustapha was by the eunuchs strangled,
Forthwith his camp grew doubtful of his absence:
The guard of Solyman himself did murmur:
People began to search their prince's counsels:
Fury gave laws: the laws of duty vanisht.
Kind fear of him they lov'd self-fear had banisht.
The headlong spirits were the heads that guided:
He that most disobeyed, was most obeyed.
Fury so suddenly became united,
As while her forces nourished confusion,
Confusion seem'd with discipline delighted.
Towards Solyman they run: and as the waters,
That meet with banks of snow, makes snow grow water:
So, even those guards, that stood to interrupt them,
Give easy passage, and pass on amongst them.
Solyman, who saw this storm of mischief coming,
Thinks absence his best argument unto them:
Retires himself, and sends me to demand,
What they demanded, or what meant their coming?
I speak: they cry'd for Mustapha and Achmat.
Some bid away; some kill; some save; some hearken.
Those that cried save, were those that sought to kill me.
Who cried hark, were those that first brake silence:

They held that bade me go. Humility was guilty ;
Words were reproach ; silence in me was scornful ;
They answer'd ere they ask'd ; assured, and doubted.
I fled ; their fury follow'd to destroy me ;
Fury made haste ; haste multiplied their fury ;
Each would do all ; none would give place to other.
The hindmost strake ; and while the foremost lifted
Their arms to strike, each weapon hinder'd other :
Their running let their strokes, strokes let their running.
Desire, mortal enemy to desire,
Made them that sought my life, give life unto me.

[These two Tragedies of Lord Brooke might with more propriety have been termed political treatises, than plays. Their author has strangely contrived to make passion, character and interest, of the highest order subservient to the expression of state dogmas and mysteries. He is nine parts Machiavel and Tacitus, for one part Sophocles or Seneca. In this writer's estimate of the faculties of his own mind, the understanding must have held a most tyrannical pre-eminence. Whether we look into his plays, or his most passionate love-poems, we shall find all frozen and made rigid with intellect. The finest movements of the human heart, the utmost grandeur of which the soul is capable, are essentially comprised in the actions and speeches of Cælica and Camena. Shakspeare, who seems to have had a peculiar delight in contemplating womanly perfection, whom for his many sweet images of female excellence all women are in an especial manner bound to love, has not raised the *ideal* of the female character higher than Lord Brooke in these two women has done. But it requires a study equivalent to the learning of a new language to understand their meaning when they speak. It is indeed hard to hit :

Much like thy riddle, Samson, in one day
Or seven though one should musing sit.

It is as if a being of pure intellect should take upon him to express the emotions of our sensitive natures. There would be all knowledge, but sympathetic expression would be wanting.]

THE CASE IS ALTERED. A COMEDY. BY BEN. JONSON

The present Humor to be followed.

AURELIA, PHŒNIXELLA, *Sister: their Mother being lately dead*

Aur. Room for a case of matrons, color'd black:
How motherly my mother's death hath made us!
I would I had some girls now to bring up;
O I could make a wench so virtuous,
She should say grace to every bit of meat,
And gape no wider than a wafer's thickness,
And she should make French court'sies so most low
That every touch should turn her over backward.
Phœn. Sister, these words become not your attire,
Nor your estate; our virtuous mother's death
Should print more deep effects of sorrow in us,
Than may be worn out in so little time.
Aur. Sister, i' faith you take too much tobacco,
It makes you black within as you 're without.
What, true-stitch sister, both your sides alike!
Be of a slighter work; for, of my word,
You shall be sold as dear, or rather dearer.
Will you be bound to customs and to rites,
Shed profitable tears, weep for advantage;
Or else do all things as you are inclined?
Eat when your stomach serves, saith the physician,
Not at eleven and six. So, if your humor
Be now affected with this heaviness,
Give it the reins, and spare not; as I do
In this my pleasurable appetite.
It is *Precisianism* to alter that,
With austere judgment, that is giv'n by nature.
I wept (you saw) too, when my mother died;
For then I found it easier to do so,
And fitter with my mode, than not to weep:
But now 'tis otherwise. Another time
Perhaps I shall have such deep thoughts of her,
That I shall weep afresh some twelvemonth hence;

And I will weep, if I be so disposed;
And put on black as grimly then as now.—
Let the mind go still with the body's stature:
Judgment is fit for judges; give me nature.

Presentiment of Treachery, vanishing at the sight of the person suspected

Lord PAULO FARNEZE. (*Speaking to himself of* ANGELO.)

—— My thoughts cannot propose a reason
Why I should fear or faint thus in my hopes
Of one so much endeared to my love:
Some spark it is, kindled within the soul,
Whose light yet breaks not to the outward sense,
That propagates this timorous suspect.
His actions never carried any force
Of change, or weakness; then I injure him,
In being thus cold-conceited of his faith.
O here he comes. [*While he speaks* ANGELO *enters.*
Angelo. How now, sweet Lord, what 's the matter?
Paul. Good faith, his presence makes me half ashamed
Of my stray'd thoughts.

Jaques (a Miser) worships his Gold.

Jac. Tis not to be told
What servile villainies men will do for gold.
O it began to have a huge strong smell,
With lying so long together in a place:
I 'll give it vent, it shall have shift enough;
And if the devil, that envies all goodness,
Have told them of my gold, and where I kept it,
I 'll set his burning nose once more a work
To smell where I removed it. Here it is;
I 'll hide and cover it with this horse-dung.
Who will suppose that such a precious nest
Is crown'd with such a dunghill excrement?
In, my dear life, sleep sweetly, my dear child,
Scarce lawfully begotten, but yet gotten,
And that 's enough. Rot all hands that come near thee,
Except mine own. Burn out all eyes that see thee,

Except mine own. All thoughts of thee be poison
To their enamor'd hearts, except mine own.
I'll take no leave, sweet prince, great emperor,
But see thee every minute: king of kings,
I 'll not be rude to thee, and turn my back
In going from thee, but go backward out,
With my face toward thee, with humble courtesies.

[The passion for wealth has worn out much of its grossness by tract of time. Our ancestors certainly conceived of money as able to confer a distinct gratification in itself, not alone considered simply as a symbol of wealth. The oldest poets, when they introduce a miser, constantly make him address his gold as his mistress; as something to be seen, felt, and hugged: as capable of satisfying two of the senses at least. The substitution of a thin unsatisfying medium for the good old tangible gold, has made avarice quite a Platonic affection in comparison with the seeing, touching, and handling pleasures of the old Chrysophilites. A bank note can no more satisfy the touch of a true sensualist in this passion, than Creusa could return her husband's embrace in the shades.—See the Cave of Mammon, in Spenser; Barabas's contemplation of his wealth, in the Jew of Malta; Luke's raptures, in the City Madam, &c. Above all, hear Guzman, in that excellent old Spanish Novel, The Rogue, expatiate on the "ruddy cheeks of your golden Ruddocks, your Spanish Pistolets, your plump and full-faced Portuguese, and your clear-skinn'd pieces of eight of Castile," which he and his fellows the beggars kept secret to themselves, and did "privately enjoy in a plentiful manner." "For to have them, for to pay them away, is not to enjoy them; to enjoy them, is to have them lying by us, having no other need of them than to use them for the clearing of the eye-sight, and the comforting of our senses. These we did carry about with us, sewing them in some patches of our doublets near unto the heart, and as close to the skin as we could handsomely quilt them in, holding them to be restorative."]

POETASTER; OR, HIS ARRAIGNMENT. A COMICAL SATYR. BY BEN JONSON.

Ovid bewails his hard condition in being banished from Court and the Society of the Princess Julia.

OVID.

Banish'd the court? let me be banish'd life,
Since the chief end of life is there concluded.

Within the court is all the kingdom bounded;
And as her sacred sphere doth comprehend
Ten thousand times so much, as so much place
In any part of all the empire else,
So every body, moving in her sphere,
Contains ten thousand times as much in him
As any other her choice orb excludes.
As in a circle a magician, then,
Is safe against tho spirit he excites,
But out of it is subject to his rage,
And loseth all the virtue of his art,
So I, exil'd the circle of the court,
Lose all the good gifts that in it I joy'd.
No virtue current is, but with her stamp;
And no vice vicious, blanch'd with her white hand.
The court's the abstract of all Rome's desert,
And my dear Julia th' abstract of the court.
Methinks, now I come near her, I respire
Some air of that late comfort I receiv'd:
And while the evening, with her modest veil,
Gives leave to such poor shadows as myself
To steal abroad, I, like a heartless ghost,
Without the living body of my love,
Will here walk, and attend her. For I know
Not far from hence she is imprison'd,
And hopes of her strict guardian to bribe
So much admittance, as to speak to me,
And cheer my fainting spirits with her breath.

Julia appears above at her Chamber-window.

Jul. Ovid! my love!
Ovid. Here, heav'nly Julia.
Jul. Here! and not here! O how that word doth play
With both our fortunes, differing, like ourselves;
But one, and yet divided, as opposed;
I high, thou low! O this our plight of place
Doubly presents the two lets of our love,
Local and ceremonial height and lowness;

Both ways, I am too high, and thou too low.
Our minds are even, yet: O why should our bodies,
That are their slaves, be so without their rule?
I 'll cast myself down to thee; if I die,
I 'll ever live with thee: no height of birth,
Of place, of duty, or of cruel power,
Shall keep me from thee; should my father lock
This body up within a tomb of brass,
Yet I'll be with thee. If the forms, I hold
Now in my soul, be made one substance with it;
That soul immortal; and the same 'tis now;
Death cannot raze the effects she now retaineth:
And then may she be anywhere she will.
The souls of parents rule not children's souls;
When death sets both in their dissolv'd estates,
Then is no child nor father: then eternity
Frees all from any temporal respect.
I come, my Ovid, take me in thine arms;
And let me breathe my soul into thy breast.
Ovid. O stay, my love; the hopes thou dost conceive
Of thy quick death, and of thy future life,
Are not authentical. Thou choosest death,
So thou might'st joy thy love in th' other life,
But know, my princely love, when thou art dead,
Thou only must survive in perfect soul;
And in the soul are no affections:
We pour out our affections with our blood;
And with our blood's affections fade our loves.
No life hath love in such sweet state as this;
No essence is so dear to moody sense,
As flesh and blood, whose quintessence is sense.
Beauty, compos'd of blood and flesh, moves more,
And is more plausible to blood and flesh,
Than spiritual beauty can be to the spirit.
Such apprehension as we have in dreams
(When sleep, the bond of senses, locks them up)
Such shall we have when death destroys them quite.
If love be then thy object, change not life;

Live high and happy still; I still below,
Close with my fortunes, in thy height shall joy.
Jul. Ay me, that virtue, whose brave eagle's wings
With every stroke blow stars in burning heaven,
Should like a swallow (preying toward storms)
Fly close to earth; and, with an eager plume
Pursue those objects which none else can see,
But seem to all the world the empty air.
Thus thou, poor Ovid, and all virtuous men,
Must prey like swallows on invisible food;
Pursuing flies, or nothing; and thus love,
And every worldly fancy, is transpos'd
By worldly tyranny to what plight it list.
O, father, since thou gav'st me not my mind,
Strive not to rule it; take but what thou gav'st
To thy disposure: thy affections
Rule not in me; I must bear all my griefs;
Let me use all my pleasures: Virtuous love
Was never scandal to a goddess' state.
But he 's inflexible! and, my dear love,
Thy life may chance be shorten'd by the length
Of my unwilling speeches to depart.
Farewell, sweet life: though thou be yet exil'd
Th' officious court, enjoy me amply still:
My soul, in this my breath, enters thine ears;
And on this turret's floor will I lie dead,
Till we may meet again. In this proud height,
I kneel beneath thee in my prostrate love,
And kiss the happy sands that kiss thy feet,
Great Jove submits a sceptre to a cell;
And lovers, ere they part, will meet in hell.
Ovid. Farewell all company, and, if I could,
All light, with thee: hell's shade should hide thy brows
Till thy dear beauty's beams redeem'd my vows.
Jul. Ovid: my love: alas! may we not stay
A little longer, think'st thou, undiscern'd?
Ovid. For thine own good, fair goddess, do not stay.
Who would engage a firmament of fires,

Shining in thee, for me, a falling star?
Begone, sweet life-blood: if I should discern
Thyself but touch'd for my sake, I should die.
Jul. I will begone then; and not heav'n itself
Shall draw me back.
Ovid. Yet, Julia, if thou wilt
A little longer stay.
Jul. I am content.
Ovid. O mighty Ovid! what the sway of heav'n
Could not retire, my breath hath turned back.
Jul. Who shall go first, my love? my passionate eyes
Will not endure to see thee turn from me.
Ovid. If thou go first, my soul will follow thee.
Jul. Then we must stay.
Ovid. Ay me, there is no stay
In amorous pleasures. If both stay, both die.
I hear thy father. Hence, my deity, [*Julia goes in.*
Fear forgeth sounds in my deluded ears;
I did not hear him: I am mad with love.
There is no spirit, under heav'n, that works
With such illusion: yet, such witchcraft kill me,
Ere a sound mind, without it, save my life.
Here on my knees I worship the blest place,
That held my goddess; and the loving air,
That clos'd her body in his silken arms.
Vain Ovid! kneel not to the place, nor air:
She's in thy heart; rise then, and worship there.
The truest wisdom, silly men can have,
Is dotage on the follies of their flesh.——

Augustus discourses with his Courtiers concerning Poetry.

CÆSAR, MECÆNAS, GALLUS, TIBULLUS, HORACE.

Equites Romani.

Cæs. We, that have conquer'd still to save the conquer'd,
And love to make inflictions fear'd, not felt;
Griev'd to reprove, and joyful to reward,
More proud of reconcilement than revenge,

Resume into the late state of our love
Worthy Cornelius Gallus and Tibullus.*
You both are gentlemen; you Cornelius,
A soldier of renown, and the first provost
That ever let our Roman Eagles fly
On swarthy Egypt, quarried with her spoils.
Yet (not to bear cold forms, nor men's out-terms,
Without the inward fires, and lives of men)
You both have virtues, shining through your shapes;
To show, your titles are not writ on posts,
Or hollow statues; which the best men are,
Without Promethean stuffings reach'd from heaven.
Sweet Poesy's sacred garlands crown your gentry:
Which is, of all the faculties on earth,
The most abstract, and perfect, if she be
True born, and nurst with all the sciences.
She can so mould Rome, and her monuments,
Within the liquid marble of her lines,
That they shall stand fresh and miraculous,
Even when they mix with innovating dust;
In her sweet streams shall our brave Roman spirits
Chase, and swim after death, with their choice deeds
Shining on their white shoulders; and therein
Shall Tyber, and our famous rivers, fall
With such attraction, that th' ambitious line
Of the round world shall to her centre shrink,
To hear their music. And for these high parts,
Cæsar shall reverence the Pierian arts.
Mec. Your majesty's high grace to poesy
Shall stand 'gainst all the dull detractions
Of leaden souls; who for the vain assumings
Of some, quite worthless of her sovereign wreaths,
Contain her worthiest prophets in contempt.
Gal. Happy is Rome of all earth's other states,
To have so true and great a president,
For her inferior spirits to imitate,

* They had offended the Emperor by concealing the love of Ovid for the Princess Julia.

As Cæsar is; who addeth to the sun
Influence and lustre, in increasing thus
His inspirations, kindling fire in us.
Hor. Phœbus himself shall kneel at Cæsar's shrine
And deck it with bay-garlands dew'd with wine,
To quit the worship Cæsar does to him:
Where other princes, hoisted to their thrones
By Fortune's passionate and disorder'd power,
Sit in their height like clouds before the sun,
Hind'ring his comforts; and (by their excess
Of cold in virtue, and cross heat in vice)
Thunder and tempest on those learned heads,
Whom Cæsar with such honor doth advance.
Tib. All human business Fortune doth command
Without all order; and with her blind hand,
She, blind, bestows blind gifts: that still have nurst,
They see not who, nor how, but still the worst.
Cæs. Cæsar, for his rule, and for so much stuff
As fortune puts in his hand, shall dispose it
(As if his hand had eyes, and soul, in it)
With worth and judgment. Hands that part with gifts,
Or will restrain their use, without desert,
Or with a misery, numb'd to Virtue's right,
Work, as they had no soul to govern them,
And quite reject her: sev'ring their estates
From human order. Whosoever can,
And will not cherish Virtue, is no man.
Eques. Virgil is now at hand, imperial Cæsar.
Cæs. Rome's honor is at hand then. Fetch a chair,
And set it on our right-hand; where 'tis fit,
Rome's honor and our own should ever sit.
Now he is come out of Campania,
I doubt not he hath finish'd all his Æneids;
Which, like another soul, I long t' enjoy.
What think you three of Virgil, gentlemen
(That are of his profession though ranked higher),
Or, Horace, what sayst thou, that art the poorest,
And likeliest to envy or to detract?

Hor. Cæsar speaks after common men in this,
To make a difference of me for my poorness:
As if the filth of poverty sunk as deep
Into a knowing spirit, as the bane
Of riches doth into an ignorant soul.
No, Cæsar; they be pathless moorish minds,
That being once made rotten with the dung
Of damned riches, ever after sink
Beneath the steps of any villainy.
But knowledge is the nectar, that keeps sweet
A perfect soul, even in this grave of sin;
And for my soul, it is as free as Cæsar's:
For what I know is due I'll give to all.
He that detracts, or envies virtuous merit,
Is still the covetous and the ignorant spirit.
Cæs. Thanks, Horace, for thy free and wholesome sharpness:
Which pleaseth Cæsar more than servile fawns.
A flatter'd prince soon turns the prince of fools.
And for thy sake we'll put no difference more
Between the great and good for being poor.
Say then, loved Horace, thy true thought of Virgil.
Hor. I judge him of a rectified spirit,
By many revolutions of discourse
(In his bright reason's influence) refined
From all the tartarous moods of common men;
Bearing the nature and similitude
Of a right heavenly body; most severe
In fashion and collection of himself:
And then as clear and confident as Jove.
Gal. And yet so chaste and tender is his ear,
In suffering any syllable to pass,
That he thinks may become the honor'd name
Of issue to his so examined self;
That all the lasting fruits of his full merit
In his own poems, he doth still distaste;
As if his mind's piece, which he strove to paint,
Could not with fleshly pencils have her right.
Tib. But to approve his works of sovereign worth,

This observation (methinks) more than serves;
And is not vulgar. That which he hath writ,
Is with such judgment labor'd, and distill'd
Through all the needful uses of our lives,
That could a man remember but his lines,
He should not touch at any serious point,
But he might breathe his spirit out of him.
Cæs. You mean he might repeat part of his works,
As fit for any conference he can use?
Tib. True, royal Cæsar.
Cæs. Worthily observed:
And a most worthy virtue in his works,
What thinks material Horace of his learning?
Hor. His learning savors not the school-like gloss,
That most consists in echoing words and terms:
And soonest wins a man an empty name:
Nor any long, or far fetch'd circumstance,
Wrapt in the curious general'ties of arts;
But a direct and analytic sum
Of all the worth and first effects of arts.
And for his poesy, 'tis so ramm'd with life,
That it shall gather strength of life, with being,
And live hereafter more admired than now.
Cæs. This one consent, in all your dooms of him,
And mutual loves of all your several merits,
Argues a truth of merit in you all.

VIRGIL *enters.*

See here comes Virgil; we will rise and greet him:
Welcome to Cæsar, Virgil. Cæsar and Virgil
Shall differ but in sound; to Cæsar, Virgil
(Of his expressed greatness) shall be made
A second sir-name; and to Virgil, Cæsar.
Where are thy famous Æneids? do us grace
To let us see, and surfeit on their sight.
Vir. Worthless they are of Cæsar's gracious eyes,
If they were perfect; much more with their wants:
Which yet are more than my time could supply.

And could great Cæsar's expectation
Be satisfied with any other service,
I would not show them.
Cæs. Virgil is too modest;
Or seeks, in vain, to make our longings more.
Show them, sweet Virgil.
Vir. Then, in such due fear
As fits presenters of great works to Cæsar,
I humbly show them.
Cæs. Let us now behold
A human soul made visible in life:
And more refulgent in a senseless paper,
Than in the sensual complement of kings.
Read, read, thyself, dear Virgil; let not me
Profane one accent with an untuned tongue:
Best matter, badly shown, shows worse than bad.
See then this chair, of purpose set for thee,
To read thy poem in; refuse it not,
Virtue, without presumption, place may take
Above best kings, whom only she should make.
Vir. It will be thought a thing ridiculous
To present eyes, and to all future times
A gross untruth; that any poet (void
Of birth, or wealth, or temporal dignity),
Should, with decorum, transcend Cæsar's chair.
Poor virtue raised, high birth and wealth set under,
Crosseth heav'n's courses, and makes worldlings wonder.
Cæs. The course of heaven, and fate itself, in this
Will Cæsar cross; much more all worldly custom.
Hor. Custom in course of honor ever errs:
And they are best, whom fortune least prefers.
Cæs. Horace hath (but more strictly) spoke our thoughts.
The vast rude swinge of general confluence
Is, in particular ends, exempt from sense:
And therefore reason (which in right should be
The special rector of all harmony)
Shall show we are a man, distinct by it
From those, whom custom rapteth in her press.

Ascend then, Virgil; and where first by chance
We here have turn'd thy book, do thou first read.
Vir. Great Cæsar hath his will: I will ascend.
'Twere simple injury to his free hand,
That sweeps the cobwebs from un-used virtue,
And makes her shine proportion'd to her worth,
To be more nice to entertain his grace,
Than he is choice and liberal to afford it.
Cæs. Gentlemen of our chamber, guard the doors,
And let none enter; peace. Begin, good Virgil.

VIRGIL *reads part of his fourth Æneid.*

Vir. Meanwhile, the skies 'gan thunder, &c.

[This Roman Play seems written to confute those enemies of Ben. Jonson in his own days and ours, who have said that he made a pedantical use of his learning. He has here revived the whole court of Augustus, by a learned spell. We are admitted to the society of the illustrious dead. Virgil, Horace, Ovid, Tibullus, converse in our own tongue more finely and poetically than they expressed themselves in their native Latin.——Nothing can be imagined more elegant, refined, and court-like than the scenes between this Louis the Fourteenth of Antiquity and his Literati.—The whole essence and secret of that kind of intercourse is contained therein. The economical liberality by which greatness, seeming to wave some part of its prerogative, takes care to lose none of the essentials; the prudential liberties of an inferior which flatter by commanded boldness and soothe with complimental sincerity.]

SEJANUS HIS FALL: A TRAGEDY. BY BEN. JONSON.

Sejanus, the morning he is condemned by the Senate, receives some tokens which presage his death.

SEJANUS. POMPONIUS. MINUTIUS. TERENTIUS, &c.

Ter. Are these things true?
Min. Thousands are gazing at it in the streets.
Sej. What 's that?
Ter. Minutius tells us here, my Lord,
That a new head being set upon your statue,

A rope is since found wreath'd about it! and
But now a fiery meteor in the form
Of a great ball was seen to roll along
The troubled air, where yet it hangs unperfect,
The amazing wonder of the multitude.
Sej. No more—
Send for the tribunes; we will straight have up
More of the soldiers for our guard. Minutius,
We pray you go for Cotta, Latiaris,
Trio the consul, or what senators
You know are sure, and ours. You, my good Natta,
For Laco provost of the watch. Now, Satrius,
The time of proof comes on. Arm all our servants,
And without tumult. You, Pomponius,
Hold some good correspondence with the consul;
Attempt him, noble friend. These things begin
To look like dangers, now, worthy my fates.
Fortune, I see thy worst: Let doubtful states
And things uncertain hang upon thy will;
Me surest death shall render certain still.
Yet why is now my thought turn'd toward death,
Whom fates have let go on so far in breath
Uncheckt or unreprov'd? I, that did help
To fell the lofty cedar of the world,
Germanicus; that at one stroke cut down
Drusus that upright elm; wither'd his vine;
Laid Silius and Sabinus, two strong oaks,
Flat on the earth; besides those other shrubs,
Cordus, and Sosia, Claudia, Pulchra,
Furnius, and Gallius, which I have grubb'd up;
And since, have set my axe so strong and deep
Into the root of spreading Agrippina;
Lopt off and scatter'd her proud branches, Nero,
Drusus, and Caius too, although replanted:
If you will, destinies, that after all
I faint now ere I touch my period,
You are but cruel; and I already have done
Things great enough. All Rome hath been my slave;

The senate sate an idle looker on,
And witness of my power; when I have blush'd
More to command, than it to suffer; all
The fathers have sate ready and prepar'd
To give me empire, temples, or their throats,
When I would ask 'em; and (what crowns the top)
Rome, senate, people, all the world, have seen
Jove but my equal, Cæsar but my second.
'Tis then your malice, Fates, who (but your own)
Envy and fear to have any power long known.

THE SAD SHEPHERD: OR, A TALE OF ROBIN HOOD. BY BEN. JONSON.

Alken, an old Shepherd, instructs Robin Hood's Men how to find a Witch, and how she is to be hunted.

ROBIN HOOD. TUCK. LITTLE JOHN. SCARLET. SCATHLOCK. GEORGE. ALKEN. CLARION.

Tuck. Hear you how
Poor Tom, the cook, is taken! all his joints
Do crack, as if his limbs were tied with points:
His whole frame slackens, and a kind of rack
Runs down along the spondils of his back;
A gout, or cramp, now seizeth on his head,
Then fall into his feet; his knees are lead;
And he can stir his either hand no more
Than a deal stump to his office, as before.
Alk. He is bewitch'd.
Cla. This is an argument
Both of her malice, and her power, we see.
Alk. She must by some device restrained be,
Or she'll go far in mischief.
Rob. Advise how,
Sage shepherd; we shall put it straight in practice.
Alk. Send forth your woodmen then into the walks,
Or let them prick her footing hence; a witch

Is sure a creature of melancholy,
And will be found, or sitting in her fourm,
Or else at relief, like a hare.
Cla. You speak,
Alken, as if you knew the sport of witch-hunting,
Or starting of a hag.
Rob. Go, Sirs, about it,
Take George here with you, he can help to find her.
John. Rare sport, I swear, this hunting of the witch
Will make us.
Scar. Let 's advise upon 't, like huntsmen.
Geo. An we can spy her once, she is our own.
Scath. First think which way she fourmeth, on what wind:
Or north, or south.
Geo. For, as the shepherd said,
A witch is a kind of hare.
Scath. And marks the weather,
As the hare does.
John. Where shall we hope to find her ?
Alk. Know you the witches dell ?
Scar. No more than I do know the walks of hell.
Alk. Within a gloomy dimble she doth dwell,
Down in a pit o'er grown with brakes and briars,
Close by the ruins of a shaken abbey,
Torn with an earthquake down unto the ground,
'Mongst graves, and grots, near an old charnel house,
Where you shall find her sitting in her fourm,
As fearful, and melancholic, as that
She is about; with caterpillars' kells,
And knotty cobwebs, rounded in with spells.
Thence she steals forth to relief, in the fogs,
And rotten mists, upon the fens and bogs,
Down to the drowned lands of Lincolnshire;
To make ewes cast their lambs, swine eat their farrow !
The house-wife's tun not work, nor the milk churn !
Writhe children's wrists, and suck their breath in sleep !
Get vials of their blood ! and where the sea
Casts up his slimy ooze, search for a weed

To open locks with, and to rivet charms,
Planted about her, in the wicked seat
Of all her mischiefs, which are manifold.
John. I wonder such a story could be told
Of her dire deeds.
Geo. I thought a witches banks
Had enclosed nothing but the merry pranks
Of some old woman.
Scar. Yes, her malice more.
Scath. As it would quickly appear, had we the store
Of his collects.
Geo. Aye, this good learned man
Can speak her right.
Scar. He knows her shifts and haunts.
Alk. And all her wiles and turns. The venom'd plants
Wherewith she kills! where the sad mandrake grows,
Whose groans are deathful! the dead numbing night-shade!
The stupifying hemlock! adder's-tongue,
And martegan! the shrieks of luckless owls,
We hear! and croaking night-crows in the air!
Green-bellied snakes! blue fire-drakes in the sky!
And giddy flitter-mice with leather wings!
The scaly beetles, with their habergeons
That make a humming murmur as they fly!
There, in the stocks of trees, white fays do dwell,
And span-long elves that dance about a pool,
With each a little changeling in their arms!
The airy spirits play with falling stars,
And mount the sphere of fire, to kiss the moon!
While she sits reading by the glow-worm's light,
Or rotten wood, o'er which the worm hath crept,
The baneful schedule of her nocent charms,
And binding characters, through which she wounds
Her puppets, the *Sigilla* of her witchcraft.
All this I know, and I will find her for you;
And show you her sitting in her fourm; I 'll lay
My hand upon her; make her throw her scut
Along her back, when she doth start before us.

But you must give her law ; and you shall see her
Make twenty leaps and doubles, cross the paths,
And then squat down beside us.
John. Crafty croan,
I long to be at the sport, and to report it.
Scar. We 'll make this hunting of the witch as famous,
As any other blast of venery.
Geo. If we could come to see her, cry *so haw* once—
Alk. That I do promise, or I 'm no good hag-finder.

CATILINE HIS CONSPIRACY : A TRAGEDY. BY BEN. JONSON.

The morning of the Conspiracy.—Lentulus, Cethegus, and Catiline meet, before the other Conspirators are ready.

Lent. It is methinks a morning full of fate,
It riseth slowly, as her sullen car
Had all the weights of sleep and death hung at it.
She is not rosy-finger'd, but swoln black.
Her face is like a water turn'd to blood,
And her sick head is bound about with clouds,
As if she threaten'd night ere noon of day.
It does not look as it would have a hail
Or health wish'd in it, as on other morns.
Cet. Why, all the fitter, Lentulus : our coming
Is not for salutation : we have business.
Cat. Said nobly, brave Cethegus. Where's Autronius ?
Cet. Is he not come ?
Cat. Not here.
Cet. Not Vargunteius ?
Cat. Neither.
Cet. A fire in their beds and bosoms,
That so well serve their sloth rather than virtue.
They are no Romans, and at such high need
As now ———
Lent. Both they, Longinus, Lecca, Curius,

Fulvius, Gabinus, gave me word last night,
By Lucius Bestia, they would all be here,
And early.
Cet. Yes! as you, had I not call'd you.
Come, we all sleep, and are mere dormice; flies
A little less than dead: more dulness hangs
On us than on the morn. We 're spirit bound,
In ribs of ice; our whole bloods are one stone:
And honor cannot thaw us, nor our wants,
Though they burn hot as fevers to our states.
Cat. I muse they would be tardy at an hour
Of so great purpose.
Cet. If the gods had call'd
Them to a purpose, they would just have come
With the same tortoise speed; that are thus slow
To such an action, which the gods will envy;
As asking no less means than all their powers
Conjoin'd to effect. I would have seen Rome burnt
By this time, and her ashes in an urn:
The kingdom of the senate rent asunder:
And the degenerate talking gown run frighted
Out of the air of Italy.
Cat. Spirit of men,
Thou heart of our great enterprise, how much
I love these voices in thee!
Cet. O the days
Of Sylla's sway, when the free sword took leave
To act all that it would!
Cat. And was familiar
With entrails, as our augurs———
Cet. Sons kill'd fathers,
Brothers their brothers———
Cat. And had price and praise:
All hate and license giv'n it; all rage reins.
Cet. Slaughter bestrid the streets, and stretch'd himself
To seem more huge: whilst to his stained thighs
The gore he drew flow'd up, and carried down
Whole heaps of limbs and bodies through his arch.

No age was spar'd, no sex.
Cat. Nay, no degree ——
Cet. Not infants in the porch of life were free.
The sick, the old, that could but hope a day
Longer by nature's bounty, not let stay.
Virgins and widows, matrons, pregnant wives,
All died.
Cat. 'Twas crime enough that they had lives.
To strike but only those that could do hurt,
Was dull and poor. Some fell, to make the number;
As some, the prey.
Cet. The rugged Charon fainted,
And ask'd a navy rather than a boat,
To ferry over the sad world that came:
The maws and dens of beasts could not receive
The bodies that those souls were frighted from;
And even the graves were fill'd with men yet living,
Whose flight and fear had mix'd them with the dead.
Cat. And this shall be again, and more, and more,
Now Lentulus, the third Cornelius,
Is to stand up in Rome.
Lent. Nay, urge not that
Is so uncertain.
Cat. How!
Lent. I mean, not clear'd;
And therefore not to be reflected on.
Cat. The Sybil's leaves uncertain! or the comments,
Of our grave, deep, divining men, not clear!
Lent. All prophecies, you know, suffer the torture.
Cat. But this already hath confess'd, without;
And so been weigh'd, examin'd, and compar'd,
As 'twere malicious ignorance in him
Would faint in the belief.
Lent. Do you believe it?
Cat. Do I love Lentulus, or pray to see it?
Lent. The augurs all are constant I am meant.
Cat. They had lost their science else.
Lent. They count from Cinna ——

Cat. And Sylla next——and so make you the third;
All that can say the sun is ris'n, must think it.
Lent. Men mark me more of late as I come forth!
Cat. Why, what can they do less? Cinna and Sylla
Are set and gone; and we must turn our eyes
On him that is, and shines. Noble Cethegus,
But view him with me here! He looks already
As if he shook a sceptre o'er the senate,
And the aw'd purple dropt their rods and axes.
The statues melt again, and household gods
In groans confess the travails of the city:
The very walls sweat blood before the change;
And stones start out to ruin, ere it comes.
Cet. But he, and we, and all, are idle still.
Lent. I am your creature, Sergius; and whate'er
The great Cornelian name shall win to be,
It is not augury, nor the Sybil's books
But Catiline, that makes it.
Cat. I am a shadow
To honor'd Lentulus, and Cethegus here;
Who are the heirs of Mars.——

THE NEW INN; OR, THE LIGHT HEART. A COMEDY. BY BEN. JONSON.

Lovel discovers to the Host of the New Inn, his Love for the Lady Frances, and his reasons for concealing his Passion from her.

Lov. There is no life on earth, but being in love!
There are no studies, no delights, no business,
No intercourse, or trade of sense, or soul,
But what is love! I was the laziest creature,
The most unprofitable sign of nothing,
The veriest drone, and slept away my life
Beyond the dormouse, till I was in love!
And now I can out-wake the nightingale,
Out-watch an usurer, and out-walk him too,

Stalk like a ghost that haunted 'bout a treasure ;
And all that fancied treasure, it is love !
Host. But is your name Love-ill, sir, or Love-well ?
I would know that.
Lov. I do not know it myself,
Whether it is. But it is love hath been
The hereditary passion of our house,
My gentle host, and, as I guess, my friend ;
The truth is, I have loved this lady long,
And impotently, with desire enough,
But no success: for I have still forborne
To express it in my person to her.
Host. How then ?
Lov. I have sent her toys, verses, and anagrams,
Trials of wit, mere trifles, she has commended,
But knew not whence they came, nor could she guess.
Host. This was a pretty riddling way of wooing !
Lov. I oft have been too in her company
And look'd upon her a whole day, admir'd her,
Loved her, and did not tell her so, loved still,
Look'd still, and loved ; and loved, and look'd, and sigh'd ;
But, as a man neglected, I came off,
And unregarded.
Host. Could you blame her, sir,
When you were silent and not said a word ?
Lov. O but I loved the more ; and she might read it
Best in my silence, had she been ——
Host. ———————— as melancholic,
As you are. Pray you, why would you stand mute, sir ?
Lov. O thereon hangs a history, mine host.
Did you ever know or hear of the Lord Beaufort,
Who serv'd so bravely in France ? I was his page,
And, ere he died, his friend ! I follow'd him
First in the wars, and in the time of peace
I waited on his studies ; which were right,
He had no Arthurs, nor no Rosicleers,
No Knights of the Sun, nor Amadis de Gauls,
Primalions, and Pantagruels, public nothings ;

Abortives of the fabulous dark cloister,
Sent out to poison courts, and infest manners:
But great Achilles', Agamemnon's acts,
Sage Nestor's counsels, and Ulysses' sleights,
Tydides' fortitude, as Homer wrought them
In his immortal fancy, for examples
Of the heroic virtue. Or, as Virgil,
That master of the Epic Poem, limn'd
Pious Æneas, his religious prince,
Bearing his aged parent on his shoulders,
Rapt from the flames of Troy, with his young son.
And these he brought to practise and to use.
He gave me first my breeding, I acknowledge,
Then shower'd his bounties on me, like the Hours,
That open-handed sit upon the clouds,
And press the liberality of heaven
Down to the laps of thankful men! But then,
The trust committed to me at his death
Was above all, and left so strong a tye
On all my powers as time shall not dissolve,
Till it dissolve itself, and bury all:
The care of his brave heir and only son!
Who being a virtuous, sweet, young, hopeful lord,
Hath cast his first affections on this lady.
And though I know, and may presume her such,
As, out of humor, will return no love,
And therefore might indifferently be made
The courting-stock for all to practise on,
As she doth practise on us all to scorn:
Yet out of a religion to my charge,
And debt profess'd, I have made a self-decree,
Ne'er to express my person though my passion
Burn me to cinders.

Lovel in the presence of the Lady Frances, the young Lord Beaufort, and other Guests of the New Inn, defines what Love is.

Lov. What else
Is love, but the most noble, pure affection

Of what is truly beautiful and fair?
Desire of union with the thing beloved?

Beau. I have read somewhere, that man and woman
Were, in the first creation, both one piece,
And being cleft asunder, ever since
Love was an appetite to be rejoin'd.

Lov. It is a fable of Plato's, in his banquet,
And utter'd there by Aristophanes.

Host. 'Twas well remember'd here, and to good use.
But on with your description what love is.
Desire of union with the thing beloved.

Lov. I meant a definition. For I make
The efficient cause, what's beautiful and fair.
The formal cause, the appetite of union.
The final cause, the union itself.
But larger, if you 'll have it, by description:
It is a flame and ardor of the mind,
Dead in the proper corps, quick in another's:
Transfers the lover into the loved.
That he, or she, that loves, engraves or stamps
The idea of what they love, first in themselves:
Or, like to glasses, so their minds take in
The forms of their belov'd, and them reflect.
It is the likeness of affections,
Is both the parent and the nurse of love.
Love is a spiritual coupling of two souls,
So much more excellent as it least relates
Unto the body; circular, eternal;
Not feign'd, or made, but born: And then, so precious,
As nought can value it but itself. So free,
As nothing can command it but itself,
And in itself so round and liberal,
As, where it favors, it bestows itself.
But we must take and understand this love
Along still as a name of dignity,
Not pleasure.
True love hath no unworthy thought, no light
Loose unbecoming appetite, or strain;

But fixed, constant, pure, immutable.
Beau. I relish not these philosophical feasts;
Give me a banquet o' sense, like that of Ovid;
A form, to take the eye; a voice, mine ear;
Pure aromatics to my scent; a soft
Smooth dainty hand to touch; and, for my taste,
Ambrosiac kisses to melt down the palate.
Lov. They are the earthly, lower form of lovers,
Are only taken with what strikes the senses,
And love by that loose scale. Altho' I grant,
We like what's fair and graceful in an object,
And (true) would use it, in them all we tend to,
Both of our civil and domestic deeds,
In ordering of an army, in our style,
Apparel, gesture, building, or what not?
All arts and actions do affect their beauty.
But put the case, in travel I may meet
Some gorgeous structure, a brave frontispiece,
Shall I stay captive in the outer court,
Surpriz'd with that, and not advanced to know
Who dwells there, and inhabiteth the house?
There is my friendship to be made, within;
With what can love me again; not with the walls,
Doors, windows, architrabes, the frieze, and cornice.
My end is lost in loving of a face,
An eye, lip, nose, hand, foot, or other part,
Whose all is but a statue if the mind
Move not, which only can make the return.
The end of love is, to have two made one
In will, and in affection, that the minds
Be first inoculated, not the bodies,
The body's love is frail, subject to change,
And alter still with it: The mind's is firm,
One and the same, proceedeth first from weighing,
And well examining what is fair and good;
Then what is like in reason, fit in manners;
That breeds good will: good will desire of union.
So knowledge first begets benevolence,

Benevolence breeds friendship, friendship love:
And where it starts or steps aside from this,
It is a mere degenerate appetite,
A lost, oblique, deprav'd affection,
And bears no mark or character of love.
Nor do they trespass within bounds of pardon,
That giving way and licence to their love,
Divest him of his noblest ornaments,
Which are his modesty and shamefac'dness:
And so they do, that have unfit designs
Upon the parties they pretend to love.
For what 's more monstrous, more a prodigy,
Than to hear me protest truth of affection
Unto a person that I would dishonor?
And what's a more dishonor, than defacing
Another's good with forfeiting mine own,
And drawing on a fellowship of sin?
From note of which though for a while we may
Be both kept safe by caution, yet the conscience
Cannot be cleans'd. For what was hitherto
Call'd by the name of love, becomes destroy'd
Then, with the fact; the innocency lost,
The bating of affection soon will follow;
And love is never true that is not lasting:
No more than any can be pure or perfect,
That entertains more than one object.

[These and the preceding extracts may serve to show the poetical fancy and elegance of mind of the supposed rugged old Bard. A thousand beautiful passages might be adduced from those numerous court masques and entertainments which he was in the daily habit of furnishing, to prove the same thing. But they do not come within my plan. That which follows is a specimen of that talent for comic humor, and the assemblage of ludicrous images, on which his reputation chiefly rests. It may serve for a variety after so many serious extracts.]

THE ALCHEMIST: A COMEDY. BY BEN. JONSON.

Epicure Mammon, a Knight, deceived by the pretensions of Subtle (the Alchemist), glories in the prospect of obtaining the Philosopher's Stone; and promises what rare things he will do with it.

MAMMON. SURLY, *his Friend.* *The Scene,* SUBTLE'S *House.*

Mam. Come on, Sir. Now you set your foot on shore
In *novo orbe.* Here's the rich Peru;
And there within, sir, are the golden mines,
Great Solomon's Ophir! He was sailing to 't
Three years, but we have reached it in ten months.
This is the day wherein to all my friends
I will pronounce the happy word, *Be rich.*
This day you shall be *spectatissimi.*
You shall no more deal with the hollow dye,
Or the frail card. No more be at charge of keeping
The livery punk for the young heir, that must
Seal at all hours in his shirt. No more,
If he deny, ha' him beaten to 't, as he is
That brings him the commodity. No more
Shall thirst of sattin, or the covetous hunger
Of velvet entrails for a rude-spun cloke
To be display'd at Madam Augusta's, make
The sons of Sword and Hazard fall before
The golden calf, and on their knees whole nights
Commit idolatry with wine and trumpets;
Or go a feasting after drum and ensign.
No more of this. You shall start up young Viceroys,
And have your punques and punquetees, my Surly:
And unto thee I speak it first, *Be rich.*
Where is my Subtle there? within ho ——

FACE *answers from within.*

Sir,
He 'll come to you by and by.
Mam. That's his fire-drake,
His Lungs, his Zephyrus, he that puffs his coals
Till he firk Nature up in her own centre.

You are not faithful, sir. This night I'll change
All that is metal in thy house to gold:
And early in the morning will I send
To all the plumbers and the pewterers,
And buy their tin and lead up; and to Lothbury,
For all the copper.

Sur. What, and turn that too?

Mam. Yes, and I'll purchase Devonshire and Cornwall,
And make them perfect Indies? You admire now?

Sur. No, faith.

Mam. But when you see the effects of the great medicine!
Of which one part projected on a hundred
Of Mercury, or Venus, or the Moon,
Shall turn it to as many of the Sun;
Nay, to a thousand, so *ad infinitum:*
You will believe me.

Sur. Yes, when I see 't, I will.

Mam. Ha! why,
Do you think I fable with you? I assure you,
He that has once the flower of the Sun,
The perfect Ruby, which we call Elixir,
Not only can do that, but by its virtue
Can confer honor, love, respect, long life,
Give safety, valor, yea, and victory,
To whom he will. In eight and twenty days
I'll make an old man of fourscore a child.

Sur. No doubt; he's that already.

Mam. Nay, I mean,
Restore his years, renew him like an eagle,
To the fifth age; make him get sons and daughters,
Young giants, as our philosophers have done
(The ancient patriarchs afore the flood)
But taking, once a week, on a knife's point
The quantity of a grain of mustard of it,
Become stout Marses, and beget young Cupids.

Sur. The decay'd vestals of Pickt-hatch would thank you,
That keep the fire alive there.

Mam. 'Tis the secret

Of Nature naturized 'gainst all infections,
Cures all diseases, coming of all causes;
A month's grief in a day: a year's in twelve;
And of what age soever, in a month:
Past all the doses of your drugging doctors.
I'll undertake withal to fright the plague
Out o' the kingdom in three months.
Sur. And I'll
Be bound, the players shall sing your praises, then,
Without their poets.
Mam. Sir, I'll do 't. Meantime,
I'll give away so much unto my man,
Shall serve th' whole city with preservative
Weekly; each house his dose, and at the rate—
Sur. As he that built the water-work, does with water?
Mam. You are incredulous.
Sur. Faith, I have a humor,
I would not willingly be gull'd. Your Stone
Cannot transmute me.
Mam. Pertinax Surly,
Will you believe antiquity? Records?
I'll show you a book, where Moses, and his sister,
And Solomon, have written of the Art?
I, and a treatise penn'd by Adam.
Sur. How?
Mam. Of the Philosopher's Stone, and in High Dutch.
Sur. Did Adam write, Sir, in High Dutch?
Mam. He did,
Which proves it was the primitive tongue.
Sur. What paper?
Mam. On cedar-board.
Sur. O that, indeed, they say,
Will last 'gainst worms.
Mam. 'Tis like your Irish wood
'Gainst cobwebs. I have a piece of Jason's Fleece too,
Which was no other than a book of Alchemy,
Writ in large sheep-skin, a good fat ram-vellum.
Such was Pythagoras' Thigh, Pandora's Tub,

And all that fable of Medea's charms,
The manner of our work: the bulls, our furnace,
Still breathing fire: our *Argent-vive*, the Dragon:
The Dragon's teeth, Mercury sublimate,
That keeps the whiteness, hardness, and the biting:
And they are gather'd into Jason's helm
(Th' Alembick) and then sow'd in Mars his field,
And thence sublim'd so often, till they are fix'd.
Both this, the Hesperian Garden, Cadmus' Story,
Jove's Shower, the Boon of Midas, Argus' Eyes,
Boccace his Demogorgon, thousands more,
All abstract riddles of our Stone.

FACE *enters.*

How now?
Do we succeed? is our day come? and holds it?
Face. The evening will set red upon you, sir;
You have color for it, crimson: the red ferment
Has done his office. Three hours hence prepare you
To see projection.
Mam. Pertinax, my Surly,
Again I say to thee aloud, *Be rich.*
This day thou shalt have ingots, and to-morrow
Give lords th' affront. Is it, my Zephyrus, right?
Blushes the Bolt's-head?
Face. Like a wench with child, sir,
That were but now discover'd to her master.
Mam. Excellent witty Lungs! My only care is,
Where to get stuff enough now, to project on.
This town will not half serve me.
Face. No, sir? buy
The covering off o' churches.
Mam. That's true.
Face. Yes.
Let 'em stand bare, as do their auditory;
Or cap 'em new with shingles.
Mam. No; good thatch:
Thatch will lie light upon the rafters, Lungs.

Lungs, I will manumit thee from the furnace;
I will restore thee thy complexion, Puffe,
Lost in the embers; and repair this brain
Hurt with the fume o' the metals.
Face. I have blown, sir,
Hard for your worship; thrown by many a coal,
When 'twas not beech; weigh'd those I put in, just,
To keep your heat still even; these blear'd eyes
Have waked to read your several colors, sir,
Of the *pale citron*, the *green lyon*, the *crow*,
The *peacock's tail*, the *plumed swan* ——
Mam. And lastly,
Thou hast described the *flower*, the *sanguis agni?*
Face. Yes, sir.
Mam. Where's master?
Face. At his prayers, sir, he,
Good man, he's doing his devotions
For his success.
Mam. Lungs, I will set a period
To all thy labors: thou shalt be the master
Of my seraglio. For I do mean
To have a list of wives and concubines
Equal with Solomon, who had the Stone
Alike with me: and I will make me a back
With the Elixir, that shall be as tough
As Hercules, to encounter fifty a night.
Thou art sure thou saw'st it *blood?*
Face. Both *blood* and *spirit*, sir.
Mam. I will have all my beds blown up; not stuft:
Down is too hard. And then, mine oval room
Fill'd with such pictures as Tiberius took
From Elephantis, and dull Aretine
But coldly imitated. Then, my glasses
Cut in more subtle angles, to disperse
And multiply the figures, as I walk
Naked between my *Succubæ*. My mists
I'll have of perfume, vapor'd 'bout the room,
To lose ourselves in; and my baths, like pits

To fall into; from whence we will come forth,
And roll us dry in gossamour and roses.
(Is it arrived at Ruby?)—Where I spy
A wealthy citizen, or rich lawyer,
Have a sublim'd pure wife, unto that fellow
I'll send a thousand pound to be my cuckold.
Face. And I shall carry it?
Mam. No, I'll have no bawds,
But fathers and mothers. They will do it best,
Best of all others. And my flatterers
Shall be the pure and gravest of divines
That I can get for money. My meet fools,
Eloquent burgesses; and then my poets,
The same that writ so subtly of the Fart:
Whom I will entertain still for that subject.
The few that would give out themselves to be
Court and town stallions, and each-where belie
Ladies, who are known most innocent (for them)
Those will I beg, to make me eunuchs of:
And they shall fan me with ten estrich tails
A piece, made in a plume, to gather wind.
We will be brave, Puffe, now we ha' the medicine
My meat shall all come in in Indian shells,
Dishes of Agate set in gold, and studded
With emeralds, sapphires, hyacinths, and rubies:
The tongues of carps, dormice, and camels' heels,
Boil'd i' the spirit of Sol, and dissolv'd pearl
(Apicius' diet 'gainst the epilepsy),
And I will eat these broths with spoons of amber,
Headed with diamant and carbuncle.
My foot-boy shall eat pheasants, calver'd salmons,
Knots, godwits, lampreys: I myself will have
The beards of barbels serv'd, in stead of sallads;
Oil'd mushrooms; and the swelling unctuous paps
Of a fat pregnant sow, newly cut off,
Drest with an exquisite and poignant sauce:
For which, I'll say unto my cook, "There's gold,
Go forth, and be a knight."

Face. Sir, I'll go look
A little, how it heightens.
Mam. Do.—My shirts
I'll have of taffata-sarsnet, soft and light
As cobwebs ; and, for all my other raiment,
It shall be such as might provoke the Persian,
Were he to teach the world riot anew.
My gloves of fishes' and birds' skins, perfum'd
With gums of paradise, and eastern air.
Sur. And do you think to have the Stone with this ?
Mam. No, I do think to have all this with the Stone.
Sur. Why, I have heard, he must be *homo frugi*,
A pious, holy, and religious man,
One free from mortal sin, a very virgin ——
Mam. That makes it —— Sir, he is so. But I buy it.
My venture brings it me. He, honest wretch,
A notable, superstitious, good soul,
Has worn his knees bare, and his slippers bald,
With prayer and fasting for it: and, sir, let him
Do it alone, for me, still. Here he comes.
Not a profane word, afore him: 'tis poison.

[The judgment is perfectly overwhelmed by the torrent of images, words, and book-knowledge with which Mammon confounds and stuns his incredulous hearer. They come pouring out like the successive strokes of Nilus They "doubly redouble strokes upon the foe." Description outstrides proof. We are made to believe effects before we have testimony for their causes : as a lively description of the joys of heaven sometimes passes for an argument to prove the existence of such a place. If there be no one image which rises to the height of the sublime, yet the confluence and assemblage of them all produces an effect equal to the grandest poetry. Xerxes' army that drank up whole rivers from their numbers may stand for single Achilles. Epicure Mammon is the most determined offspring of the author. It has the whole "matter and copy of the father, eye, nose, lip, the trick of his frown." It is just such a swaggerer as contemporaries have described old Ben to be. Meercraft, Bobadil, the Host of the New Inn, have all his "image and superscription :" but Mammon is arrogant pretension personified. Sir Sampson Legend, in Love for Love, is such another lying overbearing character, but he does not come up to Epicure Mammon. What a "tow'ring bravery" there is in his sensuality ! He affects no pleasure under a Sultan. It is as if "Egypt with Assyria strove in luxury."]

VOLPONE; OR, THE FOX: A COMEDY. BY BEN. JONSON.

Volpone, a rich Venetian nobleman, who is without children, feigns himself to be dying, to draw gifts from such as pay their court to him in the expectation of becoming his heirs. Mosca, his knavish confederate, persuades each of these men in turn, that he is named for the inheritance, and by this means extracts from their credulity many costly presents.

VOLPONE, *as on his death-bed.* MOSCA. CORBACCIO, *an old gentleman.*

Mos. Signior Corbaccio,
You are very welcome, sir.
Corb. How does your patron?
Mos. Troth, as he did, sir, no amends.
Corb. What? mends he?
Mos. No, sir, he is rather worse.
Corb. That's well. Where is he?
Mos. Upon his couch, sir, newly fall'n asleep.
Corb. Does he sleep well?
Mos. No wink, sir, all this night,
Nor yesterday; but slumbers.
Corb. Good! he shall take
Some counsel of physicians: I have brought him
An opiate here, from mine own doctor—
Mos. He will not hear of drugs.
Corb. Why? I myself
Stood by, while 'twas made; saw all th' ingredients;
And know it cannot but most gently work.
My life for his, 'tis but to make him sleep.
Volp. I, his last sleep if he would take it.
Mos. Sir,
He has no faith in physic.
Corb. Say you, say you?
Mos. He has no faith in physic: he does think,
Most of your doctors are the greatest danger,
A worst disease t' escape. I often have
Heard him protest, that your physician
Should never be his heir.

Corb. Not I his heir?
Mos. Not your physician, sir.
Corb. O, no, no, no,
I do not mean it.
Mos. No, sir, nor their fees
He cannot brook; he says they flay a man,
Before they kill him.
Corb. Right, I do conceive you.
Mos. And then, they do it by experiment:
For which the law not only doth absolve 'em,
But gives them great reward; and he is loth
To hire his death so.
Corb. It is true, they kill,
With as much license as a Judge.
Mos. Nay, more:
For he but kills, sir, where the law condemns,
And these can kill him too.
Corb. I, or me;
Or any man. How does his apoplex?
Is that strong on him still?
Mos. Most violent,
His speech is broken, and his eyes are set,
His face drawn longer than 'twas wont.——
Corb. How? how?
Stronger than he was wont?
Mos. No, sir: his face
Drawn longer than 'twas wont.
Corb. O, good.
Mos. His mouth
Is ever gaping, and his eyelids hang.
Corb. Good.
Mos. A freezing numbness stiffens all his joints,
And makes the color of his flesh like lead.
Corb. 'Tis good.
Mos. His pulse beats slow, and dull.
Corb. Good symptoms still.
Mos. And from his brain—
Corb. Ha? how? not from his brain?

Mos. Yes, sir, and from his brain—
Corb. I conceive you, good.
Mos. Flows a cold sweat, with a continual rheum
Forth the resolved corners of his eyes.
Corb. Is 't possible? yet I am better, ha!
How does he with the swimming of his head?
Mos. O, sir, 'tis past the scotomy; he now
Hath lost his feeling, and hath left to snort:
You hardly can perceive him that he breathes.
Corb. Excellent, excellent, sure I shall outlast him:
This makes me young again a score of years.
Mos. I was coming for you, sir.
Corb. Has he made his will?
What has he giv'n me?
Mos. No, sir.
Corb. Nothing? ha?
Mos. He has not made his will, sir.
Corb. Oh, oh, oh.
What then did Voltore the lawyer here?
Mos. He smelt a carcase, sir, when he but heard
My master was about his testament;
As I did urge him to it for your good—
Corb. He came unto him, did he? I thought so.
Mos. Yes, and presented him this piece of plate.
Corb. To be his heir?
Mos. I do not know, sir.
Corb. True,
I know it too.
Mos. By your own scale, sir.
Corb. Well, I shall prevent him yet. See, Mosca, look
Here I have brought a bag of bright cecchines,
Will quite weigh down his plate.
Mos. Yea marry, sir,
This is true physic, this your sacred medicine;
No talk of opiates, to this great elixir.
Corb. Tis aurum palpabile, if not potabile.
Mos. It shall be minister'd to him in his bowl?
Corb. I, do, do, do.

Mos. Most blessed cordial.
This will recover him.
Corb. Yes, do, do, do.
Mos. I think it were not best, sir.
Corb. What?
Mos. To recover him.
Corb. O, no, no, no; by no means.
Mos. Why, sir, this
Will work some strange effect if he but feel it.
Corb. 'Tis true, therefore forbear, I'll take my venture;
Give me 't again.
Mos. At no hand; pardon me
You shall not do yourself that wrong, sir.
Will so advise you, you shall have it all.
Corb. How?
Mos. All sir, 'tis your right, your own; no man
Can claim a part; 'tis yours without a rival,
Decreed by destiny.
Corb. How? ho w, good Mosca?
Mos. I 'll tell you, sir. This fit he shall recover.
Corb. I do conceive you.
Mos. And on first advantage
Of his gain'd sense, will I re-importune him
Unto the making of his testament:
And show him this.
Corb. Good, good.
Mos. 'Tis better yet,
If you will hear, sir.
Corb. Yes, with all my heart.
Mos. Now would I counsel you, make home with speed;
There frame a will; whereto you shall inscribe
My master your sole heir.
Corb. And disinherit
My son?
Mos. O sir, the better; for that color
Shall make it much more taking.
Corb. O, but color?
Mos. This will, sir, you shall send it unto me.

Now, when I come to inforce (as I will do)
Your cares, your watchings, and your many prayers,
Your more than many gifts, your this day's present,
And last produce your will; where (without thought,
Or least regard unto your proper issue,
A son so brave, and highly meriting)
The stream of your diverted love hath thrown you
Upon my master, and made him your heir;
He cannot be so stupid, or stone-dead,
But out of conscience, and mere gratitude——

Corb. He must pronounce me his?

Mos. 'Tis true.

Corb. This plot
Did I think on before.

Mos. I do believe it.

Corb. Do you not believe it?

Mos. Yes, sir.

Corb. Mine own project.

Mos. Which when he hath done, sir—

Corb. Published me his heir?

Mos. And you so certain to survive him—

Corb. I.

Mos. Being so lusty a man—

Corb. 'Tis true.

Mos. Yes, sir—

Corb. I thought on that too. See how he should be
The very organ to express my thoughts!

Mos. You have not only done yourself a good——

Corb. But multiplied it on my son.

Mos. 'Tis right, sir.

Corb. Still my invention.

Mos. 'Las, sir, heaven knows,
It hath been all my study, all my care
(I e'en grow grey with all) how to work things——

Corb. I do conceive, sweet Mosca.

Mos. You are he,
For whom I labor, here.

Corb. I, do, do, do:

I 'll straight about it.

Mos. Rook go with you, raven.

Corb. I know thee honest.

Mos. You do lie, sir—

Corb. And——

Mos. Your knowledge is no better than your ears, sir.

Corb. I do not doubt to be a father to thee.

Mos. Nor I to gull my brother of his blessing.

Corb. I may ha' my youth restored to me, why not?

Mos. Your worship is a precious ass——

Corb. What say'st thou?

Mos. I do desire your worship to make haste, sir.

Corb. 'Tis done, 'tis done, I go. [*Exit.*

Volp. O, I shall burst;
Let out my sides, let out my sides ——

Mos. Contain
Your flux of laughter, sir: you know this hope
Is such a bait it covers any hook.

Volp. O, but thy working, and thy placing it!
I cannot hold: good rascal, let me kiss thee:
I never knew thee in so rare a humor.

Mos. Alas, sir, I but do, as I am taught;
Follow your grave instructions; give 'em words:
Pour oil into their ears: and send them hence.

Volp. 'Tis true, 'tis true. What a rare punishment
Is avarice to itself!

Mos. I, with our help, sir.

Volp. So many cares, so many maladies,
So many fears attending on old age,
Yea, death so often call'd on, as no wish
Can be more frequent with 'em, their limbs faint,
Their senses dull, their seeing, hearing, going,
All dead before them; yea their very teeth,
Their instruments of eating, failing them:
Yet this is reckon'd life! Nay here was one,
Is now gone home, that wishes to live longer!
Feels not his gout, not palsy, feigns himself
Younger by scores of years, flatters his age,

With confident belying it, hopes he may
With charms, like Æson, have his youth restored:
And with these thoughts so battens, as if Fate
Would be as easily cheated on as he:
And all turns air! Who 's that there, now? a third?
[*Another knocks.*

Mos. Close to your couch again: I hear his voice.
It is Corvino, our spruce merchant.
Volp. Dead.
Mos. Another bout, sir, with your eyes. Who 's there?

CORVINO, *a Merchant, enters.*

Mos. Signior Corvino! come most wisht for! O,
How happy were you, if you knew it now!
Corv. Why? what? wherein?
Mos. The tardy hour is come, sir.
Corv. He is not dead?
Mos. Not dead, sir, but as good;
He knows no man.
Corv. How shall I do then?
Mos. Why, sir?
Corv. I have brought him here a pearl.
Mos. Perhaps he has
So much remembrance left, as to know you, sir:
He still calls on you: nothing but your name
Is in his mouth; is your pearl orient, sir?
Corv. Venice was never owner of the like.
Volp. Signior Corvino.
Mos. Hark.
Volp. Signior Corvino.
Mos. He calls you, step and give it him. He 's here, sir.
And he has brought you a rich pearl.
Corv. How do you, sir?
Tell him it doubles the twelfth caract.
Mos. Sir.
He cannot understand, his hearing 's gone:
And yet it comforts him to see you ——
Corv. Say,

I have a diamond for him too.
Mos. Best show 't, sir,
Put it into his hand; 'tis only there
He apprehends: he has his feeling yet.
See how he grasps it!
Corv. 'Las, good gentleman!
How pitiful the sight is!
Mos. Tut, forget, sir.
The weeping of an heir should still be laughter,
Under a visor.
Corv. Why, am I his heir?
Mos. Sir, I am sworn, I may not show the will,
Till he be dead: but, here has been Corbaccio,
Here has been Voltore, here were others too,
I cannot number 'em, they were so many,
All gaping here for legacies; but I,
Taking the vantage of his naming you
(Signior Corvino, Signior Corvino), took
Paper, and pen, and ink, and there I ask'd him,
Whom he would have his heir? Corvino. Who
Should be executor? Corvino. And
To any question he was silent to,
I still interpreted the nods, he made
Through weakness, for consent: and sent home the others,
Nothing bequeath'd them, but to cry, and curse.
Corv. O, my dear Mosca. Does he not perceive us?
Mos. No more than a blind harper. He knows no man,
No face of friend, nor name of any servant,
Who 't was that fed him last, or gave him drink;
Not those he hath begotten, or brought up,
Can ne remember.
Corv. Has he children?
Mos. Bastards.
Some dozen, or more, that he begot on beggars,
Gypsies, and Jews, and black-moors, when he was drunk:
Knew you not that, sir? 'Tis the common fable,
The dwarf, the fool, the eunuch, are all his:
He 's the true father of his family,

In all, save me : but he has given 'em nothing.
Corv. That 's well, that 's well. Art sure he does not hear us ?
Mos. Sure, sir ? why look you, credit your own sense.
The pox approach, and add to your diseases,
If it would send you hence the sooner, sir,
For your incontinence, it hath deserv'd it
Throughly, and throughly, and the plague to boot.
(You may come near, sir) would you would once close
Those filthy eyes of your's that flow with slime,
Like two frog-pits : and those same hanging cheeks,
Cover'd with hide, instead of skin : (nay help, sir)
That look like frozen dish-clouts set on end.
Corv. Or, like an old smok'd wall, on which the rain
Ran down in streaks.
Mos. Excellent, sir, speak out ;
You may be louder yet : a culvering
Discharged in his ear, would hardly bore it.
Corv. His nose is like a common sewer, still running.
Mos. 'Tis good ; and what his mouth ?
Corv. A very draught.
Mos. O, stop it up ——
Corv. By no means.
Mos. Pray you let me.
Faith I could stifle him rarely with a pillow,
As well as any woman that should keep him.
Corv. Do as you will, but I 'll begone.
Mos. Be so ;
It is your presence makes him last so long.
Corv. I pray you use no violence.
Mos. No, sir, why ?
Why should you be thus scrupulous ? 'Pray you, sir.
Corv. Nay, at your discretion.
Mos. Well, good sir, be gone.
Corv. I will not trouble him now, to take my pearl.
Mos. Puh, nor your diamond. What a needless care
Is this afflicts you ? Is not all here yours ?
Am not I here, whom you have made your creature,
That owe my being to you ?

Corv. Grateful Mosca!
Thou art my friend, my fellow, my companion,
My partner, and shall share in all my fortunes. [*Exit.*
Volp. My divine Mosca!
Thou hast to-day out gone thyself.

THE TRIUMPH OF LOVE: BEING THE SECOND OF FOUR PLAYS, OR MORAL REPRESENTATIONS. BY FRANCIS BEAUMONT.

Violanta, Daughter to a Nobleman of Milan, is with child by Gerrard, supposed to be of mean descent: an offence which by the laws of Milan is made capital to both parties.

VIOLANTA. GERRARD.

Viol. Why does my Gerrard grieve?
Ger. O my sweet mistress,
It is not life (which by our Milan law
My fact hath forfeited) makes me thus pensive;
That I would lose to save the little finger
Of this your noble burthen from least hurt,
Because your blood is in it. But since your love
Made poor incompatible me the parent
(Being we are not married) your dear blood
Falls under the same cruel penalty:
And can heaven think fit ye die for me?
For Heaven's sake say I ravish'd you; I'll swear it,
To keep your life and repute unstain'd.
Viol. O Gerrard, thou art my life and faculties,
And if I lose thee, I'll not keep mine own;
The thought of whom sweetens all miseries.
Would'st have me murder thee beyond thy death?
Unjustly scandal thee with ravishment?
It was so far from rape, that heaven doth know,
If ever tne first lovers, ere they fell,
Knew simply in the state of innocence,
Such was this act, this, that doth ask no blush.
Ger. Oh! but my rarest Violanta, when

My lord Randulpho, brother to your father,
Shall understand this, how will he exclaim,
That my poor aunt and me, which his free alms
Hath nurs'd, since Milan by the duke of Mantua,
Who now usurps it, was surpriz'd —— that time
My father and my mother both were slain;
With my aunt's husband, as she says; their states
Despoil'd and seized; 'tis past my memory,
But thus she told me: only thus I know,
Since I could understand, your honor'd uncle
Hath giv'n me all the liberal education
That his own son might look for, had he one;
Now will he say, dost thou requite me thus?
O! the thought kills me.
Viol. Gentle, gentle Gerrard,
Be cheer'd and hope the best. My mother, father,
And uncle, love me most indulgently,
Being the only branch of all their stocks:
But neither they, nor he thou would'st not grieve
With this unwelcome news, shall ever hear
Violanta's tongue reveal, much less accuse
Gerrard to be the father of his own.
I'll rather silent die, that thou may'st live
To see thy little offspring grow and thrive.——

Violanta is attended in Childbed by her mother Angelina

Viol. Mother, I'd not offend you; might not Gerrard
Steal in and see me in the evening?
Angel. Well,
Bid him do so.
Viol. Heaven's blessing on your heart.
Do ye not call child-bearing *travel*, mother?
Angel. Yes.
Viol. It well may be. The bare-foot traveller
That's born a prince, and walks his pilgrimage,
Whose tender feet kiss the remorseless stones
Only, ne'er felt a travel like to it.
Alas, dear mother, you groan'd thus for me,

And yet how disobedient have I been!
Angel. Peace, Violanta: thou hast always been
Gentle and good.
Viol. Gerrard is better, mother:
O if you knew the implicit innocency
Dwells in his breast, you'd love him like your prayers.
I see no reason but my father might
Be told the truth, being pleas'd for Ferdinand
To woo himself: and Gerrard ever was
His full comparative; my uncle loves him,
As he loves Ferdinand.
Angel. No, not for the world,
Since his intent is cross'd: lov'd Ferdinand
Thus ruin'd, and a child got out of wedlock,
His madness would pursue ye both to death.
Viol. As you please, mother. I am now, methinks,
Even in the land of ease; I'll sleep.
Angel. Draw in
The bed nearer the fire: silken rest
Tie all thy cares up.*

Violanta describes how her love for Gerrard began.

Viol. Gerrard's and my affection began
In infancy: my uncle brought him oft
In long coats hither.
The little boy would kiss me, being a child,
And say he lov'd me; give me all his toys,
Bracelets, rings, sweetmeats, all his rosy smiles:
I then would stand and stare upon his eyes,
Play with his locks, and swear I loved him too;
For sure methought he was a little Love,
He wooed so prettily in innocence,
That then he warm'd my fancy.

* Violanta's prattle is very pretty and so natural *in her situation*, that I could not resist giving it a place. Juno Lucina was never invoked with more elegance. Pope has been praised for giving dignity to a game of cards. It required at least as much address to ennoble a lying-in.

THE MAID'S TRAGEDY. BY FRANCIS BEAUMONT, AND JOHN FLETCHER.

Amintor, a noble Gentleman, promises marriage to Aspatia, and forsakes her by the King's command to wed Evadne.—The grief of Aspatia at being forsaken, described.

This lady
Walks discontented, with her watry eyes
Bent on the earth: the unfrequented woods
Are her delight; and when she sees a bank
Stuck full of flowers, she with a sigh will tell
Her servants what a pretty place it were
To bury lovers in; and make her maids
Pluck 'em, and strew her over like a corse.
She carries with her an infectious grief
That strikes all her beholders, she will sing
The mournfull'st things that ever ear have heard.
And sigh, and sing again; and when the rest
Of our young ladies in their wanton blood,
Tell mirthful tales in course that fill the room
With laughter, she will with so sad a look
Bring forth a story of the silent death
Of some forsaken virgin, which her grief
Will put in such a phrase, that, ere she end,
She'll send them weeping one by one away.

The marriage-night of Amintor and Evadne.

EVADNE. ASPATIA. DULA, *and other Ladies.*

Evad. Would thou could'st instill [*To* DULA.
Some of thy mirth into Aspatia.
Asp. It were a timeless smile should prove my cheek;
It were a fitter hour for me to laugh,
When at the altar the religious priest
Were pacifying the offended powers
With sacrifice, than now. This should have been
My night, and all your hands have been employ'd
In giving me a spotless offering

To young Amintor's bed, as we are now
For you: pardon, Evadne, would my worth
Were great as your's, or that the King, or he,
Or both thought so; perhaps he found me worthless,
But till he did so, in these ears of mine
(These credulous ears) he pour'd the sweetest words
That art or love could frame.
Evad. Nay, leave this sad talk, madam.
Asp. Would I could, then should I leave the cause.
Lay a garland on my hearse of the dismal yew.
Evad. That's one of your sad songs, madam.
Asp. Believe me, 'tis a very pretty one.
Evad. How is it, madam?
Asp. Lay a garland on my hearse of the dismal yew;
Maidens, willow branches bear; say I died true:
My love was false, but I was firm from my hour of birth;
Upon my buried body lay lightly gentle earth.
Madam, good night;—may no discontent
Grow 'twixt your love and you; but if there do,
Inquire of me, and I will guide your moan,
Teach you an artificial way to grieve,
To keep your sorrow waking. Love your lord
No worse than I; but if you love so well,
Alas, you may displease him, so did I.
This is the last time you shall look on me:
Ladies, farewell; as soon as I am dead,
Come all and watch one night about my hearse;
Bring each a mournful story and a tear
To offer at it when I go to earth:
With flattering ivy clasp my coffin round,
Write on my brow my fortune, let my bier
Be borne by virgins that shall sing by course
The truth of maids and perjuries of men.
Evad. Alas, I pity thee. [AMINTOR *enters.*
Asp. Go and be happy in your lady's love; [*To* AMINTOR.
May all the wrongs that you have done to me,
Be utterly forgotten in my death.
I 'll trouble you no more, yet I will take

A parting kiss, and will not be denied.
You 'll come, my lord, and see the virgins weep
When I am laid in earth, though you yourself
Can know no pity : thus I wind myself
Into this willow garland, and am prouder,
That I was once your love (though now refus'd)
Than to have had another true to me. ——

Aspatia wills her Maidens to be sorrowful, because she is so

ASPATIA. ANTIPHILA. OLYMPIAS.

Asp. Come, let 's be sad, my girls,
That down-cast of thine eye, Olympias,
Shows a fine sorrow ; mark, Antiphila,
Just such another was the nymph Oenone,
When Paris brought home Helen : now a tear,
And then thou art a piece expressing fully
The Carthage Queen, when from a cold sea rock,
Full with her sorrow, she tied fast her eyes
To the fair Trojan ships, and having lost them,
Just as thine eyes do, down stole a tear, Antiphila.
What would this wench do, if she were Aspatia ?
Here she would stand, till some more pitying god
Turn'd her to marble : 'tis enough, my wench ;
Show me the piece of needle-work you wrought.
Ant. Of Ariadne, madam ?
Asp. Yes, that piece.
This should be Theseus, h' as a cozening face ;
You meant him for a man ?
Ant. He was so, madam,
Asp. Why then 'tis well enough. Never look back,
You have a full wind, and a false heart, Theseus.
Does not the story say, his keel was split,
Or his masts spent, or some kind rock or other
Met with his vessel ?
Ant. Not as I remember.
Asp. It should ha' been so : could the gods know this,
And not of all their number raise a storm ?

But they are all as ill. This false smile was well exprest,
Just such another caught me; you shall not go so, Antiphila;
In this place work a quicksand,
And over it a shallow smiling water,
And his ship ploughing it, and then a fear.
Do that fear to the life, wench.
Ant. 'Twill wrong the story.
Asp. 'Twill make the story, wrong'd by wanton poets,
Live long and be believ'd; but where's the lady?
Ant. There, Madam.
Asp. Fie, you have miss'd it here, Antiphila,
You are much mistaken, wench;
These colors are not dull and pale enough,
To show a soul so full of misery
As this sad lady's was; do it by me,
Do it again by me the lost Aspatia,
And you shall find all true but the wild island.
I stand upon the sea-beach now, and think
Mine arms thus, and mine hair blown with the wind,
Wild as that desart, and let all about me
Tell that I am forsaken, do my face
(If thou hadst ever feeling of a sorrow)
Thus, thus, Antiphila, strive to make me look
Like Sorrow's monument; and the trees about me,
Let them be dry and leaveless; let the rocks
Groan with continual surges, and behind me
Make all a desolation; look, look, wenches,
A miserable life of this poor picture.
Olym. Dear madam!
Asp. I have done, sit down, and let us
Upon that point fix all our eyes, that point there;
Make a dull silence, till you feel a sudden sadness
Give us new souls.*

* One characteristic of the excellent old poets is their being able to bestow grace upon subjects which naturally do not seem susceptible of any. I will mention two instances: Zelmane, in the Arcadia of Sidney; and Helena, in the All 's Well that Ends Well of Shakspeare. What can be more unpromising at first sight than the idea of a young man disguising

Evadne implores forgiveness of Amintor for marrying him while she was the King's Mistress.

Evad. O my lord.
Amin. How now!
Evad. My much abused lord! [*Kneels.*
Amin. This cannot be.
Evad. I do not kneel to live, I dare not hope it;
The wrongs I did are greater; look upon me,
Though I appear with all my faults.
Amin. Stand up.
This is no new way to beget more sorrow:
Heaven knows I have too many; do not mock me;
Though I am tame and bred up with my wrongs,
Which are my foster-brothers, I may leap
Like a hand-wolf into my natural wilderness,
And do an outrage: pray thee do not mock me.
Evad. My whole life is so leprous, it infects

himself in woman's attire, and passing himself off for a woman among women? and that too for a long space of time? yet Sir Philip has preserved such a matchless decorum, that neither does Pyrocles' manhood suffer any stain for the effeminacy of Zelmane, nor is the respect due to the princesses at all diminished when the deception comes to be known. In the sweetly constituted mind of Sir Philip Sidney, it seems as if no ugly thought nor unhandsome meditation could find a harbor. He turned all that he touched into images of honor and virtue. Helena, in Shakspeare, is a young woman seeking a man in marriage. The ordinary laws of courtship are reversed; the habitual feelings are violated. Yet with such exquisite address this dangerous subject is handled, that Helena's forwardness loses her no honor; delicacy dispenses with her laws in her favor, and Nature in her single case seems content to suffer a sweet violation.

Aspatia, in this tragedy, is a character equally difficult with Helena of being managed with grace. She, too, is a slighted woman, refused by the man who had once engaged to marry her. Yet it is artfully contrived that while we pity her, we respect her, and she descends without degradation, So much true poetry and passion can do to confer dignity upon subjects which do not seem capable of it. But Aspatia must not be compared at all points with Helena; she does not so absolutely predominate over her situation but she suffers some diminution, some abatement of the full lustre of the female character; which Helena never does: her character has many degrees of sweetness, some of delicacy, but it has weakness which, if we do not despise, we are sorry for. After all, Beaumont and Fletcher were but an inferior sort of Shakspeares and Sidneys.

All my repentance: I would buy your pardon
Though at the highest set, even with my life.
That slight contrition, that 's no sacrifice
For what I have committed.

Amin. Sure I dazzle:
There cannot be a faith in that foul woman,
That knows no god more mighty than her mischiefs.
Thou dost still worse, still number on thy faults,
To press my poor heart thus. Can I believe
There's any seed of virtue in that woman
Left to shoot up, that dares go on in sin
Known, and so known as thine is? O Evadne!
Would there were any safety in thy sex,
That I might put a thousand sorrows off,
And credit thy repentance: but I must not;
Thou hast brought me to the dull calamity,
To that strange misbelief of all the world,
And all things that are in it, that I fear
I shall fall like a tree, and find my grave,
Only rememb'ring that I grieve.

Evad. My lord,
Give me your griefs: you are an innocent,
A soul as white as heaven; let not my sins
Perish your noble youth: I do not fall here
To shadow by dissembling with my tears,
As all say women can, or to make less
What my hot will hath done, which heaven and you
Knows to be tougher than the hand of time
Can cut from man's remembrance; no I do not;
I do appear the same, the same Evadne,
Drest in the shames I liv'd in, the same monster.
But these are names of honor, to what I am;
I do present myself the foulest creature,
Most poisonous, dangerous, and despis'd of men,
Lerna e'er bred, or Nilus; I am hell,
Till you, my dear lord, shoot your light into me,
The beams of your forgiveness: I am soul-sick,
And wither with the fear of one condemn'd,

Till I have got your pardon.
Amin. Rise, Evadne.
Those heavenly powers that put this good into thee,
Grant a continuance of it: I forgive thee;
Make thyself worthy of it, and take heed,
Take heed, Evadne, this be serious;
Mock not the powers above, that can and dare
Give thee a great example of their justice
To all ensuing eyes, if thou play'st
With thy repentance, the best sacrifice.
Evad. I have done nothing good to win belief,
My life hath been so faithless; all the creatures
Made for heaven's honors have their ends, and good ones,
All but the cozening Crocodiles, false women;
They reign here like those plagues, those killing sores,
Men pray against; and when they die, like tales
Ill told, and unbeliev'd, they pass away
And go to dust forgotten: but, my lord,
Those short days I shall number to my rest
(As many must not see me) shall, though too late,
Though in my evening, yet perceive a will,
Since I can do no good because a woman,
Reach constantly at something that is near it;
I will redeem one minute of my age,
Or like another Niobe I'll weep
Till I am water.
Amin. I am now dissolved:
My frozen soul melts: may each sin thou hast,
Find a new mercy: rise, I am at peace:
Had'st thou been thus, thus excellently good,
Before that devil king tempted thy frailty,
Sure thou had'st made a star: give me thy hand;
From this time I will know thee, and as far
As honor gives me leave, be thy Amintor:
When we meet next, I will salute thee fairly,
And pray the gods to give thee happy days:
My charity shall go along with thee,
Though my embraces must be far from thee.——

Men's Natures more hard and subtle than Women's.

How stubbornly this fellow answer'd me!
There is a vile dishonest trick in man,
More than in women: all the men I meet
Appear thus to me, are harsh and rude,
And have a subtilty in everything,
Which love could never know; but we fond women
Harbor the easiest and smoothest thoughts,
And think all shall go so; it is unjust
That men and women should be matcht together.

PHILASTER; OR, LOVE LIES A BLEEDING: A TRAGI-COMEDY. BY FRANCIS BEAUMONT AND JOHN FLETCHER.

Philaster tells the Princess Arethusa how he first found the boy Bellario

I have a boy sent by the gods,
Not yet seen in the court; hunting the buck,
found him sitting by a fountain side,
Of which he borrow'd some to quench his thirst,
And paid the nymph again as much in tears;
A garland lay him by, made by himself,
Of many several flowers, bred in the bay,
Stuck in that mystic order, that the rareness
Delighted me: but ever when he turn'd
His tender eyes upon them, he would weep,
As if he meant to make them grow again.
Seeing such pretty helpless innocence
Dwell in his face, I ask'd him all his story;
He told me that his parents gentle died,
Leaving him to the mercy of the fields,
Which gave him roots; and of the crystal springs,
Which did not stop their courses; and the sun,
Which still, he thank'd him, yielded him his light.
Then took he up his garland and did show,
What every flower, as country people hold,
Did signify; and how all order'd thus,
Exprest his grief: and to my thoughts did read

The prettiest lecture of his country art
That could be wish'd, so that, methought, I could
Have studied it. I gladly entertain'd him,
Who was as glad to follow; and have got
The trustiest, loving'st, and the gentlest boy,
That ever master kept: him will I send
To wait on you, and bear our hidden love.

Philaster prefers Bellario to the Service of the Princess Arethusa.

Phi. And thou shalt find her honorable, boy,
Full of regard unto thy tender youth,
For thine own modesty; and for my sake,
Apter to give, than thou wilt be to ask, aye, or deserve.
Bell. Sir, you did take me up when I was nothing,
And only yet am something by being yours;
You trusted me unknown; and that which you are apt
To construe a simple innocence in me,
Perhaps might have been craft, the cunning of a boy
Harden'd in lies and theft; yet ventur'd you
To part my miseries and me: for which,
I never can expect to serve a lady
That bears more honor in her breast than you.
Phi. But, boy, it will prefer thee; thou art young,
And bear 'st a childish overflowing love
To them that clap thy cheeks and speak thee fair yet.
But when thy judgment comes to rule those passions,
Thou wilt remember best those careful friends
That placed thee in the noblest way of life:
She is a princess I prefer thee to.
Bell. In that small time that I have seen the world,
I never knew a man hasty to part
With a servant he thought trusty; I remember,
My father would prefer the boys he kept
To greater men than he, but did it not
Till they were grown too saucy for himself.
Phi. Why, gentle boy, I find no fault at all
In thy behavior.
Bell. Sir, if I have made

A fault of ignorance, instruct my youth ;
I shall be willing, if not apt, to learn.
Age and experience will adorn my mind
With larger knowledge : and if I have done
A wilful fault, think me not past all hope
For once ; what master holds so strict a hand
Over his boy, that he will part with him
Without one warning ? Let me be corrected
To break my stubbornness if it be so,
Rather than turn me off, and I shall mend.
  Phi. Thy love doth plead so prettily to stay,
That (trust me) I could weep to part with thee.
Alas, I do not turn thee off; thou knowest
It is my business that doth call thee hence,
And when thou art with her thou dwell'st with me:
Think so, and 'tis so ; and when time is full,
That thou hast well discharg'd this heavy trust,
Laid on so weak a one, I will again
With joy receive thee ; as I live, I will ;
Nay weep not, gentle boy ; 'tis more than time
Thou didst attend the princess.
  Bell. I am gone ;
But since I am to part with you, my lord,
And none knows whether I shall live to do
More service for you, take this little prayer ;
Heaven bless your loves, your fights, all your designs.
May sick men, if they have your wish, be well ;
And heav'n hate those you curse, though I be one.

BELLARIO *describes to the* PRINCESS ARETHUSA *the manner of his master* PHILASTER'S *love for her.*

  Are. Sir, you are sad to change your service, is 't not so ?
  Bell. Madam, I have not chang'd : I wait on you,
To do him service.
  Are. Thou disclaim'st in me ;
Tell me thy name.
  Bell. Bellario.
  Are. Thou canst sing and play ?

Bell. If grief will give me leave, madam, I can.
Are. Alas! what kind of grief can thy years know?
Had'st thou a curst master when thou went'st to school?
Thou art not capable of any other grief;
Thy brows and cheeks are smooth as waters be,
When no breath troubles them: believe me, boy,
Care seeks out wrinkled brows, and hollow eyes,
And builds himself caves to abide in them.
Come, sir, tell me truly, does your lord love me?
Bell. Love, madam? I know not what it is.
Are. Canst thou know grief, and never yet knew'st love?
Thou art deceiv'd, boy. Does he speak of me
As if he wish'd me well?
Bell. If it be love,
To forget all respect of his own friends,
In thinking of your face; if it be love,
To sit cross-arm'd and sigh away the day,
Mingled with starts, crying your name as loud
And hastily, as men i' the streets do fire;
If it be love to weep himself away,
When he but hears of any lady dead,
Or kill'd, because it might have been your chance;
If when he goes to rest (which will not be)
'Twixt every prayer he says to name you once,
As others drop a bead, be to be in love;
Then, madam, I dare swear he loves you.
Are. O you 're a cunning boy, and taught to lie
For your lord's credit; but thou know'st a lie
That bears this sound, is welcomer to me
Than any truth that says he loves me not.

PHILASTER *is jealous of* BELLARIO *with the* PRINCESS.

Bell. Health to you, my lord;
The princess doth commend her love, her life,
And this unto you.
Phi. O Bellario,
Now I perceive she loves me, she does show it
In loving thee, my boy, she has made thee brave.

Bell. My lord, she has attired me past my wish,
Past my desert, more fit for her attendant,
Though far unfit for me who do attend.
Phi. Thou art grown courtly, boy. O let all women
That love black deeds learn to dissemble here.
Here by this paper she does write to me
As if her heart were mines of adamant
To all the world besides, but unto me
A maiden snow that melted with my looks.
Tell me, my boy, how doth the princess use thee?
For I shall guess her love to me by that.
Bell. Scarce like her servant, but as if I were
Something allied to her; or had preserv'd
Her life three times by my fidelity;
As mothers fond do use their only sons;
As I 'd use one that 's left unto my trust,
For whom my life should pay if he met harm,
So she does use me.
Phi. Why, this is wond'rous well:
But what kind language does she feed thee with?
Bell. Why, she does tell me, she will trust my youth
With all her loving secrets, and does call me
Her pretty servant, bids me weep no more
For leaving you; she 'll see my services
Regarded: and such words of that soft strain,
That I am nearer weeping when she ends
Than ere she spake.
Phi. This is much better still.
Bell. Are you ill, my lord?
Phi. Ill? No, Bellario.
Bell. Methinks your words
Fall not from off your tongue so evenly,
Nor is there in your looks that quietness,
That I was wont to see.
Phi. Thou art deceiv'd, boy.—And she strokes thy head?
Bell. Yes.
Phi. And she does clap thy cheeks?
Bell. She does, my lord.

Phi. And she does kiss thee, boy, ha ?
Bell. How, my lord ?
Phi. She kisses thee ?
Bell. Not so, my lord.
Phi. Come, come, I know she does.
Bell. No, by my life.
Aye, now I see why my disturbed thoughts
Were so perplext when first I went to her ;
My heart held augury. You are abus'd,
Some villain has abus'd you ; I do see
Whereto you tend ; fall rocks upon his head,
That put this to you ; 'tis some subtle train
To bring that noble frame of yours to nought.
Phi. Thou think'st I will be angry with thee. Come,
Thou shalt know all my drift. I hate her more
Than I love happiness, and plac'd thee there
To pry with narrow eyes into her deeds.
Hast thou discover'd ? is she fal'n to lust,
As I would wish her ? Speak some comfort to me.
Bell. My lord, you did mistake the boy you sent ;
Had she a sin that way, hid from the world,
I would not aid
Her base desires ; but what I came to know
As servant to her, I would not reveal,
To make my life last ages.
Phi. O my heart!
This is a salve worse than the main disease.
Tell me thy thoughts ; for I will know the least
That dwells within thee, or will rip thy heart
To know it ; I will see thy thoughts as plain
As I do know thy face.
Bell. Why, so you do.
She is (for aught I know) by all the gods,
As chaste as ice ; but were she foul as hell,
And I did know it, thus ; the breath of kings,
The points of swords, tortures, nor bulls of brass,
Should draw it from me.
Phi. Then it is no time

To dally with thee ; I will take thy life,
For I do hate thee ; I could curse thee now.

Bell. If you do hate, you could not curse me worse ;
The gods have not a punishment in store
Greater for me than is your hate.

Phi. Fie, fie,
So young and so dissembling ! fear'st thou not death ?
Can boys contemn that ?

Bell. O, what a boy is he
Can be content to live to be a man,
That sees the best of men thus passionate,
Thus without reason ?

Phi. Oh, but thou dost not know what 'tis to die.

Bell. Yes, I do know, my lord.
'Tis less than to be born ; a lasting sleep,
A quiet resting from all jealousy ;
A thing we all pursue ; I know besides
It is but giving over of a game
That must be lost.

Phi. But there are pains, false boy,
For perjur'd souls ; think but on these, and then
Thy heart will melt, and thou wilt utter all.

Bell. May they fall all upon me whilst I live,
If I be perjured, or ever thought
Of that you charge me with ; if I be false,
Send me to suffer in those punishments
You speak of ; kill me.

Phi. O, what should I do ?
Why, who can but believe him ? He does swear
So earnestly, that if it were not true,
The gods would not endure him. Rise, Bellario,
Thy protestations are so deep, and thou
Dost look so truly when thou utter'st them,
That though I know them false, as were my hopes,
I cannot urge thee further ; but thou wert
To blame to injure me, for I must love
Thy honest looks, and take no revenge upon
Thy tender youth : a love from me to thee

Is firm whate'er thou dost: it troubles me
That I have call'd the blood out of thy cheeks,
That did so well become thee: but, good boy,
Let me not see thee more; something is done
That will distract me, that will make me mad,
If I behold thee; if thou tender'st me,
Let me not see thee.
  Bell. I will fly as far
As there is morning, ere I give distaste
To that most honor'd mind. But through these tears,
Shed at my hopeless parting, I can see
A world of treason practis'd upon you,
And her, and me. Farewell for ever more;
If you shall hear that sorrow struck me dead,
And after find me loyal, let there be
A tear shed from you in my memory,
And I shall rest at peace.

Bellario, discovered to be a Woman, confesses the motive for her disguise to have been Love for Prince Philaster.

My father would oft speak
Your worth and virtue, and as I did grow
More and more apprehensive, I did thirst
To see the man so prais'd, but yet all this
Was but a maiden longing, to be lost
As soon as found, till sitting in my window,
Printing my thoughts in lawn, I saw a god
I thought (but it was you) enter our gates;
My blood flew out, and back again as fast
As I had puft it forth, and suck'd it in
Like breath; then was I call'd away in haste
To entertain you. Never was a man
Heav'd from a sheep-cot to a sceptre, rais'd
So high in thoughts as I; you left a kiss
Upon these lips then, which I mean to keep
From you for ever; I did hear you talk
Far above singing; after you were gone,
I grew acquainted with my heart, and search'd

What stirr'd it so. Alas! I found it love,
Yet far from lust, for could I have but liv'd
In presence of you, I had had my end.
For this I did delude my noble father
With a feign'd pilgrimage, and drest myself
In habit of a boy, and, for I knew
My birth no match for you, I was past hope
Of having you. And understanding well,
That when I made discovery of my sex,
I could not stay with you, I made a vow
By all the most religious things a maid
Could call together, never to be known,
Whilst there was hope to hide me from men's eyes,
For other than I seem'd; that I might ever
Abide with you: then sate I by the fount
Where first you took me up.*

* The character of Bellario must have been extremely popular in its day. For many years after the date of Philaster's first exhibition on the stage, scarce a play can be found without one of these women pages in it, following in the train of some pre-engaged lover, calling on the gods to bless her happy rival (his mistress) whom no doubt she secretly curses in her heart, giving rise to many pretty *equivoques* by the way on the confusion of sex, and either made happy at last by some surprising turn of fate, or dismissed with the joint pity of the lovers and the audience. Our ancestors seem to have been wonderfully delighted with these transformations of sex. Women's parts were then acted by young men. What an odd double confusion it must have made, to see a boy play a woman playing a man: one cannot disentangle the perplexity without some violence to the imagination.

Donne has a copy of verses addrest to his mistress, dissuading her from a resolution, which she seems to have taken up from some of these scenical representations, of following him abroad as a page. It is so earnest, so weighty, so rich in poetry, in sense, in wit, and pathos, that I have thought fit to insert it, as a solemn close in future to all such sickly fancies as he there deprecates. The story of his romantic and unfortunate marriage with the daughter of Sir George Moore, the Lady here supposed to be addrest, may be read in Walton's Lives.

ELEGY.

By our first strange and fatal interview,
By all desires which thereof did ensue,
By our long striving hopes, by that remorse
Which my words' masculine persuasive force

Natural Antipathies.

Nature that loves not to be questioned
Why she did this, or that, but has her ends,

Begot in thee, and by the memory
Of hurts, which spies and rivals threatened me,
I calmly beg. But by thy father's wrath,
By all pains which want and divorcement hath,
I conjure thee; and all the oaths, which I
And thou have sworn to seal joint constancy,
I here unswear, and overswear them thus:
Thou shalt not love by means so dangerous.
Temper, O fair love, love's impetuous rage;
Be my true mistress, not my feigned page.
I'll go, and, by thy kind leave, leave behind
Thee, only worthy to nurse in my mind
Thirst to come back; O, if thou die before,
My soul from other lands to thee shall soar.
Thy (else almighty) beauty cannot move
Rage from the seas, nor thy love teach them love,
Nor tame wild Boreas' harshness; thou hast read
How roughly he in pieces shivered
The fair Orithea, whom he swore he lov'd.
Fall ill or good, 'tis madness to have prov'd
Dangers unurged; feed on this flattery,
That absent lovers one in th' other be.
Dissemble nothing, not a boy, nor change
Thy body's habit, nor mind: be not strange
To thyself only. All will spy in thy face
A blushing womanly discovering grace.
Richly cloath'd apes are call'd apes, and as soon
Eclips'd as bright we call the moon the moon.
Men of France, changeable camelions,
Spittles of diseases, shops of fashions,
Lives' fuellers, and the rightest company
Of players which upon the world's stage be,
Will too too quickly know thee: and alas,
Th' indifferent Italian, as we pass
His warm land, well content to think thee page,
Will hunt thee with such lust, and hideous rage,
As Lot's fair guests were vext. But none of these,
Nor spungy Aydroptique Dutch shall thee displease,
If thou stay here. O stay here; for, for thee
England is only a worthy gallery,
To walk in expectation, till from thence
Our greatest king call thee to his presence.

And knows she does well, never gave the world
Two things so opposite, so contrary,
As he and I am: if a bowl of blood
Drawn from this arm of mine would poison thee
A draught of his would cure thee.

Interest in Virtue.

Why, my lord, are you so moved at this?——
When any falls from virtue, I am distract,
I have an interest in 't.

CUPID'S REVENGE: A TRAGEDY. BY FRANCIS BEAUMONT AND JOHN FLETCHER.

Leucippus, the King's Son, takes to mistress Bacha, a Widow; but being questioned by his Father, to preserve her honor, swears that she is chaste. The old King admires her, and on the credit of that Oath, while his Son is absent, marries her. Leucippus, when he discovers the dreadful consequences of the deceit which he had used to his Father, counsels his friend Ismenus never to speak a falsehood in any case.

Leu. My sin, Ismenus, has wrought all this ill:
And I beseech thee to be warn'd by me,
And do not lie, if any man should ask thee
But *how thou dost*, or *what o'clock 'tis now*,
Be sure thou do not lie, make no excuse
For him that is most near thee; never let
The most officious falsehood 'scape thy tongue;
For they above (that are entirely truth)

When I am gone, dream me some happiness;
Nor let thy looks our long hid love confess;
Nor praise, nor dispraise me, nor bless, nor curse,
Openly love's force; nor in bed fright thy nurse
With midnights' startings, crying out, oh, oh,
Nurse, O my love is slain, I saw him go
O'er the white Alps alone; I saw him, I,
Assail'd, fight, taken, stabb'd, bleed, fall, and die.
Augur me better chance, except dread Jove
Think it enough for me to have had thy love

Will make that seed which thou hast sown of lies,
Yield miseries a thousand fold
Upon thine head, as they have done on mine.

Leucippus and his wicked Mother-in-law, Bacha, are left alone together for the first time after her marriage with the King, his Father.

Bach. He stands
As if he grew there, with his eyes on earth.
Sir, you and I when we were last together
Kept not this distance, as we were afraid
Of blasting by ourselves.
Leu. Madam, 'tis true,
Heaven pardon it.
Bach. Amen, sir: you may think
That I have done you wrong in this strange marriage.
Leu. 'Tis past now.
Bach. But it was no fault of mine:
The world had call'd me mad, had I refus'd
The king: nor laid I any train to catch him,
It was your own oaths did it.
Leu. 'Tis a truth,
That takes my sleep away; but would to heaven,
If it had so been pleas'd, you had refus'd him,
Though I had gratified that courtesy
With having you myself: but since 'tis thus,
I do beseech you that you will be honest
From henceforth; and not abuse his credulous age,
Which you may easily do. As for myself,
What I can say, you know alas too well,
Is tied within me; here it will sit like lead,
But shall offend no other, it will pluck me
Back from my entrance into any mirth,
As if a servant came and whisper'd with me
Of some friend's death: but I will bear myself
To you, with all the due obedience
A son owes to a mother; more than this
Is not in me, but I must leave the rest
To the just gods, who in their blessed time,

When they have given me punishment enough
For my rash sin, will mercifully find
As unexpected means to ease my grief
As they did now to bring it.
  Bach. Grown so godly?
This must not be, and I will be to you
No other than a natural mother ought;
And for my honesty, so you will swear
Never to urge me, I shall keep it safe
From any other.
  Leu. Bless me, I should urge you!
  Bach. Nay, but swear then, that I may be at peace,
For I do feel a weakness in myself
That can deny you nothing; if you tempt me
I shall embrace sin as it were a friend,
And run to meet it.
  Leu. If you knew how far
It were from me, you would not urge an oath.
But for your satisfaction, when I tempt you ——
  Bach. Swear not. I cannot move him. This sad talk
Of things past help, does not become us well.
Shall I send one for my musicians, and we'll dance?
  Leu. Dance, madam?
  Bach. Yes, a lavolta.
  Leu. I cannot dance, madam.
  Bach. Then let's be merry.
  Leu. I am as my fortunes bid me.
Do not you see me sour?
  Bach. Yes.
And why think you I smile?
  Leu. I am so far from any joy myself,
I cannot fancy a cause of mirth.
  Bach. I'll tell you. We are alone.
  Leu. Alone!
  Bach. Yes.
  Leu. 'Tis true: what then?
  Bach. What then?
You make my smiling now break into laughter:

What think you is to be done then?
Leu. We should pray to heaven for mercy.
Bach. Pray! that were a way indeed
To pass the time.
Leu. I dare not think I understand you.
Bach. I must teach you then. Come kiss me.
Leu. Kiss you?
Bach. Yes, be not asham'd:
You did it not yourself, I will forgive you.
Leu. Keep, you displeased gods, the due respect.
I ought to bear unto this wicked woman,
As she is now my mother: haste within me,
Lest I add sins to sins, till no repentance
Will cure me.
Bach. Leave these melancholy moods,
That I may swear thee welcome on thy lips
A thousand times.
Leu. Pray leave this wicked talk;
You do not know to what my father's wrong
May urge me.
Bach. I'm careless, and do weigh
The world, my life, and all my after hopes,
Nothing without thy love: mistake me not,
Thy love, as I have had it, free and open
As wedlock is within itself, what say you?
Leu. Nothing.
Bach. Pity me, behold a duchess
Kneels for thy mercy. What answer will you give?
Leu. They that can answer must be less amaz'd
Than I am now: you see my tears deliver
My meaning to you.
Bach. Shall I be contemn'd?
Thou art a beast, worse than a savage beast,
To let a lady kneel.
Leu. 'Tis your will, heaven: but let me bear me
Like myself, however she does.
Bach. How fond was I
To beg thy love! I'll force thee to my will.

Dost thou not know that I can make the king
Doat as my list? yield quickly, or, by heaven,
I'll have thee kept in prison for my purpose.
Leu. All you have nam'd, but making of me sin
With you, you may command, but never that:
Say what you will, I'll hear you as becomes me:
If you speak, I will not follow your counsel,
Neither will I tell the world to your disgrace,
But give you the just honor
That is due from me to my father's wife.
Bach. Lord, how full of wise formality you're grown
Of late: but you were telling me,
You could have wish'd that I had married you;
If you will swear so yet, I'll make away
The king.
Leu. You are a strumpet.
Bach. Nay I care not
For all your railings: they will batter walls
And take in towns as soon as trouble me:
Tell him; I care not; I shall undo you only.
Which is no matter.
Leu. I appeal to you,
Still, and for ever, that are and cannot be other.—
Madam, I see 'tis in your power
To work your will on him: and I desire you
To lay what trains you will for my wish'd death,
But suffer him to find his quiet grave
In peace; alas he never did you wrong;
And farther I beseech you pardon me
For the ill word I gave you, for however
You may deserve, it became not me
To call you so, but passion urges me
I know not whither; my heart break now, and ease me ever

THE FAITHFUL SHEPHERDESS. BY JOHN FLETCHER.

Clorin, a Shepherdess, watching by the Grave of her Lover, is found by a Satyr.

Clor. Hail holy earth, whose cold arms do embrace
The truest man that ever fed his flocks
By the fat plains of fruitful Thessaly.
Thus I salute thy grave, thus do I pay
My early vows, and tribute of mine eyes,
To thy still loved ashes; thus I free
Myself from all ensuing heats and fires
Of love: all sports, delights, and jolly games,
That shepherds hold full dear, thus put I off.
Now no more shall these smooth brows be begirt
With youthful coronals, and lead the dance.
No more the company of fresh fair maids
And wanton shepherds be to me delightful:
Nor the shrill pleasing sound of merry pipes
Under some shady dell, when the cool wind
Plays on the leaves: all be far away,
Since thou art far away, by whose dear side
How often have I sate crown'd with fresh flowers
For summer's queen, whilst every shepherd's boy
Puts on his lusty green, with gaudy hook,
And hanging script of finest cordevan.
But thou art gone, and these are gone with thee,
And all are dead but thy dear memory:
That shall out-live thee, and shall ever spring,
Whilst there are pipes, or jolly shepherds sing.
And here will I in honor of thy love,
Dwell by thy grave, forgetting all those joys
That former times made precious to mine eyes,
Only rememb'ring what my youth did gain
In the dark hidden virtuous use of herbs,
That will I practise, and as freely give
All my endeavors, as I gain'd them free.
Of all green wounds I know the remedies
In men or cattle, be they stung with snakes,

Or charm'd with powerful words of wicked art;
Or be they love-sick, or through too much heat
Grown wild, or lunatic; their eyes, or ears,
Thick'ned with misty film of dulling rheum:
These I can cure, such secret virtue lies
In herbs applied by a virgin's hand.
My meat shall be what these wild woods afford.
Berries and chestnuts, plantains, on whose cheeks
The sun sits smiling, and the lofty fruit
Pull'd from the fair head of the straight-grown pine.
On these I 'll feed with free content and rest,
When night shall blind the world, by thy side blest.

A Satyr enters.

Satyr. Through yon same bending plain
That flings his arms down to the main,
And through these thick woods have I run,
Whose bottom never kist the sun.
Since the lusty spring began
All to please my master Pan,
Have I trotted without rest
To get him fruit; for at a feast
He entertains this coming night
His paramour the Syrinx bright:
But behold a fairer sight!
By that heavenly form of thine,
Brightest fair, thou art divine,
Sprung from great immortal race
Of the gods, for in thy face
Shines more awful majesty,
Than dull weak mortality
Dare with misty eyes behold,
And live: therefore on this mold
Lowly do I bend my knee
In worship of thy deity.
Deign it, goddess, from my hand
To receive whate'er this land
From her fertile womb doth send

Of her choice fruits: and but lend
Belief to that the Satyr tells,
Fairer by the famous wells
To this present day ne'er grew,
Never better, nor more true.
Here be grapes whose lusty blood
Is the learned poet's good,
Sweeter yet did never crown
The head of Bacchus; nuts more brown
Than the squirrels teeth that crack them:
Deign, O fairest fair, to take them:
For these, black-eyed Driope
Hath oftentimes commanded me
With my clasped knee to climb.
See how well the lusty time
Hath deckt their rising cheeks in red,
Such as on your lips is spread.
Here be berries for a queen,
Some be red, some be green,
These are of that luscious meat
The great god Pan himself doth eat:
All these, and what the woods can yield,
The hanging mountain, or the field,
I freely offer, and ere long
Will bring you more, more sweet and strong;
Till when, humbly leave I take,
Lest the great Pan do awake
That sleeping lies in a deep glade,
Under a broad beeches shade.
I must go, I must run,
Swifter than the fiery sun. [*Exit.*

Clor. And all my fears go with thee
What greatness, or what private hidden power,
Is there in me to draw submission
From this rude man and beast? sure I am mortal;
The daughter of a shepherd; he was mortal,
And she that bore me mortal; prick my hand
And it will bleed; a fever shakes me, and

The self-same wind that makes the young lambs shrink,
Makes me a-cold: my fear says I am mortal:
Yet I have heard (my mother told it me)
And now I do believe it, if I keep
My virgin flower uncropt, pure, chaste, and fair;
No goblin, wood-god, fairy, elf, or fiend,
Satyr, or other power that haunts the groves,
Shall hurt my body, or by vain illusion
Draw me to wander after idle fires,
Or voices calling me in dead of night
To make me follow, and so tole me on
Through mire, and standing pools, to find my ruin.
Else why should this rough thing, who never knew
Manners nor smooth humanity, whose heats
Are rougher than himself, and more misshapen,
Thus mildly kneel to me?—Sure there 's a power
In that great name of Virgin, that binds fast
All rude uncivil bloods, all appetites
That break their confines. Then, strong Chastity,
Be thou my strongest guard; for here I 'll dwell
In opposition against fate and hell.———

PERIGOT *and* AMORET *appoint to meet at the Virtuous Well.*

Peri. Stay, gentle Amoret, thou fair-brow'd maid,
Thy shepherd prays thee stay, that holds thee dear.
Equal with his soul's good.
Amo. Speak, I give
Thee freedom, shepherd, and thy tongue be still
The same it ever was, as free from ill,
As he whose conversation never knew
The court or city, be thou ever true.
Peri. When I fall off from my affection,
Or mingle my clean thoughts with ill desires,
First let our great God cease to keep my flocks,
That being left alone without a guard,
The wolf, or winter's rage, or summer's great heat,
And want of water, rots, or what to us
Of ill is yet unknown, full speedily,

And in their general ruin, let me feel.
Amo. I pray thee, gentle shepherd, wish not so:
I do believe thee, 'tis as hard for me
To think thee false, and harder than for thee
To hold me foul.
Peri. O you are fairer far
Than the chaste blushing morn, or that fair star
That guides the wand'ring sea-men through the deep,
Straighter than straightest pine upon the steep
Head of an aged mountain, and more white
Than the new milk, we strip before day-light
From the full-freighted bags of our fair flocks.
Your hair more beauteous than those hanging locks
Of young Apollo.
Amo. Shepherd, be not lost,
Y' are sail'd too far already from the coast
Of our discourse.
Peri. Did you not tell me once
I should not love alone, I should not lose
Those many passions, vows, and holy oaths,
I' ve sent to heaven? did you not give your hand,
Even that fair hand, in hostage? Do not then
Give back again those sweets to other men,
You yourself vow'd were mine.
Amo. Shepherd, so far as maiden's modesty
May give assurance, I am once more thine.
Once more I give my hand; be ever free
From that great foe to faith, foul jealousy.
Peri. I take it as my best good; and desire,
For stronger confirmation of our love,
To meet this happy night in that fair grove,
Where all true shepherds have rewarded been
For their long service. Say, sweet, shall it hold?
Amo. Dear friend, you must not blame me if I make
A doubt of what the silent night may do—
Maids must be fearful.
Peri. O do not wrong my honest simple truth,
Myself and my affections are as pure

As those chaste flames that burn before the shrine
Of the great Dian: only my intent
To draw you thither, was to plight our troths,
With interchange of mutual chaste embraces,
And ceremonious tying of ourselves.
For to that holy wood is consecrate
A Virtuous Well, about whose flowery banks
The nimble-footed fairies dance their rounds
By the pale moon-shine, dipping oftentimes
Their stolen children, so to make them free
From dying flesh, and dull mortality.
By this fair fount hath many a shepherd sworn
And given away his freedom, many a troth
Been plight, which neither envy or old time
Could ever break, with many a chaste kiss given
In hope of coming happiness: by this
Fresh fountain many a blushing maid
Hath crown'd the head of her long loved shepherd
With gaudy flowers, whilst he happy sung
Lays of his love and dear captivity.
There grow all herbs fit to cool looser flames
Our sensual parts provoke; chiding our bloods,
And quenching by their power those hidden sparks
That else would break out, and provoke our sense
To open fires—so virtuous is that place.
Then, gentle shepherdess, believe and grant;
In troth it fits not with that face to scant
Your faithful shepherd of those chaste desires
He ever aim'd at.
  Amo. Thou hast prevail'd; farewell; this coming nigh
Shall crown thy chaste hopes with long wish'd delight.—

Thenot, admiring the constancy of Clorin to her dead Lover, rejects the suit of Cloe.

  Cloe. Shepherd, I pray thee stay, where hast thou been,
Or whither go'st thou? Here be woods as green
As any, air likewise as fresh and sweet,
As where smooth Zephyrus plays on the fleet
Face of the curled streams, with flowers as many

As the young spring gives, and as choice as any.
Here be all new delights, cool streams and wells,
Arbors o'ergrown with woodbines, caves and dells,
Choose where thou wilt, whilst I sit by and sing,
Or gather rushes to make many a ring
For thy long fingers : tell thee tales of love,
How the pale Phœbe, hunting in a grove,
First saw the boy Endymion, from whose eyes
She took eternal fire that never dies ;
How she convey'd him softly in a sleep,
His temples bound with poppy, to the steep
Head of old Latmus, where she stoops each night,
Gilding the mountains with her brother's light,
To kiss her sweetest.
The. Far from me are these
Hot flashes, bred from wanton heat and ease.
I have forgot what love and loving meant ;
Rhimes, songs, and merry rounds, that oft are sent
To the soft ears of maids, are strange to me ;
Only I live to admire a chastity,
That neither pleasing age, smooth tongue, or gold,
Could ever break upon, so pure a mold
Is that her mind was cast in ; 'tis to her
I only am reserv'd ; she is my form I stir
By, breathe and move, 'tis she and only she
Can make me happy, or give me misery.
Cloe. Good shepherd, may a stranger crave t) know
To whom this dear observance you do owe ?
The. You may, and by her virtue learn to square
And level out your life ; for to be fair
And nothing virtuous, only fits the eye
Of gaudy youth and swelling vanity.
Then know, she 's call'd the Virgin of the Grove,
She that hath long since buried her chaste love,
And now lives by his grave, for whose dear soul
She hath vow'd herself into the holy roll
Of strict virginity ; 'tis her I so admire,
Not any looser blood, or new desire. ——

Thenot loves Clorin yet fears to gain his suit.

Clor. Shepherd, how cam'st thou hither to this place?
No way is trodden; all the verdant grass
The spring shot up, stands yet unbruised here
Of any foot, only the dappled deer
Far from the feared sound of crooked horn
Dwells in this fastness.
The. Chaster than the morn,
I have not wand'red, or by strong illusion
Into this virtuous place have made intrusion.
But hither am I come (believe me, fair),
To seek you out, of whose great good the air
Is full, and strongly labors, whilst the sound
Breaks against heaven, and drives into a stound
The amazed shepherd, that such virtue can
Be resident in lesser than a man.
Clor. If any art I have, or hidden skill,
May cure thee of disease, or fester'd ill,
Whose grief or greenness to another's eye
May seem unpossible of remedy,
I dare yet undertake it.
The. 'Tis no pain
I suffer through disease, no beating vein
Conveys infection dangerous to the heart,
No part imposthumed, to be cured by art,
This body holds, and yet a feller grief
Than ever skilful hand did give relief
Dwells on my soul, and may be heal'd by you,
Fair beauteous virgin.
Clor. Then, shepherd, let me sue
To know thy grief; that man yet never knew
The way to health, that durst not show his sore.
The. Then, fairest, know I love you.
Clor. Swain, no more.
Thou hast abused the strictness of this place,
And offer'd sacrilegious foul disgrace
To the sweet rest of these interred bones
For fear of whose ascending, fly at once,

Thou and thy idle passions, that the sight
Of death and speedy vengeance may not fright
Thy very soul with horror.
The. Let me not
(Thou all perfection) merit such a blot
For my true zealous faith.
Clor. Darest thou abide
To see this holy earth at once divide
And give her body up? for sure it will,
If thou pursu'st with wanton flames to fill
This hallow'd place; therefore repent and go,
Whilst I with praise appease his ghost below;
That else would tell thee, what it were to be
A rival in that virtuous love that he
Embraces yet.
The. 'Tis not the white or red
Inhabits in your cheek, that thus can wed
My mind to adoration; nor your eye,
Though it be full and fair, your forehead high,
And smooth as Pelops' shoulder: not the smile,
Lies watching in those dimples to beguile
The easy soul; your hands and fingers long
With veins enamel'd richly; nor your tongue,
Though it spoke sweeter than Arion's harp;
Your hair, wove into many a curious warp,
Able in endless error to enfold
The wand'ring soul; nor the true perfect mold
Of all your body, which as pure doth show
In maiden whiteness as the Alpsian snow:
All these, were but your constancy away,
Would please me less than a black stormy day
The wretched seaman toiling though the deep.
But whilst this honor'd strictness you dare keep,
Though all the plagues that e'er begotten were
In the great womb of air, were settled here,
In opposition, I would, like the tree,
Shake off those drops of weakness, and be free,
Even in the arm of danger.

Clor. Wouldst thou have
Me raise again (fond man) from silent grave,
Those sparks that long ago were buried here
With my dead friend's cold ashes?
The. Dearest dear,
I dare not ask it, nor you must not grant.
Stand strongly to your vow, and do not faint.
Remember how he lov'd ye; and be still
The same, opinion speaks ye; let not will,
And that great god of women, appetite,
Set up your blood again; do not invite
Desire and Fancy from their long exile,
To set them once more in a pleasing smile,
Be like a rock made firmly up 'gainst all
The power of angry heaven, or the strong fall
Of Neptune's battery; if ye yield, I die
To all affection: 'tis that loyalty,
Ye tie unto this grave, I so admire;
And yet there's something else I would desire
If you would hear me, but withal deny.
O Pan, what an uncertain destiny
Hangs over all my hopes! I will retire,
For if I longer stay, this double fire
Will lick my life up.
Clor. The gods give quick release
And happy cure unto thy hard disease.——

The God of the River rises with Amoret in his arms, whom the sullen Shepherd has flung wounded into his spring.

River God. What powerful charms my streams do bring
Back again unto their spring,
With such force, that I their god,
Three times striking with my rod,
Could not keep them in their ranks?
My fisnes shoot into the banks,
There's not one that stays and feeds,
All have hid them in the weeds.
Here's a mortal almost dead

Fal'n into my river head,
Hallow'd so with many a spell,
That till now none ever fell.
'Tis a female young and clear,
Cast in by some ravisher.
See upon her breast a wound,
On which there is no plaister bound.
Yet she's warm, her pulses beat,
'Tis a sign of life and heat.
If thou be'st a virgin pure,
I can give a present cure.
Take a drop into thy wound
From my watry locks, more round
Than orient pearl, and far more pure
Than unchaste flesh may endure.
See she pants, and from her flesh
The warm blood gusheth out afresh.
She is an unpolluted maid;
I must have this bleeding staid.
From my banks I pluck this flower
With holy hand, whose virtuous power
Is at once to heal and draw.
The blood returns. I never saw
A fairer mortal. Now doth break
Her deadly slumber. Virgin, speak.

Amo. Who hath restored my sense, given me new breath,
And brought me back out of the arms of death?

River God. I have heal'd thy wounds.

Amo. Ah me!

River God. Fear not him that succor'd thee.
I am this fountain's god; below
My waters to a river grow,
And 'twixt two banks with osiers set,
That only prosper in the wet,
Through the meadows do they glide,
Wheeling still on every side,
Sometimes winding round about,
To find the evenest channel out;

And if thou wilt go with me,
Leaving mortal company,
In the cool streams shalt thou lie,
Free from harm as well as I.
I will give thee for thy food,
No fish that useth in the mud,
But trout and pike that love to swim
Where the gravel from the brim
Through the pure streams may be seen.
Orient pearl fit for a queen,
Will I give thy love to win,
And a shell to keep them in.
Not a fish in all my brook
That shall disobey thy look,
But when thou wilt, come sliding by,
And from thy white hand take a fly.
And to make thee understand,
How I can my waves command,
They shall bubble whilst I sing
Sweeter than the silver spring. [*Sings.*

Do not fear to put thy feet
Naked in the rivers sweet:
Think not leach, or newt, or toad,
Will bite thy foot, when thou hast trod;
Nor let the water rising high,
As thou wadest in, make thee cry
And sob, but ever live with me,
And not a wave shall trouble thee.

Amo. Immortal power, that rulest this holy flood;
I know myself unworthy to be woo'd
By thee, a god: for ere this, but for thee,
I should have shown my weak mortality.
Besides, by holy oath betwixt us twain,
I am betroth'd unto a shepherd swain,
Whose comely face, I know, the gods above
May make me leave to see, but not to love.
River God. May he prove to thee as true.—

Fairest virgin, now adieu,
I must make my waters fly,
Lest they leave their channels dry,
And beasts that come unto the spring
Miss their morning's watering:
Which I would not, for of late
All the neighbor people sate
On my banks, and from the fold
Two white lambs of three weeks old
Offer'd to my deity:
For which this year they shall be free
From raging floods, that as they pass
Leave their gravel in the grass:
Nor shall their meads be overflown,
When their grass is newly mown.
Amo. For thy kindness to me shown,
Never from thy banks be blown
Any tree, with windy force,
Cross thy streams to stop thy course:
May no beast that comes to drink,
With his horns cast down thy brink;
May none that for thy fish do look,
Cut thy banks to damm thy brook:
Bare-foot may no neighbor wade
In thy cool streams, wife nor maïd,
When the spawn on stones do lie,
To wash their hemp, and spoil the fry.
River God. Thanks, virgin, I must down again,
Thy wound will put thee to no pain:
Wonder not so soon 'tis gone;
A holy hand was laid upon.

[If all the parts of this Play had been in unison with these innocent scenes, and sweet lyric intermixtures, it had been a Poem fit to vie with Comus or the Arcadia, to have been put into the hands of boys and virgins, to have made matter for young dreams, like the loves of Hermia and Lysander. But a spot is on the face of this moon.—Nothing short of infatuation could have driven Fletcher upon mixing up with this blessedness such an ugly deformity as Cloe: the wanton shepherdess! Coarse words do but wound the ears; but a character of lewdness affronts the mind. Female lewdness at once shocks nature and morality. If Cloe was meant to set off Clorin by contrast, Fletcher should have known that such weeds by juxta-position do not set off but kill sweet flowers.]

THE FALSE ONE: A TRAGEDY. BY JOHN FLETCHER.

Ptolomy, King of Egypt, presents to Cæsar the head of Pompey. Cæsar rebukes the Egyptians for their treachery and ingratitude.

CÆSAR, ANTHONY, DOLLABELA, SCEVA, *Romans;* PTOLOMY, PHOTINUS, ACHILLAS, *Egyptians.*

Pho. Hail, conqueror and head of all the world,
Now this head's off.
Cæs. Ha!
Pho. Do not shun me, Cæsar.
From kingly Ptolomy I bring this present,
The crown and sweat of thy Pharsalian labor;
The goal and mark of high ambitious honor.
Before, thy victory had no name, Cæsar;
Thy travail and thy loss of blood no recompence;
Thou dream'dst of being worthy and of war;
And all thy furious conflicts were but slumbers;
Here they take life, here they inherit honor,
Grow fix'd and shoot up everlasting triumphs,
Take it and look upon thy humble servant,
With noble eyes look on the princely Ptolomy,
That offers with this head, most mighty Cæsar,
What thou would'st once have given for 't, all Egypt.
Ach. Nor do not question it, most royal conqueror,
Nor disesteem the benefit that meets thee,
Because 'tis easily got, it comes the safer.
Yet, let me tell thee, most imperious Cæsar,
Though he oppos'd no strength of swords to win this,
Nor labor'd through no showers of darts and lances,
Yet here he found a fort that fac'd him strongly,
An inward war: He was his grandsire's guest,

Friend to his father, and when he was expell'd
And beaten from this kingdom by strong hand,
And had none left him to restore his honor,
No hope to find a friend in such a misery;
Then in stept Pompey, took his feeble fortune,
Strengthen'd and cherish'd it, and set it right again.
This was a love to Cæsar!

Sce. Give me hate, gods.

Pho. This Cæsar may account a little wicked;
But yet remember, if thine own hands, conqueror,
Had fall'n upon him, what it had been then;
If thine own sword had touch'd his throat, what that way:
He was thy son-in-law, there to be tainted
Had been most terrible: let the worst be render'd,
We have deserv'd for keeping thy hands innocent.

Cæs. O Sceva, Sceva, see that head; see, captains,
The head of godlike Pompey.

Sce. He was basely ruin'd,
But let the gods be griev'd that suffer'd it,
And be you Cæsar.

Cæs. Oh thou conqueror,
Thou glory of the world once, now the pity,
Thou awe of nations, wherefore didst thou fall thus?
What poor fate follow'd thee, and pluck'd thee on
To trust thy sacred life to an Egyptian;
The life and light of Rome to a blind stranger,
That honorable war ne'er taught a nobleness,
Nor worthy circumstance show'd what a man was;
That never heard thy name sung but in banquets
And loose lascivious pleasures; to a boy,
That had no faith to comprehend thy greatness,
No study of thy life to know thy goodness:
And leave thy nation, nay, thy noble friend,
Leave him distrusted, that in tears falls with thee:
In soft relenting tears? Hear me, great Pompey,
If thy great spirit can hear, I must task thee:
Thou 'st most unnobly robb'd me of my victory,
My love and mercy.

Ant. O how brave these tears show!
How excellent is sorrow in an enemy!
Dol. Glory appears not greater than this goodness.
Cæs. Egyptians, dare you think your high pyramids,
Built to outdure the sun as you suppose,
Where your unworthy kings lie rak'd in ashes,
Are monuments fit for him? No, brood of Nilus,
Nothing can cover his high fame but heaven,
No pyramids set off his memories
But the eternal substance of his greatness:
To which I leave him. Take the head away,
And with the body give it noble burial.
Your earth shall now be bless'd to hold a Roman,
Whose braveries all the world's earth cannot balance—
You look now, king,
And you that have been agents in this glory,
For our especial favor?
Ptol. We desire it.
Cæs. And doubtless you expect rewards?—
I forgive you all: that's recompence.
You are young and ignorant; that pleads your pardon;
And fear, it may be, more than hate provok'd ye.
Your ministers I must think wanted judgment.
And so they err'd; I am bountiful to think this,
Believe me, most bountiful; be you most thankful,
That bounty share amongst ye: if I knew
What to send you for a present, king of Egypt,
I mean, a head of equal reputation,
And that you lov'd, though it were your brightest sister's,*
(But her you hate) I would not be behind ye.
Ptol. Hear me, great Cæsar.
Cæs. I have heard too much:
And study not with smooth shows to invade
My noble mind as you have done my conquest.
Ye are poor and open: I must tell ye roundly,
That man that could not recompence the benefits,

* Cleopatra

The great and bounteous services of Pompey,
Can never doat upon the name of Cæsar.
Though I
Had hated Pompey, and allow'd his ruin,
Hasty to please in blood are seldom trusty:
And but I stand environ'd with my victories,
My fortune never failing to befriend me,
My noble strengths and friends about my person,
I durst not try ye, nor expect a courtesy
Above the pious love you show'd to Pompey.
You 've found me merciful in arguing with you;
Swords, hangmen, fires, destructions of all natures,
Demolishments of kingdoms, and whole ruins,
Are wont to be my orators. Turn to tears,
You wretched and poor seeds of sun-burnt Egypt:
And now you 've found the nature of a conqueror,
That you cannot decline with all your flatteries,
That where the day gives light will be himself still,
Know how to meet his worth with human courtesi
Go, and embalm the bones of that great soldier;
Howl round about his pile, fling on your spices,
Make a Sabæan bed, and place this Phœnix
Where the hot sun may emulate his virtues,
And draw another Pompey from his ashes
Divinely great, and fix him 'mongst the worthies.
Ptol. We will do all.
Cæs. You 've robb'd him of those tears
His kindred and his friends kept sacred for him,
The virgins of their funeral lamentations;
And that kind earth that thought to cover him,
His country's earth, will cry out 'gainst your cruelty.
And weep unto the ocean for revenge,
Till Nilus raise his seven heads and devour ye,
My grief has stopt the rest · when Pompey lived,
He used you nobly; now he is dead, use him so.

LOVE'S PILGRIMAGE: A COMEDY. BY JOHN FLETCHER.

Leocadia leaves her Father's house, disguised in man's apparel, to travel in search of Mark-antonio, to whom she is contracted, but has been deserted by him. When at length she meets with him, she finds, that by a precontract he is the Husband of Theodosia. In this extremity, Philippo, Brother to Theodosia, offers Leocadia marriage.

PHILIPPO. LEOCADIA.

Phi. Will you not hear me?
Leo. I have heard so much,
Will keep me deaf for ever. No, Mark-antonio,
After thy sentence I may hear no more,
Thou hast pronounc'd me dead.
Phi. Appeal to reason:
She will reprieve you from the power of grief,
Which rules but in her absence; hear me say
A sovereign message from her, which in duty,
And love to your own safety, you ought hear.
Why do you strive so? whither would you fly?
You cannot wrest yourself away from care,
You may from counsel; you may shift your place,
But not your person; and another clime
Makes you no other.
Leo. Oh!
Phi. For passion's sake
(Which I do serve, honor, and love in you),
If you will sigh, sigh here; if you would vary
A sigh to tears, or out-cry, do it here.
No shade, no desart, darkness, nor the grave,
Shall be more equal to your thoughts than I.
Only but hear me speak.
Leo. What would you say?
Phi. That which shall raise your heart, or pull down mine,
Quiet your passion, or provoke mine own:
We must have both one balsam, or one wound.
For know, lov'd fair,
I have read you through,
And with a wond'ring pity look'd on you.

I have observ'd the method of your blood,
And waited on it even with sympathy
Of a like red and paleness in mine own.
I knew which blush was anger's, which was love's,
Which was the eye of sorrow, which of truth,
And could distinguish honor from disdain
In every change: and you are worth my study.
I saw your voluntary misery
Sustain'd in travel; a disguised maid,
Wearied with seeking, and with finding lost,
Neglected where you hoped most, or put by,
I saw it, and have laid it to my heart,
And though it were my sister which was righted,
Yet being by your wrong, I put off nature,
Could not be glad, where I most bound to triumph:
My care for you so drown'd respect of her.
Nor did I only apprehend your bonds,
But studied your release: and for that day
Have I made up a ransom, brought you a health,
Preservative 'gainst chance or injury,
Please you apply it to the grief; *myself.*

Leo. Ah!

Phi. Nay, do not think me less than such a cure;
Antonio was not, and 'tis possible
Philippo may succeed. My blood and house
Are as deep rooted, and as fairly spread,
As Mark-antonio's; and in that, all seek,
Fortune hath giv'n him no precedency;
As for our thanks to Nature, I may burn
Incense as much as he; I ever durst
Walk with Antonio by the self-same light
At any feast, or triumph, and ne'er cared
Which side my lady or her woman took
In their survey; I durst have told my tale too,
Though his discourse new ended.

Leo. My repulse——

Phi. Let not that torture you which makes me happy,
Nor think that conscience, fair, which is no shame;

'Twas no repulse, it was your dowry rather:
For then methought a thousand graces met
To make you lovely, and ten thousand stories
Of constant virtue, which you then out-reach'd,
In one example did proclaim you rich:
Nor do I think you wretched or disgraced
After this suffering, and do therefore take
Advantage of your need; but rather know,
You are the charge and business of those powers,
Who, like best tutors, do inflict hard tasks
Upon great natures, and of noblest hopes;
Read trivial lessons and half-lines to slugs:
They that live long, and never feel mischance,
Spend more than half their age in ignorance.
Leo. 'Tis well you think so.
Phi. You shall think so too,
You shall, sweet Leocadia, and do so.
Leo. Good sir, no more; you have too fair a shape
To play so foul a part in, as the Tempter.
Say that I could make peace with fortune; who,
Who should absolve me of my vow yet: ha?
My contract made?
Phi. Your contract?
Leo. Yes, my contract.
Am I not his? his wife?
Phi. Sweet, nothing less.
Leo. I have no name then.
Phi. Truly then you have not.
How can you be his wife, who was before
Another's husband?
Leo. Oh! though he dispense
With his faith given, I cannot with mine.
Phi. You do mistake, clear soul; his precontract
Doth annul yours, and you have giv'n no faith
That ties you, in religion, or humanity:
You rather sin against that greater precept,
To covet what's another's; sweet, you do,
Believe me, who dare not urge dishonest things.

Remove that scruple, therefore, and but take
Your dangers now into your judgment's scale,
And weigh them with your safeties. Think but whither
Now you can go; what you can do to live:
How near you have barr'd all ports to your own succor,
Except this one that I here open, love,
Should you be left alone, you were a prey
To the wild lust of any, who would look
Upon this shape like a temptation,
And think you want the man you personate;
Would not regard this shift, which love put on,
As virtue forc'd, but covet it like vice:
So should you live the slander of each sex,
And be the child of error and of shame;
And which is worse, even Mark-antonio
Would be call'd just, to turn a wanderer off,
And fame report you worthy his contempt:
Where, if you make new choice, and settle here,
There is no further tumult in this flood,
Each current keeps his course, and all suspicions
Shall return honors. Came ye forth a maid?
Go home a wife. Alone, and in disguise?
Go home a waited Leocadia.
Go home, and by the virtue of that charm,
Transform all mischiefs as you are transform'd,
Turn your offended father's wrath to wonder,
And all his loud grief to a silent welcome;
Unfold the riddles you have made.—What say you?
Now is the time; delay is but despair;
If you be chang'd, let a kiss tell me so.
Leo. I am; but how, I rather feel than know.

[This is one of the most pleasing if not the most shining scenes in Fletcher. All is sweet, natural, and unforced. It is a copy in which we may suppose Massinger to have profited by the studying.]

BONDUCA: A TRAGEDY. BY JOHN FLETCHER.

Bonduca, the British Queen, taking occasion from a Defeat of the Romans to impeach their Valor, is rebuked by Caratach.

BONDUCA, CARATACH, HENGO, NENNIUS, Soldiers.

Bon. The hardy Romans! O ye gods of Britain,
The rust of arms, the blushing shame of soldiers!
Are these the men that conquer by inheritance?
The fortune-makers? these the Julians,
That with the sun measure the end of Nature,
Making the world but one Rome and one Cæsar?
Shame, how they flee! Cæsar's soft soul dwells in them;
Their mothers got them sleeping, pleasure nurst them,
Their bodies sweat with sweet oils, love's allurements,
Not lusty arms. Dare they send these to seek us,
These Roman girls? Is Britain grown so wanton?
Twice we have beat them, Nennius, scattered them,
And though their big-boned Germans, on whose pikes
The honors of their actions sit in triumph,
Made themes for songs to shame them: and a woman,
A woman beat them, Nennius; a weak woman,
A woman beat these Romans.
Car. So it seems. A man would shame to talk so.
Bon. Who 's that?
Car. I.
Bon. Cousin, do you grieve at my fortunes?
Car. No, Bonduca,
If I grieve, 'tis at the bearing of your fortunes;
You put too much wind to your sail: discretion
And hardy valor are the twins of honor,
And nurs'd together, make a conqueror;
Divided, but a talker. 'Tis a truth,
That Rome has fled before us twice, and routed.
A truth we ought to crown the gods for, lady,
And not our tongues. A truth, is none of ours,
Nor in our ends, more than the noble bearing:
For then it leaves to be a virtue, lady,

And we that have been victors, beat ourselves,
When we insult upon our honor's subject.
Bon. My valiant cousin, is it foul to say
What liberty and honor bid us do,
And what the gods allow us?
Car. No, Bonduca,
So what we say exceed not what we do.
Ye call the Romans fearful, fleeing Romans,
And Roman girls, the lees of tainted pleasures:
Does this become a doer? are they such?
Bon. They are no more.
Car. Where is your conquest then?
Why are your altars crown'd with wreaths of flowers,
The beast with gilt horns waiting for the fire?
The holy Druids composing songs
Of everlasting life to Victory?
Why are these triumphs, lady? for a may-game?
For hunting a poor herd of wretched Romans?
Is it no more? shut up your temples, Britons,
And let the husbandman redeem his heifers;
Put out our holy fires; no timbrel ring;
Let 's home and sleep; for such great overthrows
A candle burns too bright a sacrifice;
A glow-worm's tail too full of flame. O Nennius,
Thou hast a noble uncle knew a Roman,
And how to speak to him, how to give him weight
In both his fortunes.
Bon. By the gods, I think
Ye doat upon these Romans, Caratach.
Car. Witness these wounds, I do; they were fairly given.
I love an enemy, I was born a soldier;
And he that in the head of 's troop defies me,
Bending my manly body with his sword,
I make a mistress. Yellow-tressed Hymen
Ne'er tied a longing virgin with more joy,
Than I am married to that man that wounds me:
And are not all these Romans. Ten struck battles
I suck'd these honor'd scars from, and all Roman.

Ten years of bitter nights and heavy marches,
When many a frozen storm sung through my cuirass,
And made it doubtful whether that or I
Were the more stubborn metal, have I wrought througn,
And all to try these Romans. Ten times a night
I have swum the rivers, when the stars of Rome
Shot at me as I floated, and the billows
Tumbled their watry ruins on my shoulders,
Charging my batter'd sides with troops of agues,
And still to try these Romans; whom I found
(And if I lie, my wounds be henceforth backward,
And be you witness, gods, and all my dangers)
As ready, and as full of that I brought
(Which was not fear nor flight) as valiant,
As vigilant, as wise, to do and suffer,
Ever advanc'd as forward as the Britons;
Their sleeps as short, their hopes as high as ours.
Aye, and as subtle, Lady. 'Tis dishonor,
And follow'd will be impudence, Bonduca,
And grow to no belief, to taint these Romans.
Have I not seen the Britons—
  Bon. What?
  Car. Disheart'ned,
Run, run, Bonduca, not the quick rack swifter;
The virgin from the hated ravisher
Not half so fearful;—not a flight drawn home,
A round stone from a sling, a lover's wish,
E'er made that haste that they have. By heavens,
I have seen these Britons that you magnify,
Run as they would have out-run time, and roaring,
Basely for mercy, roaring; the light shadows,
That in a thought scur o'er the fields of corn,
Halted on crutches to them.
  Bon. O ye powers,
What scandals do I suffer!
  Car. Yes, Bonduca,
I have seen thee run too, and thee, Nennius;
Yea run apace, both; then when Penyus,

The Roman girl, cut through your armed carts,
And drove them headlong on ye down the hill:
Then when he hunted ye like Britain-foxes,
More by the scent than sight: then did I see
These valiant and approved men of Britain,
Like boding owls, creep into tods of ivy,
And hoot their fears to one another nightly.
Nen. And what did you then, Caratach?
Car. I fled too,
But not so fast; your jewel had been lost then,
Young Hengo there; he trasht me, Nennius:
For when your fears out-run him, then stept I,
And in the head of all the Roman's fury
Took him, and, with my tough belt to my back,
I buckled him; behind him, my sure shield;
And then I follow'd. If I say I fought
Five times in bringing off this bud of Britain,
I lie not, Nennius. Neither had ye heard
Me speak this, or ever seen the child more,
But that the son of Virtue, Penyus,
Seeing me steer through all these storms of danger,
My helm still in my hand (my sword), my prow
Turn'd to my foe (my face), he cried out nobly,
"Go, Briton, bear thy lion's whelp off safely;
"Thy manly sword has ransom'd thee: grow strong,
"And let me meet thee once again in arms:
"Then if thou stand'st, thou art mine." I took his offer,
And here I am to honor him.

THE BLOODY BROTHER; OR, ROLLO: A TRAGEDY. BY JOHN FLETCHER.

Rollo, Duke of Normandy, a bloody tyrant, puts to death his tutor Baldwin, for too freely reproving him for his crimes; but afterwards falls in love with Edith, daughter to the man he has slain. She makes a show of returning his love, and invites him to a banquet; her design being to train him there, that she may kill him: but overcome by his flatteries and real or dissembled remorse, she faints in her resolution.

ROLLO. EDITH.

Rol. What bright star, taking beauty's form upon her,
In all the happy lustre of heaven's glory,
Has dropt down from the sky to comfort me?
Wonder of Nature, let it not profane thee
My rude hand touch thy beauty, nor this kiss,
The gentle sacrifice of love and service,
Be offer'd to the honor of thy sweetness.
Edi. My gracious lord, no deity dwells here,
Nor nothing of that virtue but obedience;
The servant to your will affects no flattery.
Rol. Can it be flattery to swear those eyes
Are Love's eternal lamps he fires all hearts with:
That tongue the smart string to his bow? those sighs
The deadly shafts he sends into our souls?
Oh, look upon me with thy spring of beauty.
Edi. Your grace is full of game.
Rol. By heaven, my Edith,
Thy mother fed on roses when she bred thee.
The sweetness of the Arabian wind still blowing
Upon the treasures of perfumes and spices,
In all their pride and pleasures, call thee mistress.
Edi. Wil 't please you sit, sir?
Rol. So you please sit by me.
Fair gentle maid, there is no speaking to thee,
The excellency that appears upon thee
Ties up my tongue: pray speak to me.
Edi. Of what, sir?
Rol. Of anything, anything is excellent.
Will you take my directions? speak of love then;
Speak of thy fair self, Edith: and while thou speak'st,
Let me thus languishing give up myself, wench.
Edi. H'as a strange cunning tongue. Why do you sigh, sir?
How masterly he turns himself to catch me!
Rol. The way to paradise, my gentle maid,

Is hard and crooked: scarce repentance finding,
With all her holy helps, the door to enter.
Give me thy hand, what dost thou feel?
Edi. Your tears, sir;
You weep extremely; strengthen me now, justice.
Why are these sorrows, sir?
Rol. Thou'lt never love me,
If I should tell thee; yet there's no way left
Ever to purchase this blest paradise,
But swimming thither in these tears.
Edi. I stagger.
Rol. Are they not drops of blood?
Edi. No.
Rol. They're for blood then,
For guiltless blood; and they must drop, my Edith,
They must thus drop, till I have drown'd my mischiefs.
Edi. If this be true, I have no strength to touch him.
Rol. I prithee look upon me, turn not from me;
Alas I do confess I'm made of mischiefs,
Begot with all man's miseries upon me:
But see my sorrows, maid, and do not thou,
Whose only sweetest sacrifice is softness,
Whose true condition, tenderness of nature——
Edi. My anger melts, oh, I shall lose my justice.
Rol. Do not thou learn to kill with cruelty,
As I have done, to murder with thine eyes,
(Those blessed eyes) as I have done with malice.
When thou hast wounded me to death with scorn,
(As I deserve it, lady) for my true love,
When thou hast loaden me with earth for ever,
Take heed my sorrows, and the stings I suffer,
Take heed my nightly dreams of death and horror
Pursue thee not: no time shall tell thy griefs then,
Nor shall an hour of joy add to thy beauties,
Look not upon me as I kill'd thy father,
As I was smear'd in blood, do not thou hate me;
But thus in whiteness of my wash'd repentance,

In my heart's tears and truth of love to Edith,
In my fair life hereafter.
Edi. He will fool me.
Rol. Oh, with thine angel eyes behold and bless me·
On heaven we call for mercy and obtain it,
To justice for our right on earth and have it,
Of thee I beg for love, save me, and give it.
Edi. Now, heaven, thy help, or I am gone for ever!
His tongue has turn'd me into melting pity.

THIERRY AND THEODORET: A TRAGEDY. BY JOHN FLETCHER.

Thierry, King of France, being childless, is foretold by an Astrologer, that he shall have children if he sacrifice the first Woman that he shall meet at sun-rise coming out of the Temple of Diana. He waits before the Temple, and the first Woman he sees proves to be his own Wife Ordella.

THIERRY. MARTEL, *a Nobleman.*

Mart. Your grace is early stirring.
Thier. How can he sleep
Whose happiness is laid up in an hour
He knows comes stealing towards him? Oh Martel!
Is't possible the longing bride, whose wishes
Out-run her fears, can on that day she is married
Consume in slumbers; or his arms rust in ease
That hears the charge, and sees the honor'd purchase
Ready to guild his valor? Mine is more,
A power above these passions: this day France,
France, that in want of issue withers with us,
And like an aged river, runs his head
Into forgotten ways, again I ransom,
And his fair course turn right.
Mart. Happy woman, that dies to do these things.

Thier. The Gods have heard me now, and those that scorn'd me,
Mothers of many children and blest fathers
That see their issue like the stars unnumber'd,
Their comfort more than them, shall in my praise
Now teach their infants songs; and tell their ages
From such a son of mine, or such a queen,
That chaste Ordella brings me.
Mart. The day wears,
And those that have been offering early prayers,
Are now retiring homeward.
Thier. Stand and mark then.
Mart. Is it the first must suffer?
Thier. The first woman.
Mart. What hand shall do it, sir?
Thier. This hand, Martel:
For who less dare presume to give the gods
An incense of this offering?
Mart. Would I were she,
For such a way to die, and such a blessing,
Can never crown my parting.
Here comes a woman.

ORDELLA *comes out of the Temple veiled.*

Thier. Stand and behold her then.
Mart. I think a fair one.
Thier. Move not whilst I prepare her: may her peace,
Like his whose innocence the gods are pleas'd with,
And offering at their altars, gives his soul
Far purer than those fires, pull heaven upon her;
You holy powers, no human spot dwell in her;
No love of anything, but you and goodness,
Tie her to earth; fear be a stranger to her,
And all weak blood's affections, but thy hope,
Let her bequeath to women: hear me, heaven,
Give her a spirit masculine and noble,
Fit for yourselves to ask, and me to offer.
O let her meet my blow, doat on her death;
And as a wanton vine bows to the pruner,

That by his cutting off more may increase,
So let her fall to raise me fruit. Hail woman!
The happiest and the best (if the dull will
Do not abuse thy fortune) France e'er found yet.
Ordel. She's more than dull, sir, less and worse than woman,
That may inherit such an infinite
As you propound, a greatness so near goodness,
And brings a will to rob her.
Thier. Tell me this then,
Was there e'er woman yet, or may be found,
That for fair fame, unspotted memory,
For virtue's sake, and only for its self sake
Has, or dare make a story ?
Ordel. Many dead, sir, living I think as many.
Thier. Say the kingdom
May from a woman's will receive a blessing,
The king and kingdom, not a private safety ;
A general blessing, lady.
Ordel. A general curse light on her heart denies it.
Thier. Full of honor ;
And such examples as the former ages
Were but dim shadows of and empty figures,
Ordel. You strangely stir me, sir, and were my weakness
In any other flesh but modest woman's,
You should not ask more questions ; may I do it ?
Thier. You may, and which is more, you must.
Ordel. I joy in't,
Above a moderate gladness ; sir, you promise
It shall be honest.
Thier. As ever time discover'd.
Ordel. Let it be what it may then, what it dare,
I have a mind will hazard it.
Thier. But hark ye,
What may that woman merit, makes this blessing ?
Ordel. Only her duty, sir.
Thier. 'Tis terrible.
Ordel. 'Tis so much the more noble.
Thier. 'Tis full of fearful shadows.

Ordel. So is sleep, sir,
Or anything that's merely ours and mortal;
We were begotten gods else: but those fears,
Feeling but once the fires of nobler thoughts,
Fly, like the shapes of clouds we form, to nothing.
Thier. Suppose it death.
Ordel. I do.
Thier. And endless parting
With all we can call ours, with all our sweetness,
With youth, strength, pleasure, people, time, nay reason:
For in the silent grave, no conversation,*
No joyful tread of friends, no voice of lovers,
No careful father's counsel, nothing's heard,
Nor nothing is, but all oblivion,
Dust and an endless darkness: and dare you, woman,
Desire this place?
Ordel. 'Tis of all sleeps the sweetest;
Children begin it to us, strong men seek it,
And kings from height of all their painted glories
Fall like spent exhalations to this centre:
And those are fools that fear it, or imagine,
A few unhandsome pleasures, or life's profits,
Can recompense this place; and mad that stay it,
Till age blow out their lights, or rotten humors
Bring them dispersed to the earth.
Thier. Then you can suffer?
Ordel. As willingly as say it.
Thier. Martel, a wonder!
Here is a woman that dares die. Yet tell me,
Are you a wife?
Ordel. I am, sir?
Thier. And have children? She sighs and weeps.
Ordel. O none, sir.
Thier. Dare you venture,
For a poor barren praise you ne'er shall hear,

* There is no work, no device, nor knowledge, nor wisdom, in the grave, whither thou goest. *Ecclesiastes.*

To part with these sweet hopes?
Ordel. With all but heaven,
And yet die full of children; he that reads me
When I am ashes, is my son in wishes:
And those chaste dames that keep my memory,
Singing my yearly requiems, are my daughters.
Thier. Then there is nothing wanting but my knowledge,
And what I must do, lady.
Ordel. You are the king, sir,
And what you do I'll suffer, and that blessing
That you desire, the gods shower on the kingdom.
Thier. Thus much before I strike then, for I must kill you,
The gods have will'd it so, they've made the blessing
Must make France young again, and me a man.
Keep up your strength still nobly.
Ordel. Fear me not.
Thier. And meet death like a measure.
Ordel. I am stedfast.
Thier. Thou shalt be sainted, woman, and thy tomb
Cut out in crystal pure and good as thou art;
And on it shall be graven every age
Succeeding peers of France that rise by thy fall,
Till thou liest there like old and fruitful Nature.
Darest thou behold thy happiness?
Ordel. I dare, sir.
[*Pulls off her veil; he lets fall his sword.*
Thier. Ha!
Mar. O, sir, you must not do it.
Thier. No, I dare not.
There is an angel keeps that paradise,
A fiery angel friend: O virtue, virtue,
Ever and endless virtue.
Ordel. Strike, sir, strike.
And if in my poor death fair France may merit,
Give me a thousand blows, be killing me
A thousand days.
Thier. First let the earth be barren,
And man no more remember'd. Rise, Ordella,

The nearest to thy Maker, and the purest
That ever dull flesh show'd us,—Oh my heart-strings.*

Martel relates to Thierry the manner of Ordella's death.

Mar. The griev'd Ordella (for all other titles
But take away from that) having from me,
Prompted by your last parting groan, enquir'd
What drew it from you, and the cause soon learn'd :
For she whom barbarism could deny nothing,
With such prevailing earnestness desir'd it,
'Twas not in me, though it had been my death,
To hide it from her ; she, I say, in whom,
All was, that Athens, Rome, or warlike Sparta,
Have register'd for good in their best women,
But nothing of their ill ; knowing herself
Mark'd out (I know not by what power, but sure
A cruel one), to die, to give you children ;
Having first with a settled countenance
Look'd up to heaven, and then upon herself
(It being the next best object), and then smil'd,
As if her joy in death to do you service,
Would break forth, in despite of the much sorrow

* I have always considered this to be the finest scene in Fletcher, and Ordella the most perfect idea of the female heroic character, next to Calantha in the Broken Heart of Ford, that has been embodied in fiction. She is a piece of sainted nature. Yet noble as the whole scene is, it must be confessed that the manner of it, compared with Shakspeare's finest scenes, is slow and languid. Its motion is circular, not progressive. Each line revolves on itself in a sort of separate orbit. They do not join into one another like a running hand. Every step that we go we are stopped to admire some single object, like walking in beautiful scenery with a guide. This slowness I shall elsewhere have occasion to remark as characteristic of Fletcher. Another striking difference perceivable between Fletcher and Shakspeare, is the fondness of the former for unnatural and violent situations, like that in the scene before us. He seems to have thought that nothing great could be produced in an ordinary way. The chief incidents in the Wife for a Month, in Cupid's Revenge, in the Double Marriage, and in many more of his Tragedies, show this. Shakspeare had nothing of this contortion in his mind, none of that craving after romantic incidents, and flights of strained and improbable virtue, which I think always betrays an imperfect moral sensibility.

She show'd she had to leave you ; and then taking
Me by the hand, this hand which I must ever
Love better than I have done, since she touch'd it,
" Go," said she, " to my lord (and to go to him
" Is such a happiness I must not hope for),
" And tell him that he too much priz'd a trifle
" Made only worthy in his love, and her
" Thankful acceptance, for her sake to rob
" The orphan kingdom of such guardians, as
" Must of necessity descend from him ;
" And therefore in some part of recompence
" Of his much love, and to show to the world
" That 'twas not her fault only, but her fate,
" That did deny to let her be the mother
" Of such most certain blessings : yet for proof,
" She did not envy her, that happy her,
" That is appointed to them ; her quick end
" Should make way for her :" which no sooner spoke,
But in a moment this too ready engine
Made such a battery in the choicest castle
That ever Nature made to defend life,
That straight it shook and sunk.

WIT WITHOUT MONEY : A COMEDY. BY JOHN FLETCHER.

The humor of a Gallant who will not be persuaded to keep his Lands, but chooses to live by his Wits rather.

VALENTINE'S *Uncle.* MERCHANT, *who has his Mortgage.*

Mer. When saw you Valentine ?
Unc. Not since the horse race.
He's taken up with those that woo the widow.
Mer. How can he live by snatches from such people ?
He bore a worthy mind.
Unc. Alas, he's sunk,
His means are gone, he wants ; and, which is worse,
Takes a delight in doing so.

Mer. That's strange.
Unc. Runs lunatic if you but talk of states;
He can't be brought (now he has spent his own)
To think there is inheritance, or means,
But all a common riches; all men bound
To be his bailiffs.
Mer. This is something dangerous.
Unc. No gentleman, that has estate, to use it
In keeping house or followers: for those ways
He cries against for eating sins, dull surfeits,
Cramming of serving-men, mustering of beggars,
Maintaining hospitals for kites and curs,
Grounding their fat faiths upon old country proverbs,
"God bless the founders:" these he would have ventur'd
Into more manly uses, wit and carriage;
And never thinks of state or means, the ground-works:
Holding it monstrous, men should feed their bodies,
And starve their understandings.

VALENTINE *joins them.*

Val. Now to your business, uncle.
Unc. To your state then.
Val. 'Tis gone, and I am glad on 't, name 't no more,
'Tis that I pray against, and heaven has heard me;
I tell you, sir, I am more fearful of it
(I mean, of thinking of more lands or livings),
Than sickly men are o' travelling o' Sundays,
For being quell'd with carriers; out upon 't;
Caveat emptor; let the fool out-sweat it,
That thinks he has got a catch on 't.
Unc. This is madness,
To be a wilful beggar.
Val. I am mad then,
And so I mean to be; will that content you?
How bravely now I live! how jocund!
How near the first inheritance! without fears!
How free from title troubles!
Unc. And from means too!

Val. Means——
Why, all good men's my means; my wit 's my plough;
The town 's my stock, tavern 's my standing-house
(And all the world know, there 's no want): all gentlemen
That love society, love me; all purses
That wit and pleasure opens, are my tenants;
Every man's clothes fit me; the next fair lodging
Is but my next remove; and when I please
To be more eminent, and take the air,
A piece is levied, and a coach prepar'd,
And I go I care not whither; what need state here?
Unc. But say these means were honest, will they last, sir?
Val. Far longer than your jerkin, and wear fairer.
Your mind 's enclos'd, nothing lies open nobly;
Your very thoughts are hinds, that work on nothing
But daily sweat and trouble: were my way
So full of dirt as this ('tis true) I 'd shift it.
Are my acquaintance Graziers? But, sir, know;
No man that I 'm allied to in my living,
But makes it equal whether his own use
Or my necessity pull first; nor is this forc'd,
But the meer quality and poisure of goodness.
And do you think I venture nothing equal?
Unc. You pose me, cousin.
Val. What 's my knowledge, uncle?
Is 't not worth money? what's my understanding?
Travel? reading? wit? all these digested? my daily
Making men, some to speak, that too much phlegm
Had froz'n up; some, that spoke too much, to hold
Their peace, and put their tongues to pensions; some
To wear their cloaths, and some to keep 'em: these
Are nothing, uncle? besides these ways, to teach
The way of nature, a manly love, community
To all that are deservers, not examining
How much or what 's done for them; it is wicked.
Are not these ways as honest, as persecuting
The starv'd inheritance with musty corn,
The very rats were fain to run away from?

Or selling rotten wood by the pound, like spices,
Which gentlemen do after burn by the ounces?
Do not I know your way of feeding beasts
With grains, and windy stuff, to blow up butchers?
Your racking pastures, that have eaten up
As many singing shepherds, and their issues,
As Andaluzia breeds? These are authentic.
I tell you, sir, I would not change way with you;
Unless it were to sell your state that hour,
And (if 'twere possible) to spend it then too;
For all your beans in Rumnillo: now you know me.

[The wit of Fletcher is excellent, like his serious scenes: but there is something strained and far-fetched in both. He is too mistrustfnl of Nature; he always goes a little on one side of her. Shakspeare chose her without a reserve: and had riches, power, understanding, and long life, with her, for a dowry.]

THE TWO NOBLE KINSMEN. A TRAGEDY. BY JOHN FLETCHER.*

Three Queens, whose Lords were slain and their bodies denied burial by Creon, the cruel King of Thebes, seek redress from Theseus, Duke of Athens, on the day of his marriage with Hippolita, Queen of the Amazons. The first Queen falls down at the feet of Theseus; the second at the feet of Hippolita, his bride; and the third implores the mediation of Emilia, his Sister.

1*st Qu. to Thes.* For pity's sake, and true gentility,
Hear and respect me.
2*d Qu. to Hip.* For your mother's sake,
And as you wish your womb may thrive with fair ones,
Hear and respect me.
3*rd Qu. to Emil.* Now for the love of him whom Jove hath mark'd
The honor of your bed, and for the sake
Of clear virginity, be advocate

* Fletcher is said to have been assisted in this Play by Shakspeare

For us and our distresses : this good deed
Shall raze you out of the book of trespasses
All you are set down there.

Thes. Sad lady, rise.

Hip. Stand up.

Emil. No knees to me.
What woman I may stead, that is distrest,
Does bind me to her.

Thes. What's your request ? Deliver you for al..

1*st Qu.* We are three queens, whose sovereigns fell before
The wrath of cruel Creon ; who endure
The beaks of ravens, talons of the kites,
And peck of crows, in the foul field of Thebes.
He will not suffer us to burn their bones,
To urn their ashes, nor to take th' offence
Of mortal loathsomeness from the blest eye
Of holy Phœbus, but infects the winds
With stench of our slain lords. Oh pity, duke,
Thou purger of the earth, draw thy fear'd sword
That does good turns to th' world ; give us the bones
Of our dead kings, that we may chapel them ;
And, of thy boundless goodness, take some note
That for our crowned heads we have no roof,
Save this which is the lion's and the bear's,
And vault to everything.

Thes. Pray you kneel not,
I was transported with your speech, and suffer'd
Your knees to wrong themselves : I have heard the fortunes
Of your dead lords, which gives me such lamenting,
As wakes my vengeance and revenge for them.
King Capaneus was your lord : the day
That he should marry you, at such a season
As now it is with me, I met your groom ;
By Mars's altar, you were that time fair,
Not Juno's mantle fairer than your tresses,
Nor in more bounty spread her. Your wheaten wreath
Was not then thrash'd nor blasted : Fortune at you
Dimpled her cheek with smiles : Hercules, our kinsman,

(Then weaker than your eyes) laid by his club;
He tumbled down upon his Nemean hide,
And swore his sinews thaw'd. Oh, grief, and time,
Fearful consumers, you will all devour.

1st Qu. Oh I hope some god,
Some god hath put his mercy in your manhood,
Whereto he 'll infuse power, and press you forth
Our undertaker.

Thes. Oh, no knees, none, widow;
Unto the helmeted Bellona use them,
And pray for me your soldier.
Troubled I am.

2d Qu. Honor'd Hippolita,
Most dreaded Amazonian, that hast slain
The scythe-tusk'd boar; that with thy arm, as strong
As it is white, wast near to make the male
To thy sex captive, but that this thy lord,
Born to uphold creation in that honor
First Nature styled it in, shrunk thee into
The bound thou wast o'erflowing, at once subduing
Thy force and thy affection: Soldieress,
That equally canst poise sternness with pity,
Who now I know hast much more power on him
Than ever he had on thee, who ow'st his strength
And his love too; who is a servant for
The tenor of the speech: Dear glass of ladies,
Bid him that we, whom flaming war doth scorch,
Under the shadow of his sword may cool us:
Require him he advance it o'er our heads;
Speak 't in a woman's key, like such a woman
As any of us three: weep ere you fail; lend us a knee,
But touch the ground for us no longer time
Than a dove's motion when the head 's pluckt off:
Tell him if he i' th' blood-siz'd field lay swoln,
Showing the sun his teeth, grinning at the moon,
What you would do.

Hip. Poor lady, say no more;
I had as lieve trace this good action with you,

As that whereto I 'm going, and never yet
Went I so willing 'way. My lord is taken
Heart-deep with your distress; let him consider;
I 'll speak anon.
3rd Qu. to Emil. O my petition was
Set down in ice, which by hot grief uncandied
Melts into drops, so sorrow wanting form
Is prest with deeper matter.
Emil. Pray stand up,
Your grief is written in your cheek.
3rd Qu. Oh wo,
You cannot read it there; there through my tears,
Like wrinkled pebbles in a glassy stream,
You may behold them. Lady, lady, alack!
He that will all the treasures know o' th' earth.
Must know the centre too; he that will fish
For my least minnow, let him lead his line
To catch one at my heart. O pardon me;
Extremity that sharpens sundry wits
Makes me a fool.
Emil. Pray you say nothing, pray you;
Who cannot feel, nor see the rain, being in 't,
Knows neither wet, nor dry: if that you were
The ground-piece of some painter, I would buy you
T' instruct me 'gainst a capital grief indeed,
Such heart-pierc'd demonstration; but alas
Being a natural sister of our sex,
Your sorrow beats so ardently upon me,
That it shall make a counter-reflect 'gainst
My brother's heart, and warm it to some pity,
Though it were made of stone: pray have good comfort.
Thes. Forward to th' temple, leave not out a jot
O' th' sacred ceremony.
1st. Qu. Oh this celebration
Will longer last, and be more costly than
Your suppliants' war. Remember that your fame
Knolls in the ear o' th' world: what you do quickly,
Is not done rashly; your first thought is more

Than others' labor'd meditance ; your premeditating
More than their actions ; but oh Jove, your actions,
Soon as they move, as Asprays do the fish,
Subdue before they touch. Think, dear duke, think,
What beds our slain kings have.
2nd. Qu. What griefs our beds,
That our dear lords have none.
3rd. Qu. None fit for the dead ;
Those that with cords, knives, drams, precipitance,
Weary of this world's light, have to themselves
Been death's most horrid agents, human grace
Affords them dust and shadow.
1st. Qu. But our lords
Lie blistering 'fore the visitating sun,
And were good kings when living.
Thes. It is true, and I will give you comfort,
To give your dead lords graves :
The which to do must make some work with Creon.
1st. Qu. And that work presents itself to th' doing :
Now 'twill take form, the heats are gone to-morrow,
Then bootless toil must recompence itself
With its own sweat ; now he 's secure,
Not dreams we stand before your puissance,
Rincing our holy begging in our eyes
To make petition clear.
2nd. Qu. Now you may take him
Drunk with his victory.
3rd. Qu. And his army full.
Of bread and sloth.
Thes. Artesis, that best knowest
How to draw out, fit to this enterprize,
The prim'st for this proceeding, and the number
To carry such a business forth ; and levy
Our worthiest instruments, whilst we dispatch
This grand act of our life, this daring deed
Of fate in wedlock.
1st. Qu. Dowagers, take hands ;
Let us be widows to our woes, delay

Commends us to a famishing hope.
All. Farewell.
2nd. Qu. We come unseasonably. But when could grief
Cull forth, as unpang'd judgment can, fit'st time
For best solicitation?
Thes. Why good ladies,
This is a service, whereto I am going,
Greater than any was; it more imports me
Than all the actions that I have foregone,
Or futurely can cope.
1st. Qu. The more proclaiming
Our suit shall be neglected, when her arms,
Able to lock Jove from a synod, shall
By warranting moon-light corslet thee. Oh when
Her twining cherries shall their sweetness fall
Upon thy tasteful lips, what wilt thou think
Of rotten kings, or blubber'd queens? what care
For what thou feel'st not? what thou feel'st being able
To make Mars spurn his drum. Oh if thou couch
But one night with her, every hour in 't will
Take hostage of thee for a hundred, and
Thou shalt remember nothing more, than what
That banquet bids thee to.
Hip. Though much unliking
You should be so transported, as much sorry
I should be such a suitor, yet I think
Did I not by th' abstaining of my joy
Which breeds a deeper longing, cure their surfeı
That craves a present med'cine, I should pluck
All ladies' scandal on me. Therefore, sir,
As I shall here make trial of my prayers,
Either presuming them to have some force,
Or sentencing for aye their vigor dumb,
Prorogue this business we are going about, and hang
Your shield afore your heart, about that neck
Which is my fee, and which I freely lend
To do those poor queens service.
All Qu's. to Emil. Oh help now,

Our cause cries for your knee.
Emil. If you grant not
My sister her petition in that force,
With that celerity and nature which
She makes it in, from henceforth I 'll not dare
To ask you anything, nor be so hardy
Ever to take a husband.
Thes. Pray stand up.
I am entreating of myself to do
That which you kneel to have me; Perithous,
Lead on the bride; get you and pray the gods
For success and return; omit not anything
In the pretended celebration; queens,
Follow your soldier (as before); hence you,
And at the banks of Anly meet us with
The forces you can raise, where we shall find
The moiety of a number, for a business
More bigger look 't. Since that our theme is haste,
I stamp this kiss upon thy currant lip;
Sweet, keep it as my token. Set you forward,
For I will see you gone.

Hippolita and Emilia discoursing of the friendship between Perithous and Theseus, Emilia relates a parallel instance of the love between herself and Flavia being girls.

Emil. I was acquainted
Once with a time, when I enjoy'd a play-fellow;
You were at wars, when she the grave enrich'd,
Who made too proud the bed, took leave o' th' moon
(Which then look'd pale at parting) when our count
Was each eleven.
Hip. 'Twas Flavia.
Emil. Yes.
You talk of Perithous and Theseus' love;
Theirs has more ground, is more maturely season'd,
More buckled with strong judgment, and their needs
The one of th' other may be said to water
Their intertangled roots of love; but I

And she (I sigh and spoke of) were things innocent,
Loved for we did, and like the elements,
That know not what, nor why, yet do effect
Rare issues by their operance, our souls
Did so to one another; what she liked,
Was then of me approved; what not condemned,
No more arraignment; the flower that I would pluck,
And put between my breasts (Oh then but beginning
To swell about the bosom) she would long
Till she had such another, and commit it
To the like innocent cradle, where phœnix-like
They died in perfume: on my head no toy
But was her pattern; her affections pretty,
Though happily hers careless were, I followed
For my most serious decking; had mine ear
Stolen some new air, or at adventure humm'd on
From musical coinage, why it was a note
Whereon her spirits would sojourn (rather dwell on)
And sing it in her slumbers; this rehearsal
(Which every innocent wots well) comes in
Like old Importment's bastard, has this end:
That the true love 'tween maid and maid may be
More than in sex dividual. ——

Palamon and Arcite repining at their hard condition, in being made captives for life in Athens, derive consolation from the enjoyment of each other's company in prison.

Pal. How do you, noble cousin?
Arc. How do you, sir?
Pal. Why strong enough to laugh at misery,
And bear the chance of war yet; we are prisoners
I fear for ever, cousin.
Arc. I believe it,
And to that destiny have patiently
Laid up my hour to come.
Pal. Oh cousin Arcite,
Where is Thebes now? where is our noble country?
Where are our friends and kindreds? never more
Must we behold those comforts, never see

The hardy youths strive for the games of honor,
Hung with the painted favors of their ladies
Like tall ships under sail; then start amongst them,
And as an east wind leave them all behind us
Like lazy clouds, whilst Palamon and Arcite,
Even in the wagging of a wanton leg,
Out-stript the people's praises, won the garlands
Ere they have time to wish them ours. Oh never
Shall we two exercise, like twins of honor,
Our arms again, and feel our fiery horses
Like proud seas under us, our good swords now
(Better the red-eyed god of war ne'er wore)
Ravish'd our sides, like age, must run to rust,
And deck the temples of those gods that hate us;
These hands shall never draw them out like lightning
To blast whole armies more.

Arc. No, Palamon,
Those hopes are prisoners with us; here we are,
And here the graces of our youths must wither
Like a too timely spring; here age must find us,
And (which is heaviest) Palamon, unmarried;
The sweet embraces of a loving wife
Loaden with kisses, arm'd with thousand cupids,
Shall never clasp our necks, no issue know us,
No figures of ourselves shall we e'er see,
To glad our age, and like young eagles teach them
Boldly to gaze against bright arms, and say,
"Remember what your fathers were, and conquer."
The fair-eyed maids shall weep our banishments,
And in their songs curse ever-blinded Fortune,
Till she for shame see what a wrong she has done
To youth and nature. This is all our world:
We shall know nothing here, but one another;
Hear nothing, but the clock that tells our woes.
The vine shall grow, but we shall never see it:
Summer shall come, and with her all delights,
But dead-cold winter must inhabit here still.

Pal. 'Tis too true, Arcite. To our Theban hounds,

That shook the aged forest with their echoes,
No more now must we halloo, no more shake
Our pointed javelins, whilst the angry swine
Flies like a Parthian quiver from our rages,
Struck with our well-steel'd darts. All valiant uses
(The food and nourishment of noble minds)
In us two here shall perish: we shall die
(Which is the curse of honor) lastly
Children of grief and ignorance.
Arc. Yet cousin,
Even from the bottom of these miseries,
From all that fortune can inflict upon us,
I see two comforts rising, two mere blessings,
If the gods please to hold here; a brave patience,
And the enjoying of our griefs together.
Whilst Palamon is with me, let me perish
If I think this our prison.
Pal. Certainly
'Tis a main goodness, cousin, that our fortunes
Were twin'd together; 'tis most true, two souls
Put in two noble bodies, let them suffer
The gall of hazard, so they grow together,
Will never sink; they must not; say they could,
A willing man dies sleeping, and all 's done.
Arc. Shall we make worthy uses of this place
That all men hate so much?
Pal. How, gentle cousin?
Arc. Let 's think this prison holy sanctuary,
To keep us from corruption of worse men;
We are young, and yet desire the ways of honor,
That liberty and common conversation,
The poison of pure spirits, might (like women)
Woo us to wander from. What worthy blessing
Can be, but our imaginations
May make it ours? And here being thus together,
We are an endless mine to one another;
We are one another's wife, ever begetting
New births of love; we are father, friends, acquaintance;

We are, in one another, families;
I am your heir, and you are mine. This place
Is our inheritance; no hard oppressor
Dare take this from us; here with a little patience
We shall live long, and loving; no surfeits seek us;
The hand of war hurts none here, nor the seas
Swallow their youth. Were we at liberty,
A wife might part us lawfully, or business;
Quarrels consume us; envy of ill men
Crave our acquaintance; I might sicken, cousin,
Where you should never know it, and so perish
Without your noble hand to close mine eyes,
Or prayers to the gods: a thousand chances,
Were we from hence, would sever us.

Pal. You have made me
(I thank you, Cousin Arcite) almost wanton
With my captivity: what a misery
It is to live abroad, and everywhere!
'Tis like a beast methinks! I find the court here,
I 'm sure a more content; and all those pleasures,
That woo the wills of men to vanity,
I see through now; and am sufficient
To tell the world, 'tis but a gaudy shadow,
That old Time, as he passes by, takes with him.
What, had we been old in the Court of Creon,
Where sin is justice, lust and ignorance
The virtues of the great ones? Cousin Arcite,
Had not the loving gods found this place for us,
We had died, as they do, ill old men, unwept,
And had their epitaphs, the people's curses.

[This scene bears indubitable marks of Fletcher: the two which precede it give strong countenance to the tradition that Shakspeare had a hand in this play. The same judgment may be formed of the death of Arcite, and some other passages, not here given. They have a luxuriance in them which strongly resembles Shakspeare's manner in those parts of his plays where, the progress of the interest being subordinate, the poet was at leisure for description. I might fetch instances from Troilus and Timon. That Fletcher should have copied Shakspeare's manner through so many entire scenes (which is the theory of Mr. Steevens) is not very probable, that he could have done it with such facility is to me not certain. His ideas move slow; his versification, though sweet, is tedious, it stops every moment; he lays line upon line, making up one after the other, adding image to image so deliberately that we see where they join: Shakspeare mingles everything, he runs line into line, embarrasses sentences and metaphors: before one idea has burst its shell, another is hatched and clamorous for disclosure. If Fletcher wrote some scenes in imitation, why did he stop? or shall we say that Shakspeare wrote the other scenes in imitation of Fletcher? that he gave Shakspeare a curb and a bridle, and that Shakspeare gave him a pair of spurs: as Blackmore and Lucan are brought in exchanging gifts in the Battle of the Books?]

THE CITY MADAM: A COMEDY. BY PHILIP MASSINGER.

Luke, from a state of indigence and dependence, is suddenly raised into immense affluence by a deed of gift of the estates of his brother, Sir John Frugal, a merchant, retired from the world. He enters, from taking a survey of his new riches.

Luke. 'Twas no fantastic object but a truth,
A real truth, no dream. I did not slumber;
And could wake ever with a brooding eye
To gaze upon 't! it did endure the touch,
I saw, and felt it. Yet what I beheld
And handled oft, did so transcend belief
(My wonder and astonishment pass'd o'er)
I faintly could give credit to my senses.
Thou dumb magician, [*To the Key.*
That without a charm
Didst make my entrance easy to possess
What wise men wish and toil for. Hermes' Moly;
Sybilla's golden bough; the great elixir
Imagin'd only by the alchymist;
Compar'd with thee, are shadows, thou the substance
And guardian of felicity. No marvel,
My brother made thy place of rest his bosom,
Thou being the keeper of his heart, a mistress
To be hugg'd ever. In by-corners of
This sacred room, silver, in bags heap'd up

Like billets saw'd and ready for the fire,
Unworthy to hold fellowship with bright gold,
That flow'd about the room, conceal'd itself.
There needs no artificial light, the splendor
Makes a perpetual day there, night and darkness
By that still-burning lamp for ever banish'd.
But when, guided by that, my eyes had made
Discovery of the caskets, and they open'd,
Each sparkling diamond from itself shot forth
A pyramid of flames, and in the roof
Fix'd it a glorious star, and made the place
Heaven's abstract, or epitome ; Rubies, sapphires,
And robes of orient pearl, these seen, I could not
But look on gold with contempt. And yet I found,
What weak credulity could have no faith in,
A treasure far exceeding these. Here lay
A manor bound fast in a skin of parchment ;
The wax continuing hard, the acres melting.
Here a sure deed of gift for a market town,
If not redeem'd this day ; which is not in
The unthrift's power. There being scarce one shire
In Wales or England, where my monies are not
Lent out at usury, the certain hook
To draw in more.

The extravagance of the City Madams aping court fashions reprehended.

Luke, having come into the possession of his brother Sir John Frugal's estates. Lady, wife to Sir John Frugal, and two daughters, in homely attire.

Luke, Save you, sister ;
I now dare style you so. You were before
Too glorious to be look'd on : now you appear
Like a city matron, and my pretty nieces
Such things
As they were born and bred there. Why should you ape
The fashions of court ladies, whose high titles
And pedigrees of long descent give warrant

For their superfluous bravery? 'twas monstrous.
Till now you ne'er look'd lovely.
Lady. Is this spoken
In scorn?
Luke. Fie, no; with judgment, I make good
My promise, and now show you like yourselves,
In your own natural shapes.
Lady. We acknowledge
We have deserv'd ill from you,* yet despair not,
Though we 're at your disposure, you 'll maintain us
Like your brother's wife and daughters.
Luke. 'Tis my purpose.
Lady. And not make us ridiculous.
Luke. Admir'd rather
As fair examples for our proud city dames
And their proud brood to imitate. Hear
Gently, and in gentle phrase I 'll reprehend
Your late disguis'd deformity.
Your father was
An honest country farmer, Goodman Humble,
By his neighbors ne'er call'd master. Did your pride
Descend from him? but let that pass. Your fortune,
Or rather your husband's industry, advanc'd you
To the rank of merchant's wife. He made a knight,
And your sweet mistress-ship ladyfy'd, you wore
Satin on solemn days, a chain of gold,
A velvet hood, rich borders, and sometimes
A dainty miniver cap, a silver pin
Headed with a pearl worth three-pence; and thus far
You were privileg'd, and no man envied it:
It being for the city's honor that
There should be distinction between
The wife of a patrician and a plebeian.——
But when the height
And dignity of London's blessings grew

* In his dependent state they had treated him very cruelly. They are now dependent on him

Contemptible, and the name lady mayoress
Became a by-word, and you scorn'd the means
By which you were rais'd (my brother's fond indulgence
Giving the reins to 't) and no object pleas'd you
But the glitt'ring pomp and bravery of the court;
What a strange, nay monstrous metamorphosis follow'd!
No English workmen then could please your fancy;
The French and Tuscan dress, your whole discourse;
This bawd to prodigality entertain'd,
To buz into your ears, what shape this countess
Appear'd in, the last mask; and how it drew
The young lord's eyes upon her: and this usher
Succeeded in the eldest 'prentice's place,
To walk before you. Then, as I said
(The reverend hood cast off), your borrow'd hair,
Powder'd and curl'd, was by your dresser's art
Form'd like a coronet, hang'd with diamonds,
And the richest orient pearl: your carkanets,
That did adorn your neck, of equal value;
Your Hungerland bands, and Spanish Quellio ruffs:
Great lords and ladies feasted, to survey
Embroider'd petticoats; and sickness feign'd,
That your nightrails of forty pounds a-piece
Might be seen with envy of the visitants:
Rich pantables in ostentation shown,
And roses worth a family. You were serv'd
In plate;
Stirr'd not a foot without a coach; and going
To church, not for devotion, but to show
Your pomp, you were tickled when the beggars cried
Heaven save your honor. This idolatry
Paid to a painted room. And, when you lay
In childbed, at the christening of this minx,
I well remember it, as you had been
An absolute princess (since they have no more)
Three several chambers hung: the first with arras,
And that for waiters; the second, crimson satin,
For the meaner sort of guests; the third of scarlet

Of the rich Tyrian dye: a canopy
To cover the brat's cradle; you in state,
Like Pompey's Julia.
Lady. No more, I pray you.
Luke. Of this be sure you shall not. I 'll cut off
Whatever is exorbitant in you,
Or in your daughters; and reduce you to
Your natural forms and habits: not in revenge
Of your base usage of me; but to fright
Others by your example.

[This bitter satire against the city women for aping the fashions of the court ladies, must have been peculiarly gratifying to the females of the Herbert family and the rest of Massinger's noble patrons and patronesses.

A NEW WAY TO PAY OLD DEBTS: A COMEDY. BY PHILIP MASSINGER.

Overreach (a cruel extortioner) treats about marrying his daughter with Lord Lovell.

LOVELL. OVERREACH.

Over. To my wish we are private.
I come not to make offer with my daughter
A certain portion; that were poor and trivial:
In one word I pronounce all that is mine,
In lands or leases, ready coin or goods,
With her, my lord, comes to you; nor shall you have
One motive to induce you to believe
I live too long, since every year I'll add
Something unto the heap, which shall be yours too.
Lov. You are a right kind father.
Over. You shall have reason
To think me such. How do you like this seat?
It is well-wooded and well-water'd, the acres
Fertile and rich: would it not serve for change,
To entertain your friends in a summer's progress?
What thinks my noble lord?

Lov. 'Tis a wholesome air,
And well built, and she,* that is mistress of it,
Worthy the large revenues.
Over. She the mistress?
It may be so for a time: but let my lord
Say only that he but like it, and would have it;
I say, ere long 'tis his.
Lov. Impossible.
Over. You do conclude too fast; not knowing me,
Nor the engines that I work by. 'Tis not alone
The lady Allworth's lands: but point out any man's
In all the shire, and say they lie convenient
And useful for your lordship; and once more
I say aloud, they are yours.
Lov. I dare not own
What's by unjust and cruel means extorted:
My fame and credit are more dear to me,
Than so to expose 'em to be censur'd by
The public voice.
Over. You run, my lord, no hazard:
Your reputation shall stand as fair
In all good men's opinions as now:
Nor can my actions, though condemn'd for ill,
Cast any foul aspersion upon yours.
For though I do contemn report myself,
As a mere sound; I still will be so tender
Of what concerns you in all points of honor,
That the immaculate whiteness of your fame,
Nor your unquestioned integrity,
Shall e'er be sullied with one taint or spot
That may take from your innocence and candor
As my ambition is to have my daughter
Right honorable; which my lord can make her:
And might I live to dance upon my knee
A young lord Lovell, born by her unto you,
I write *nil ultra* to my proudest hopes.

* The Lady Allworth.

As for possessions and annual rents,
Equivalent to maintain you in the port
Your noble birth and present state require,
I do remove that burden from your shoulders,
And take it on mine own: for though I ruin
The country to supply your riotous waste,
The scourge of prodigals (want) shall never find you.
Lov. Are you not frighted with the imprecations
And curses of whole families, made wretched
By your sinister practices?
Over. Yes, as rocks are
When foamy billows split themselves against
Their flinty ribs; or as the moon is mov'd
When wolves, with hunger pined, howl at her brightness.
I am of a solid temper, and, like these,
Steer on a constant course: with mine own sword,
If call'd into the field, I can make that right,
Which fearful enemies murmur'd at as wrong.
Now, for those other piddling complaints,
Breath'd out in bitterness; as, when they call me
Extortioner, tyrant, cormorant, or intruder
On my poor neighbor's right, or grand encloser
Of what was common to my private use;
Nay, when my ears are pierc'd with widows' cries,
And undone orphans wash with tears my threshold:
I only think what 'tis to have my daughter
Right honorable; and 'tis a powerful charm,
Makes me insensible of remorse or pity,
Or the least sting of conscience.
Lov. I admire
The toughness of your nature.
Over. 'Tis for you,
My lord and for my daughter, I am marble.

THE PICTURE: A TRAGI-COMEDY. BY PHILIP MASSINGER.

Matthias, a knight of Bohemia, going to the wars; in parting with his wife, shows her substantial reasons why he should go.

MATTHIAS. SOPHIA.

Mat. Since we must part, Sophia, to pass further
Is not alone impertinent, but dangerous.
We are not distant from the Turkish camp
Above five leagues; and who knows but some party
Of his Timariots, that scour the country,
May fall upon us? Be now, as thy name
Truly interpreted* hath ever spoke thee,
Wise and discreet; and to thy understanding
Marry thy constant patience.
Soph. You put me, sir,
To the utmost trial of it.
Mat. Nay, no melting:
Since the necessity, that now separates us,
We have long since disputed; and the reasons,
Forcing me to it, too oft wash'd in tears.
I grant that you in birth were far above me,
And great men my superiors rivals for you;
But mutual consent of heart, as hands
Join'd by true love, hath made us one and equal:
Nor is it in me mere desire of fame,
Or to be cried up by the public voice
For a brave soldier, that puts on my armor;
Such airy tumors take not me: you know
How narrow our demeans are; and what's more,
Having as yet no charge of children on us,
We hardly can subsist.
Soph. In you alone, sir,
I have all abundance.
Mat. For my mind's content,
In your own language I could answer you.

* Sophia; wisdom.

You have been an obedient wife, a right one;
And to my power, though short of your desert,
I have been ever an indulgent husband.
We have long enjoy'd the sweets of love, and though
Not to satiety or loathing, yet
We must not live such dotards on our pleasures,
As still to hug them to the certain loss
Of profit and preferment. Competent means
Maintains a quiet bed, want breeds dissension
Even in good women.
Soph. Have you found in me, sir,
Any distaste or sign of discontent,
For want of what's superfluous?
Mat. No, Sophia;
Nor shalt thou ever have cause to repent
Thy constant course in goodness, if heaven bless
My honest undertakings. 'Tis for thee,
That I turn soldier, and put forth, dearest,
Upon this sea of action as a factor,
To trade for rich materials to adorn
Thy noble parts, and show 'em in full lustre.
I blush that other ladies, less in beauty
And outward form, but, in the harmony
Of the soul's ravishing music, the same age
Not to be named with thee, should so outshine thee
In jewels and variety of wardrobes;
While you, to whose sweet innocence both Indies
Compar'd are of no value, wanting these,
Pass unregarded.
Soph. If I am so rich,
Or in your opinion so, why should you borrow
Additions for me?
Mat. Why? I should be censur'd
Of ignorance, possessing such a jewel,
Above all prices, if I forbear to give it
The best of ornaments. Therefore, Sophia,
In a few words know my pleasure, and obey me;
As you have ever done. To your discretion

I leave the government of my family,
And our poor fortunes, and from these command
Obedience to you as to myself:
To th' utmost of what's mine, live plentifully:
And, ere the remnant of our store be spent,
With my good sword I hope I shall reap for you
A harvest in such full abundance, as
Shall make a merry winter.
Soph. Since you are not
To be diverted, sir, from what you purpose,
All arguments to stay you here are useless.
Go when you please, sir. Eyes, I charge you, waste not
One drop of sorrow; look you hoard all up,
Till in my widow'd bed I call upon you:
But then be sure you fail not. You blest angels,
Guardians of human life, I at this instant
Forbear t' invoke you at our parting; 'twere
To personate devotion. My soul
Shall go along with you; and when you are
Circled with death and horror, seek and find you;
And then I will not leave a saint unsued to
For your protection. To tell you what
I will do in your absence, would show poorly;
My actions shall speak me. 'Twere to doubt you,
To beg I may hear from you where you are;
You cannot live obscure: nor shall one post,
By night or day, pass unexamin'd by me.
If I dwell long upon your lips, consider
After this feast the griping fast that follows;
And it will be excusable; pray, turn from me:
All that I can is spoken.

[The good sense, rational fondness, and chastised feeling, of this dialogue, make it more valuable than many of those scenes in which this writer has attempted a deeper passion and more tragical interest. Massinger had not the higher requisites of his art in anything like the degree in which they were possessed by Ford, Webster, Tourneur, Heywood, and others. He never shakes or disturbs the mind with grief. He is read with composure and placid delight. He wrote with that equability of all the passions, which made his English style the purest and most free from violent metaphors and harsh constructions, of any of the dramatists who were his contemporaries.]

THE PARLIAMENT OF LOVE: A COMEDY. BY PHILIP MASSINGER.

Cleremond takes an oath to perform his mistress Leonora's pleasure. She enjoins him to kill his best friend. He invites Montrose to the field, under pretence of wanting him for a second: then shows, that he must fight with him.

Cler. This is the place.
Mont. An even piece of ground,
Without advantage; but be jocund, friend:
The honor to have enter'd first the field,
However we come off, is ours.
Cler. I need not,
So well I am acquainted with your valor,
To dare, in a good cause, as much as man,
Lend you encouragement; and should I add,
Your power to do, which Fortune, howe'er blind,
Hath ever seconded, I cannot doubt
But victory still sits upon your sword,
And must not now forsake you.
Mont. You shall see me
Come boldly up; nor will I shame your cause,
By parting with an inch of ground not bought
With blood on my part.
Cler. 'Tis not to be question'd:
That which I would entreat (and pray you grant it),
Is, that you would forget your usual softness,
Your foe being at your mercy; it hath been
A custom in you, which I dare not praise,
Having disarm'd your enemy of his sword,
To tempt your fate, by yielding it again;
Then run a second hazard.
Mont. When we encounter

A noble foe, we cannot be too noble.
Cler. That I confess; but he that 's now to oppose you,
I know for an arch villain; one that hath lost
All feeling of humanity, one that hates
Goodness in others, 'cause he 's ill himself;
A most ungrateful wretch (the name 's too gentle,
All attributes of wickedness cannot reach him),
Of whom to have deserved, beyond example,
Or precedent of friendship, is a wrong
Which only death can satisfy.
Mont. You describe
A monster to me.
Cler. True, Montrose, he is so.
Africk, though fertile of strange prodigies,
Never produced his equal; be wise, therefore,
And if he fall into your hands, dispatch him:
Pity to him is cruelty. The sad father,
That sees his son stung by a snake to death,
May, with more justice, stay his vengeful hand
And let the worm escape, than you vouchsafe him
A minute to repent: for 'tis a slave
So sold to hell and mischief, that a traitor
To his most lawful prince, a church-robber,
A parricide, who, when his garners are
Cramm'd with the purest grain, suffers his parents,
Being old, and weak, to starve for want of bread,
Compared to him are innocent.
Mont. I ne'er heard
Of such a cursed nature; if long-lived,
He would infect mankind: rest you assured,
He finds from me small courtesy.
Cler. And expect
As little from him; blood is that he thirsts for,
Not honorable wounds.
Mont. I would I had him
Within my sword's length!
Cler. Have thy wish: Thou hast!
[*Cleremond draws his sword.*

Nay draw thy sword and suddenly ; I am
That monster, temple-robber, parricide,
Ingrateful wretch, friend-hater, or what else
Makes up the perfect figure of the devil,
Should he appear like man. Banish amazement,
And call thy ablest spirits up to guard thee
From him that 's turn'd a fury. I am made
Her minister, whose cruelty but named
Would with more horror strike the pale-cheek'd stars,
Than all those dreadful words which conjurors use
To fright their damn'd familiars. Look not on me
As I am Cleremond ; I have parted with
The essence that was his, and entertain'd
The soul of some fierce tigress, or a wolf's
New-hang'd for human slaughter, and 'tis fit:
I could not else be an apt instrument
To bloody Leonora.
Mont. To my knowledge
I never wrong'd her.
Cler. Yes, in being a friend
To me, she hated my best friend, her malice
Would look no lower :—and for being such,
By her commands, Montrose, I am to kill thee
Oh, that thou hadst, like others, been all words,
And no performance ! or that thou hadst made
Some little stop in thy career of kindness !
Why wouldst thou, to confirm the name of friend,
Snatch at this fatal office of a second,
Which others fled from ?——'Tis in vain to mourn now,
When there 's no help ! and therefore, good Montrose,
Rouse thy most manly parts, and think thou stand'st now,
A champion for more than king or country ;
Since in thy fall, goodness itself must suffer.
Remember too, the baseness of the wrong
Offer'd to friendship ; let it edge thy sword,
And kill compassion in thee ; and forget not
I will take all advantages : and so,
Without reply, have at thee. [*They fight, Cleremond falls.*

Mont. See, how weak
An ill cause is! you are already fallen:
What can you look for now?
Cler. Fool, use thy fortune:
And so he counsels thee, that, if we had
Changed places, instantly would have cut thy throat,
Or digg'd thy heart out.
Mont. In requital of
That savage purpose, I must pity you:
Witness these tears, not tears of joy for conquest;
But of true sorrow for your misery.
Live, O live, Cleremond, and, like a man,
Make use of reason, as an exorcist
To cast this devil out, that does abuse you;
This fiend of false affection.

A VERY WOMAN; OR, THE PRINCE OF TARENT: A TRAGI-COMEDY. BY PHILIP MASSINGER.

Don John Antonio, Prince of Tarent, in the disguise of a slave, recounts to the Lady Almira, she not knowing him in that disguise, the story of his own passion for her, and of the unworthy treatment which he found from her.

John. Not far from where my father lives, a lady,
A neighbor by, blest with as great a beauty
As Nature durst bestow without undoing,
Dwelt, and most happily, as I thought then,
And bless'd the house a thousand times she dwelt in.
This beauty, in the blossom of my youth,
When my first fire knew no adulterate incense,
Nor I no way to flatter but my fondness,
In all the bravery my friends could show me,
In all the faith my innocence could give me,
In the best language my true tongue could tell me,
And all the broken sighs my sick heart lent me,
I sued, and serv'd. Long did I love this lady,
Long was my travail, long my trade, to win her:

With all the duty of my soul I serv'd her.
Alm. How feelingly he speaks! And she loved you too?
It must be so.
John. I would it had, dear lady.
This story had been needless; and this place,
I think, unknown to me.
Alm. Were your bloods equal?
John. Yes; and, I thought, our hearts too.
Alm. Then she must love.
John. She did; but never me: she could not love me;
She would not love; she hated; more, she scorn'd me:
And in so poor and base a way abused me,
For all my services, for all my bounties,
So bold neglects flung on me ——
Alm. An ill woman!
Belike you found some rival in your love then?
John. How perfectly she points me to my story! [*Aside.*
Madam, I did; and one whose pride and anger,
Ill manners, and worse mein, she doated on;
Doated, to my undoing and my ruin.
And, but for honor to your sacred beauty,
And reverence to the noble sex, though she fall
(As she must fall, that durst be so unnoble),
I should say something unbeseeming me.
What out of love, and worthy love, I gave her
(Shame to her most unworthy mind), to fools,
To girls, and fiddlers, to her boys she flung,
And in disdain of me.
Last, to blot me
From all rememb'rance, what I have been to her,
And how, how honestly, how nobly serv'd her,
'Twas thought she set her gallant to dispatch me.
'Tis true, he quarrell'd, without place, or reason;
We fought, I kill'd him; heaven's strong hand was with me ·
For which I lost my country, friends, acquaintance,
And put myself to sea, where a pirate took me,
And sold me here.

THE UNNATURAL COMBAT: A TRAGEDY. BY PHILIP MASSINGER.

Malefort senior, Admiral of Marseilles, poisons his first wife to make way for a second. This coming to the knowledge of his son, Malefort junior, he challenges his father to fight him. This unnatural combat is performed before the Governor and the Court of Marseilles. The spectators retiring to some distance, the father and son parley before the fight commences.

MALEFORT *senior*. MALEFORT *junior*.

Mal. sen. Now we are alone, sir;
And thou hast liberty to unload the burden
Which thou groan'st under. Speak thy griefs.
Mal. jun. I shall, sir;
But in a perplext form and method, which
You only can interpret: would you had not
A guilty knowledge in your bosom of
The language which you force me to deliver,
So I were nothing! As you are my father,
I bend my knee, and uncompell'd profess,
My life and all that's mine to be your gift,
And that in a son's duty I stand bound
To lay this head beneath your feet, and run
All desperate hazards for your ease and safety.
But, this confess'd on my part, I rise up;
And not as with a father (all respect,
Love, fear, and reverence, cast off) but as
A wicked man, I thus expostulate with you.
Why have you done that which I dare not speak?
And in the action chang'd the humble shape
Of my obedience to rebellious rage
And insolent pride? and with shut eyes constrain'd me
To run my bark of honor on a shelf,
I must not see, nor, if I saw it, shun it?
In my wrongs nature suffers, and looks backward;
And mankind trembles to see me pursue
What beasts would fly from. For when I advance
This sword, as I must do, against your head,

Piety will weep, and filial duty mourn,
To see their altars, which you built up in me,
In a moment raz'd and ruin'd. That you could
(From my griev'd soul I wish it) but produce
To qualify, not excuse, your deed of horror,
One seeming reason : that I might fix here,
And move no further !

Mal. sen. Have I so far lost
A father's power, that I must give account
Of my actions to my son ? or must I plead
As a fearful prisoner at the bar, while he
That owes his being to me sits as judge
To censure that, which only by myself
Ought to be question'd ? mountains sooner fall
Beneath their valleys, and the lofty pine
Pay homage to the bramble, or what else is
Preposterous in nature, ere my tongue
In one short syllable yields satisfaction
To any doubt of thine; nay, though it were
A certainty, disdaining argument :
Since, though my deeds wore hell's black livery,
To thee they should appear triumphant robes,
Set off with glorious honor : thou being bound
To see with my eyes, and to hold *that* reason
That takes or birth or fashion from my will.

Mal. jun. This sword divides that slavish knot.

Mal. sen. It cannot,
It cannot, wretch; and thou but remember
From whom thou hadst this spirit, thou dar'st not hope it.
Who train'd thee up in arms, but I ? who taught thee
Men were men only when they durst look down
With scorn on death and danger, and contemn'd
All opposition, till plum'd victory
Had made her constant stand upon their helmets ?
Under my shield thou hast fought as securely
As the young eaglet, covered with the wings
Of her fierce dam, learns how and where to prey.
All that is manly in thee, I call mine ;

But what is weak and womanish, thine own.
And what I gave (since thou art proud, ungrateful,
Presuming to contend with him, to whom
Submission is due) I will take from thee.
Look therefore for extremities, and expect not
I will correct thee as a son, but kill thee
As a serpent swoln with poison; who surviving
A little longer, with infectious breath,
Would render all things near him, like itself,
Contagious.

Mal. jun. Thou incensed power,
Awhile forbear thy thunder: let me have
No aid in my revenge, if from the grave
My mother ———

Mal. sen. Thou shalt never name her more ——
(*They fight, and the son is slain.*)

Mal. sen. Die all my fears,
And waking jealousies, which have so long
Been my tormentors; there 's now no suspicion:
A fact, which I alone am conscious of,
Can never be discover'd, or the cause
That call'd this duel on; I being above
All perturbations; nor is it in
The power of fate again to make me wretched.

THE VIRGIN MARTYR: A TRAGEDY. BY PHILIP MASSINGER AND THOMAS DECKER.

Angelo, an angel, attends Dorothea, as a page.

ANGELO. DOROTHEA. *The time, midnight.*

Dor. My book and taper.

Ang. Here, most holy mistress.

Dor. Thy voice sends forth such music, that I never
Was ravished with a more celestial sound.
Were every servant in the world like thee,
So full of goodness, angels would come down

To dwell with us: thy name is *Angelo*,
And like that name thou art. Get thee to rest;
Thy youth with too much watching is opprest.
Ang. No, my dear lady. I could weary stars,
And force the wakeful moon to lose her eyes,
By my late watching, but to wait on you.
When at your prayers you kneel before the altar,
Methinks I 'm singing with some quire in heaven,
So blest I hold me in your company.
Therefore, my most lov'd mistress, do not bid
Your boy, so serviceable, to get hence;
For then you break his heart.
Dor. Be nigh me still, then.
In golden letters down I 'll set that day,
Which gave thee to me. Little did I hope
To meet such worlds of comfort in thyself,
This little, pretty body, when I coming
Forth of the temple, heard my beggar-boy,
My sweet-fac'd, godly beggar-boy, crave an alms,
Which with glad hand I gave, with lucky hand;
And when I took thee home, my most chaste bosom
Methought was fill'd with no hot wanton fire,
But with a holy flame, mounting since higher,
On wings of cherubims, than it did before.
Ang. Proud am I that my lady's modest eye
So likes so poor a servant.
Dor. I have offer'd
Handfuls of gold but to behold thy parents.
I would leave kingdoms, were I queen of some,
To dwell with thy good father; for, the son
Bewitching me so deeply with his presence,
He that begot him must do 't ten times more.
I pray thee, my sweet boy, show me thy parents;
Be not ashamed.
Ang. I am not: I did never
Know who my mother was; but, by yon palace,
Fill'd with bright heav'nly courtiers, I dare assure you,
And pawn these eyes upon it, and this hand,

My father is in heav'n ; and, pretty mistress
If your illustrious hour-glass spend his sand
No worse, than yet it doth, upon my life,
You and I both shall meet my father there,
And he shall bid you welcome.
Dor. A bless'd day !

[This scene has beauties of so very high an order that, with all my respect for Massinger, I do not think he had poetical enthusiasm capable of furnishing them. His associate Decker, who wrote Old Fortunatus, had poetry enough for anything. The very impurities which obtrude themselves among the sweet pieties of this play (like Satan among the Sons of Heaven) and which the brief scope of my plan fortunately enables me to leave out, have a strength of contrast, a raciness, and a glow in them, which are above Massinger. They set off the religion of the rest, somehow as Caliban serves to show Miranda.]

THE FATAL DOWRY; A TRAGEDY. BY PHILIP MASSINGER AND NATHANIEL FIELD.

The Marshal of Burgundy dies in prison at Dijon for debts contracted by him for the service of the state in the wars. His dead body is arrested and denied burial by his creditors. His son, young Charalois, gives up himself to prison to redeem his father's body, that it may have honorable burial. He has leave from his prison doors to view the ceremony of the funeral, but to go no further.

Enter three gentlemen, PONTALIER, MALOTIN, *and* BEAUMONT, *as spectators of the funeral.*

Mal. 'Tis strange.
Beaum. Methinks so.
Pont. In a man but young,
Yet old in judgment; theoric and practic
In all humanity; and, to increase the wonder,
Religious, yet a soldier,—that he should
Yield his free-living youth a captive, for
The freedom of his aged father's corpse ;
And rather choose to want life's necessaries,
Liberty, hope of fortune, than it should
In death be kept from christian ceremony.

Mal. Come, 'tis a golden precedent in a son,
To let strong nature have the better hand,
In such a case, of all affected reason.
What years sit on this Charalois?
Beaum. Twenty-eight.
For since the clock did strike him seventeen old,
Under his father's wing this son hath fought,
Serv'd and commanded, and so aptly both,
That sometimes he appeared his father's father,
And never less than his son; the old man's virtues
So recent in him, as the world may swear
Nought but a fair tree could such fair fruit bear.
Mal. This morning is the funeral?
Pont. Certainly,
And from this prison,—'twas the son's request.
[CHARALOIS *appears at the door of the prison.*
That his dear father might interment have,
See, the young son enter'd a lively grave.
Beaum. They come. Observe their order.

The funeral procession enters. Captain and soldiers, mourners. Romont, friend to the deceased. Three creditors are among the spectators Charalois speaks.

Char. How like a silent stream shaded with night,
And gliding softly with our windy sighs,
Moves the whole frame of this solemnity!
Tears, sighs, and blacks, filling the simile;
Whilst I, the only murmur in this grove
Of death, thus hollowly break forth!—vouchsafe
To stay awhile. Rest, rest in peace, dear earth!
Thou that broughtst rest to their unthankful lives,
Whose cruelty denied thee rest in death!
Here stands thy poor executor, thy son,
That makes his life prisoner to bail thy death;
Who gladlier puts on this captivity,
Than virgins, long in love, their wedding weeds.
Of all that ever thou hast done good to,
These only have good memories; for they

Remember best, forget not gratitude.
I thank you for this last and friendly love,
And though this country, like a viperous mother,
Not only hath eat up ungratefully
All means of thee, her son, but last thyself,
Leaving thy heir so bare and indigent,
He cannot raise thee a poor monument,
Such as a flatterer or an usurer hath;
Thy worth in every honest breast builds one,
Making their friendly hearts thy funeral stone.
Pont. Sir!
Char. Peace! O peace! This scene is wholly mine—
What! weep you, soldiers?—blanch not.—Romont weeps.—
Ha! let me see! my miracle is eas'd;
The jailors and the creditors do weep;
E'en they that make us weep, do weep themselves.
Be these thy body's balm: these, and thy virtue,—
Keep thy fame ever odoriferous,
Whilst the great, proud, rich, undeserving man
Alive stinks in his vices, and, being vanish'd,
The golden calf that was an idol, deck'd
With marble pillars, jet and porphyry,
Shall quickly both in bone and name consume,
Tho' wrapt in lead, spice, cerecloth, and perfume.
Creditor. Sir!
Char. What!—away for shame,—you, profane rogues,
Must not be mingled with these holy relics:
This is a sacrifice—our show'r shall crown
His sepulchre with olive, myrrh, and bays,
The plants of peace, of sorrow, victory:
Your tears would spring but weeds.
Rom. Look, look, you slaves! your thankless cruelty,
And savage manners of unkind Dijon,
Exhaust these floods, and not his father's death.
Priest. On.
Char. One moment more,
But to bestow a few poor legacies,
All I have left in my dead father's right,

And I have done. Captain, wear thou these spurs,
That yet ne'er made his horse run from a foe.
Lieutenant, thou this scarf; and may it tie
Thy valor and thy honesty together,
For so it did in him. Ensign, this cuirass,
Your general's necklace once. You, gentle bearers,
Divide this purse of gold: this other strew
Among the poor. 'Tis all I have. Romont,
Wear thou this medal of himself, that like
A hearty oak grew'st close to this tall pine,
E'en in the wildest wilderness of war,
Whereon foes broke their swords, and tir'd themselves:
Wounded and hack'd ye were, but never fell'd.
For me, my portion provide in heaven:
My root is earth'd, and I, a desolate branch,
Left scatter'd in the highway of the world,
Trod under foot, that might have been a column
Mainly supporting our demolish'd house.
This* would I wear as my inheritance,—
And what hope can arise to me from it,
When I and it are here both prisoners?
Only may this, if ever we be free,
Keep or redeem me from all infamy.
Jailor. You must no farther.—
The prison limits you, and the creditors
Exact the strictness.—

THE OLD LAW: A COMEDY. BY PHILIP MASSINGER, THOMAS MIDDLETON, AND WILLIAM ROWLEY.

The Duke of Epire enacts a law, that all men who have reached the age of fourscore, shall be put to death, as being adjudged useless to the commonwealth. Simonides, the bad, and Cleanthes, the good son, are differently affected by the promulgation of the edict.

Sim. Cleanthes,
Oh, lad, here's a spring for young plants to flourish!

* His father's sword.

The old trees must down, kept the sun from us.
We shall rise now, boy.
Cle. Whither, sir, I pray?
To the bleak air of storms, among those trees
Which we had shelter from.
Sim. Yes, from our growth,
Our sap and livelihood, and from our fruit.
What! 'tis not jubilee with thee yet, I think;
Thou look'st so sad on 't. How old is thy father?
Cle. Jubilee! no, indeed; 'tis a bad year with me.
Sim. Prithee, how old's thy father? then I can tell thee.
Cle. I know not how to answer you, Simonides.
He is too old, being now expos'd
Unto the rigor of a cruel edict;
And yet not old enough by many years,
'Cause I 'd not see him go an hour before me.
Sim. These very passions I speak to my father.

* * * * * * * *

Cle. Why, here's a villain,
Able to corrupt a thousand by example.
Does the kind root bleed out its livelihood
In parent distribution to his branches,
Adorning them with all his glorious fruits,
Proud that his pride is seen when he's unseen,
And must not gratitude descend again
To comfort his old limbs in fruitless winter?

Cleanthes, to save his old father, Leonides, from the operation of the law, gives out that he is dead, celebrating a pretended funeral, to make it believed.

DUKE. COURTIERS. CLEANTHES, *as following his father's body to the grave.*

Duke. Cleanthes?
Court. 'Tis, my lord, and in the place
Of a chief mourner too, but strangely habited.
Duke. Yet suitable to his behavior, mark it;
He comes all the way smiling, do you observe it?
I never saw a corse so joyfully follow'd,

Light colors and light cheeks—who should this be ?
'Tis a thing worth resolving,—Cleanthes ——
Cle. O my lord !
Duke. He laugh'd outright now.
Was ever such a contrariety seen
In natural courses yet, nay, profess'd openly ?
Cle. 'Tis, of a heavy time, the joyfull'st day
That ever son was born to.
Duke. How can that be ?
Cle. I joy—to make it plain—my father's dead.
Duke. Dead ?
Court. Old Leonides ?
Cle. In his last month dead.
He beguil'd cruel law the sweetliest
That ever age was blest to.
It grieves me that a tear should fall upon 't,
Being a thing so joyful, but his memory
Will work it out, I see; when his poor heart
Broke, I did not so much, but leap'd for joy
So mountingly, I touch'd the stars, methought.
I would not hear of blacks, I was so light,
But chose a color orient, like my mind :
For blacks are often such dissembling mourners,
There is no credit giv'n to 't, it has lost
All reputation by false sons and widows.
Now I would have men know what I resemble,
A truth, indeed ; 'tis joy clad like a joy,
Which is more honest than a cunning grief
That's only fac'd with sables for a show,
But gawdy-hearted. When I saw death come
So ready to deceive you, sir, forgive me,
I could not choose but be entirely merry ;
And yet too, see now, of a sudden,
Naming but death, I show myself a mortal,
That's never constant to one passion long ;
I wonder whence that tear came, when I smil'd
In the production on 't : Sorrow's a thief,
That can, when joy looks on, steal forth a grief.

But, gracious leave, my lord; when I've perform'd
My last poor duty to my father's bones,
I shall return your servant.
Duke. Well, perform it,
The law is satisfied: they can but die.

Cleanthes conceals Leonides in a secret apartment within a wood, where himself, and his wife Hippolita, keep watch for the safety of the old man. This coming to the Duke's knowledge, he repairs to the wood and makes discovery of the place where they have hid Leonides.

The Wood.—CLEANTHES *listening, as fearing every sound.*

Cle. What's that? Oh, nothing but the whisp'ring wind
Breathes thro' yon churlish hawthorn, that grew rude
As if it chid the gentle breath that kiss'd it.
I cannot be too circumspect, too careful,
For in these woods lies hid all my life's treasure,
Which is too much ever to fear to lose,
Though it be never lost; and if our watchfulness
Ought to be wise and serious 'gainst a thief
That comes to steal our goods, things all without us,
That prove vexation often more than comfort,
How mighty ought our providence to be
To prevent those, if any such there were,
That come to rob our bosom of our joys,
That only make poor man delight to live!
Pshaw, I 'm too fearful—fie, fie, who can hurt me?
But 'tis a general cowardice, that shakes
The nerves of confidence; he that hides treasure,
Imagines every one thinks of that place,
When 'tis a thing least minded; nay, let him change
The place continually, where'er it keeps,
There will the fear keep still. Yonder 's the storehouse
Of all my comfort now—and, see, it sends forth

HIPPOLITA *enters.*

A dear one to me. Precious chief of women!
How does the good old soul? has he fed well?
Hip. Beshrew me, sir, he made the heartiest meal to-day,

Much good may 't do his health.
Cle. A blessing on thee,
Both for thy news and wish.
Hip. His stomach, sir,
Is better'd wond'rously, since his concealment.
Cle. Heav'n has a blessed work in 't. Come, we 're safe here.
I prithee, call him forth, the air is much wholesomer.
Hip. Father.

LEONIDES *comes forth.*

Leon. How sweetly sounds the voice of a good woman!
It is so seldom heard, that, when it speaks,
It ravishes all senses. Lists of honor!
I 've a joy weeps to see you, 'tis so full,
So fairly fruitful.
Cle. I hope to see you often, and return
Loaden with blessing, still to pour on some.
I find them all in my contented peace,
And lose not one in thousands, they 're dispers'd
So gloriously, I know not which are brightest;
I find them, as angels are found, by legions.

A horn is heard.

Ha!—
Leon. What was 't disturb'd my joy?
Cle. Did you not hear,
As afar off?
Hip. What, my excellent consort?
Cle. Nor you——
Hip. I heard a——
Cle. Hark again——
Leon. Bless my joy,
What ails it on a sudden?
Cle. Now since——lately——
Leon. 'Tis nothing but a symptom of thy care, man.
Cle. Alas, you do not hear well.
Leon. What was 't, daughter?
Hip. I heard a sound twice.
Cle. Hark! louder and nearer.

In, for the precious good of virtue, quick, sir,
Louder and nearer yet; at hand, at hand;
A hunting here! 'tis strange! I never knew
Game follow'd in these woods before. [LEONIDES *goes in.*

Hip. Now let them come, and spare not.

Enter DUKE, *Courtiers, Attendants, as if hunting.*

Cle. Ha! 'tis——is 't not the Duke?——look sparingly.

Hip. 'Tis he, but what of that? alas! take heed, sir;
Your care will overthrow us.

Cle. Come, it shall not.
Let 's set a pleasant face upon our fears,
Though our hearts shake with horror. Ha! ha! ha!

Duke. Hark!

Cle. Prithee, proceed;
I 'm taken with these light things infinitely,
Since the old man's decease.—Ha! ha! ha!

Duke. Why, how should I believe this? Look, he 's merry,
As if he had no such charge. One with that care
Could never be so still; he holds his temper,
And 'tis the same still; with no difference,
He brought his father's corpse to the grave with.
He laugh'd thus then, you know.

Court. Aye, he may laugh, my lord;
That shows but how he glories in his cunning;
And, perhaps, done more to advance his wit,
Than to express affection to his father,
That only he has over-reach'd the law.

Duke. If a contempt can be so neatly carried,
It gives me cause of wonder.——
Cleanthes——

Cle. My lov'd lord—

Duke. Not mov'd a whit!
Constant to lightning still!——'tis strange to meet you
Upon a ground so unfrequented, sir:
This does not fit your passion; you are for mirth,
Or I mistake you much.

Cle. But finding it

Grow to a noted imperfection in me
(For anything too much is vicious),
I come to these disconsolate walks of purpose
Only to dull and take away the edge on 't.
I ever had a greater zeal to sadness,
A natural propension, I confess, my lord,
Before that chearful accident fell out,—
If I may call a father's funeral chearful,
Without wrong done to duty or my love.
Duke. It seems then you take pleasure in these walks, sir?
Cle. Contemplative content I do, my lord:
They bring into my mind oft meditations
So sweetly precious, that in the parting
I find a shower of grace upon my cheeks,
They take their leave so feelingly.
Duke. So, sir——
Cle. Which is a kind of grave delight, my lord.
Duke. And I 've small cause, Cleanthes, to afford you
The least delight that has a name.
Cle. My lord——
Duke. In your excess of joy you have express'd
Your rancor and contempt against my law:
Your smiles deserve fining; you have profess'd
Derision openly ev'n to my face,
Which might be death, a little more incensed.
You do not come for any freedom here,
But for a project of your own;
But all that's known to be contentful to thee,
Shall in the use prove deadly. Your life 's mine,
If ever thy presumption do but lead thee
Into these walks again——aye, or that woman——
I 'll have them watch'd a purpose.
1st Court. Now, now, his color ebbs and flows.
2d Court. Mark hers too.
Hip. Oh! who shall bring food to the poor old man now?
Speak somewhat, good sir, or we are lost for ever.
[*Apart to* CLEANTHES.
Cle. Oh! you did wondrous ill to call me again.

There are not words to help us. If I entreat,
'Tis found; that will betray us worse than silence.
Prithee, let heaven alone, and let's say nothing.
[*Apart to* HIPPOLITA.

1st Court. You have struck them dumb, my lord.
2d Court. Look how guilt looks!
Cle. He is safe still, is he not? } *Apart.*
Hip. Oh! you do ill to doubt it. }
Cle. Thou art all goodness. }
2d Court. Now does your grace believe?
Duke. 'Tis too apparent.
Search, make a speedy search; for the imposture
Cannot be far off, by the fear it sends.
Cle. Ha!
2d Court. He has the lapwing's cunning, I'm afraid, my lord,
That cries most when she is farthest from the nest.
Cle. Oh! we are betrayed.

[There is an exquisiteness of moral sensibility, making one to gush out tears of delight, and a poetical strangeness in all the improbable circumstances of this wild play, which are unlike anything in the dramas which Massinger wrote alone. The pathos is of a subtler edge. Middleton and Rowley, who assisted in this play, had both of them finer geniuses than their associate.]

THE TRAGEDY OF PHILIP CHABOT, ADMIRAL OF FRANCE. BY GEORGE CHAPMAN, AND JAMES SHIRLEY.

The Admiral is accused of treason, a criminal process is instituted against him, and his faithful servant Allegre is put on the rack to make him discover: his innocence is at length established by the confession of his enemies; but the disgrace of having been suspected for a traitor by his royal Master, sinks so deep into him, that he falls into a mortal sickness.

ADMIRAL. ALLEGRE, *supported between two.*

Adm. Welcome my injured servant: what a misery
Have they made on thee!
Al. Though some change appear
Upon my body, whose severe affliction
Hath brought it thus to be sustain'd by others,

My heart is still the same in faith to you,
Not broken with their rage.

Adm. Alas poor man.
Were all my joys essential, and so mighty,
As the affected world believes I taste,
This object were enough t' unsweeten all.
Though, in thy absence, I had suffering,
And felt within me a strong sympathy,
While for my sake their cruelty did vex
And fright thy nerves with horror of thy sense,
Yet in this spectacle I apprehend
More grief, than all my imagination
Could let before into me. Didst not curse me
Upon the torture?

Al. Good my lord, let not
That thought of what I suffer'd dwell upon
Your memory; they could not punish more
Than what my duty did oblige to bear
For you and justice: but there's something in
Your looks presents more fear, than all the malice
Of my tormentors could affect my soul with.
That paleness, and the other forms you wear,
Would well become a guilty admiral, one
Lost to his hopes and honor, not the man
Upon whose life the fury of injustice,
Arm'd with fierce lightning and the power of thunder,
Can make no breach. I was not rack'd till now.
There's more death in that falling eye, than all
Rage ever yet brought forth. What accident, sir, can blast,
Can be so black and fatal, to distract
The calm, the triumph, that should sit upon
Your noble brow: misfortune could have no
Time to conspire with fate, since you were rescued
By the great arm of Providence; nor can
Those garlands, that now grow about your forehead,
With all the poison of the world be blasted.

Adm. Allegre, thou dost bear thy wounds upon thee
In wide and spacious characters, but in

The volume of my sadness thou dost want
An eye to read. An open force hath torn
Thy manly sinews, which some time may cure.
The engine is not seen that wounds thy master;
Past all the remedy of art, or time,
The flatteries of court, of fame, or honors.
Thus in the summer a tall flourishing tree,
Transplanted by strong hand, with all her leaves
And blooming pride upon her, makes a show
Of spring, tempting the eye with wanton blossoms;
But not the sun with all her amorous smiles,
The dews of morning, or the tears of night,
Can root her fibres in the earth again;
Or make her bosom kind, to growth and bearing:
But the tree withers; and those very beams,
That once were natural warmth to her soft verdure,
Dry up her sap, and shoot a fever through
The bark and rind, till she becomes a burden
To that which gave her life: so Chabot, Chabot—
Al. Wander in apprehension! I must
Suspect your health indeed.
Adm. No, no, thou shalt not
Be troubled: I but stirr'd thee with a moral,
That's empty; contains nothing. I am well:
See, I can walk; poor man, thou hast not strength yet.

The father of the Admiral makes known the condition his son is in to the king.

FATHER. KING.

King. Say, how is my admiral?
The truth upon thy life.
Fath. To secure his, I would you had.
King. Ha! who durst oppose him?
Fath. One that hath power enough, hath practis'd on him,
And made his great heart stoop.
King. I will revenge it
With crushing, crushing that rebellious power
To nothing. Name him.

Fath. He was his friend.
King. What mischief hath engender'd
New storms ?
Fath. 'Tis the old tempest.
King. Did not we
Appease all horrors that look'd wild upon him ?
Fath. You drest his wounds, I must confess, but made
No cure ; they bleed afresh : pardon me, sir ;
Although your conscience have closed too soon,
He is in danger, and doth want new surgery :
Though he be right in fame, and your opinion,
He thinks you were unkind.
King. Alas, poor Chabot :
Doth that afflict him ?
Fath. So much, though he strive
With most resolv'd and adamantine nerves,
As ever human fire in flesh and blood
Forg'd for example, to bear all ; so killing
The arrows that you shot were (still, your pardon)
No centaur's blood could rankle so.
King. If this
Be all, I'll cure him. Kings retain
More balsam in their soul, than hurt in anger.
Fath. Far short, sir ; with one breath they uncreate :
And kings, with only words, more wounds can make
Than all their kingdom made in balm can heal.
'Tis dangerous to play too wild a descant
On numerous virtue ; though it become princes
To assure their adventures made in everything.
Goodness, confin'd within poor flesh and blood,
Hath but a queazy and still sickly state ;
A musical hand should only play on her,
Fluent as air, yet every touch command.
King. No more :
Commend us to the admiral, and say
The king will visit him, and bring health.
Fath. I will not doubt that blessing, and shall move
Nimbly with this command.

The King visits the Admiral.

KING. ADMIRAL. *His wife, and father.*

King. No ceremonial knees:
Give me thy heart, my dear, my honest Chabot;
And yet in vain I challenge that; 'tis here
Already in my own, and shall be cherish'd
With care of my best life: no violence
Shall ravish it from my possession;
Not those distempers that infirm my blood
And spirits, shall betray it to a fear;
When time and nature join to dispossess
My body of a cold and languishing breath;
No stroke in all my arteries, but silence
In every faculty; yet dissect me then,
And in my heart the world shall read thee living;
And, by the virtue of thy name writ there,
That part of me shall never putrify,
When I am lost in all my other dust.
Adm. You too much honor your poor servant, sir;
My heart despairs so rich a monument,
But when it dies—
King. I wo' not hear a sound
Of anything that trenched upon death.
He speaks the funeral of my crown, that prophesies
So unkind a fate: we'll live and die together.
And by that duty, which hath taught you hitherto
All loyal and just services, I charge thee,
Preserve thy heart for me, and thy reward,
Which now shall crown thy merits.
Adm. I have found
A glorious harvest in your favor, sir;
And by this overflow of royal grace,
All my deserts are shadows and fly from me:
I have not in the wealth of my desires
Enough to pay you now——
King. Express it in some joy then.
Adm. I will strive

To show that pious gratitude to you, but——
King. But what?
Adm. My frame hath lately, sir, been ta'en a pieces,
And but now put together; the least force
Of mirth will shake and unjoint all my reason.
Your patience, royal sir.
King. I 'll have no patience,
If thou forget the courage of a man.
Adm. My strength would flatter me.
King. Physicians,
Now I begin to fear his apprehension.
Why how is Chabot's spirit fall'n?
Adm. Who would not wish to live to serve your goodness?
Stand from me. You betray me with your fears.
The plummets may fall off that hang upon
My heart, they were but thoughts at first; or if
They weigh me down to death, let not my eyes
Close with another object than the king.
King. In a prince
What a swift executioner is a frown,
Especially of great and noble souls!
How is it with my Philip?
Adm. I must beg
One other boon.
King. Upon condition
My Chabot will collect his scatter'd spirits,
And be himself again, he shall divide
My kingdom with me.
Adm. I observe
A fierce and killing wrath engender'd in you;
For my sake, as you wish me strength to serve you,
Forgive your chancellor;* let not the story
Of Philip Chabot, read hereafter, draw
A tear from any family; I beseech
Your royal mercy on his life, and free
Remission of all seizure upon his state.

* Chabot's accuser.

I have no comfort else.
King. Endeavor
But thy own health ; and pronounce general pardon
To all through France.
Adm. Sir, I must kneel to thank you ;
It is not seal'd else. Your blest hand : live happy,
May all your trust have no less faith than Chabot.
Oh! [*Dies*.
Wife. His heart is broken.
Father. And kneeling, sir ;
As his ambition were in death to show
The truth of his obedience.

THE MAID'S REVENGE ; A TRAGEDY. BY JAMES SHIRLEY *

Sebastiano invites Antonio to Avero Castle.

SEBASTIANO. ANTONIO.

Seb. The noble courtesies I have receiv'd
At Lisbon, worthy friend, so much engage me,
That I must die indebted to your worth,
Unless you mean to accept what I have studied,
Although but partly, to discharge the sum
Due to your honor'd love.
Ant. How now, Sebastiano, will you forfeit
The name of friend, then ? I did hope our love
Had out-grown compliment.
Seb. I spake my thoughts ;
My tongue and heart are relatives ; I think
I have deserv'd no base opinion from you ;
I wish not only to perpetuate
Our friendship, but t' exchange that common name
Of friend for—

* Shirley claims a place amongst the worthies of this period, not so much for any transcendent genius in himself, as that he was the last of a great race, all of whom spoke nearly the same language, and had a set of moral feelings and notions in common. A new language and quite a new turn of tragic and comic interest came in with the Restoration.

Ant. What? take heed, do not profane:
Wouldst thou be more than friend? it is a name
Virtue can only answer to: couldst thou
Unite into one all goodness whatsoe'er
Mortality can boast of, thou shalt find
The circle narrow-bounded to contain
This swelling treasure; every good admits
Degrees, but this being so good, it cannot:
For he 's no friend is not superlative.
Indulgent parents, brethren, kindred, tied
By the natural flow of blood, alliances,
And what you can imagine, is too light
To weigh with name of friend: they execute
At best but what a nature prompts them to;
Are often less than friends, when they remain
Our kinsmen still: but friend is never lost.
Seb. Nay then, Antonio, you mistake; I mean not
To leave off friend, which, with another title,
Would not be lost. Come, then, I 'll tell you, sir;
I would be friend and brother: thus our friendship
Shall, like a diamond set in gold, not lose
His sparkling, but show fairer: I have a pair
Of sisters, which I would commend, but that
I might seem partial, their birth and fortunes
Deserving noble love; if thou be'st free
From other fair engagement, I would be proud
To speak them worthy: come, shalt go and see them.
I would not beg them suitors; fame hath spread
Through Portugal their persons, and drawn to Avero
Many affectionate gallants.
Ant. Catalina and Berinthia.
Seb. The same.
Ant. Report speaks loud their beauties, and no less
Virtue in either. Well, I see you strive
To leave no merit where you mean to honor.
I cannot otherwise escape the censure
Of one ungrateful, but by waiting on you
Home to Avero.

Seb. You shall honor me,
And glad my noble father, to whom you are
No stranger; your own worth before hath been
Sufficient preparation.
Ant. Ha!
I have not so much choice, Sebastiano:
But if one sister of Antonio's
May have a commendation to your thoughts
(I will not spend much art in praising her,
Her virtue speak itself) I shall be happy;
And be confirm'd your brother, though I miss
Acceptance at Avero.
Seb. Still you out-do me. I could never wish
My service better placed. At opportunity
I 'll visit you at Elvas; i' the mean time
Let's haste to Avero, where with you I 'll bring
My double welcome, and not fail to second
Any design.
Ant. You shall teach me a lesson
Against we meet at Elvas castle, sir.

Sebastiano's father welcomes Antonio to Avero Castle.

VILLAREZO. CATALINA. BERINTHIA. SEBASTIANO. ANTONIO.

Vil. Old Gaspar's house is honor'd by such guests.
Now, by the tomb of my progenitors,
I envied that your fame should visit me
So oft without your person. Sebastiano
Hath been long happy in your noble friendship,
And cannot but improve himself in virtues,
That lives so near your love.—You shall dishonor me,
Unless you think yourself as welcome here
As at your Elvas castle. Villarezo
Was once as you are, sprightly; and though I say it,
Maintain'd my father's reputation,
And honor of our house, with actions
Worthy our name and family: but now
Time hath let fall cold snow upon my hairs,
Plough'd on my brows the furrows of his anger,

Disfurnish'd me of active blood, and wrapt me
Half in my sear-cloth, yet I have a mind
That bids me honor virtue, where I see it
Bud forth and spring so hopefully.

Ant. You speak all nobleness, and encourage me
To spend the greenness of my rising years
So to th' advantage, that at last I may
Be old like you.

Vil. Daughters, speak his welcome.—

Antonio loves and is beloved by Berinthia, the younger sister. Catalina the elder is jealous, and plots to take off her sister by poison. Antonio rescues Berinthia from the vindictive jealousy of her sister, and carries her off to Elvas Castle; where his sister Castabella and his cousin Villandras welcome her.

ANTONIO. BERINTHIA. CASTABELLA. VILLANDRAS. SFORZA, *a domestic.*

Ant. The welcom'st guest that ever Elvas had.
Sister—Villandras——you 're not sensible
What treasure you possess. I have no loves
I would not here divide.

Cast. Indeed, madam,
You are as welcome here as e'er my mother was.

Vill. And you are here as safe,
As if you had an army for your guard.
Nor think my noble cousin meaneth you
Any dishonor here.

Ant. Dishonor! 'tis a language
I never understood yet. Throw off your fears,
Berinthia, you 're in the power of him,
That dares not think the least dishonor to you.—
Come, be not sad.

Cast. Put on fresh blood; you are not chearful, how do you?

Ber. I know not how, nor what to answer you;
Your loves I cannot be ungrateful to;
You 're my best friends I think, but yet I know not
With what consent you brought my body hither,

Ant. Can you be ignorant what plot was laid
To take your fair life from you?

Ber. If all be not a dream, I do remember
Your servant Diego told me wonders, and
I owe you for my preservation, but—
Cast. It is your happiness you have escaped
The malice of your sister.
Vill. And it is worth
A noble gratitude to have been quit
By such an honorer as Antonio is
Of fair Berinthia.
Ber. Oh, but my father; under whose displeasure
I ever sink.
Ant. You are secure—
Ber. As the poor deer that being pursued, for safety
Gets up a rock that overhangs the sea,
Where all that she can see is her destruction;
Before, the waves; behind, her enemies,
Promise her certain ruin.
Ant. Feign not yourself so hapless, my Berinthia.
Raise your dejected thoughts, be merry, come,
Think I am your Antonio.
Cast. 'Tis not wisdom
To let our passed fortunes trouble us;
Since, were they bad, the memory is sweet
That we have past them. Look before you, lady;
The future most concerneth.

DIEGO, *a domestic, enters, and announces that* SEBASTIANO *is at the gate.*

Aut. Your brother, lady, and my honor'd friend.
Why do the gates not spread themselves to open
At his arrival? Sforza, 'tis Berinthia's brother;
Sebastiano, th' example of all worth
And friendship, is come after his sweet sister.
Ber. Alas, I fear.
Ant. Be not such a coward, lady, he cannot come
Without all goodness waiting on him. Sforza,
Sforza, I say, what precious time we lose!
Sebastiano—I almost lose myself

In joy to meet him. Break the iron bars,
And give him entrance,—Sebastiano's come——

Ber. Sent by my father to——

Ant. What? to see thee. He shall see thee here,
Respected like thyself, Berinthia,
Attended with Antonio, begirt
With armies of thy servants.

SEBASTIANO *enters, with* COUNT DE MONTE NIGRO, *his friend.*

Ant. Oh, my friend.

Seb. 'Tis yet in question, sir, and will not be
So easily prov'd.

Ant. What face have you put on? am I awake,
Or do I dream Sebastiano frowns?

Seb. Antonio (for here I throw off all
The ties of love), I come to fetch a sister
Dishonorably taken from her father;
Or with my sword to force thee render her:
Now if thou be'st a soldier, redeliver,
Or keep her with the danger of thy person.

Ant. Promise me the hearing,
And shalt have any satisfaction,
Becomes my fame.—
Wer't in your power, would you not account it
A precious victory, in your sister's cause,
To dye your sword with any blood of him,
Sav'd both her life and honor?

Seb. Why, would you have me think
My sister owes to you such preservation?

Ant. Oh Sebastiano!
Thou dost not think what devil lies at home
Within a sister's bosom. Catalina
(I know not with what worst of envy) laid
Force to this goodly building, and through poison
Had robb'd the earth of more than all the world,
Her virtue.—
Valasco was the man appointed by
That goodly sister to steal Berinthia,

And lord himself of this possession,
Just at that time ; but hear, and tremble at it,
She by a cunning poison should have breath'd
Her soul into his arms within two hours,
And so Valasco should have borne the shame
Of theft and murder.

Seb. You amaze me, sir.

Ant. 'Tis true, by honor's self: hear it confirm'd;
And when you will, I am ready.

Seb. I cannot but believe it. Oh Berinthia,
I 'm wounded ere I fight.

Ant. Holds your resolve yet constant? if you have
Better opinion of your sword, than truth,
I am bound to answer: but I would I had
Such an advantage 'gainst another man,
As the justice of my cause; all valor fights
But with a sail against it.

Seb. But will you back with me then?

Ber. Excuse me, brother: I shall fall too soon
Upon my sister's malice, whose foul guilt
Will make me expect more certain ruin.

Ant. Now Sebastiano
Puts on his judgment, and assumes his nobleness
Whilst he loves equity.

Seb. And shall I carry shame
To Villarezo's house, neglect of father,
Whose precepts bind me to return with her,
Or leave my life at Elvas? I must on.
I have heard you to no purpose. Shall Berinthia
Back to Avero?

Ant. Sir, she must not yet;
'Tis dangerous.

Seb. Choose thee a second then: this count and I
Mean to leave honor here.

Vill. Honor me, sir.

Ant. 'Tis done. Sebastiano shall report
Antonio just: and, noble Sforza, swear
Upon my sword (Oh, do not hinder me)

If victory crown Sebastiano's arm,
I charge thee by thy honesty restore
This lady to him; on whose lip I seal
My unstain'd faith.

Antonio falls in a duel by the sword of Sebastiano. Sebastiano is disconsolate for having killed his friend. In his penitence, he is visited by Antonio's sister, Castabella, disguised as a page.

CASTABELLA. SEBASTIANO.

Cast. He that hath sent you, sir, this gift, did love you;
You 'll say yourself he did.
Seb. Ha, name him prithee.
Cast. The friend I came from was Antonio.
Seb. Who hath sent thee
To tempt Sebastiano's soul to act on thee
Another death, for thus affrighting me?
Cast. Indeed I do not mock, nor come to affright you;
Heaven knows my heart. I know Antonio's dead.
But 'twas a gift he in his life design'd
To you, and I have brought it.
Seb. Thou dost not promise cozenage: what gift is 't?
Cast. It is myself, sir; whilst Antonio liv'd,
I was his boy; but never did boy lose
So kind a master; in his life he promis'd
He would bestow me (so much was his love
To my poor merit) on his dearest friend,
And named you, sir, if heaven should point out
To over-live him, for he knew you would
Love me the better for his sake: indeed
I will be very honest to you, and
Refuse no service to procure your love
And good opinion to me.
Seb. Can it be
Thou wert his boy? Oh, thou shouldst hate me then.
Thou art false, I dare not trust thee; unto him
Thou show'st thee now unfaithful, to accept
Of me: I kill'd thy master. 'Twas a friend
He could commit thee to; I only was,

Of all the stock of men, his enemy,
His cruel'st enemy.
Cast. Indeed I am sure it was ; he spoke all truth ;
And, had he liv'd to have made his will, I know
He had bequeath'd me as a legacy,
To be your boy ; alas, I am willing, sir,
To obey him in it : had he laid on me
Command, to have mingled with his sacred dust
My unprofitable blood, it should have been
A most glad sacrifice, and 't had been honor
To have done him such a duty : sir, I know
You did not kill him with a heart of malice,
But in contention with your very soul
To part with him.
Seb. All is as true
As oracle by heaven ; dost thou believe so?
Cast. Indeed I do.
Seb. Yet be not rash ;
'Tis no advantage to belong to me ;
I have no power nor greatness in the court
To raise thee to a fortune worthy of
So much observance, as I shall expect
When thou art mine.
Cast. All the ambition of my thoughts shall be
To do my duty, sir.
Seb. Besides, I shall afflict thy tenderness
With solitude and passion : for I am
Only in love with sorrow, never merry,
Wear out the day in telling of sad tales,
Delight in sighs and tears ; sometimes I walk
To a wood or river, purposely to challenge
The boldest echo to send back my groans
In th' height I break them. Come, I shall undo thee.
Cast. Sir, I shall be most happy to bear part
In any of your sorrows ; I ne'er had
So hard a heart but I could shed a tear
To bear my master company.
Seb. I will not leave thee, if thou 'lt dwell with me,

For wealth of Indies: be my loved boy,
Come in with me; thus I'll begin to do
Some recompence for dead Antonio.

Berinthia kills her brother Sebastiano sleeping.

CASTABELLA. SEBASTIANO.

Cast. Sir, if the opportunity I use
To comfort you be held a fault, and that
I need not distance of a servant, lay it
Upon my love; indeed, if it be an error,
It springs out of my duty.
Seb. Prithee, boy, be patient.
The more I strive to throw off the remembrance
Of dead Antonio, love still rubs the wounds
To make them bleed afresh.
Cast. Alas, they are past;
Bind up your own for honor's sake, and show
Love to yourself; pray do not lose your reason.
To make your grief so fruitless. I have procur'd
Some music, sir, to quiet those sad thoughts
That make such war within you.
Seb. Alas, good boy, it will but add more weight
Of dullness on me! I am stung with worse
Than the tarantula, to be cured with music;
It has th' exactest unity, but it cannot
Accord my thoughts.
Cast. Sir, this your couch
Seems to invite some small repose:
Oh, I beseech you taste it. I will beg
A little leave to sing. [*She sings.*

BERINTHIA *enters softly.*

Cast. Sweet sleep charm his sad senses:
And gentle thoughts let fall
Your flowing numbers here; and round about
Hover celestial angels with your wings
That none offend his quiet. Sleep begins
To cast his nets o'er me too; I'll obey,

And dream on him that dreams not what I am.
[*She lies down by him.*

Ber. Nature doth wrestle with me, but revenge
Doth arm my love against it; justice is
Above all tie of blood. Sebastiano,
Thou art the first shall tell Antonio's ghost,
How much I lov'd him.
[*She stabs him upon his couch.*

Seb. (*waking.*) Oh, stay thy hand, Berinthia! no:
Thou 'st done 't. I wish thee heaven's forgiveness. I cannot
Tarry to hear thy reasons; at many doors
My life runs out, and yet Berinthia
Doth in her name give me more wounds than these.
Antonio, Oh, Antonio: we shall now
Be friends again. [*Dies.*

THE POLITICIAN: A TRAGEDY. BY JAMES SHIRLEY.

Marpisa widow of Count Altomarus is advanced to be Queen to the King of Norway, by the practices of her paramour Gotharus. She has by her first husband a young son Haraldus; to secure whose succession to the crown by the aid of Gotharus (in prejudice of the king's son, the lawful heir) she tells Gotharus that the child is his. He believes her, and tells Haraldus; who taking to heart his mother's dishonor, and his own stain of bastardy, falls into a mortal sickness.

QUEEN. HARALDUS.

Queen. How is it with my child?

Har. I know you love me:
Yet I must tell you truth, I cannot live.
And let this comfort you, death will not come
Unwelcome to your son. I do not die
Against my will; and having my desires,
You have less cause to mourn.

Queen. What is 't hath made
The thought of life unpleasant? which does court
Thy dwelling here, with all delights that nature

And art can study for thee, rich in all things
Thy wish can be ambitious of, yet all
These treasures nothing to thy mother's love,
Which to enjoy thee would defer a while
Her thought of going to heaven.
Har. O take heed, mother.
Heaven has a specious ear, and power to punish
Your too much love with my eternal absence.
I beg your prayers and blessing.
Queen. Thou art dejected.
Have but a will, and live.
Har. 'Tis in vain, mother.
Queen. Sink with a fever into earth!
Look up, thou shalt not die.
Har. I have a wound within,
You do not see, more killing than all fevers.
Queen. A wound? where? who has murther'd thee?
Har. Gotharus ——
Queen. Ha! furies persecute him.
Har. O pray for him:
It is my duty, though he gave me death.
He is my father.
Queen. How, thy father?
Har. He told me so, and with that breath destroy'd me.
I felt it strike upon my spirits, mother;
Would I had ne'er been born!
Queen. Believe him not.
Har. Oh do not add another sin to what
Is done already; death is charitable,
To quit me from the scorn of all the world.
Queen. By all my hopes, Gotharus has abused thee.
Thou art the lawful burthen of my womb;
Thy father Altomarus.
Har. Ha!
Queen. Before whose spirit (long since taken up
To meet with saints and troops angelical)
I dare again repeat, thou art his son.
Har. Ten thousand blessings now reward my mother!

Speak it again, and I may live : a stream
Of pious joy runs through me ; to my soul
You've struck a harmony, next that in heaven.
Can you without a blush call me your child,
And son of Altomarus ? all that's holy
Dwell in your blood for ever : speak it once,
But once again.
Queen. Were it my latest breath ;
Thou'rt his and mine.
Har. Enough, my tears do flow
To give you thanks for 't ; I would you could resolve me
But one truth more : why did my lord Gotharus
Call me the issue of his blood ?
Queen. Alas,
He thinks thou art.
Har. What are those words ? I am
Undone again.
Queen. Ha !
Har. 'Tis too late
To call 'em back. He thinks I am his son.
Queen. I have confess'd too much, and tremble with
The imagination. Forgive me, child,
And heaven, if there be mercy to a crime
So black, as I must now, to quit thy fears,
Say I've been guilty of : we have been sinful,
And I was not unwilling to oblige
His active brain for thy advancement, by
Abusing his belief thou wert his own.
But thou hast no such stain ; thy birth is innocent,
Or may I perish ever : 'tis a strange
Confession to a child, but it may drop
A balsam to thy wound. Live, my Haraldus,
If not, for this, to see my penitence,
And with what tears I'll wash away my sin.
Har. I am no bastard then ———
Queen. Thou art not.
Har. But
I am not found, while you are lost. No time

Can restore you. My spirits faint ——
Queen. Will nothing comfort thee?
Har. Give me your blessing; and, within my heart,
I'll pray you may have many. My soul flies
'Bove this vain world: good mother, close mine eyes.
Queen. Never died so much sweetness in his years.*

THE BROTHERS: A COMEDY. BY JAMES SHIRLEY.

Don Ramires leaves his son Fernando with a heavy curse, and a threat of disinheriting, if he do not renounce Felisarda, the poor niece of Don Carlos, whom he courts, when by his father's command he should address Jacinta, the daughter and rich heiress of Carlos, his younger brother Francisco's Mistress.

FERNANDO. FRANCISCO.

Fer. Why does not all the stock of thunder fall?
Or the fierce winds, from their close caves let loose,
Now shake me into atoms?
Fran. Fie, noble brother, what can so deject
Your masculine thoughts? is this done like Fernando,
Whose resolute soul so late was arm'd to fight
With all the miseries of man, and triumph
With patience of a martyr? I observed
My father late come from you.
Fer. Yes, Francisco:
He hath left his curse upon me.
Fran. How?
Fer. His curse: dost comprehend what that word carries,
Shot from a father's angry breath? unless
I tear poor Felisarda from my heart,
He hath pronounc'd me heir to all his curses.
Does this fright thee, Francisco? Thou hast cause
To dance in soul for this: 'tis only I
Must lose, and mourn; thou shalt have all; I am

* Mamillus in the Winter's Tale in this manner droops and dies from a conceit of his mother's dishonor.

Degraded from my birth, while he affects
Thy forward youth, and only calls thee son,
Son of his active spirit, and applauds
Thy progress with Jacinta, in whose smiles
Thou may'st see all thy wishes waiting for thee;
Whilst poor Fernando for her sake must stand
An excommunicate from every blessing,
A thing that dare not give myself a name,
But flung into the world's necessities,
Until in time, with wonder of my wants,
I turn a ragged statue, on whose forehead
Each clown may carve his motto.

Don Ramires is seized with a mortal sickness, but forbids Fernando to approach his chamber till he shall send for him, on pain of his dying curse.

FERNANDO.

Fer. This turn is fatal, and affrights me; but
Heaven has more charity than to let him die
With such a hard heart; 'twere a sin, next his
Want of compassion, to suspect he can
Take his eternal flight, and leave Fernando
This desperate legacy; he will change the curse
Into some little prayer, I hope; and then ——

Enter Servant and Physician.

Ser. Make haste, I beseech you, doctor.
Phy. Noble Fernando.
Fer. As you would have men think your art is meant
Not to abuse mankind, employ it all
To cure my poor sick father.
Phy. Fear it not, sir.
[*Exeunt Physician and Servant*
Fer. But there is more than your thin skill requir'd,
To state a health; your recipes, perplext
With tough names, are but mockeries and noise,
Without some dew from heaven, to mix and make 'em
Thrive in the application: what now?

Enter Servant.

Ser. Oh sir, I am sent for the confessor,
The doctor fears him much; your brother says
You must have patience; and not enter, sir;
Your father is a going, good old man,
And, having made him heir, he's loth your presence
Should interrupt his journey. [*Exit.*

Fer. Francisco may be honest, yet methinks
It would become his love to interpose
For my access, at such a needful hour,
And mediate for my blessing; not assist
Unkindly thus my banishment. I'll not
Be lost so tamely. Shall my father die,
And not Fernando take his leave? —— I dare not.
'If thou dost hope I should take off this curse,
Do not approach until I send:" 'twas so;
And 'tis a law that binds above my blood.

Enter Confessor and Servant.

Make haste, good father, and if heaven deny
Him life, let not his charity die too:
One curse may sink us both. Say how I kneel,
And beg he would bequeath me but his blessing.
Then, though Francisco be his heir, I shall
Live happy, and take comfort in my tears,
When I remember him so kind a father.

Conf. It is your duty. [*Exit.*

Fer. Do my holy office.
Those fond philosophers that magnify
Our human nature, and did boast we had
Such a prerogative in our rational soul,
Convers'd but little with the world, confin'd
To cells, and unfrequented woods, they knew not
The fierce vexation of community;
Else they had taught, our reason is our loss,
And but a privilege that exceedeth sense
By nearer apprehension of what wounds,
To know ourselves most miserable. My heart

Enter Physician and Francisco.

Is teeming with new fears.—Ha! is he dead?
Phy. Not dead, but in a desperate condition;
And so that little breath remains we have
Remitted to this confessor, whose office
Is all that's left.
Fer. Is he not merciful to Fernando yet?
No talk of me?
Phy. I find he takes no pleasure
To hear you named: Francisco to us all
He did confirm his heir, with many blessings.
Fer. And not left one for me? Oh take me in,
Thou gentle earth, and let me creep through all
Thy dark and hollow crannies, till I find
Another way to come into the world;
For all the air I breathe in here is poison'd.
Fran. We must have patience, brother, it was no
Ambitious thought of mine to supplant you;
He may live yet, and you be reconcil'd.
Fer. That was some kindness yet, Francisco: but
I charge thee by the nearness of our blood,
When I am made this mockery and wonder,
I know not where to find out charity,
If unawares a chance direct my weary
And wither'd feet to some fair house of thine,
Where plenty with full blessings crowns thy table,
If my thin face betray my want of food,
Do not despise me, 'cause I was thy brother.

Enter Confessor.

Fran. Leave these imagin'd horrors, I must not
Live when my brother is thus miserable.
Fer. There's something in that face looks comfortably.
Conf. Your father, sir, is dead. His will to make
Francisco the sole master of his fortunes
Is now irrevocable: a small pension
He hath given you for life, which, with his blessing,
Is all the benefit I bring.

Fer. Ha! blessing! speak it again, good father.
Conf. I did apply some lenitives to soften
His anger, and prevail'd; your father hath
Reversed that heavy censure of his curse,
And in the place bequeath'd his prayer and blessing.
Fer. I am new created by his charity.
Conf. Some ceremonies are behind: He did
Desire to be interr'd within our convent,
And left his sepulture to me; I am confident,
Your pieties will give me leave——
Fran. His will in all things I obey, and yours
Most reverend father: order as you please
His body; we may after celebrate
With all due obsequies his funeral.
Fer. Why you alone obey? I am your brother:
My father's eldest son, though not his heir.
Fran. It pleas'd my father, sir, to think me worthy
Of such a title; you shall find me kind,
If you can look on matters without envy.
Fer. If I can look on matters without envy!
Fran. You may live here still.
Fer. I may live here, Francisco!

Enter a Gentleman with a letter.

Conditions! I w uld not understand
This dialect.
Fran. With me, from madam——?
Gent. If you be signior Francisco.
Fer. Slighted!—
I find my father was not dead till now.
Crowd not, you jealous thoughts, so thick into
My brain, lest you do tempt me to an act,
Will forfeit all again.——

Fernando tells Felisarda that his father is dead.

Fer. I have a story to deliver;
A tale, will make thee sad: but I must tell it.
There is one dead, that lov'd thee not.

Fel. One dead.
That lov'd not me? this carries, sir, in nature
No killing sound;* I shall be sad to know
I did deserve an enemy or he want
A charity at death.
Fer. Thy cruel enemy,
And my best friend, hath took eternal leave,
And 's gone, to heaven, I hope: excuse my tears;
It is a tribute I must pay his memory;
For I did love my father.
Fel. Ha! your father!
Fer. Yes, Felisarda, he is gone, that in
The morning promis'd many years, but death
Hath in a few hours made him as stiff, as all
The winds and winter had thrown cold upon him,
And whisper'd him to marble.——

Francisco offers to restore Fernando his birthright. Fernando dares not take it.

FRANCISCO. FERNANDO. DON CARLOS.

Fran. What demands
Fernando?
Fer. My inheritance, wrought from me
By thy sly creeping to supplant my birth,
And cheat our father's easy soul, unworthily
Betraying to his anger, for thy lust
Of wealth, the love and promise of two hearts.
Poor Felisarda and Fernando now
Wither at soul, and robb'd by thee of that
Should cherish virtue, like to rifled pilgrims
Met on the way, and having told their story,
And dropt their even tears for both their loss,
Wander from one another.
Fran. 'Tis not sure
Fernando, but his passion (that obeys not

* Like the reply of Manoah in Samson Agonistes: "Sad, but not saddest, the desolation of a hostile city."

The counsel of his reason) would accuse me:
And if my father now (since spirits lose not
Intelligence, but more active when they have
Shook off their chains of flesh), would leave his dwelling,
And visit this coarse* orb again! my innocence
Should dare the appeal, and make Fernando see
His empty accusations.

Fer. He that thrives
By wicked art, has confidence to dress
His action with simplicity and shapes,
To cheat our credulous natures: 'tis my wonder
Thou durst do so much injury, Francisco,
As must provoke my justice to revenge,
Yet wear no sword.

Fran. I need no guard, I know
Thou dar'st not kill me.

Fer. Dare I not?

Fran. And name
Thy cause: 'tis thy suspicion, not Francisco,
Hath wrought thee high and passionate. To assure it;
If you dare violate, I dare possess you
With all my title to your land.

Car. How is that?

Fran. Let him receive it at his peril.

Fer. Ha!

Fran. It was my father's act, not mine: he trembled
To hear his curse alive; what horror will
His conscience feel, when he shall spurn his dust,
And call the reverend shade from his blest seat
To this bad world again, to walk and fright him!

Fer. Can this be more than a dream?

Fran. (*Gives him the will.*) Sir, you may cancel it. But think withal,
How you can answer him that's dead, when he
Shall charge your timorous soul for this contempt
To nature and religion; to break

* Dirty Planet.—*Sterne.*

His last bequest, and breath, that seal'd your blessings!
Car. These are fine fancies.
Fer. (*Returns the will.*) Here; and may it prosper,
Where my good father meant it: I'm overcome!
Forgive me, and enjoy it. [*Is going.*

His father RAMIRES (*supposed dead*) *appears above, with* FELISARDA.

Ram. Fernando, stay.
Fer. Ha, my father and Felisarda: [*Kneels.*
Are they both dead!—I did not think
To find thee in this pale society
Of ghosts so soon.
Fel. I am alive, Fernando:
And Don Ramires still thy living father.
Fran. You may believe it, sir, I was of the council.
Car. Men thought you dead.
Ram. I lay within
The knowledge of Francisco, and some few,
By this device to advance my younger son
To a marriage with Jacinta, sir, and try
Fernando's piety, and his mistress' virtue:
Which I have found worth him, and my acceptance.
With her I give thee what thy birth did challenge:
Receive thy Felisarda.
Fer. 'Tis a joy
So flowing, it drowns all my faculties.
My soul will not contain, I fear, but loose,
And leave me in this extacy.

THE LADY OF PLEASURE: A COMEDY. BY JAMES SHIRLEY

Sir Thomas Bornewell expostulates with his Lady on her extravagance and love of pleasure.

BORNEWELL. ARETINA, *his lady.*

Are. I am angry with myself;

To be so miserably restrained in things,
Wherein it doth concern your love and honor
To see me satisfied.
Bor. In what, Aretina,
Dost thou accuse me? have I not obey'd
All thy desires, against mine own opinion;
Quitted the country, and remov'd the hope
Of our return, by sale of that fair lordship
We liv'd in: chang'd a calm and retire life
For this wild town, compos'd of noise and charge?
Are. What charge, more than is necessary
For a lady of my birth and education?
Bor. I am not ignorant how much nobility
Flows in your blood, your kinsmen great and powerful
In the state; but with this lose not your memory
Of being my wife: I shall be studious,
Madam, to give the dignity of your birth
All the best ornaments which become my fortune;
But would not flatter it, to ruin both,
And be the fable of the town, to teach
Other men wit by loss of mine, employ'd
To serve your vast expences.
Are. Am I then
Brought in the balance? so, sir.
Bor. Though you weigh
Me in a partial scale, my heart is honest:
And must take liberty to think, you have
Obey'd no modest counsel to effect,
Nay, study ways of pride and costly ceremony;
Your change of gaudy furniture, and pictures,
Of this Italian master, and that Dutchman's;
Your mighty looking-glasses, like artillery
Brought home on engines; the superfluous plate
Antick and novel; vanities of tires,
Four score pound suppers for my lord your kinsman,
Banquets for t' other lady, aunt, and cousins;
And perfumes, that exceed all; train of servants,
To stifle us at home, and show abroad

More motly than the French, or the Venetian,
About your coach, whose rude postilion
Must pester every narrow lane, till passengers
And tradesmen curse your choaking up their stalls,
And common cries pursue your ladyship
For hindering of their market.
Are. Have you done, sir?
Bor. I could accuse the gaity of your wardrobe,
And prodigal embroideries, under which,
Rich satins, plushes, cloth of silver, dare
Not show their own complexions; your jewels,
Able to burn out the spectators' eyes,
And show like bonfires on you by the tapers:
Something might here be spared, with safety of
Your birth and honor, since the truest wealth
Shines from the soul, and draws up just admirers.
I could urge something more.
Are. Pray, do. I like
Your homily of thrift.
Bor. I could wish, madam,
You would not game so much.
Are. A gamester, too!——
Bor. But are not come to that repentance yet,
Should teach you skill enough to raise your profit;
You look not through the subtilty of cards,
And mysteries of dice, nor can you save
Charge with the box, buy petticoats and pearls,
And keep your family by the precious income;
Nor do I wish you should: my poorest servant
Shall not upbraid my tables, nor his hire
Purchas'd beneath my honor: you make play
Not a pastime but a tyranny, and vex
Yourself and my estate by 't.
Are. Good, proceed.
Bor. Another game you have, which consumes more
Your fame than purse, your revels in the night,
Your meetings, call'd the ball, to which appear,
As to the court of pleasure, all your gallants

And ladies, thither bound by a subpœna
Of Venus and small Cupid's high displeasure:
'Tis but the Family of Love, translated
Into more costly sin; there was a play on 't;
And had the poet not been brib'd to a modest
Expression of your antic gambols in 't,
Some darks had been discover'd; and the deeds too;
In time he may repent, and make some blush,
To see the second part danc'd on the stage.
My thoughts acquit you for dishonoring me
By any foul act; but the virtuous know,
'Tis not enough to clear ourselves, but the
Suspicions of our shame.
Are. Have you concluded
Your lecture?
Bor. I have done; and howsoever
My language may appear to you, it carries
No other than my fair and just intent
To your delights, without curb to their modest
And noble freedom.
Are. I 'll not be so tedious
In my reply, but, without art or elegance,
Assure you I keep still my first opinion;
And though you veil your avaricious meaning
With handsome names of modesty and thrift,
I find you would intrench and wound the liberty
I was born with. Were my desires unprivileged
By example; while my judgment thought 'em fit,
You ought not to oppose: but when the practice
And tract of every honorable lady
Authorize me, I take it great injustice
To have my pleasures circumscrib'd and taught me.

[This dialogue is in the very spirit of the recriminating scenes between Lord and Lady Townley in the Provoked Husband. It is difficult to believe, but it must have been Vanbrugh's prototype.]

END OF PART II.

www.ingramcontent.com/pod-product-compliance
Lightning Source LLC
LaVergne TN
LVHW020936110826
845150LV00004B/878

9781425551834